D1568453

Beyond Our Control?

Beyond Our Control?

Confronting the Limits of Our Legal System in the Age of Cyberspace

Stuart Biegel

The MIT Press
Cambridge, Massachusetts
London, England

This book was set in Sabon by Achorn Graphic Services, Inc.
Printed and bound in the United States of America.

Library of Congress Cataloging-in-Publication Data

Biegel, Stuart.
Beyond our control? confronting the limits of our legal system in the age of cyberspace/Stuart Biegel.
p. cm.
Includes bibliographical references and index.
ISBN 0-262-02504-3 (hc.: alk. paper)
1. Internet—Law and legislation—United States. 2. Computer networks—Law and legislation—United States. 3. Cyberspace—United States. I. Title.
KF390.5.C6 B495 2001
343.7309'944—dc21

2001030601

Contents

Acknowledgments

A project of this size and scope cannot be completed without the assistance, encouragement, and support of many people. During the time I spent working on this book—and even earlier, when the ideas were just taking shape—I was very fortunate indeed to be able to benefit from ongoing contact with so many special individuals.

Looking back, the foundation for this project was established through my participation in a series of online discussion forums, real-time panels, and memorable conferences. In particular, I would like to thank Trotter Hardy and the participants in his *Cyberia* mailing list (circa 1995)—especially Dan Burk, Ed Cavazos, Julie Cohen, Michael Froomkin, and David Post—whose enthusiasm, knowledge, and willingness to push the proverbial envelope moved us all forward. Larry Lessig and John Perry Barlow—fellow panelists at events in 1996 and 1997—played key roles (both through their writings and their in-person comments) in helping me formulate my first theories regarding cyberspace regulation. I would also like to thank those who organized and participated in the Computers, Freedom & Privacy (CFP) Conferences of 1997 (in the San Francisco Bay Area) and 1998 (in Austin). And the active contributors to the *CyberProf* mailing list have not only been an important source of timely knowledge but have also provided all of us with a great sense of perspective.

Once this project became an outline and pen began to be put to paper, I benefited in particular from the comments, encouragement, and advice of Ethan Katsh, David Johnson, Mark Lemley, Pam Samuelson, and Jonathan Zittrain. And their own valuable research in this area continues to inform my work. In addition, at the University of California Office of the President, Stuart Lynn was an ongoing source of valuable information and feedback.

At UCLA, I have benefited greatly from contact with a very special group of people. Jerry Kang, Richard Steinberg, and Eugene Volokh have always been there to provide insights and encouragement, and to challenge me with their own innovative approaches to this material. Conversations about the project with Phil Agre, Dan Bussel, and John Wiley have been a continuing delight. The support of the administration—and in particular, Robert Goldstein at the UCLA School of Law and Pat McDonough at the UCLA Graduate School of Education and Information Studies—has been a very important component of this picture. And Christine Borgman played a central role from the beginning, both as the Department Chair who encouraged me to teach the first cyberspace law classes on campus and later as the colleague who paved the way for me to move forward with this project.

On an international level, I have been fortunate to have come into contact with a large number of scholars—both online and in real time—who have helped me maintain a global perspective on all these issues. In this regard, I would like to thank Rafi Cohen-Almagor and Rolf Weber for their advice and encouragement. And special thanks must go the Cristina Fernandez and Carlos Rohrmann, who—even when they were still my students in our Master of Laws (LL.M.) Program—were able to bring to these emerging questions a wonderful ability to make sense of the larger picture.

Finally, I would like to thank those who worked with me directly on this project. My research assistants—Carolyn Ko and Allen Seto—contributed in many important ways with their meticulous and thoughtful work. And I benefited greatly from the feedback and ongoing support I received in all my interactions with MIT Press editors Deborah Cantor-Adams, Bob Prior, and Doug Sery—professionals in every sense of the word.

Los Angeles, California
Spring 2001

Introduction

Keen instruments, strung to a vast precision
Bind town to town and dream to ticking dream . . .
Through the bound cable strands, the arching path . . .
Taut miles of shuttling moonlight syncopate . . .
White tempest nets file upward . . .
And synergy of waters ever fuse, recast
In myriad symbols . . .

—Hart Crane, *The Bridge,* Circa 1930

. . . [T]he data has passed out of the physical plane and into the mathematical, a higher and purer universe where different laws apply.

—Neal Stephenson, on the first "Turing" computer of the 1940s, *Cryptonomicon,* 1999

There are now more than a billion pages on the World Wide Web, all loosely tied together by seven billion annotated links . . . which is at least one link for every person on the planet. Each day, more than a million pages are added. . . . For the first time in history, people everywhere have access to the thoughts, products, and writing of a large—and growing—percentage of the earth's population.

—Michael Specter, "Postcard from Silicon Valley," *The New Yorker,* Spring 2000

In a recent novel focusing on a mythical agrarian community, Emily Barton tells the story of an invention that ultimately changes everything for people who had once led relatively simple lives. The invention is the harness, and the narrative describing the transformative events that follow can serve as a remarkable parable for our own era.

At first glance, a harness might not strike the reader as a particularly innovative development. But a detailed examination of a farmer's day-to-day existence before the harness reveals a primitive lifestyle severely impacted by an inability to employ horses for anything other than basic transportation. In an age when horsepower was the most potent source of energy available, horses were attached to rudimentary, one-wheel carts by pieces of flaxen rope or leather thong tied around their necks. Predictably, only a little extra weight beyond a moderate load could result in the strangling death of the animals. And the farmers themselves devoted tremendous amounts of time to the most elementary tasks, using sharp sticks to dig holes for each seed and furrowing their fields by actually dragging their fingernails through them and picking out each small stone.

After the invention of the harness, however, one breakthrough led to another. Suddenly, large amounts of goods could be transported all at once, and at speeds no one would have thought possible. Larger two-wheel carts soon replaced the primitive one-wheel variety, and profits from the sale of crops that had been brought to town increased dramatically. Soon the entire architecture and infrastructure of the area began to change. Roads were built, gates were widened, and major areas of the village were cleared to make way for the wider vehicles and the booming new marketplace that had developed. Then, in yet another significant breakthrough, the inventor realized that he no longer needed to pull a plow, but could instead attach it to his horse with the very same harness that he had created.

At first, the results were dazzling. Unprecedented changes were happening on a regular basis, new social norms emerged, basic rules were identified, and pastoral visions of a halcyon future were the order of the day. But it was not long before the unintended consequences of these transformative developments soon became apparent, and the residents of the area proved unable to understand what had transpired or to take control of subsequent events.

In the end, the story Emily Barton tells in *The Testament of Yves Gundron* is yet another example of a scenario that has been played out over and over again throughout history. At some level, the new developments take on a life of their own, events spiral out of control, and an uncertain state of affairs ensues. Upon reflection, it is not evident that things are any better overall than they had been before it all began.

As we enter a new century, many believe that the emergence of the Internet as a central feature of our daily lifestyle will lead to an analogous set of circumstances and a similar end result. Others dispute this view, pointing to all the ways that things are not only different this time but incrementally better across the board. Still others have adopted a more agnostic approach, taking the position that perhaps no one really understands just exactly what is going on here. But no matter which view of cyberspace a person or group might adopt, the question of regulation has proven to be central. Everyone, in fact, has been asking the same questions. How can we get a handle on this reality? What might be done to control it? Should anything be done to control it? Will some level of greater control actually make a difference?

At the heart of these questions are the same issues that are raised by the parable of the harness. Can we truly understand the implications of the recent changes when we are right in the middle of the transformation? Is it possible to ascertain the nature and extent of the new social norms, the pattern of the emerging rules, and the potential unintended consequences of any effort to aggressively regulate this territory? Or is the Internet the latest version of an old story, with a life of its own, and beyond our control?

One of the most compelling issues in this context has been the development and proliferation of MP3 file sharing. Indeed, no single Internet-related dispute exemplifies the nature and extent of the current regulation debate more completely than the MP3 controversy.

MP3 itself is no more than a file format that enables online users to store audio files on a computer. Before MP3, audio files were usually very large, and the sound quality was inconsistent at best. But after MP3 technology was introduced, not only could large audio files be compressed, but the resulting sound was near-CD quality.

By 1998, MP3 music files could be created easily by copying or "ripping" existing digital files from CDs, using software that was available at no charge on the World Wide Web. As a result, a very large number of free MP3 files have proliferated in cyberspace—some posted with permission, but many others without permission.

Once MP3 files are posted online or made available through simple file-sharing programs, any Internet user can download perfect copies and then choose from several convenient listening formats. High-quality MP3 players, for example, continue to be available as shareware or freeware and enable music lovers to listen to their files on their computers. And a growing selection of digital tools can be purchased and used to transfer MP3 files from a computer to a variety of stationary and portable devices.

Both the sound quality and the convenience of the MP3 format have made this technology very attractive, and the resulting ability of online users to save money by essentially downloading free music has caused an ongoing uproar in the offices of music executives worldwide.

From the beginning, the Recording Industry Association of America (RIAA) attempted to employ a variety of strategies to counter these developments. These strategies ranged from cease-and-desist letters to full-blown lawsuits to technology-based initiatives that would limit the ability of users to create and exchange MP3 files. By late 1999, its efforts appeared to be increasingly successful. Searches for MP3 files that had typically been posted on Web sites, FTP sites, and newsgroups often proved fruitless, and many commentators predicted that the controversy was ending and that the RIAA had won. While people generally agreed that MP3 technology was here to stay, the potent combination of legal remedies and imminent technological solutions appeared to have enabled copyright holders to bring the problem under control.

Yet even as pundits and prognosticators were agreeing with each other that the powers-that-be had prevailed, increasing numbers of online users had begun to take advantage of Internet Relay Chat and ICQ instant-messaging software to transfer files more covertly. At the same time, a new file-sharing technology emerged, which soon changed the entire equation. This technology was Napster, and it enabled people to exchange MP3 files in cyberspace without anyone actually having to post anything online.

Napster software facilitated the sharing of music files through a central server by providing Netizens with the ability to search the hard drives of other Napster users who might be connected at any given moment. And using Napster on a regular basis was as easy as using a basic search engine.

Predictably, numerous lawsuits were filed against Napster, seeking to put a stop to these practices. But while the litigation worked its way through the courts, use of the file sharing service continued to increase dramatically. In January 2001, for example, and estimated 50 to 60 million users downloaded 2.7 *billion* songs through Napster. And any optimism on the part of the record companies—based on initial court decisions that had come down in their favor—was tempered by the knowledge that other file-sharing programs building on the Napster model had also proliferated in the online world.

Indeed, software developers had come up with even more anarchic methods of exchanging MP3 files. Gnutella, for example, accomplished the same thing as Napster without using a central server. Instead, it was based on the same "distributed" or "peer-to-peer" approach that was increasingly being used by both law enforcement officials attempting to monitor individual user activity and by lawbreakers who sought to shut down certain Internet-based operations by employing unwitting computers to flood the sites with data requests. In addition, because Gnutella-like software could be used to exchange all sorts of files—from documents to software to digital photographs—the threat of even greater anarchy loomed on the horizon by 2001.

A detailed examination of MP3 issues reveals many of the same patterns identified in the parable of the harness. As a result of innovative and incremental advances in technology—from the building of a networked environment to the creation of the MP3 file format to the development of automated file-sharing software—everything changed for the persons and institutions involved. Lifestyles were transformed, industry operations faced dramatic restructuring, and intractable regulation issues moved to the forefront.

Given the inherent limits of our legal system and the persistence of the rule of unintended consequences, many have expressed doubt that a workable legal solution can be found for this controversy. And the tenacious ability of software code writers to come up with "architectural" answers to just about any new technological fix generates a similar level of skepticism regarding the potential value of a code-based solution. Thus, people are not only wondering whether the situation is beyond our control, but also whether some level of greater control will actually make any difference—especially if there is no buy-in and no consensus among the major stakeholders in the field.

This is a book about the control of the online world, focusing in particular on the Internet. It examines both the extent to which the Internet is currently under control and the extent to which its various components can or should be brought under control.

The book recognizes that in general things are working quite well in cyberspace on a day-to-day level, and that many things should probably be left alone. But it also seeks to come to grips with the range of problematic conduct that has been identified by various stakeholders over the past six to eight years. While it cannot cover every major problem in detail, it strives to discuss enough representative examples so that a comprehensive overview of current regulation issues emerges.

The term *regulation* is defined very broadly to include case decisions, legislation, relevant policies, administrative agency activity, international cooperation, architectural changes, private ordering, self-regulation, and any other methods that might be employed to control various portions of cyberspace. Through an examination of three broad regulatory models, the book provides an overview of how relevant legal principles can operate in cyberspace, even as it identifies the inherent limits of our legal system and the pitfalls that would-be regulators must face.

Informed by the rich and wide-ranging body of "cyberspace regulation" scholarship that has appeared in law journals and essay collections since the mid-1990s, the book recognizes that the online world is not monolithic but instead contains many different cyber spaces. It therefore shies away from generalizations regarding the overall status quo, and urges the reader to consider the importance of examining each representative problem separately—even as it attempts to provide an overarching context that can be employed to address new Internet-related questions in a proactive manner.

The book is designed as a series of building blocks that lead from an examination of who might be in charge and an analysis of just how unique cyberspace might be to the sorting out of representative problem areas, the identification of major regulatory models, and the application of these models to some of the most volatile Internet-related topics of our era.

These topics include cybersecurity, consumer fraud, free speech rights, intellectual property rights, and the prospective impact of file-sharing programs such as Napster and Gnutella on both the development of the law and the future of the Internet itself.

Part I

1

Controlling the Internet: Is Anyone in Charge?

I didn't expect to find any fences around here.

—*Shane,* directed by George Stevens, Hollywood (1954)

We doubt that the Internet should be governed by one plan or one body or even by a series of plans and bodies.

—U.S. Government Proposal to Improve Technical Management of Internet Names and Addresses—Discussion Draft (Green Paper), January 30, 1998

We're your cyber-neighborhood watch. We find and report illegal material online, educate families about online safety and how to enjoy cyberspace together, work with schools and libraries, and share basic Internet tips . . .

—http://www.cyberangels.org, visited November 15, 1998

When historians look back on this era, they will probably determine that the "age of cyberspace" began in the early 1990s, fueled by the development of the World Wide Web and the statutory authority granted to the National Science Foundation (NSF) to commercialize what was then called the NSFNET.[1] The "new" Internet soon became the central feature in what has come to be known as *cyberspace* or the *online world.*

The term *online world* can be defined broadly to include not only the Internet but also commercial online services (such as America Online), private databases (such as Lexis-Nexis and Westlaw), and private networks (sometimes called "Intranets"). The Internet itself today includes e-mail, the World Wide Web, file transfer protocol (FTP), newsgroups (Usenet), and Internet Relay Chat (IRC).

From the beginning, as the new Internet emerged, a significant aspect of its mystique was the commonly accepted notion that no one is in charge.[2] Indeed, in the popular culture of the past decade, the entire online world has often been viewed as a loosely coupled and somewhat mysterious conglomeration of virtual communities. The Wild West metaphor is typically seen as most appropriate in this regard, with cyberspace depicted as a lawless frontier where anarchy and vigilantism are alive and well.[3]

Yet, even in the beginning, this romantic image may have amounted to little more than a myth. For a close examination of the Internet over the past ten years reveals a changing world that is, at least in part, under a significant degree of control.

In attempting to ascertain just exactly which persons and groups might be in charge here, it is instructive to begin with a broad overview of the emerging field of cyberspace law. In general, cyberspace law or "cyberlaw" typically encompasses all the cases, statutes, and constitutional provisions that impact persons and institutions who control the entry to cyberspace, provide access to cyberspace, create the hardware and software that enable people to access cyberspace, or use their own computers to go online and enter cyberspace. Key stakeholders in cyberlaw disputes thus may include phone companies, regulatory agencies, personal-computer companies, software companies, major online services, Internet service providers, K-12 schools, colleges and universities, persons and companies that have established a presence on the Internet, and of course the growing number of users themselves. Given the parameters of these recent disputes, an inquiry regarding the control of the Internet logically begins with an examination of the role that many of these stakeholders continue to play in this context.

Governments Not only did the U.S. government participate in the founding of the Internet, but it maintains a significant presence in the online world and through a variety of major policy initiatives continues to play a role in its growth and development.[4] While the White House has chosen in recent years to delegate such tasks as the building of the Internet backbone and the assignment of domain names and IP addresses to private entities, it retains a tremendous amount of power from a regulatory perspective.

Other governments worldwide are playing an increasingly important role in this area, both individually and through a growing number of collaborative efforts. Some governments have chosen a more laissez-faire, free-market approach to the online world, while others remain convinced that they can and should maintain tight control over the flow of information and the online interaction that takes place in their countries. In any case, given the power of political leaders, legislative bodies, and courts, governments certainly cannot be ignored.

Internet Service Providers For the average person, Internet service providers (ISPs) continue to serve as gatekeepers to cyberspace. Most people who wish to send and receive e-mail and access the World Wide Web must first sign up with a service provider before they can connect to the Internet. By the year 2000, the ISP industry had grown to encompass over four thousand companies, even as commentators predicted a significant trend toward consolidation.[5]

The central role of the Internet service provider has been recognized in a growing number of statutes, case decisions, and policy directives. Since the ISPs can immediately and directly let a person in or remove a person from the online world, they have been viewed by many as an important focal point of control. Debates regarding the legal responsibility of ISPs thus continue unabated.

Local Telephone Companies In a changing technological environment, it is unclear at this point in time just how central a role local telephone companies will play in the future, given the potential for expanded cable modem service and wireless satellite communication. But, at least at the present time, telephone companies still serve—along with the ISPs—as major gatekeepers to cyberspace. Without phone connections, many people must remain offline. And the emergence of digital subscriber line (DSL) services may serve to enhance the role of telephone companies in this context.

Hardware and Software Companies Beyond the governments and the primary telecommunications gatekeepers, other entities that may play a central role in the control of cyberspace include the hardware and software companies. Hardware is often taken for granted in this context, but it must be noted that without it, online connections are virtually impossible. And as the hardware changes, the entire experience of going online can be transformed.

In the late 1990s, for example, a new kind of telecommunications hardware—the "information appliance"—began to proliferate.[6] Seen by many as the logical extension of the palmtop computing technology, these appliances included smart phones, smart navigation cards, digital television boxes, car navigation systems, and digital recording devices. Most have the ability to connect to at least some portion of the online world. As a connection with cyberspace becomes for many a more natural part of day-to-day life, the nature of the online world itself may inevitably change.

The role of software companies is much more complex and direct, with disputes in recent years ranging from anti-trust lawsuits to controversies regarding the architecture of the Internet itself. The *U.S. v. Microsoft* case—which focused in great part on the bitter disputes between Microsoft and Netscape regarding Internet browsers and between Microsoft and Sun Microsystems regarding Java—has been viewed by many as a fight for the control of cyberspace itself. In both the briefs themselves and in oral arguments at trial, much of the case against Microsoft was based on an often implicit assumption that if one company were to control the software that enables users to access the World Wide Web, then that company would, at least on some level, control the Web itself.[7] For many, such extensive control has always been unacceptable.

A related controversy has focused on adjustments in browser software that might succeed—intentionally or otherwise—in filtering out certain content. While it is generally accepted that individual persons and families should have the right to filter out objectionable online content, there has been great concern in many quarters that such software-based modifications may have a significantly adverse effect on the nature of cyberspace itself.[8]

Colleges and Universities Any analysis of controlling forces must also include colleges and universities worldwide. The Internet began at the university level, and for many years was viewed as almost the exclusive province of higher education.[9] Even today, colleges and universities play a dominant role by providing a large number of computers that serve as hosts, generating important policy initiatives, developing a variety of new programs, posting a tremendous amount of valuable information online, and providing easy access for a very large number of regular users.

Builders and Custodians of the Internet Backbone Less well-known but arguably just as important in this picture are those who directly control the Internet backbone lines and hubs. Backbone lines are the high-speed fiber optic cables that transfer information through the Internet at speeds that can reach 155 million bits per second.[10] These backbones—originally controlled essentially by the National Science Foundation (NSF)—are today developed and maintained individually or in concert by such companies as MCI WorldCom, Cable & Wireless (C&W), Genuity, Sprint, and PSINet.[11]

Commentators have noted in recent years that the ever-changing backbone system has become so complex that there is now only a general consensus on what constitutes it and who its top players are. The original Internet as administered by the NSF evolved into a network linking a handful of university-based supercomputers, but in April 1995, the proverbial keys were turned over to the private sector.

The backbone today has been called the "commercial descendant" of the original Internet framework. While major telecommunications companies own most of the high-speed fiber optic lines and lease these lines to other backbone firms, no single company or group controls the entire network. Indeed, competing companies move data by a cooperative arrangement called "peering," which involves an agreement to send each other's data through their own networks at no charge. Thus, at this level of control, companies compete and cooperate at the same time.[12]

The backbone system also consists of large hubs through which all the high-speed lines merge to reroute billions of packets of data and send them either to a requesting Internet service provider or to another hub for further rerouting. And companies such as Cisco Systems, Juniper Networks, and Avici that supply equipment to backbone companies continue to play an important role in this context.

Internet Organizations Probably the least well-known but arguably among the most important persons and groups in this inquiry are those who participate in key Internet organizations. These interrelated organizations have become more prominent in recent years as their longstanding roles began to collide—or at least interface—with the growing power of the Information Technology (IT) industry.[13]

Major Internet organizations at the turn of the century include (1) the Internet Society (ISOC), which sees itself as the "ambassador of the Internet" and works "to assure the open development, evolution and use of the Internet for the benefit of all people throughout the world"; (2) the Internet Architecture Board (IAB), which serves as the technical advisory group of the Internet Society, providing oversight of the process used to create Internet standards, and serving as an appeal board for complaints; (3) the Internet Engineering Task Force (IETF), which grew out of the IAB and decides on technical standards for the Internet; and (4) the World Wide Web Consortium (W3C), an international organization that works to maximize the full potential of the Web by "developing common protocols that promote its evolution and ensure its interoperability."[14]

The IETF, in particular, has been at the center of controversy in recent years, as disputes regarding the possible adjustment of technical Internet standards continue unabated. Internet law scholar Michael Froomkin has documented the IETF's remarkably decentralized standard-setting process, which "allows unlimited grassroots participation and operates under a relatively large, open agenda." The IETF is made up primarily of volunteers, meetings are open to all, and anyone can join its electronic mailing list in which potential standards are discussed. Froomkin notes that

> although the IETF plays a role in the selection of other groups that help define the basic Internet protocols, the IETF is not part of or subject to those groups. Indeed, it is not entirely clear to the membership who if anyone "owns" the IETF or for that matter who is liable if it is sued. An amorphous body of this sort may be difficult to sue; it is even harder to control.[15]

In the aftermath of widespread "denial-of-service" attacks against major Web sites and portals in early 2000, a new focus on technical standards as a vehicle for tightening up Internet security led to a reassessment of the IETF's role and suggestions that perhaps it should be granted more power. Commentators noted that "despite its importance to the Internet's operations, the IETF has no power to enforce its recommendations, and instead must lead by example and moral suasion." And Marcus Leech, a codirector of the IETF's security section, emphasized that the organization could "issue statements all we like, but unless we get buy-in from service providers and application providers—all the people with irons in the fire—nothing happens."[16]

The Internet Corporation for Assigned Names and Numbers (ICANN)
In late 1998, the U.S. government announced its intention to delegate certain tasks relating to the assignment of domain names and IP addresses to ICANN.[17] The announcement generated great concern among certain Internet stakeholders, and the new entity has been the focal point of significant controversy ever since. Debates concerning ICANN range from the parameters of its ultimate role to the extent of its actual power. And by 2001, it was still unclear whether ICANN should appropriately be characterized as yet another "volunteer" Internet organization with similar indeterminate power, a fledgling international body that could serve as an Internet UN, or a quasi-governmental body inextricably tied on some level to the U.S. Everyone agreed, however, that ICANN cannot be ignored, and that developments at its meetings should continue to be monitored very closely.[18]

At the present time, in spite of all the jockeying for positions of power between and among persons, groups, corporations, and government entities, it is still very easy for literally anyone to access cyberspace and to establish a presence in the online world. In addition, it is still relatively easy to break laws in cyberspace and get away with it.

On the other hand, there is growing evidence to indicate that cyberspace may no longer be as freewheeling and open as it used to be. With the increased popularity of the online world has come a broad-based demand for greater structure, an intensified push for a more reliable level of security, and a growing emphasis on what may loosely be called "law-abiding behavior."

Although the U.S. Federal Bureau of Investigation (FBI) initially maintained a fairly low profile in this area, specific agents in FBI offices throughout the country are now assigned to Internet-related law enforcement activities. Some agents work for the National Computer Crime Squad, investigating violations of the Federal Computer Fraud and Abuse Act. Others "patrol" the Internet by going online, visiting Web sites, and participating in chat rooms or newsgroup discussions.[19] Still others participate in the National Infrastructure Protection Center (NIPC), located in the FBI's national headquarters and established in 1998 to bring together representatives from the FBI, other U.S. government agencies, state and local governments, and the private sector. NIPC's mission is to protect the nation's critical infrastructure by serving as the government's focal point for "threat assessment, warning, investigation, and response."[20]

Other government agencies have stepped up their efforts to monitor the online world and ferret out criminal activity. Both the U.S. Securities and Exchange Commission (SEC) and the Federal Trade Commission (FTC) served notice in the late 1990s that they were working hard to crack down on Internet fraud and privacy violations. A series of highly publicized investigations, indictments, and arrests were announced, and details regarding SEC and FTC operations in this area were released. By 1998 the SEC employed more than one hundred staff attorneys, analysts, and accountants who received special training in Internet surveillance. Each member of this team was responsible for searching Web sites, chat rooms, and bulletin boards on a regular basis, looking for telltale signs of online securities fraud.[21]

In addition to the active role played by the U.S. government, international law enforcement efforts have also been stepped up. One of the more publicized early efforts, for example, was the International Internet Sweep Day. This sweep was sponsored by a worldwide association of consumer-protection law enforcement agencies and coordinated by the Australian Competition and Consumer Commission. On the same day—October 16, 1997—consumer protection officials in twenty-five countries warned hundreds of Web site operators that their get-rich-quick business opportunities and pyramid schemes might be illegal. In the U.S., the Federal Trade Commission, the Securities and Exchange Commission, and the Commodity Futures Trading Commission joined consumer protection agencies and securities regulators in twenty-two states to target suspected Web sites and issue warnings.[22]

Another notable international effort in this regard was the multinational crackdown on members of a secret, exclusive pedophile chat room known as "Wonderland," the largest Internet child-pornography ring discovered to date. Over the course of two days in September 1998,

U.S. Customs Service computer experts worked closely with local law enforcement and several foreign police agencies to conduct one hundred raids in twenty-two states and twelve countries, including Australia, France, Germany, Italy, Spain, and the United Kingdom.[23]

Increasingly, surveillance of the online world is also being conducted by individuals and groups that are not connected with traditional law enforcement. One such group is the Cyberangels, founded in the mid-1990s by Curtis Sliwa, head of the Guardian Angels for the past twenty years. Sliwa views the Cyberangels as a natural extension of the controversial street patrols and neighborhood watch groups that he has coordinated in urban areas.

Attorney Parry Aftab, executive director of the group, insists that the Cyberangels are not vigilantes but "caring community volunteers" who "look out for their neighbors." The mission of the Cyberangels includes (1) looking for and finding online fraud and scams that prey on seniors and the innocent, (2) finding and reporting sites that use children in sexually provocative ways, (3) watching over children in child chat areas online, and (4) helping victims of harassment and online stalking find and report their harassers and stalkers.[24]

A different type of cyber-patrolling is conducted by groups of online detectives on behalf of software publishers and other major companies. Such private "corporate web police" are hired to protect intellectual property and combat piracy by guarding everything from corporate logos and comic strips to music and software.[25] Infringatek, one of the earliest private police forces, gained national prominence by focusing on intellectual property searches but later expanded its operations to include undercover activities and the prevention of computer misuse on the job. The Online Monitoring Service (OMS), which charged a minimum of $1,500 a month in the late 1990s for its services, was one of several companies using specialized search-engine technology to find copyright and trademark abusers.[26] Other similar services included eWatch and MarkWatch.

Yet another form of online surveillance is conducted by Internet filtering companies, which constantly seek to update their files by identifying sites that their customers might find objectionable.

With the increased monitoring of cyberspace by law-enforcement officials and security agencies, the online world has become a less private place. One of the early attractions of the Internet for many people was the opportunity to achieve a certain level of anonymity and even build a new persona in ways that simply were not possible offline. But this level of privacy has been increasingly threatened by a combination of surveillance and technological advances. Ironically, at this point in time, people in many ways have more privacy offline than they have online—given the ability of persons and agencies to retrieve copies of deleted e-mail and track visits by Netizens to different portions of the online world.

As cyberspace continued to evolve in the late 1990s, it became clear that in certain ways it was no longer the "level playing field" it once had been. For many, one of the greatest strengths of the online world had been its openness. Anyone could settle in cyberspace. Individuals and corporations were on an equal footing. Twelve-year-old Jamie's Web site describing his favorite fishing gear and costing virtually nothing to set up could be accessed as easily as the Ford Motor Company Web site that costs many thousands of dollars to create and maintain. In addition, both jamie.net and ford.com could be accessed in the same way, by typing in their respective uniform resource locators (URLs).

Today, it is still possible to access radically different Web sites in the same way, but in the eyes of many observers, high-profile sites are gaining an inexorable advantage through mechanisms ranging from Internet portals to Web browser channels to modified search engines. And travel through cyberspace is no longer unimpeded in the way it once was. Netizens increasingly come up against firewalls, copy management systems, demands for digital signatures, digital watermarks, and downloading opportunities that may be accomplished only by providing a credit card number.

Although some commentators continue to compare the online world to a "new frontier," others feel that in light of the changes documented above the Wild West analogy is no longer valid.[27] Yet it can be argued that recent changes in cyberspace have made the West an even more appropriate starting place.

It is generally agreed that the Wild West imagery of popular culture comes not from history books but from the western film. Focusing primarily on the years 1865–1890, the western presents a romanticized and often only marginally accurate view of a very complex period in American history. Scholars believe that the film genre is itself derived from the western literature of the 1800s, rooted in the works of James Fenimore Cooper, but ultimately exemplified by the dime novels of the late-nineteenth century.[28] These novels, written by popular authors who may have spent little or no time in the West, feature a series of familiar stock characters and events.

Sophisticated screenwriters and filmmakers built upon this tradition and succeeded in creating what some have called a national American mythology. Indeed, succeeding generations continue to find great meaning in the milieu and mores of the western, where the adventures of larger-than-life heroes and heroines are played out against the backdrop of a pristine, magnificent landscape. The historical events depicted in the western—the last days of the U.S. Civil War, the construction of the railroad, the Indian Wars, cattle drives, the growth of agriculture—have taken on a metaphorical, almost archetypal quality. Artists and poets worldwide have found great symbolism in these events. And American icons from John F. Kennedy to the Grateful Dead have successfully invoked western imagery in their greatest work.

Cyberspace—seen by many as an ultimate next step—fits right in with "the idea of the West" as both a direction and a place. Not only did great empires typically develop in a westerly direction, but it was in the West that one might find the Elysian fields, Atlantis, El Dorado, and the fountain of youth. And from a legal perspective, it was in the archetypal American West, after all, where everything was wide-open . . . where rugged individuals either created their own rules or chose not to have any rules at all.

Jim Kitses, in his classic 1969 essay on the western film genre, argues that what gives the western its "particular thrust and centrality is its historical setting; its being placed at exactly that moment when options are still open, the dream of a primitivistic individualism, the ambivalence of at once beneficient and threatening horizons, still tenable." While Kitses could not have anticipated the emergence of cyberspace two decades later, his words pinpoint the appropriateness of western imagery for the online world, which at the turn of the century is arguably at a "moment when options [are] still open. . ." in a classic western sense.

An examination of selected western films may therefore provide some insights into the nature of an online world that may still be beyond our control, even as a large number of persons and groups attempt to establish control.

Interestingly, the classic western film was only rarely about rugged individuals interacting in a pristine environment with no rules in a *Lord of the Flies* manner.[29] More often, it focused in some way on the coming of civilization, and on the conflicts that arose between the original pioneers and those who came afterward, bringing their families, their farms, their Eastern businesses, and their rules. This clash can be viewed as a precise analogy for the online world at the beginning of the twenty-first century, a time when the original Internet pioneers and Netizens find themselves wrestling with the coming of "civilization" and its inevitable regulations.

In *Shane* (1953), the coming of civilization and the battle for control are exemplified by the violent feud between cattlemen and "sodbusters." The cattlemen—who got there first—relied upon an open range, where they could drive their cattle unimpeded from one vast location to the next. The sodbusters, or would-be farmers, came later, brought their families, and built fences.

Shane (played by Alan Ladd) is a dark, lonely, mythic figure with a mysterious and apparently violent past who rides into a magnificent valley that is about to explode into confrontation. The cattlemen, led by Ryker and his boys, are growing increasingly frustrated by the establishment and development of five to six farms on what they view as *their* open range. The farmers, led by Joe Starrett and his family, are determined to settle that range and build a community.

The town in this film consists of perhaps six ramshackle wood-frame buildings all in a row, dwarfed by the surrounding mountains and the vastness of the surrounding land. There is no law at all, so to speak. "That's the trouble with this country," one of the farmers says, "There ain't a marshal within a hundred-mile ride."[30] The closest thing to a controlling figure is Grafton, an aging, soft-spoken gentleman who does not even pack a gun but owns the main building in town—a combination saloon and general store. In some sort of unspoken understanding, Ryker believes that he must justify his actions to Grafton at every step, even though Grafton can only reason with others but has no apparent enforcement powers.

The confrontation between the cattlemen and the sodbusters grows increasingly violent as Ryker takes the offensive to try to restore the open range. Farms are burned down, and a hired gun (played by Jack Palance) is brought into town. One farmer is killed. Shane, who—for a variety of complicated reasons—has begun working on Starrett's farm, becomes the hero of the story as he faces down Ryker with his fists and his guns. In the end, the threat to the farmers is removed, the fences remain, civilization can grow, and community values prevail. Shane rides off, not into the sunset, but into the coming dawn.

In *The Man Who Shot Liberty Valance,* directed by John Ford (1962), the omnipresent feud between cattlemen and sodbusters is viewed within the context of a much more complex set of characters and themes. Fresh out of law school, Ransom Stoddard (played by James Stewart) decides to heed Horace Greely's advice and heads West, symbolically packing not a gun but a bag filled with law books. Yet even before reaching his destination, his stagecoach is held up by the ruthless Liberty Valance. When Stoddard tries to protect his fellow passenger and then declares that he is an attorney and that he'll see Valance in jail for this, he is brutally beaten, his law books are torn up, and he is left for dead by the side of the road. "I'll teach you law," Valance exclaims as he takes out his whip. "Western law!"[31]

Rescued by Tom Donovan (played by John Wayne), Stoddard is brought to Shinbone, where he soon begins to exert great influence. Before long, he has started the first public school in the area, teaching everyone from young children to grizzled adults how to read and write. He also paints his own shingle—Ransom Stoddard, Attorney at Law—and hangs it outside the local newspaper office. Yet there is little or no law enforcement in the Wild West town of Shinbone. The Marshal (played by Andy Devine) is a gentle, friendly man who is happiest when eating large portions of steak and potatoes. The people are generally law-abiding and good-natured, but when Valance and his band of outlaws come into town, it is only through the gunfighting skills of Tom Donovan that the uneasy status quo is maintained.

Against the backdrop of the territorial feud between the cattlemen and the sodbusters and the personal feud between Valance and Stoddard, civilization continues to emerge in Shinbone. A mass election meeting is held in the town saloon, and Stoddard is chosen as a delegate for the territorial convention in Capital City. But it becomes clear that Valance, who has been hired by the cattlemen, will not tolerate these developments. Stoddard—who has been taught to shoot by Tom Donovan—has no choice but to confront Liberty Valance with a gun, or get out of town. In the end, Stoddard prevails, and he goes on to become governor of the new state and later a three-term U.S. senator. The land is settled, and—in the words of Stoddard's wife Hallie—is transformed into a "garden."[32]

Similar themes can be found in *Cimarron* (1960), although the focus in Anthony Mann's adaptation of Edna Ferber's novel is slightly different. Unlike *Shane* and *Liberty Valance,* all the settlers in this tale of the Oklahoma land rush arrive in the West at the same time. And the epic story itself extends into the twentieth century and the World War I era, against the background of inevitable "progress" and the sudden industrialization brought about by the discovery of oil.

The defining event of the film is the dramatic land rush itself, when portions of "the last unsettled territories in America" are given free on a first-come, first-served basis.[33] The film focuses on the new town of Osage and the surrounding area, where Yancy Cravat, known as Cimarron, is a central figure from the beginning. A lawyer by training, but later an entrepreneur, would-be farmer, rough rider at San Juan Hill, and highly influential journalist, Yancy serves as the closest thing to the law in Osage as it grows and develops in the 1890s. On several occasions, he is called upon to enforce law and order through the barrel of a gun. When a Native American is lynched, for example, Yancy breaks up the mob and kills the bigoted ringleader. There are no arrests, and no trials. Based on an unspoken understanding within the community, Yancy *is* the law. And when the Cherokee Kid and his friends rob a train and then hold young pupils hostage in the schoolhouse, it is Yancy and only Yancy who ultimately comes to the rescue.

Soon, oil is discovered, and the area is transformed by industrialization and sudden wealth. Yancy maintains his role as the conscience of the community by becoming an even more aggressive and, indeed, fiercely independent newspaper editor. When the powers-that-be attempt to co-opt him by offering to make him the governor of Oklahoma, he rejects the offer and leaves the territory. His wife, however, continues his work, and after he is killed fighting in World War I, the town memorializes his contributions by erecting a statue depicting him as the honored symbol of the pioneer spirit.

All three of these classic westerns thus provide appropriate metaphors for the emerging online world. On some level, at the heart of each story, it is unclear who really is in charge and what the rules actually are. In addition, the realities depicted in each setting are unusually complex and multifaceted, with the relationship between individuals and the community exemplifying a whole host of conflicting values and themes. Such conflicts are typical in the western film, as Kitses points out in a chart depicting the "shifting ideological play" inherent in the tension between the individual (representing the wilderness) and the community (representing civilization). While the conflict between wilderness and civilization can embody the tension between freedom and restriction, it can also represent integrity versus compromise, tradition versus change, and the past versus the future.

It is instructive, therefore, to examine the nature of the community in each film. In *Shane,* the new community at first glance seems to be comprised entirely of the five to six families who are settling the land. But Ryker and his men are arguably part of the community as well. They are always around, visiting settlers' homes and interacting with the sodbusters. In addition, the line between good and evil is often blurred in this story. Chris, for example, starts off as one of the meanest of Ryker's hired hands, but eventually shifts sides and befriends Shane. Ryker himself tries to be reasonable at times, and indicates in conversations with Grafton that it is very important to him to be seen as complying with "the law."

In *Liberty Valance,* the Shinbone community is depicted as a group of good-hearted, genial men and women who want nothing more than to live their lives in peace. The cattlemen are clearly outside the community. We never even see them until right near the end at the territorial convention, but we know that they have hired Liberty Valance as their enforcer, and Valance is the embodiment of arrogance, intolerance, and ultimate evil. Stoddard, on the other hand, grows to exemplify the community and becomes in the end its most important citizen.

In *Cimarron,* where the community begins its existence together on the day of the land rush, there are different sorts of complications from the start. Bigotry and intolerance persist over time, and things only get worse with the corruption that follows in the wake of progress and industrialization. Yancy, like Shane, is highly respected but never really becomes part of the community.

Shane is arguably the most appropriate metaphor for the online community in this context. Although the people in *Shane* might seem at first glance to be divided into two groups—the original pioneers who want to maintain an open range and the more recent settlers who want to build fences—in actuality, the lines between the two groups are shifting and not clearly drawn. As Kitses argues, the wilderness individual can be seen as exemplifying savagery, as opposed to the humanity of civilization and community, but conversely, he can also be seen as exemplifying purity, as opposed to the corruption of civilization and community.

In the end, the community remains a force to be reckoned with, as it is in cyberspace, where a dynamic community of online users continues to play a key role. In the online world all Netizens have the opportunity to be much more than passive observers. Not only can they actively interact with highly influential persons and groups on a regular basis, but they can also stake out their own ground by establishing their own Web sites and portals. Ultimately, then, the online community qualifies as yet another group that should be added to the list of those who arguably control the online world.

It has become a complex and multi-faceted community, reflecting contradictory values that are remarkably similar to those described by Kitses. "The community in the western," he writes, "can be seen as a positive force, a movement of refinement, order, and local democracy in the wilds, or as a harbinger of corruption in the form of Eastern values which threaten frontier ways." In this manner, the emerging online community embodies the contradictions inherent in the West itself. For it is never really clear in western mythology whether the West is "a Garden of natural dignity and innocence offering refuge from the decadence of civilization" or "a treacherous Desert stubbornly resisting the gradual sweep of agrarian progress and community values."[34]

Given the influence that the online community has demonstrated, it can be argued that—at least at certain times—it should be viewed as the most powerful of all the forces controlling cyberspace. In the *Reno v. ACLU* litigation, for example, an amazingly potent coalition of representatives from the online community came together to challenge and ultimately overturn certain key portions of the 1996 Communications Decency Act.[35] Plaintiffs in the initial lawsuit included the Electronic Privacy Information Center, the Electronic Frontier Foundation, Computer Professionals for Social Responsibility, the National Writers Union, and the Planned Parenthood Federation of America. A second group soon filed a similar First Amendment suit, led by the American Library Association (ALA) and the newly formed Citizens Internet Empowerment Coalition (CIEC). Plaintiffs in this lawsuit included not only such highly respected groups as the ALA, the American Booksellers Association, the American Society of Newspaper Editors, the Association of American Publishers, and the Center for Democracy and Technology, but also such major companies as America Online, Apple Computer, CompuServe, Microsoft Corporation, Netcom, Prodigy, and Wired Ventures. The two lawsuits were eventually consolidated, and these high-powered representatives of the online community eventually prevailed in the U.S. Supreme Court.

At other times, however—particularly when intellectual property is at issue—the online community has been much more fragmented. Lobbying efforts in the U.S. Congress during the deliberations regarding both the "No Electronic Theft" Act of 1997 and the Digital Millennium Copyright Act of 1998, for example, often pitted representatives of the software and entertainment industries against scientists, academics, and librarians, with many other persons and groups unsure about the role they were supposed be playing.

This split—coinciding as it did with a rapid increase in advertising, Internet commerce, and the general commercialization of cyberspace—may have marked a key turning point in the recent history of the online world. Arguably the major companies that had, at least occasionally, worked together with grassroots organizations and day-to-day Net users, arguably, transitioned out of the online community at this point in time and formally joined the powers-that-be. Whether a separate and independent online community of users able to build on the emerging social norms could still be identified after 1998 is a question that has generated substantial debate.[36]

The question is particularly significant because many believe that any attempt to regulate the online world must take social norms into account. Those advocating a reliance on social norms in this context look to the work of scholars such as Robert C. Ellickson, who addresses the relationship between social norms and control in the American and British legal systems. A central point of this research is that the role of social norms and social change simply cannot be ignored.[37]

In *Order without Law: How Neighbors Settle Disputes,* Ellickson focuses on Shasta County, California, an environment remarkably similar in many ways to the world of the western film. Feuds between cattlemen and farmers apparently continue in Shasta County even to this day, and often involve legal disputes relating to ownership, liability, and the role of fences on the open range.

Interviewing the stakeholders in the area, Ellickson found that when disputes arise, informal social norms are significantly more important than either real or perceived legal principles. There appear to be definite social rules for sharing the costs of fence-building along common boundaries, and when one of these boundaries is violated, Shasta residents rely upon self-help measures such as phone calls to the owner of trespassing cattle, gossip, subtle threats, and "mild retaliation." If these methods fail, reports are sometimes filed with county authorities, or informal claims for compensation are submitted, but typically without the assistance of lawyers. Ellickson's research, according to Robert Cooter, demonstrates that "social norms, not law, constrain behavior and tilt the balance."[38]

For Ellickson, the Shasta County findings support important conclusions regarding "decentralized law" and "the extent that people can cooperate together without coercion from central authorities." The natural parallel between his subject matter and the online world has been noted by major scholars throughout the 1990s. Indeed, it has become almost obligatory for those confronting questions of cyberspace regulation to cite Ellickson's work on a decentralized "social norm" model of governance. Some, however, suggest a more restrained approach that relies on social norms to develop and refine legal principles within the more traditional regulatory models.

Internet law scholar Mark Lemley not only questions the existence of an identifiable online community at the turn of the century, but challenges the view that social norms can be pinpointed precisely enough to influence the development of cyberspace regulation:

Even a brief look at the Net should dispel any notion that Netizens are a homogenous group with a strong community of interest. White supremacists, libertarians, communitarians, and communists all coexist on the Net; so do rich and poor, black and white, nerds and literati. If we brought them all together in a room, virtual or real, it is doubtful they would reach even a rough consensus on virtually any subject. Norms that purport to emanate from the Net as a whole are necessarily suspect"[39]

Lemley suggests that a more logical approach might focus on the norms of smaller, close-knit "virtual communities" that can be identified. He believes that "the existence and strength of norms "vary from issue to issue and sub-community to sub-community."[40] He concludes, however, that not only can it be unclear which community's norms should influence the development of new legal principles, but that the individual communities themselves may change too quickly to serve as stable reference points.[41]

Other commentators are more sanguine in this regard. Sociologist Amitai Etzioni agrees that building and maintaining virtual communities are not simple tasks, but he contends that certain steps can be taken to build a lasting level of inclusion and intimacy that may not exist offline.[42] And Gary Chapman, director of the 21st Century Project at the University of Texas, Austin, continues to view collaborative efforts by Internet-based community organizations with both an online and an offline presence as central to maintaining an online world closely "aligned with the public interest."[43]

Although the boundaries of identifiable online communities and their prospective role in developing and maintaining viable social norms are still the subject of significant debate, it is useful at this point in our inquiry to proceed from the premise that community is indeed a potentially powerful force in cyberspace that cannot be ignored. In some areas, online users are quite fragmented, and patterns are very difficult to discern. In others, it may sometimes be feasible to locate the profile of the average Netizen and the range of practices that she might embrace. And in certain situations, it is still possible to identify clear social norms that cannot be ignored in any analysis of prospective regulatory changes.

Such norms are reflected in some very basic online practices that may have already influenced the development of the law in this area. They include the generally accepted activity of linking without permission, the aggressive commitment to a libertarian view of free-speech rights, and the ongoing consensus regarding the perceived right to remain anonymous. In addition, many believe that digital copyright law will inevitably be impacted by a culture that continues to embrace the unrestricted copying and distribution of documents, music files, and other intellectual property that may still be protected under traditional legal principles.[44]

Of course, these norms have often encountered great resistance from certain Internet stakeholders who, like the sodbusters of the Old West, have resorted to digital "fences" as a means of separation and control. Indeed, a review of recent scholarship reveals that the fence analogy is applicable to a range of disputes, including those that focus on free speech (virtual fences restricting access to information), copyright (digital barriers protecting intellectual property), privacy (using software code to create private space), safety (building firewalls to foil hackers), and jurisdiction (digital fences as the potential equivalent of new borders in the online world).

On a larger and more symbolic level, fences do not simply represent ominous barriers restricting access, protective walls guaranteeing some form of security, or new types of national and international boundaries. Ultimately, they represent law, order, and control. And as different types of fences are built in cyberspace, new social norms reflecting these changing dimensions of control may inevitably emerge.

In *Mending Wall,* written by Robert Frost in 1914, the poet tells of an old stone fence in rural New England that has been worn down by the forces of time and nature. One spring morning, the neighbors meet to repair the fence between them, and the poet wonders aloud whether and to what extent the wall is needed. "Good fences make good neighbors," his counterpart responds. But the poet is not convinced. "Before I built a wall," he declares, "I'd ask to know what I was walling in or walling out." Unmoved, the neighbor continues to rebuild the wall. "I see him there," the poet writes, "bringing a stone grasped firmly by the top in each hand . . . He will not go behind his father's saying, and he likes having thought of it so well. He says again, 'Good fences make good neighbors.'"

Do good fences make good neighbors? In the western film, the answer is not always a simple one. In *Shane,* fences are not necessarily a good thing. Shane himself ultimately fights on behalf of fences, but he does so in an ambivalent and hesitant manner, and arguably for reasons having nothing to do with his feelings regarding the true value of fenced-off land. In *Liberty Valance,* fences are central to the development of the garden of civilization, whereas, in *Cimarron,* they represent the first step toward crass industrialization and a not entirely positive view of progress.

The answer is no simpler in cyberspace, and commentators have certainly not reached a consensus as they continue to examine the role of social norms, the value of digital fences, and the nature of control in the online world. Indeed, in light of the analysis in this chapter, cyberspace emerges as highly protean, defying easy analysis and certainly resisting control. An in-depth exploration of parallels to the world of the western film yields not only some remarkable similarities, but also a range of interesting perspectives on the character and scope of the cyberspace community itself and on the continuing role of certain day-to-day Net users in seeking to maintain control over the online world. The popularity of Ellickson's emphasis on the importance of socialization and the primacy of social norms suggests that his research goes to the heart of the debate regarding the role of law in an environment where no one person or group appears to be in charge.

Before we continue our inquiry into this debate, it is important to ascertain the nature of cyberspace itself. What exactly is cyberspace? Is it really a different place, or simply a hackneyed, geography-based metaphor? How different is human interaction on the Internet, and how much more different will it become? In chapter 2, we turn to an exploration of these questions.

2

Just How Different Is Cyberspace?

Rise into a new world of wonders on IBM's "People Wall." ... [S]oon you are soaring into a fantastic new world called the "Information Machine." Here, you find a new kind of living picture entertainment.... Suddenly you're sharing the reactions of a racing car driver at 120 M.P.H. Then you plan strategy with a football coach. You join famous scientists at work.

—Advertisement for IBM Pavilion, *Official Guide to the New York World's Fair,* 1964–1965

There is no such thing as a single, monolithic, online subculture; it's more like an ecosystem of subcultures, some frivolous, others serious. The cutting edge of scientific discourse is migrating to virtual communities, where you can read the electronic pre-printed reports of molecular biologists and cognitive scientists. At the same time, activists and educational reformers are using the same medium as a political tool. You can use virtual communities to find a date, sell a lawnmower, publish a novel, conduct a meeting.

—Howard Rheingold, *The Virtual Community: Homesteading on the Electronic Frontier,* Circa 1993

And where is law going? ... To a place where there are new opportunities for interacting with the law and where there are also significant challenges to the legal profession and to traditional legal practices and concepts. To an unfamiliar and rapidly changing information environment. ... To a world of flexible spaces, of new relationships, and of greater possibilities for individual and group communication. To a place where law faces new meanings and new expectations.

—M. Ethan Katsh, *Law in a Digital World,* 1995

For those who seek to regulate cyberspace, the question of how different it is becomes a central component of the inquiry. If the Internet is simply another high-tech method of sending and receiving information, then arguably the same legal and policy principles that apply to other forms of communication are applicable here. If the differences are only a matter of degree, then minor adjustments can be made in the law and the task still remains relatively straightforward. But if the online world is different enough to be distinguishable from the offline world in significant ways—and noted commentators have argued as much—then the task of would-be regulators becomes much more complicated indeed.

At the most basic level, everyone agrees. The 1990s version of the Internet has become a new, widely used form of communication with three distinguishing features. It has provided the means for instantaneous global transmission of written messages, which may also be accompanied by graphic and audio-visual material. It has expanded the ability to communicate easily with large numbers of people. And it has emerged as a vehicle for unprecedented access to information. Although fax machines and various other forms of telephone, radio, and satellite transmission provide similar benefits, the scope of Internet communication via e-mail, newsgroups, and the World Wide Web—combined with its relatively low cost for those who already have the hardware—makes it at least somewhat different from anything that has come before.

For the majority of people, however, the Internet is more than just a bit different. Most would concede that it is different enough to merit a level of attention that very few other modes of communications have received. And many see the Internet as something more than simply another communication tool, although just how one might classify this new medium has been the subject of debate at the highest levels of government and industry.

The controversy surrounding the correct classification of the Internet came to the forefront during the *Reno v. ACLU* litigation of 1996–1997.[1] At the oral arguments for the first Internet-related case to reach the U.S. Supreme Court, both attorneys and justices focused extensively on the nature of cyberspace and sought to identify the most relevant analogy for it.

Deputy Solicitor General Seth P. Waxman, representing the government, argued that the Internet might be viewed as analogous to a library. Building on the fact that many people use the Internet as a research tool, he argued that the Communications Decency Act (CDA) simply required that certain indecent material be put in "a different room" of the library.[2] Plaintiffs also liked the library analogy, but for different reasons. Judith Krug of the American Library Association noted with pleasure that during the oral arguments in the *Reno* case, "the justices paid special attention to the threat that the CDA would pose to libraries around the country seeking to use the Internet to provide greater public access to information."[3]

Justice Stephen Breyer wondered aloud at the oral argument whether the Internet might simply be more like a telephone. Given that a large percentage of online users at the time communicated via modems over telephone lines, the analogy seemed quite appropriate. Breyer asked whether a group of high school students discussing their sexual experiences online might appropriately be characterized as simply teenagers talking on the telephone, and he appeared genuinely concerned about the prospect of criminalizing such behavior.[4]

Justices Sandra Day O'Connor and Anthony Kennedy suggested in their questions to Mr. Waxman that the Internet might be considered analogous to "a street corner or a park," raising the question of whether the online world could be viewed as a traditional public forum for purposes of First Amendment analysis.[5] Commentators have wrestled extensively with this issue, seeking to determine whether the Internet might best be characterized as a public street corner or more akin to a private shopping mall.[6]

The government, however, appeared at other times to prefer that the Internet be viewed as more akin to broadcast media. The Justice Department's brief in *Reno* relied heavily on *FCC v. Pacifica,*[7] the case that considered the complaints of a father who heard the broadcast of George Carlin's "Seven Dirty Words" monologue with his young son. In *Pacifica,* the Court found that "broadcasting . . . has received the most limited First Amendment protection" both because of its pervasiveness and because of child accessibility.[8] Building on *Pacifica* in its brief, the government argued that it should be able to regulate online speech because there is a "danger of inadvertent exposure to indecent material on the Internet as well."[9] Plaintiffs countered, however, with the argument that if the Internet is analogous to any form of media, it is newspapers and magazines—which are afforded much greater First Amendment protection under constitutional law.[10]

While in the end the Court found that the Internet—at least for purposes of deciding the *Reno* case—is more analogous to both a library *and* a shopping mall, it can be argued that every one of the analogies raised in the oral arguments might apply at some point depending on the circumstances. Indeed, at the turn of the century, the Internet can probably be viewed as all of the above, and more: a library, a telephone, a public park, a local bar, a shopping mall, a broadcast medium, a print medium, a medical clinic, a private living room, and a public educational institution. No previous mode of communication in the history of humankind has served so many purposes all at once. And Internet law scholars are increasingly building on this conception of cyberspace, arguing persuasively that it should no longer be viewed as one space, but as a series of separate "cyberspaces" which may be very different from one another.[11]

Beyond the identification of analogies that highlight unique aspects of these networked environments, it is also instructive to consider the lifestyle changes that have been triggered by the Internet over the past ten years. These changes have been documented extensively in the media, and they include a dependence on e-mail for essential work-related and family-related communication, a reliance on the World Wide Web as a basic information resource, and the subsequent emergence of desktop and laptop computers as fundamental components of people's lives.

A 1998 study of online users conducted by Roper Starch Worldwide, for example, found that once Americans hook up to the Internet, they develop a strong passion for the online world and begin to view their Internet connections as indispensable. Ninety percent of the poll's respondents said that they use the Internet to stay in touch with family and friends, and more than seventy percent said that they regularly access the Web and newsgroups to obtain information about products to purchase. Even more significantly, most said that, if stranded on a desert island, they would pick the Internet over a telephone or a television. And eighty percent described the computer as the most important invention of the twentieth century.[12]

Indeed, online users are now using the Internet from the safety and convenience of their own homes to meet people, share photographs and other artistic creations, maintain personal and professional contact, advertise, seek out and obtain jobs, engage in comparison shopping, and participate in an emerging online health-care industry. Inevitably, these sorts of lifestyle changes have in turn triggered numerous changes in certain key businesses and professions as well.

With regard to business in general, not only has the information technology field become the largest industry in the U.S.,[13] but the long-recognized potential for making money in cyberspace through advertising and e-commerce has now been realized. By late 1998, for example, online business trade in the U.S. had reached $43 billion for the year. In addition, a highly publicized report by Forrester Research, Inc., concluded that the value of participating in Internet commerce would increase dramatically as more companies join in and as the "efficiencies of Internet trading" become even more apparent. And even after the dot-com shakeout in the year 2000, Forrester predicted that North American e-commerce alone "would reach $3.2 trillion in 2004."[14]

As far back as 1995, a report by the U.S. government's Office of Technology Assessment (OTA) sought to address the wide-ranging implications of these business-related changes. The OTA report explained that new technology was in the process of creating "footloose" companies that no longer needed to be based in costly and congested city centers. "Metros, cities or parts of cities that will not or cannot adapt run the risk of being left behind to face stagnation or decline," the OTA report concluded.[15]

In the legal profession, the Internet has provided a vast array of new options for practitioners, serving as a vehicle for discovering information about courtroom foes, posting queries on bulletin boards to identify expert witnesses, conferring with clients, accessing primary sources, and seeking out new business.[16] Class-action lawsuits have actually coalesced in cyberspace.[17]

Not only have lawyers and law firms established a presence in the online world through an array of Web sites, but a growing number of academics, practitioners, and entrepreneurs in the legal community have posted valuable legal information online. Primary legal documents and high-quality legal analysis are now more readily accessible to the general public than at any time in history.

In the medical profession, the online world has clearly become a gold mine of interactive, health-related information and activity. Customizable health-care directories are available through the portals of all the major search engines, including updated links to a range of health-related Web sites. Chat rooms and newsgroups engage persons in online discussions about their respective medical problems, and participants are encouraged to share sensitive personal information. Individual doctors exchange e-mail messages with their patients, sometimes tying their conversations to the results of simple tests that patients can perform by themselves at home.

And technology that combines e-mail with audio and video—enabling online patients to communicate their physical symptoms in great detail—continues to be developed worldwide. By early 2001, for example, Eastman Kodak had already launched such a system for the health-care market.[18]

The health-care providers of the online world include a growing number of medical doctors who have been urged by the American Medical Association to create their own Web sites. Some of these doctors have been answering questions online, and a few have been charging fees for the service. In addition, medical schools across the globe are now posting incredible amounts of information. Medical journals are online, as are many medical organizations and pharmaceutical companies. There is also a vast amount of information online regarding alternative medical practices and therapies. Acupuncturists, chiropractors, massage therapists, and reflexologists are now populating the web, as are herbalists and homeopathic medicine specialists.

In the education community, changes have been particularly noticeable at the college and university level. Not only has Internet technology changed the way faculty members communicate with each other and with their students, but many institutions have been experimenting with different methods of using cyberspace to facilitate the education process. These methods have ranged from the posting of syllabi, course material, links, and resources to such elaborate learning activities as course projects involving the creation of interactive web pages.

An interesting development in this area of higher education has been the growing prevalence of online-discussion forums via e-mail, newsgroups, and/or the World Wide Web. Some professors, for example, have required students to participate in e-mail exchanges, either through existing mailing lists or through relatively private vehicles that they have set up. Others have set up Web-based electronic bulletin boards, where students participate in online inquiry by posting responses to questions by professors and to the posts of other students.[19] And some professors have also set up real-time chat rooms, where, at specific times, students are expected to go online and participate in discussions led by professors or other facilitators. Educators often find that these sorts of activities help maximize student interaction and add valuable new dimensions to in-class discussions.[20]

But perhaps the most significant—and controversial—education-related development in cyberspace has been the emergence of distance education. A growing number of new and existing educational institutions are beginning to offer course credit for work that can be completed online.[21] While some institutions require at least some in-person contact, others allow students to participate solely via computer. Such participation may include a combination of e-mail, online discussion forums, and Web-based tools for the dissemination of material via text, graphics, audio, and/or video. Educators who recognize the importance of in-person contact have warned that such an approach is filled with dangerous pitfalls, but others believe that distance education—if done correctly—can only spread knowledge and build valuable skills for more people across the globe.[22]

Other professions, and indeed the daily offline activities of people everywhere, continue to change dramatically as a result of ongoing technological innovations and recent Internet-related developments.[23] And experts have gone to great lengths to document the far-reaching implications of these changes. A significant body of literature focusing on the Internet and society had, in fact, emerged by 2001.[24]

In light of all this compelling evidence, it is virtually impossible for anyone to view today's Internet as anything other than "different." But there is significant disagreement among commentators, policymakers, and members of the legal community regarding the nature and extent of this difference. At one end of the spectrum are those who recognize occasional differences, conceding in certain limited cases that some new rules and regulations may be necessary.[25] Others may go much further, arguing that today's networked computer environment is *different enough*—both in its design and in the nature of the online activity that takes place—to merit new and different approaches to regulatory issues that inevitably arise.[26] Finally, at the other end of the spectrum, are those who would go so far as to argue that the online world is metaphysically both a different place and time, transcending commonly accepted notions of geography and duration.[27]

For commentators who argue that the Internet is only slightly different, *cyberspace* may itself be a troublesome term. The word denotes, or at least connotes, a different space, and many believe that this may be an attractive metaphor but not an appropriate description of the reality.[28] According to this view, the Internet is wonderfully unique in many ways, but it is, in the end, nothing more than a network of computer networks. There is no separate or different reality. People are never *in* cyberspace, but simply sitting at their computers and connected to other computers. A Web site or interactive discussion forum is not located in some virtual reality, but is simply a digitized representation stored on a server that exists physically in a particular geographical location. Lifestyles may have changed as a result of this new medium, but existing rules and regulations are more than adequate in most cases to address problems and disputes that may arise. After all, proponents of this view may argue, we were certainly able to adapt existing regulatory principles to other new types of communications—from the telegraph and telephone to radio and television. We can do the same here. People are still behaving as people, doing the same sorts of things via the Internet that they did before the Internet existed.

Eugene Volokh's research on cyberspace issues often exemplifies this *traditionalist* view. While Volokh has been an enthusiastic participant in the communications revolution and has not hesitated to predict even greater changes in this context, he often challenges those who would view the Internet as some sort of different space. In a 1995 article, for example, he takes issue with the view that the "digital world" is in the process of triggering such radical changes that it requires the development of a new set of rules.

Although occasionally using the term *cyberspace,* Volokh appears to prefer terms such as *computer networks, electronic environment,* and *the new technologies* to describe Internet communication. He concedes the significance of these new technologies, but foresees much more modest changes in the legal profession as a result, thus challenging the view that "computers will substantially alter the way we think about law, the way we do law, and the role of law in society." In a brief discussion of copyright issues, he rejects the view that "the new technologies are basically incompatible with existing copyright law." The basic policy of copyright law, Volokh argues, is to compensate authors so that they have more incentive to create, and he insists that this policy is as applicable to the "dynamic works" of new media as it is to "static" ones.[29]

Commentators who share this view make similar arguments with regard to Internet commerce. They reject the view, for example, that shopping on the Internet is different enough to merit an entirely new regulatory structure.[30] Yes, they concede, purchases are often made without actually seeing or touching or testing out the item under consideration. Buyers may wonder whether the seller got the order right, or whether a contract has been consummated. High-pressure salespersons are avoided, and interaction occurs in a different manner. But similar differences may be apparent in other alternative methods of shopping, such as catalogue sales. According to this view, online shopping is just a fancier version of an old-fashioned method of buying and selling, and thus does not generally qualify for new forms of regulation.

A second broad view of computer networks is located somewhere in the middle of the continuum between those who view the Internet as only slightly different and those who view it as so radically different as to constitute another time zone and/or geographical location. Most commentators favoring this *moderate* view are very comfortable with the term *cyberspace,* and, indeed, would adopt the definition set forth by Howard Rheingold in 1993:

> *Cyberspace* . . . is the name some people use for the conceptual space where words, human relationships, data, wealth, and power are manifested by people using computer-mediated communications technology.[31]

According to this view, at least some portions of cyberspace are significantly different in both their architectural design and the type of activity that occurs there. From a design perspective, many of the differences in networked environments are a function of the "unique combination of features" governing interaction in this medium, including "the ability to communicate instantaneously on a one-to-one, one-to-many, and many-to-many basis, the independence of communication from physical distance, the relatively low barriers to entry to communication, and the entirely software-mediated nature of all communication and interaction."[32]

In addition to recognizing these basic features, some moderates actually view portions of the networked environment as more akin to a separate virtual reality. According to this perspective, persons who log on do not just establish a connection to servers and to computer networks along with other persons and computers, but actually become participants in a unique digital setting. By connecting simultaneously and engaging in varying levels of simultaneous communication across many geographical barriers, people take part in activity where things begin to happen in a very different manner. Proponents of this view argue that at a certain point, it is only logical to refer to the place where all this is happening as a different place. It may be different conceptually, or it may be different legally, or for some, it may even be different physically, but the acceptance of the term *cyberspace* as an appropriate and popular designation arguably implies at least a tacit recognition of its *separate* nature in certain cases and for certain types of online interaction.

For those whose work reflects this view in at least some fashion, the term *cyberspace* is more than just a metaphor. Some, for example, see *cyberspace* as a broad, descriptive scientific term, encompassing a range of networked environments that have developed over time. Buford Terrell, for instance, argues that "cyberspace was first visited when Morse sent his first telegraph message." For him, "cyberspace is that venue in which immediate interactions, including asynchronous ones, can occur without physical presence."[33]

Science fiction writer William Gibson, who coined the term *cyberspace* in a 1982 *Omni* magazine piece, traces its history back to the 1940s. Although, on some level, he still views it as a metaphor, it is, for him, "a metaphor that allows us to grasp . . . this place where since about the time of the second world war we've increasingly done so many of the things that we think of as civilization."

Gibson goes on to argue in a 1994 interview that "in a very real sense cyberspace is the place where any telephone call takes place, and where the bank keeps your money these days because it's all direct electronic transfer." He also contends that it is where much of the stock market actually takes place, "in the electronic communication between the worlds' stock-exchanges." And he believes that "when people use the Internet, that's when they're most obviously navigating in cyberspace"[34]

There are certainly enough differences in the nature of the cyberspace experience to provide support for those who designate portions of the online world as unique and perhaps even separate. In cyberspace, one can achieve a level of anonymity that is generally not possible in most day-to-day activities. While on some level, there is less privacy in cyberspace, on another level, a person can change her age, gender, race, and/or socio-economic status and present a completely different persona to others in online chat rooms and discussion forums. People become less inhibited and feel more free to act in ways that they might not think of acting in the actual physical presence of others. Countless stories have emerged of people with minimal social skills who have raised havoc in cyberspace, relying implicitly or explicitly on the apparent lack of accountability for their actions. A certain level of anarchy has in fact been tolerated in many parts of the online world, reflecting a libertarian Net culture that insists on freedom of expression at all times and in all contexts.

The level of openness that has emerged in cyberspace can also lead to some very extreme and unsettling experiences. Laws are broken with impunity, unsubstantiated rumors take on an inappropriate level of credibility, young people have unprecedented access to adult information, and people witness things they may not have chosen to witness. While the debate regarding the extent of society's willingness to tolerate a certain level of anarchic and unlawful behavior in some parts of the online world continues, the simple recognition that such behavior may exist *there and not here* leads inexorably to the conclusion that cyberspace is different enough to be viewed not only as unique but, at times, even as a separate place.

Jerry Kang provides support for this view through an analysis of race relations and the prospective impact of networked environments in this context. He demonstrates how "cyberspace—by helping people meet—enables new forms of social interaction." He also writes of cyberspace facilitating ongoing relationships, often through "virtual communities of common interests, experiences, and fates . . . Examples include academic e-mail distribution lists, Usenet newsgroups, chat rooms, and instant messaging." In these examples, Kang argues, cyberspace functions more like a series of sidewalk cafes, and the activity taking place *there* can play a very important role in bringing people together.[35]

Lawrence Lessig apparently takes a similar view, while emphasizing that cyberspace is both a separate and not separate place. Believing cyberspace to have existed as early as the 1920s—or even earlier—he writes that "even in 1928, much of life had moved onto the wires . . . those first steps into cyberspace."[36] Today, it is indeed "a place," he concedes. "People live there. They experience all the sorts of things that they experience in real space, there. For some, they experience more. They experience this not as isolated individuals, playing some high tech computer game; they experience it in groups, in communities, among strangers, among people they come to know, and sometimes like . . . [But] while they are in that place, cyberspace, they are also here."[37]

David Post would go even farther. In 1996, he and David Johnson defined *cyberspace* as "the global aggregate of digital, interactive, electronic communication networks," excluding the worldwide telephone network, "non-interactive media" such as television, and "non-networked" computer applications such as computer games.[38] Post continues to believe that a definition of cyberspace that "focuses on its 'place-ness'—the persistence of interactions between individuals over time, a characteristic not shared with telegraph or telephone systems—is a useful one for helping to focus attention on certain legally-significant aspects of interactions 'there.'"[39]

Post's emphasis on the unique separateness of cyberspace for purposes of approaching regulation issues has been embraced by a significant number of commentators, jurists, and policy makers.[40] And for those who have adopted this view, the extent of the differences in the online world is often the key factor in distinguishing such a position from the more traditionalist approach. U.S. District Court Judge Nancy Gertner, for example, addressing issues of personal jurisdiction and trademark infringement in the 1997 case of *Digital Equipment Corporation v. AltaVista Technology*, considered the question of how legal analysis in these types of disputes might require different paradigms. She concluded that the changes in communication brought about by the emergence of cyberspace are so significant that a different concept of territory may very well be in order:

> The change is significant. Physical boundaries typically have framed legal boundaries, in effect creating signposts that warn that we will be required after crossing to abide by different rules. . . . To impose traditional territorial concepts on the commercial uses of the Internet has dramatic implications, opening the Web user up to inconsistent regulations throughout the fifty states, indeed, throughout the globe. It also raises the possibility of dramatically chilling what may well be the most participatory marketplace of mass speech that this country—and indeed the world—has yet seen. As a result courts have been, and should be, cautious in applying traditional concepts.[41]

It must be emphasized, however, that in this broad middle ground, the level of "separateness" or territoriality that may be identified is not necessarily a determining or distinguishing factor in the inquiry. Just how different cyberspace—or a portion of cyberspace—might be is necessarily a function of design and activity. Those who view an online space as different enough will focus on the uniqueness of Internet architecture and the differences in the type of activity that takes place there. They may or may not also believe that cyberspace should be viewed as a separate place.

Thus Andrew Shapiro and Phil Agre—who have identified unique nuances and wide-ranging implications in the growth and development of networked environments—both believe that it is inappropriate to view cyberspace as a separate reality —either metaphorically or from the perspective of legal boundaries.

Shapiro, for example, insists that "we are not well served by the idea that cyberspace is an autonomous 'place.' . . . It suggests that what happens 'there' is in some way unconnected to what happens 'here.'" He argues that "the real significance of cyberspace is not in its being elsewhere but . . . in its coming increasingly closer to us" as we integrate it more and more into our daily lives. For Shapiro, cyberspace is "a locus of control":

> It is not so much a space as it is a lens through which we can see the world. It is a filter through which we can do almost anything: learn, work, socialize, transact, participate in politics. It is an interface that allows us to control other things. . . .[42]

Agre, even as he continues to develop innovative constructs for viewing the major technological developments of our time,[43] rejects both the idea of cyberspace as a separate legal space and the use of the term *cyberspace* as a "utopian" metaphor. Taking issue with Johnson and Post's view of the online world as a separate place, he argues that their "border problems get worse as the Internet becomes integrated into the world around it." Agre wonders why a corporate Intranet, for example, should be reckoned part of cyberspace? "And where are the borders of cyberspace," he asks, "when the Internet protocols begin flowing in cars and kitchen appliances? The borders between cyberspace and real life are less obvious than they seem, and they are getting less distinct every day."

Because the Internet is becoming integrated with the institutional world around it, Agre concludes, "the concept of cyberspace . . . may have had its day." What is needed, he believes, is "a post-utopian imagination that embraces the complexity of human institutions and a critical technical practice that embraces the coevolution of institutions and technologies."[44]

A third broad view of cyberspace can be discerned in the work of commentators such as Ethan Katsh and John Perry Barlow, who argue that the online world is so different that it might appropriately be characterized as another geographical space and/or time zone. While some adherents of this position are content to focus on the impact that such a radically different new medium might have, others emphasize the importance of aggressively rejecting any sort of regulation for this separate entity.

In his writings, Katsh appears to have adopted the view that at some level cyberspace is a separate metaphysical space capable of transcending both distance and time. "The computer is a space machine," he declares, "negating physical distance and creating new spaces in which novel relationships and activities can occur. . . . [It is also] . . . a time machine, creating a new environment in which our relationship with time becomes different from what it has been."[45]

With regard to space, for example, every online user has equal access to the Internet and is located at the same distance from the online world. Cyberspace is just as close to an online user in Japan as it is to an online user in the United Kingdom, and it can be accessed with the same ease by simply logging on and connecting up. Katsh argues that "cyberspace does not mean that all territorial, institutional, doctrinal, or conceptual boundaries are replaced and become irrelevant, but cyberspace does overlay a whole new set of opportunities for overcoming physical distances and creating and shaping virtual spaces." And with regard to time, Katsh contends that the online world "has brought us new ways of speaking and thinking about time, of 'time shifting,' of 'real time,' of relying more on and appreciating the value of asynchronous communication."[46]

Cyberspace is seen by proponents of this view as having a transformative effect—fostering new growth, encouraging experimentation, and maximizing human potential. Thus, the online world is more than just different; it is very special indeed. And outsiders who would tamper with it must be resisted. Science fiction imagery is often invoked in this context, with any regulatory body seen as alien and all proposed rules viewed as particularly threatening.

Barlow claims to be the first person to name Cyberspace, a word which he insists must be capitalized because he continues to view it as a place. He explains that he was participating in an online discussion on The Well in early 1990 when he conceived of cyberspace as "any 'space' in which people can gather their minds without bringing their bodies."[47]

A noted libertarian and former lyricist for the legendary rock group The Grateful Dead, Barlow cofounded the Electronic Frontier Foundation and has been a tireless spokesperson for an expansive view of the rights of Netizens. In his writings, he has sought to popularize the term *cyberspace,* most notably, in "Crime and Puzzlement," which appeared in the Spring 1990 issue of the *Whole Earth Review.* "The important thing was to name it," he explained years later. "Once it had a name, then the people who met there could have a society and a stake in that society."[48]

Perhaps Barlow's most famous work in this area is "The Economy of Ideas" (1994), a *Wired* magazine article in which he argues that copyright law has become irrelevant in the information age.[49] In 1996, on the day that the Communications Decency Act became law in the U.S., he posted a "Declaration of the Independence of Cyberspace." In an oft-quoted passage, he addresses the "governments of the industrial world" and declares that:

> Cyberspace does not lie within your borders. Do not think that you can build it, as though it were a public construction project. You cannot. . . . You do not know our culture, our ethics, or the unwritten codes that already provide our society more order than could be obtained by any of your impositions. . . . You claim there are problems among us that you need to solve. . . . Many of these problems don't exist. Where there are real conflicts, where there are wrongs, we will identify them and address them by our means. We are forming our own Social Contract. This governance will arise according to the conditions of our world, not yours. Our world is different. Cyberspace consists of transactions, relationships, and thought itself, arrayed like a standing wave in the web of our communications. . . .[50]

If we examine the online world as a whole, the debate regarding conceptions of cyberspace and the nature and extent of the differences brought about by information technology remains unresolved. Three broad positions can be identified, even as it must be noted that their advocates often disagree with each other while adopting similar views of the larger picture.[51]

If we examine individual cyber spaces, it quickly becomes apparent that a resolution of the larger debate may not be necessary at all. Indeed, all three positions are often applicable—and the suggestions of individual commentators for prospective action within those positions appropriate—depending on differences in architectural design and the online activities that have been identified with particular problems on a case-by-case basis.

For example, in determining the rules regarding copyright in cyberspace, would-be regulators must examine the level of ease with which material is currently copied in the online world vis-à-vis the level of ease with which material is currently copied outside the online world. With regard to privacy, they should try to ascertain what—if anything—is different about cyberspace in that context. The same holds true for free-speech controversies, and for other high-profile disputes that have arisen or are likely to arise in the near future. In some cases, it may be determined that things are not a whole lot different here than they have been in the offline world, and thus the conclusions of the traditionalists would be most directly applicable. In other cases, it may be determined that there are significant differences, and that the suggestions of those in the broad middle ground should be considered. In a third category of cases, it may be determined that both the online space and the activity taking place in that space are so different as to constitute a separate virtual reality, in which case the countercultural views of Katsh and Barlow would be most directly relevant.

In addition to the differences in architectural design and online activity that can be found in at least some cyberspaces and the relevant changes in lifestyle that have often been triggered, one other key difference has arisen in certain cases at the jurisdiction and enforcement level. Not only are national and international borders crossed easily in cyberspace, but they are crossed indiscriminately. This is arguably very different from other forms of either high-tech or low-tech communication. Phone calls, faxes, and broadcasts all cross borders fairly easily these days, but, as a general rule, signals are given in advance as to which borders are being crossed, and who the likely recipient might be. In cyberspace, that is not necessarily the case.

Thus novel questions of jurisdiction have quickly emerged. If it is not clear which borders might be crossed, and who the recipient of the communication might be, then it certainly follows that it may not be clear which governing entity has jurisdiction over a dispute that may arise as a result of such communication. And if it is not clear who has jurisdiction over a dispute, then it is certainly not clear whose rules might apply, and in what context. Finally, if it is not clear whose rules apply, then it may be even more problematic to ascertain how these rules might be enforced—even if one can determine who the wrongdoer might be in a particular situation.

Several paradigmatic legal disputes in recent years have served to crystallize many of these interrelated questions. One is the *Thomas* case, a criminal controversy involving pornography dealers in Northern California who were convicted in Tennessee. The second is the CompuServe Germany case, in which the company's general manager was prosecuted and convicted in Munich for simply letting the Internet "come through" to Bavaria. And then there are two highly problematic e-mail and instant-messaging cases, which sought to punish senders for "crossing state lines" because the messages, although sent to someone in the same state, actually crossed several state borders via cyberspace.

The highly publicized case of *U.S. v. Thomas* has been analyzed and discussed at great length, and is seen by many as a watershed event in the development of cyberspace law.[52] Working out of their Northern California home, the Thomases operated a highly profitable bulletin board system (BBS). Through this system, online customers who registered and paid a membership fee were able to access sexually explicit pictures via computer. Responding to a complaint from a person in Tennessee, an undercover postal inspector signed on to the system and downloaded sexually explicit Graphic Interchange Format (GIF) files. Based primarily on that evidence, the Thomases were indicted in the U.S. District Court for the Western District of Tennessee and convicted under a variety of federal obscenity statutes, including 18 U.S. Code Section 1465, which prohibited "*knowingly* using and causing to be used a facility and means of interstate commerce—a combined computer/telephone system—for the purpose of *transporting* obscene computer-generated materials (the GIF files) in interstate commerce" (emphasis added).[53] The U.S. Court of Appeals for the Sixth Circuit upheld the conviction, and the U.S. Supreme Court declined to hear the case.

Perhaps the most central and, indeed, the most controversial aspect of the *Thomas* decision[54] was its treatment of the jurisdiction and community-standards questions. This court was one of the first to be presented with the proposition that transborder issues in cyberspace trigger a variety of unresolved considerations. Given that, as a matter of course, items posted on a computer in one part of the world can be accessed by persons in other parts of the world where laws might be entirely different, it is unclear whether a different state or a different country should have jurisdiction over the original actor in this regard.

In addition, the Thomases focused on the fact that while the GIFs may have been obscene in Tennessee, they were arguably not obscene in Northern California. Under the first prong of the three-part First Amendment test for obscenity set forth in *Miller v. California,* courts inquire as to whether "the average person applying contemporary community standards would find that the work, taken as a whole, appeals to the prurient interest."[55]

Both defendants and attorneys who filed friend-of-the-court briefs in this case argued that recent developments in technology require a new definition of community, one based on "the broad-ranging connections among people in cyberspace." Without such a definition, they contended, there would be "an impossible chill on protected speech" because creators of materials in cyberspace cannot select who will access the created items, and will necessarily be forced to censor their materials so as not to run afoul of more restrictive community standards.[56]

The Sixth Circuit, however, concluded that the question of whether to recognize community standards for cyberspace under the First Amendment did not need to be addressed. The court did not believe that the Thomases were mistreated by virtue of the fact that the standard of obscenity was different in Tennessee than it might have been in Northern California. After all, the court reasoned, the Thomases must have anticipated when setting up the BBS that people from all over the country would sign up. A registration system for the BBS had been established, and the Thomases arguably could have rejected potential customers from a given location where the obscenity standards might have posed a problem.

Did the Thomases actually *know* they were sending picture files to Tennessee, or at least making them available to be copied in Tennessee? Legal scholars have debated this question in the aftermath of the Thomas decision, and the results of this debate may ultimately turn on a definition of *knowledge.* Although the Thomases knew that they had one or more customers in Tennessee, they probably did not know that copies of the software had been downloaded. And not only did they probably not know it at the time, but they may not have known it afterward—at least until they reviewed their financial balance sheets. But the Thomases' software knew that this was happening, even if the Thomases themselves did not. If your software knows, does that mean that you know? Should that mean that you know?

Clearly, the Thomases were not the best defendants to help sort out these issues. As commentators have pointed out, courts in general have little sympathy for pornography dealers, especially those who can control the distribution of the pornographic material and who know beforehand where it might be headed.[57] An entirely different set of circumstances might be anticipated in the future, however, with a different type of defendant, particularly if the interaction takes place on the World Wide Web rather than a bulletin board service, and if it involves anonymous strangers rather than registered subscribers.

Consider, for example, the hypothetical case of a respectable professor in Northern California who posts an example of a controversial work of art on her class Web site for her students to view and discuss. If a copy of this work is viewed and/or downloaded in Tennessee, and judged to be obscene under Tennessee community standards, would the professor be convicted in the same way that the Thomases had been convicted? Would the professor be viewed as having knowledge—on some level—that anything on her Web site could be copied and downloaded in Tennessee, or in any other location across the globe for that matter? And would it make any difference that the defendant is a respectable professor who is not making any money off of her site rather than an unrespectable pornography dealer who is clearing $200,000 a year? Should it make any difference?

Similar questions on an international level were raised by the prosecution and conviction of Felix Bruno Somm, then General Manager of CompuServe Deutschland, for simply allowing the Internet to be completely accessible in Germany via CompuServe.[58]

In December 1995, the police in Munich (the capital of the conservative state of Bavaria) raided the CompuServe offices, and in response, the online service temporarily barred access to two hundred Internet Usenet sites for some four million subscribers worldwide.[59] A huge outcry ensued, with many customers and free-speech activists protesting CompuServe's policy decision in online discussion forums. Particularly troublesome to many of these online protesters was the fact that some of the prohibited sites focused on issues like breast cancer and AIDS.

After a long investigation that followed the police raid, criminal charges were brought against Mr. Somm. According to the Munich prosecutor's office, Mr. Somm was accused of trafficking in pornography and neo-Nazi propaganda. The office said that he "*knowingly* allowed images of child pornography, violent sex and sex with animals from newsgroups . . . to be made accessible to customers of CompuServe Germany" (emphasis added). In addition, prosecutors said that subscribers were also given access to computer games that contained forbidden images of Hitler and Nazi symbols such as swastikas.[60]

Somm and CompuServe both argued that the commercial online service could not shape Internet content specifically for the German market. Apparently, at that point in time, were it to restrict access to certain sites, these restrictions would be in force for all subscribers worldwide.

Despite a global outcry, Somm was convicted in 1998 of violating local pornography laws. The defendant was convicted even though the prosecutors had actually asked for his acquittal in the end. Judge Wilhelm Hubbert apparently disagreed with the arguments of both the prosecution and the defendant. In his decision, Hubbert said that CompuServe had let "protecting the young . . . take second place to maximizing profits." Somm was sentenced to two years probation and ordered to pay one hundred thousand marks to charity. An appeal followed.

Like the Thomas case, the conviction of Mr. Somm at the trial-court level serves to highlight the range of unresolved issues in the interrelated areas of jurisdiction, regulation, and enforcement. Somm and the Thomases were convicted for similar reasons—knowingly allowing material to be accessed across borders—even though they arguably did not know that certain material was accessed at a given time. Ultimately, defendants in both cases were caught up in the tricky legal dilemma regarding the applicability of particular laws in particular jurisdictions. And while Somm's conviction was ultimately overturned on appeal, with his legal team taking advantage of a new multimedia law that absolved him of responsibility if it could be shown that he did all he could to block the material, the larger question of Internet service provider liability at the global level remains unresolved.[61]

With online events taking place—at least conceptually—beyond state lines and international borders, it remains unclear which laws are applicable, and in what context. And laws can indeed be very different from place to place. For example, while all countries generally have laws prohibiting the distribution and sale of certain types of pornography, definitions and penalties may vary in a significant fashion. With regard to neo-Nazi propaganda, the situation is even more complicated, given that its dissemination is not a crime in many countries, including the United States.

Because it raises these questions on an international level, and with regard to an arguably respectable defendant who was doing nothing more than managing a large commercial online service, the CompuServe Germany prosecution—even though it was overturned on appeal—may prove to be more important than *Thomas* in the end, affecting issues far beyond pornography alone.

A third example of the new dilemmas affecting would-be regulators and law-enforcement officials is the question of jurisdiction over messages that are sent between persons located in the same state but happen to cross over several state borders in the process. Two recent convictions in local disputes—one in Utah and the other in Texas, under a 1934 federal statute prohibiting the knowing transmission of a threat in "interstate commerce"—highlight some of the complexities that have arisen.

In the Utah case, defendant Matthew Kammersell had sent an instant message from his home computer in Riverdale to the America Online center in Ogden, four miles away.[62] The message, reportedly nothing more than a prank intended to get his girlfriend off work early, was characterized by the prosecution as a bomb threat and included the following language: "We are sick of your censorship and bad service. You can kiss your assess [*sic*] goodbye."[63]

Had the Kammersell incident been deemed a local dispute, the penalties would probably have been much less severe. But the defendant was convicted under the federal statute with the more stringent penalties because prosecutors were able to establish that Kammersell's message actually crossed state lines and went through the AOL servers in Virginia before coming back to Utah. Kammersell had sent the message through his

America Online account, and in 1997, *every* AOL message went through Virginia. The defendant contended that no one saw the message in Virginia, but the court reasoned that the threat does not have to be received or seen by someone across state lines for the requirements of the federal statute to be satisfied. Kammersell was convicted and had to serve time in a federal penitentiary.[64]

In the Texas case, defendant John Murillo, a disgruntled postal worker in Laredo, had sent an e-mail message to a friend who lived across town, but the message actually passed through Tennessee cyberspace, Georgia cyberspace, and New Jersey cyberspace before reaching its destination. The message included the following words: "They are trying everything to make me go postal . . . [I] . . . can only take so much. You kick a dog so much and sooner or later that chain will snap. I have been very patient with them but I am tired and making plans. Judgment day will come. It will be a shootout at the O.K. Corral."[65]

Prosecutors in the Laredo case were also successful in getting the court to recognize the message as a true threat within the meaning of the more stringent federal statute. Murillo, too, was convicted.

With current technology, e-mail messages may literally bounce uncontrollably from server to server across state lines and even international borders before reaching their destination. Indeed, the path a person takes as she travels through cyberspace via e-mail or the World Wide Web is rarely predictable. A person's Internet connection may take her through Canada or Mexico, for example, en route from Los Angeles to Denver. Or an e-mail message from San Francisco to Jerusalem may travel through computers in Italy and Turkey in one direction, while the response may bounce up through Russia, down to Egypt, across to Brazil, and then back to the Bay Area. There is typically no way to predict which international borders will be crossed.

Experts have noted that technologically savvy users may actually be able to control the direction in which their messages travel. When e-mail messages are transmitted, they are divided into packets of digital data, and, as Attorney Diane Cabell explains, there is a method called "strict source routing" that may enable senders to establish total control over "each and every IP address" visited by their packets. However, Cabell notes that this method is not foolproof, because for one reason or another "a lot of the Internet does not honor source routing."[66] Thus, even the most technologically adept may not always be successful in their efforts to keep their messages from crossing state lines. And policymakers continue to wonder whether laws that were promulgated in another era are adequate or appropriate to address such realities.

Of course, regulation questions in this context are made even more complicated by the rapidly changing technological environment. Given the extent of the recent changes and the fact that few people could anticipate the scope of these changes during the past decade, an understanding of how the online world might be further transformed over the next ten to twenty years is essential if appropriate rules and viable governance mechanisms are to be established.

As a starting point, many people believe that there are significant parallels between the technological developments that took place during the years 1890–1910 and those of today. For example, in *Martin Dressler* (1996), Pulitzer-Prize-winning novelist Steven Millhauser presents a picture of New York City at the turn of the century, and the similarities between that time and our own are striking.[67] Through the eyes of Martin Dressler, a pleasant and engaging entrepreneur, we see how the advent of electricity, the development of new construction techniques, and a wide variety of major inventions combined to transform both the face of the city and its way of life.

If, in fact, we are in the midst of changes that are at least as rapid and far-reaching as those at the beginning of the twentieth century, then arguably we have only begun to see the extent of the revolutionary developments that will be brought about by information technology. Particularly now, at the beginning of the new millennium, an unending series of predictions have been set forth . . . and it is often unclear where science fiction ends and nonfiction begins in this regard.

All agree, for example, that the twenty-first century will bring a greater level of interconnectivity, both within the basic *real-world* context of day-to-day pursuits and within the framework of a growing virtual-reality industry. Devices connecting people to cyberspace will inevitably become smaller, more efficient, and less expensive, presenting us with viable opportunities for an even greater integration of Internet-based technology into our daily affairs.

And it is certainly clear that no one knows just how far all this will go, or, in fact, to what extent current technology will actually be replaced by inventions and discoveries that we may not even be able to imagine at the present time. Two recent books—one fiction and the other ostensibly nonfiction—provide some interesting examples of possible developments that will undoubtedly trigger the same sorts of debates concerning regulation that we are seeing today.

In *The Truth Machine* (1996), novelist James Halperin presents a picture of the years 2000–2050 through the story of computer genius Pete Armstrong, who, as an inventor and entrepreneur, becomes the most influential person of his era.[68] The meticulously researched novel, which is narrated by a computer looking back on the story from the mid-2000s, presents a series of logical predictions that flow naturally from the current growth and development of technology. Armstrong's most important invention is the computer-based truth machine, which is able to determine with complete accuracy whether or not a person is telling the truth. Not only is the truth machine used by employers and law-enforcement officials, but most people eventually wear a wristwatch version of the device, thus ensuring that all conversations are indeed truthful. The implications for the transformation of society are astonishing.

Ray Kurzweil's *The Age of Spiritual Machines* (1999) is in many ways very similar to *The Truth Machine,* in that it also presents twenty-first-century scenarios that may seem outrageous but could be viewed as logical outgrowths of current developments.[69] Kurzweil presents a fascinating series of predictions focusing on specific years and linked to a highly informed analysis of trends in current technology. Tiny portable computers and widespread interconnectivity via a wireless Internet are only the beginning. Kurzweil envisions the proliferation of computer-chip implants, the inevitable growth of nanotechnology, and developments in virtual reality that stretch the limits of human imagination. Perhaps his most significant prediction is that, at some point in the first half of the century, computers will have exceeded human intelligence and will on some level qualify as living entities.

Like Halperin, Kurzweil is optimistic, painting a highly positive picture of an exciting future. But both authors make it clear that there are significant dangers inherent in this environment of great interconnectivity and rapid technological change. And the role of the law in safeguarding basic human interests will arguably become more important than ever.

In light of the evidence presented in this chapter regarding the transformative effect of information technology, the innovative character of certain networked environments, the unique nature of some online activity, the complex questions of jurisdiction and enforcement that have arisen, and the prospects for even more significant development and change in the near future, it is clear that policymakers across the globe are faced with an online world that often defies easy characterization and, in some cases, may be different enough to merit either new regulatory approaches or no regulation at all. Certainly, no one approach is likely to work for this diverse and multifaceted medium.

Before examining such prospective approaches, however, day-to-day online issues and problems must be identified and sorted out. For some, the Internet is working wonderfully, and is the greatest thing to happen to mankind since the invention of the wheel. For others, the Internet is a highly problematic development that resists any efforts by lawmakers to bring it under control. Are there many problems in cyberspace, or have exaggerated and dystopian scenarios been set forth by those who fear and distrust the new technology? We consider these central questions in chapter 3.

3

Is There Really a Problem Here? Sorting Out Categories of Allegedly Problematic Conduct

It's very exciting for us to be part of this. There are no regulations or laws right now, so we're just going to take things very slowly.

—Dr. Steven Kohler, cofounder of Cyberdocs (www.cyberdocs.com), April 1997

Is MP3 legal? Absolutely Yes! MP3 is an audio compression algorithm, so there is no point discussing its legality. . . . It's perfectly legal to create your own MP3s.

—Is MP3 Legal? (www.mp3now.com), Circa 1999

You already have zero privacy. Get over it.

—Scott McNealy, CEO, Sun Microsystems, Inc., March 1999

For most of the past decade, many people have viewed the debate regarding the regulation of cyberspace in *all-or-nothing* terms. Control or no control. Censorship or no censorship. Rules or no rules. Order or no order.

It has become increasingly clear, however, that the online world has become too complex to be viewed in such a fashion.

First, as discussed in chapters 1 and 2, cyberspace can no longer be viewed as a monolithic entity. There are in fact many different cyber spaces. Some of these spaces are analogous to offline neighborhoods, such as shopping districts or red light districts. Others may resemble insular offline communities and reflect a range of carefully defined social norms. Circumstances and controlling points may therefore be quite different depending on which portions of the online world might be addressed.

In addition, those who wish to control cyberspace must recognize how difficult such a task can sometimes be. As far back as 1995, Gary Chapman noted that the amount of data alone is perhaps an insurmountable challenge:

> [T]erabytes, or trillions of bytes, are circulating on the net at any given time. Trying to locate illegal or offensive data on the net would be harder than trying to isolate two paired words in all the world's telephone conversations and TV transmissions at once. And this difficulty grows worse every hour.

Chapman concluded that the combination of anonymity, encryption, the global nature of cyberspace, and overwhelming data volume makes "censorship of the Internet technically impossible."[1] Today, powerful search engines and other devices have made things much easier to find, but the striking increase in the amount of online data at any given moment has arguably resulted in a standstill with regard to the ability of any regulatory agency to control the online world.

Further complicating matters is the possibility that many rules already exist in cyberspace simply by virtue of the fact that so many *existing* laws apparently apply. And the scope of these traditional rules has become even less clear as state, federal, and international regulatory bodies begin to set forth specific *new* laws in this area.

Finally, the prospective role of litigation in this context must be recognized. Lawsuits will happen with or without regulation. And it is likely that less regulation will lead to even more lawsuits, since a greater number of unresolved issues will have to be sorted out. In the end, under such a scenario, there will indeed be specific rules and regulations governing the online world. But it will be the courts and the judicial process that dictate the shape of many of these controls.

In light of these complexities, our inquiry will proceed from the premise that regulation is inevitable, and that no matter how different cyberspace might be, a reasonable set of national and international guidelines can and should ultimately be established. Yet our exploration will also be based on the principle that the unique features of the online world identified in chapter 2 must be taken into account, and that the challenges faced by regulators in this context cannot be ignored.

The inquiry at this point inevitably begins with an analysis of just what sorts of specific problems currently exist in the online world. At the outset, it must be recognized that in general the online world is working quite well. People from all walks of life and very different cultural backgrounds are interacting freely and openly in a way that would have been unimaginable only a short time ago. Given the mushrooming number of online users, it is on some level remarkable that so few problems have arisen. But issues have emerged that cannot easily be ignored. Ultimately, strategies for addressing these problem areas will depend to a great degree on our ability to reach a consensus on the "harm" we wish to prevent.

Agreement regarding just what is harmful in cyberspace is an essential first step in the regulatory process, and such an approach has often been overlooked. If, for example, some view cyberspace as dangerous and unprotected territory while others feel completely comfortable and see few problems, it will be difficult to reach any sort of consensus as to the purpose of certain proposed rules. And without such a consensus—particularly given the highly participatory nature of the online world today—even rules that are ultimately adopted may not make a whole lot of difference . . . or may end up causing more problems than they resolve.

Consensus, then, is necessary both at the rule-generating stage and at the enforcement stage. If it cannot be established that a consensus is possible regarding both the nature and extent of an alleged dilemma and the prospects for any sort of regulatory approach to the dilemma, then the particular problem area is likely to remain beyond our control.

There are in fact many ways to sort out allegedly problematic Internet-related conduct. One common approach, for example, is to separate the problems out by traditional areas of the law. Contracts might therefore be one area, torts might be a second, civil procedure might be a third, etc. A second common approach is to discuss problematic conduct under recognized sub-categories of "cyberlaw," such as freedom of expression, intellectual property, and privacy. Other organizational rubrics might divide problems based on types of perpetrators or categories of victims. And certain commentators have identified still other methods of classification that may reflect their own particular "world views" of cyberspace. Thus Internet law scholar Timothy Wu argues in favor of an "application-based" approach. Wu contends that the legal analysis should typically begin "at the level of the Internet's individual applications, and not at the level of 'Cyberspace.' What this ultimately means is an analysis that focuses on the user, and how the Internet actually appears to the user, rather than the abstract focus on the network as a whole."[2]

Yet these organizational frameworks may prove either too broad or too narrow for our purposes. In light of the analysis in the first two chapters and the complexities described above, it is essential to begin constructing a comprehensive framework that is broad enough to embrace both current and future problems, but narrow enough to be geared specifically to cyberspace regulation issues. Such a framework would not only have to help us identify representative characteristics of alleged problems, but also point toward proactive strategies that could lead to a reasonable resolution. It would therefore need to be structured based on the potential for consensus regarding both the parameters of the problem and the prospects for any possible regulatory solution down the road.

A viable approach in this context is to divide current problem areas into four categories, ranging in order from conduct that most would consider harmful and threatening to acts that may be much less hazardous and troubling to the average stakeholder: (1) dangerous conduct, (2) fraudulent conduct, (3) unlawful anarchic conduct, and (4) inappropriate conduct.

Under this framework, a roadmap for prospective regulation can be identified based on representative characteristics that would be established for each broad category. The categories are designed to be both flexible and fluid, with certain types of generic behavior fitting under more than one category depending on specific factors that might be present in a given situation.

In addition, it must be emphasized that the harm represented by each category may not always affect everybody in the same way. It may be real and palpable for certain stakeholders, and only identified as possible for others at some point down the road. But these considerations can all be factored into the inquiry.

In any case, once the category has been identified for a specific problem, regulation questions can become more precise. The simplistic and arguably anachronistic inquiry regarding whether or not cyberspace can or should be regulated in general can then be replaced by a much more sophisticated inquiry addressing the parameters of appropriate regulation for a particular category of problems that may arise. We turn now to a detailed exploration of these categories, examining typical problem areas and pointing toward the identification of representative characteristics.

Dangerous Conduct

The *dangerous conduct* category is composed of acts and behaviors that may impact physical or national safety. Such conduct includes threatening behavior, creating and trafficking in child pornography, unlicensed online health care, and certain types of hacking activity that may be considered "cyberterrorism" or "acts of cyberwar."

Threatening Behavior

Threatening behavior can be loosely defined as any activity which—if unchecked—may lead to physical injury. It would include "true threats" communicated via e-mail or the World Wide Web, as well as activity that some have labeled "cyberstalking."

Several highly publicized cases involving online threats have reached the U.S. federal courts in recent years. In 1998, Richard Machado, who had flunked out of UC Irvine, was found guilty of violating federal civil rights laws after sending a hateful and threatening e-mail message to fifty-nine UCI students with Asian surnames. The message, signed "Asian Hater," warned that all Asians should leave UC Irvine or the sender would "hunt all of you down and kill your stupid asses." He also wrote: "I personally will make it my life's work to find and kill every one of you personally. OK? That's how determined I am. Do you hear me?"[3] At trial, the defense attempted to portray Machado's actions as "a classic flame," and argued that no reasonable person should have felt threatened by it. Indeed, this author was originally contacted by the defense attorneys and asked to testify as an expert witness that the message was well within the range of acceptable behaviors in the online world. Since I did not agree with this assertion, I respectfully declined the offer.

A frighteningly similar case was resolved without a trial in 1999 when Kingman Quon, a Cal Poly Pomona student, pled guilty to seven misdemeanor counts of interfering with federally protected activities. Quon had sent his message to persons with Hispanic surnames across the United States, including fourty-two professors at California State University, Los Angeles (CSULA), twenty-five students at MIT, and employees of Indiana University, Xerox Corporation, the Texas Hispanic Journal, the Internal

Revenue Service, and NASA's Ames Research Center. The message was two-pages long, strewn with profanity, and began with the words: "I hate your race. I want you all to die." It also included such phrases as "kill all wetbacks."[4]

Perhaps the most highly publicized of all these cases in the late 1990s was the Oregon anti-abortion Web site case, *Planned Parenthood of the Columbia/Willamette v. The American Coalition of Life Activists.* At issue in this case was a "Nuremberg Files" Web site that posted the actual names and whereabouts of doctors who performed abortions. This information was presented as a series of lists within a highly inflammatory context that described the doctors as persons "working in the baby slaughter business" and characterized them as akin to Nazi war criminals who must be punished. Particularly troubling was the Web site owners' practice of drawing a line through the names of those doctors who had been killed in anti-abortion violence, and listing in gray those doctors who had been wounded. In fact, the name of a New York doctor slain in October 1998 had appeared on this site, and was crossed out soon after his death. At trial in early 1999, the plaintiff doctors argued that the publication of such detailed information on this type of Web site amounted to a threat of bodily harm in heated atmosphere of clinic bombings, burnings, shootings, and acid attacks. The federal jury agreed, and ordered the anti-abortion activists to pay the doctors over one hundred million dollars in damages.[5]

On appeal, however, the Ninth Circuit reversed the decision and held in favor of the abortion foes. Judge Alex Kozinski, applying basic First Amendment principles, wrote that "[d]efendants can only be held liable if they authorized, ratified or directly threatened violence. . . . But if their statements merely encouraged unrelated terrorists, then their words are protected by the First Amendment."[6]

While Net libertarians and most First Amendment scholars took the position that under the circumstances this was the only correct decision, other reactions ranged from concern to outrage. The *New York Times,* for example, called for a Juctice Department investigation into "whether the site is part of a conspiracy to single out doctors and clinics for intimidation and violence." And, in a highly unusual move, 43 members of the U.S. Congress asked the court to revisit its ruling.[7]

A more nebulous type of threatening activity may involve acts very similar in nature to the predatory behavior that occurs in the offline world. Such activity, sometimes grouped under the heading "cyberstalking," can range from the stalking of a former girlfriend to the extreme and highly dangerous pursuit and intimidation of minors by adults with serious problems. Several states have passed laws prohibiting cyberstalking or have extended existing antistalking statutes to the online world.[8] In early 1999, a Los Angeles man was indicted under such a law for first harassing a former girlfriend and then going online to pose as her and pretending to solicit sex. According to the L.A. District Attorney's Office, six men actually arrived at the woman's home in North Hollywood after they read Internet ads or received e-mail messages through chat rooms suggesting that she fantasized about being raped. Some of the e-mail messages gave out not just her phone number but also her address, driving directions to her home, and information on how to circumvent the home's security system. Several men also called the woman, saying they were responding to ads.[9]

Creating and Trafficking in Child Pornography

While not typically posing a direct threat to the average online user per se, the utilization of cyberspace for the distribution of child pornography is an area of great concern. The practice is arguably less prevalent now than it was before international law-enforcement officials began to focus on it, but digital images of persons under the age of eighteen engaging in sexually explicit conduct continue to be exchanged in great quantity via e-mail, Usenet, IRC, and file-sharing software. Posting is often tantamount to distributing, because Internet technology typically enables users to copy these pictures easily by clicking on the image and saving it to their hard drives. Usenet has been particularly troubling in this regard. Even in 2001, the alt.binaries.pictures groups are often filled with nude and suggestive images of young people who are clearly under eighteen. It is generally believed that the emergence of cyberspace has resulted in the widespread and, indeed, unprecedented availability of child pornography worldwide.[10]

At the third hearing of the International Tribunal of Children's Rights, held in Sri Lanka in early 1999, experts bemoaned the fact that computer technology has transformed the production of child pornography into a global cottage industry, and that thousands of persons visit pornographic Web sites containing pictures of children. It was reported that "more and more children are being raped and tortured as fixed images give way to live shows on computers." Pierre Dionne, director-general of the Montreal-based International Bureau for Children's Rights (IBCR), claimed that not only are "children . . . being exploited as the subject of pornography on the Internet," but that pedophiles are building on the availability of this pornography to exchange information on children and arrange international tours that offer children as part of the 'package.'"[11]

While it is generally agreed that child pornography is unacceptable on any level, there has been an ongoing debate in recent years regarding certain features of child pornography laws that may do more to exacerbate the problem than they do to address it. For example, the penalties under U.S. law are apparently the same for possessing or selling a picture of two seventeen-year-olds having sex as they are for possessing or selling a picture of a four-year-old and an adult in a sexually suggestive pose.[12] And while the federal sentencing guidelines mandate a "2 level enhancement" if the minor depicted is prepubescent or under the age of 12, the resulting difference in penalties at the sentencing level is only about 6 months of jail time.[13]

In addition, the U.S. Child Pornography Prevention Act of 1996 mandated new penalites for creating, distributing, or possessing digital images that do not depict real people but are simply computer-generated creations. Even pictures of persons who *appear to be* under 18 can constitute child pornography.[14] These laws have been challenged in several federal courts, and the U.S. Supreme Court has agreed to address the dispute during the 2001–2002 term.[15]

Unlicensed Online Health Care

Many people would not at first glance place online health care in the "dangerous conduct" category. Yet activity by health-care practitioners, which is so tightly regulated offline, continues to be relatively unregulated in the online world. And persons who have not been licensed to practice medicine of any type can be found on the Internet providing medical advice. Some of this activity—particularly if no fees are being charged—may be viewed as "unlawful anarchic conduct," and other behavior may even fit more appropriately under "inappropriate conduct." But persons relying on faulty medical advice can in fact get hurt . . . sometimes very badly. Thus certain online health care would indeed qualify as dangerous conduct.

In addition, to the extent that online drug sales also constitute health care, the growing practice of filling prescriptions in cyberspace also fits in here. These practices can pose great danger to the average online user.[16]

As discussed earlier, the burgeoning practice of online health care includes everything from customizable, information-rich directories on major portals to chat rooms and interactive sites that enable persons to seek out the advice and support of both fellow Netizens and health-care practitioners. In addition, enterprising professionals are setting up online versions of "telemedicine" that will increasingly enable physical exams to take place in cyberspace, complete with audio and video input. These online health care providers include traditional medical doctors and pharmacists as well as alternative practitioners such as herbalists and New Age therapists. An analysis of recent developments in this area reveals a series of unresolved legal and policy issues, ranging from the reliability of the online "care" itself to the rights and responsibilities of online patients.

The accuracy and reliability of online care is probably the single most important issue in this context, because reliance on health-related information and advice may have a significantly negative impact on health and well-being. Indeed, no other topic area in this chapter evidences a similar level of concern regarding the precision and truth of the information obtained. Yet at the present time there are few rules addressing the dispensing of medical care online, no quality control, and minimal licensing requirements at best. Information obtained by online patients in this area may be neither accurate nor timely.

With the situation so different in cyberspace than it is in the offline world, issues relating to the rights and responsibilities of Netizens in this context become paramount. Certainly, for example, online users need to exercise great caution here, yet at this point in time there are no "warning" requirements on health-related sites. In fact, the only sort of warning typically found on these sites is a disclaimer seeking to absolve the online practitioner of any legal liability.

From a legal perspective, it may be very important to determine whether a health-related Web site, newsgroup, bulletin board, or chat room is characterized as *information* or *care*. If it is viewed as *information,* then it may be much harder to show that the online provider was negligent or that any unauthorized practice of medicine took place. Statements or documents posted on the Internet might then be viewed by the public as no more or less reliable than private conversation or articles in newspapers and magazines. However, if the online interaction is characterized as *care,* then negligence or unauthorized practice of medicine might be much easier to demonstrate.[17]

The legal impact of disclaimers is itself the subject of some controversy. As a general rule, a person cannot avoid liability by simply declaring that what he or she is doing is not really what people think he or she is doing. Thus, a lawyer cannot avoid liability by saying that she is not really representing a client when, in fact, she is representing a client. An architect cannot avoid liability by saying that he is not really designing a house when, in fact, he is designing a house. And a doctor cannot avoid liability by saying that she is not really practicing medicine online when, in fact, she is practicing medicine online.

Of course, it is still not clear that even the most interactive medical sites are the equivalent of medical practice. Whether disclaimers will insulate a Web site owner from liability may very well depend on how the legal system ultimately characterizes such online activity.

In addition to issues of negligence and disclaimers, owners and users of health-related Web sites are currently faced with questions regarding the unauthorized practice of medicine. Currently in the United States, M.D.s are typically licensed to practice medicine only in a particular state. With the development of the online world and the advent of virtual health care, a range of questions related to "unauthorized practice" laws must be addressed.

Over the years, case decisions have included broad general definitions of the term *practice of medicine.* In its broadest sense, the term has been defined as "the practice of the art of healing disease and preserving health." Although it might be interesting to speculate as to whether a particular type of online health care qualifies as the practice of medicine under this definition, a more appropriate inquiry would focus on an individual state's definition of the term. In the United States, each state has the power and right to determine what constitutes the practice of medicine, and these state-by-state definitions can vary significantly.

No matter how individual definitions are worded, the problem in every state and every country is, of course, the fact that the online world has no borders. Assuming that the "unauthorized practice of medicine" statutes do apply to at least some forms of online health care, owners of medical Web sites may simply be unable to refrain from violating the law. Licensed practitioners may find it impossible to limit the scope of their information or care to persons in their own state, and unlicensed practitioners may conceivably be charged with violating these laws no matter what state they are in.

The telemedicine analogy may prove useful here, at least for those already licensed to practice somewhere. Telemedicine has existed for some time now, and several commentators have raised concerns regarding the unauthorized practice of telemedicine across state lines. Proposals to address this problem include the development of a limited license to practice in more than one state, but by the beginning of the new century there had been little apparent movement toward this novel and arguably simple form of regulation.[18]

Although there is no evidence that anyone is currently seeking to punish health-care practitioners for the violation of these laws, it is clear that at some point the more egregious violations may have to be addressed. If, for example, an increasing number of virtual practitioners start charging for online medical advice to persons in other states—or, indeed, other countries—there is likely to be some sort of outcry. In fact, doctors themselves may begin to complain if it becomes apparent that a growing number of private, unlicensed citizens are charging others for health-related advice.

If online health care were regulated in any way, then the answers to the issues raised in these pages might be found in published guidelines. Other than the stepped-up legal activity focusing on Internet pharmacies, however, few relevant regulations had been written in this area by 2001. Analogous laws in related areas might be consulted, but these doctrines come from a different era, when most people could not even imagine such a thing as cyberspace. Some propose a new legal framework to address online health-care issues, but it must be noted that members of the medical community often distrust the legal system, and are therefore likely to resist any sort of additional regulation unless it is clear that they would stand to benefit from it.[19]

While as recently as 1998 many would have argued that things are just fine in this area and that only members of the legal community are raising these thorny questions, it is now clear that more and more of the activity we have traditionally associated with a visit to a doctor's office will be moving to cyberspace. In light of this reality, some sort of regulatory scheme addressing online health care seems essential for the protection of online users.

Cyberterrorism and Cyberwar

The word *hacker* was coined at MIT in the 1960s, and at that time it apparently meant "computer virtuoso." Even in the 1994 edition of the *New Hacker's Dictionary, hacker* was defined as someone "who enjoys exploring the details of programmatic systems and how to stretch their capabilities; one who programs enthusiastically, even obsessively."[20]

Much has been written in the past ten years regarding hackers and the real or perceived threat they pose to online users, other stakeholders, and national security in general. It is clear that there are different types of hackers and that their activity often reflects a range of motives. A relatively gentle hacker culture has certainly existed for some time, and many hackers pose little or no threat to anyone. Nevertheless, there is an ongoing concern that too many people can too easily wreak havoc in both the public and private portions of the online world should they desire to do so.

While the exact parameters of this territory are uncertain (and the perceptions of commentators colored by ongoing distortions and sensationalized news reports) several key trends have become apparent: (1) playful and inherently moral hacking may have had a "brief heyday" in the 1980s and early 1990s, but malicious computer meddling has apparently increased in scope since then;[21] (2) veteran hackers from the earlier years have been hired in increasingly large numbers by governments and corporations to shore up protection against hacking and cracking;[22] (3) the rise of e-commerce has seen a concurrent improvement in the power and sophistication of online security measures;[23] (4) for many teens across the globe, hacking is still viewed as an attractive and relatively innocuous form of mischief;[24] and (5) there are growing concerns worldwide regarding the danger of cyberterrorism, cyberattacks, and cyberwars.[25]

In 1997, the U.S. President's Commission on Critical Infrastructure released a report warning of increased danger from "new cyber-threats." The commission reported that "the right command sent over a network to a power generating station's control computer could be just as effective as a backpack full of explosives, and the perpetrator would be harder to identify and apprehend." It warned that the rapid growth of a computer-literate population means that an increasingly large number of persons now possess "the skills necessary to consider such an attack," particularly in light of "the wide adoption of public protocols for system interconnection and the availability of 'hacker tool' libraries." In fact, the commission declared that "a personal computer and a simple telephone connection to an Internet service provider anywhere in the world are enough to cause a great deal of harm."[26]

A U.S. Senate committee investigating these matters in May 1998 heard testimony from seven of the nation's top computer hackers. According to reports, the hackers claimed they could "cripple the Internet in a half-hour," and with more time and money, they could "interrupt satellite transmissions or electricity grids and snoop on the president's movements." Although some experts dismissed these claims as excessive, members of the Senate Governmental Affairs Committee were convinced that they had been presented with evidence of threats to national security. This evidence included details from the report by the President's Commission on Critical Infrastructure itself, which cited an "unprecedented national risk" because computer and telephone systems have linked such national public works as power plants, rail lines, and banking networks. It also included a study by the General Accounting Office (GAO) of Congress that was critical of computer security at both the State Department and the Federal Aviation Administration. The State Department's unclassified automated information systems "are very susceptible to hackers, [and] terrorists," the GAO stated.[27]

In other venues, experts have warned of potential problems with the vulnerability of the 911 emergency-telephone system, and with the archiving of medical records. At one point, a hacker from Sweden succeeded in jamming the 911 system throughout west-central Florida, prompting FBI Director Louis Freeh to call the 1997 incident "a dress rehearsal for a national disaster."[28] And a 1999 incident at the University of Michigan, in which a student was able to tap into the university's health care systems database, crystallized ongoing concerns about the availability of private records online and fears of a prospective impact on the physical safety of individuals. According to the University of Michigan Health Care Systems, only a few unauthorized people saw records that included everything from names and addresses to social security numbers and diagnosis codes before the database was moved off the Internet. But hospitals in this era have apparently been quite lax with regard to online security, often failing to put appropriate safeguards in place.[29]

Indeed, by the year 2000, a growing number of reports in this context generated heightened concern across the globe. In Israel, for example, the *Jerusalem Report* published a wide-ranging study of "information warfare," reminding its readers at the outset that throughout history, armies have attempted to manipulate the information their enemies receive.[30] The study defined information warfare as acts that could "cripple an enemy by bringing down the computer systems on which his army and his civilian population depend." Areas of vulnerability identified by the author included Internet sites, phones, emergency services, electricity, water, financial systems, airports, and vital records.

"Hacktivism," a form of online activism involving cyberprotests, also added to the concerns of government officials. While arguably not a form of cyberterrorism per se, the vandalizing of Web sites for the purpose of making a political statement only "underscores the risk to companies and governments that increasingly rely on the Internet for commerce and communication."[31] On December 31, 1998, for example a small group of hackers called "Legions of the Underground" (LoU) released a statement "declaring cyberwar" on China and Iraq:

> In a very heated and emotional discussion, Legions of the Underground declared cyberwar on the information infrastructure of China and Iraq Monday night. They cited severe civil rites [*sic*] abuses by the governments of both countries as well as the recent sentencing to death of two bank robbers in China and the production of weapons of mass destruction by Iraq as the reasons for their outrage.[32]

Against this backdrop, new drives against information warfare were launched in Canada, the United Kingdom, and other countries around the world.[33] President Clinton, in his 1999 State of the Union address, called specifically for funding "to defend the U.S. from threats to critical computer networks by combating terrorism and protecting the infrastructures." Clinton's plan included a study of how to recruit technology experts to safeguard government computers. Initiatives were aimed at "thwarting hackers armed with destructive computer codes and terrorists intent on sabotaging America's electricity grid and its increasingly computer-dependent banking and financial networks." "We will improve systems designed to monitor computer intrusions," he declared in his speech. "We will develop better ways of sharing information between public and private sectors so that we better prepare for possible cyber-attacks."[34]

Fraudulent Conduct

The second category of problematic acts in the online world—fraudulent conduct—is comprised of behavior that may impact the *economic safety* of persons, businesses, institutions, and governments. The generic term *fraudulent* can refer to a wide-range of generally dishonest activity, and conduct that falls under this category might, therefore, include hacking that poses the threat of financial loss, deceitful business practices (including certain privacy invasions), and online fraud in general.

Hacking Activity Posing the Threat of Financial Loss

Much of the activity currently classified as hacking or cracking has no potential impact on physical or national safety, but may have a significant impact on the financial well-being of persons and institutions. This activity may range from simple mischief to political protest to truly malicious attempts to alter online realities.

Sometimes, for example, the relatively innocuous attempts by young hackers to disable password protection and break through firewalls for no purpose other than to see if it can be done will trigger direct or indirect financial costs. Even if no repairs are needed, the time spent by employees to address the results of the hacking or cracking can become a financial burden. Hacktivism, may also sometimes inflict financial damage, with activities ranging from the sending of thousands of e-mail messages to the disabling of Web sites. In late 1998, the *New York Times* reported that an Internet distribution hub featuring "tools to assist others in subversive digital activism had been set up." Online activists participating in a particular operation could apparently access such a hub by visiting a Web site and clicking on an icon that launches a program called "FloodNet." The software would then point the hacktivist's web browser to the target of the attack, where it would request the same page over and over again at a rate of about ten times per minute.[35] These protests invariably cause financial hardship, which can range from time spent addressing the attack to money spent updating equipment.

There is, of course, a fine line separating hacking activity that may impact physical or national safety from activity that may only have a financial impact. Most hacking incidents, however, have the potential to cause economic hardship, and officials at businesses and institutions worldwide are beginning to pay much more attention to these threats.[36]

Deceitful Business Practices

Activity under this subcategory may range from highly questionable and generally dishonest business promotion to egregious invasions of privacy carried out for the purpose of gaining commercial advantage. Although most of this behavior violates current law, some types of deceitful acts—particularly in the area of privacy infringement—are still legal, to the dismay of many Netizens.

Many commentators saw 1997 as the year that e-commerce had "arrived." No longer was the idea of conducting business in the online world little more than a pipe dream. Significant profits were being realized for the first time in a wide variety of business-related ventures, and it was easy for experts to predict that the trend would continue. In this heady entrepreneurial environment, corporate leaders took the initiative to warn against any form of e-commerce regulation.[37] The Clinton administration soon issued a directive adopting this very position.[38] Things were going well, the government argued, and there was no need to step in.

By the year 2000, however, it had become clear that a blanket prohibition against any sort of regulation would not only be unrealistic but also unacceptable. Not only were certain practices already violative of existing laws in this context, but other business activities—particularly those that impacted personal privacy—had begun to generate a significant backlash across the board.

Privacy in the online world is a complex and multifaceted area of concern; discussion about it is marked by unexplored nuances, ironies, and inherent contradictions. One of the most fascinating contradictions is the fact that online users appear to have both more privacy and less privacy than they typically do in the offline world. They have more privacy because they can assume other identities and take advantage of the technology to maintain a certain level of anonymity in certain situations. They also have less privacy because both their e-mail and Web-surfing activities can be subject to extensive monitoring without permission by a variety of public and private entities. Even their own hard drives can betray them, given that documents and picture files placed in "recycle bins" can often be retrieved even after those bins have been "emptied."[39]

On some level, these invasions can be viewed as part and parcel of the same erosion of privacy rights that has taken place in society as a whole. In other ways, however, the tampering with the privacy interests of persons in cyberspace is arguably much more egregious. With regard to personal communications, for example, U.S. residents have come to expect a basic level of protection from intrusion in the offline world, and they are likely to assume that this protection extends to their cyberspace activity. From a technological perspective, however, online communications today are significantly less private and secure than either the U.S. Postal Service or the typical telephone conversation.

The monitoring of an individual's Web activities may prove to be the most important focal point for Netizens concerned with deceitful business practices. In 1998, Internet law scholar Jerry Kang explored the basic ways that a person's footprints can be tracked in cyberspace. He found that certain personal information is generally disclosed when someone visits any given Web site. And the active entry of additional data—such as site registration and/or the purchase of products—typically triggers a much more thorough and sophisticated monitoring process.[40]

The architecture of the World Wide Web itself currently requires that a person's computer reveal something about its identity, configuration, and browsing activity when it accesses a particular Web site's server. This is done through the providing of the IP address (which includes the domain name), the type of Web browser, the operating system, the hardware platform, and the most recently visited place on the Web (the referrer). By giving up this information, an online user does not typically reveal her identity per se, but as a general rule, she is identifying both her geographic location and certain personal tastes. If a person has used a search engine to access the site, this engine will be revealed as well, along with the keywords used to generate the search.

Once a person begins to access particular pages on a given site, this trail itself can be recorded by the site owner. In addition, if the visitor enters any sort of data at all, the Web site owner may keep that data on the person's hard drive in the form of a "cookie." The cookie retains the information so that when the person accesses the site again, the server can connect to the cookie and provide access and services automatically.[41]

Much of this information is collected simply for the convenience of the parties involved, and at first, many Netizens were either unaware of the process or not particularly bothered by it. Even revelations regarding extensive "data mining" by online entrepreneurs who sought to gather unprecedented marketing information by creating profiles of Web site visitors' personal tastes initially generated a limited outcry. After all, the argument goes, merchants have been gathering information regarding the personal tastes of their customers from time immemorial.

In early 2000, however, a turning point was reached when DoubleClick, a large Internet advertising firm, disclosed plans to create a program that would match consumers' identities with anonymous data that had been gathered. Protest against any sort of data mining had already increased by that point in time, fueled not only by important scholarship[42] but by the ongoing efforts of online grassroots-advocacy organizations such as the Electronic Privacy Information Center (EPIC) and Junkbusters.[43] Once it became clear that companies would soon be able to pinpoint exactly who was visiting key websites, a major backlash occurred.

Legal complaints were filed; government investigations were instigated, and DoubleClick's stock price dropped precipitously as investors reacted to the outrage. By mid-2000, federal legislation was being considered to address this volatile area, and cover stories focusing on the dangers inherent in a lack of online privacy seemed to be appearing in every major U.S. magazine.[44] Commentators predicted that the days of unrestricted "data mining" were over, and that many questionable but heretofore largely ignored practices were about to be viewed as fraudulent by both online users and the powers-that-be. The increased efforts of the U.S. Federal Trade Commission only served to support these predictions.

Events in mid-2000 demonstrated, however, that even in the aftermath of the DoubleClick controversy, privacy advocates seeking to limit the opportunity for deceitful online-business practices had a long road ahead of them. The FTC—after finding that less than half of the most popular Web sites were complying with voluntary privacy-protection standards—voted to recommend new federal legislation that would give it new power to oversee how companies handle private information they obtain about consumers.

The FTC report called for new rules "in conjunction with continuing self-regulatory programs," and one FTC official insisted that this was not "a drastic bid for regulating the Internet." But IT-industry opposition was immediate. "This is the first step down the slippery slope of government regulation of the Internet," said Harris Miller, president of the Information Technology Association of America. "The marketplace has responded to the important privacy concerns of consumers and will continue to do so in practical ways." Industry officials continued to insist that privacy concerns could be addressed through public-awareness campaigns and new software. And two of the five FTC commissioners opposed the proposed legislation, leading the White House itself to question the efficacy of backing such an initiative.[45]

While egregious privacy violations have been the subject of much discussion in recent years, domain-name disputes have also garnered a great deal of attention.[46] Initially it was thought that traditional trademark law sets forth clear parameters regarding the nature and extent of acceptable business practices, but the early domain-name cases continued to highlight gaps in the existing legal doctrine. Ultimately, certain practices such as "cybersquatting" that had been legal under existing law were prohibited under subsequent legislation. And the dispute-resolution process adopted by ICANN under its 1999 Uniform Dispute Resolution Policy generated great controversy, but provided many aggrieved parties with a viable alternative to the courts.[47]

Other areas of e-commerce have also been the focus of relatively extensive regulatory efforts. The Uniform Computer Information Transactions

Act (UCITA), for example, focusing on rules for electronic contracts, has been a prime example of controversy in this regard.[48] The Electronic Signatures in Global and National Commerce Act (E-Sign Act)—by contrast—is an example of federal legislation in this area that garnered widespread support. Signed into law by President Clinton, the "E-Sign Act" became effective in October 2000 and allowed businesses and consumers to seal a variety of legally binding arrangements with electronic rather than handwritten signatures.[49]

Online Fraud in General

While the word *fraudulent* may encompass a broad range of criminal, quasi-criminal, or generally dishonest acts, the legal term *fraud* has a very specific and well-developed operative meaning. Under common law, for example, fraud can be the basis of either a civil lawsuit or a criminal prosecution. Lawsuits can be pursued by victims of fraud (i.e., intentional misrepresentation) in civil court, and defendants can be prosecuted in criminal court for either acts of fraud or the intent to defraud during the commission of theft.

The common-law "tort" (civil wrong)[50] of *intentional misrepresentation* is defined as the false representation of a material fact or opinion by someone who either knows it to be false or makes it with reckless disregard for the truth, and intends to induce reliance on the representation. In addition, the victim must prove that the representation played a substantial part in inducing him to act as he did (actual reliance), and that the victim was justified in relying on the representation (justifiable reliance).[51]

Common-law crimes that may contain an element of fraud include *larceny* (if the property is taken through consent obtained by fraud), *embezzlement* (intent to defraud required), and *false pretenses* (intent to defraud also required).[52]

Such behaviors appear to have become more prevalent in the online world over time. In Los Angeles, for example, a sheriff's captain who ran a regional anti-car-theft unit reported that in 1997, about sixty people in his area alone were arrested for "hacking into credit files, . . . fabricating drivers' licenses, [and] . . . then walking into car dealerships and buying luxury cars under assumed identities."[53] In the San Francisco Bay Area, a man whom local authorities called the "cyberspace bandit" was arrested in late 1998 after allegedly using his high-tech skills to steal more than fifty thousand dollars, and possibly as much as one million dollars, from a dozen or more victims. Apparently, his crime spree had begun when he obtained a box of housing applications from a friend who worked at an off-campus student dormitory in Sonoma County. Using the basic information included on the applications—social security numbers, addresses, and dates of birth—he "electronically assumed other people's identities, broke into their bank and credit-card accounts, and either withdrew cash or bought things for himself." He was able to elude law enforcement officials for a good period of time by moving from hotel to hotel and eventually by traveling to different countries as well.[54]

Online-auction fraud has also emerged as a potential problem area in cyberspace. In recent years, Internet auction houses have become very popular, with over fifteen hundred online operations reportedly conducting business by early 1999. eBay (www.ebay.com), a company founded in 1995 by a man whose original motivation was to sell his girlfriend's Pez dispensers, has become the most widely known of these operations. For the most part, online auctions appear to have been very successful, but some people have reported problems at both the buyer and seller end. While eBay continues to insist that fraud is extremely rare among its millions of users, some believe that this is because problems are reported elsewhere. In 1999, for example, the FTC's Bureau of Consumer Protection recorded approximately six thousand complaints, which represented a two thousand precent increase in just one year's time. During the same time period, the National Consumers League reportedly recieved 600 complaints a month about Internet fraud, and two out of three were auction fraud cases.[55]

Arguably, the most significant problem in this area is online stock fraud, which has been closely monitored by both the government and the media since the Internet became a central component of the financial world. According to the market research firm NFO Worldwide, Inc., for example, the number of investors trading online grew by 2.2 million to more than 5.2 million in 1998, and by March 1999, more than twenty-five percent of all stock trades were completed over the Internet. Large numbers of individuals began coming online for the first time, new to online trading and starved for financial information and hot stock tips. Such individuals can be easy prey for savvy con artists.[56]

In the first of several highly publicized sweeps conducted in the late 1990s, the U.S. Securities and Exchange Commission accused forty-four stock promoters of "fraudulently recommending more than 235 small companies on the Internet." Describing the alleged behaviors, the SEC said that the promoters "illegally touted securities" and misled investors about their relationships with the companies they were promoting. "Not only did they lie about their own independence," Richard H. Walker, director of enforcement at the SEC, said, "[but] . . . some of them lied about the companies they featured and then took advantage of any quick spike in price to sell their shares for a fast and easy profit." The promoters—who wrote for online newsletters, posted messages on Web sites and sent out a great deal of unsolicited e-mail—were apparently paid more than $6.2 million in cash and were given 1.8 million shares of stock or stock options for their work. And John R. Stark, head of the SEC Office of Internet Enforcement, reported in this context that "all types of scams are . . . [now] . . . finding their way to the Internet. You have Ponzi schemes, pyramid schemes, public offerings, oil and gas fraud, every kind of fraud."[57]

Money laundering may also be a component of such schemes. In the first criminal case involving Internet stock fraud, for example, federal officials uncovered a stock-manipulation and money-laundering scheme by Systems of Excellence, Inc. that resulted in criminal prosecution and jail sentences for the perpetrators.[58]

Despite the ongoing federal crackdown, online stock-fraud problems continue to plague the financial world. The nature of cyberspace itself has been particularly conducive to this type of fraud, with "fast-moving con artists" taking advantage of opportunities to reach large numbers of people in an inexpensive, low-key, and relatively anonymous fashion. The sheer volume of stock touts and old-fashioned "rumor mongering" on the Internet has generated great concern. By the year 2000, the SEC was, in fact, receiving upwards of three-hundred complaints a day in this area.[59]

Addressing the parameters of cybercrime at the turn of the century, a leading international expert stated that "[p]olice are losing the fight against criminals in cyberspace and will have to take giant strides to catch up." Paul Higdon, head of the criminal intelligence directorate at Interpol—an organization that coordinates the activities of 177 police forces from around the world—voiced the same concern at an international conference in London. "We recognize that technology has outpaced us," he said. "Tomorrow's challenge today is for law enforcement to catch up and close the gap."[60]

Unlawful Anarchic Conduct

The third category is in many ways the most controversial because there is frequently so little agreement regarding the nature and extent of the problems. When confronted with conduct that falls into this category, many people will insist that it is not a problem at all. For others, there may indeed be problems, but the problems are typically viewed as the direct result of an inconsistent, overbearing, or anachronistic legal system. Less regulation is often seen as a panacea in this context.

The areas of conduct that fit under this category include digital copying, pornographic expression, and online defamation. Such activity—which may, at times, be illegal but may not necessarily be criminal—is often carried out by individual Netizens rather than by commercial entities, and is consistently cited by commentators bemoaning the lawlessness of cyberspace. Indeed, leaders of governments, churches, and big businesses continue to insist that such conduct must be brought under control, while many online users remain adamant in their defense of the freedom to do as they wish here.

Other distinguishing features of "category 3" behavior are that the behavior is not generally fraudulent or dishonest, that there is no danger to physical safety or national security, and that the potential impact on the economic well-being of other persons and groups may not be very clear. In addition, the behavior exemplifies the anarchic image of the online world.

Copyright Violations in Cyberspace

Under legal frameworks governing the volatile area of copyright, there are typically two broad types of infringement—civil and criminal. Most run-of-the-mill copyright violations are not crimes, and the only remedy available to an alleged victim is a lawsuit in civil court. But some copyright violations do indeed amount to criminal behavior, and this area of the law has been expanded in the United States by the "No Electronic Theft" Act of 1997.[61]

The nature and extent of a person's right to copy material in the online world has become for many *the* paradigmatic cyberspace-related inquiry.[62] And it has been a truly contentious inquiry, with little apparent resolution in sight. The contours of the debate are very familiar by now, and go to the heart of what people believe cyberspace to be. For both the communitarians who migrated to the Internet in the early days and the many libertarian online users who came to cyberspace in the mid-to-late 1990s, one of the great advantages of the online world is its openness—an openness that includes the unrestricted sharing of information.

Particularly galling to these users is the suggestion that information in cyberspace is not there for the taking. After all, every person with a computer—and the standard bundled software package that comes with it—has the ability simply to take material posted online. If you post something online, the argument goes, you are implicitly sharing it, and you should expect that it will be copied, printed, and/or downloaded without your permission by people across the globe. In addition, supporters of this view see parallels between the architecture that facilitates the copying of computer files and other technological advances that enable persons to xerox documents, record music, and tape television programs. How, they ask, can such copying logically be restricted?

In fact, it is clear that an entire generation has now had easy access to a range of devices that can be used to infringe copyrights. As Eric Goldman points out:

> [T]he under-thirty generation has grown up being able to freely expropriate intellectual property easily and at little cost. As college students, how many of them bought most (or even some) of the software on their computer, rather than "borrowing" it from their folks or from a friend down the hall? How many of them put together a compilation tape of their favorite songs? How many of them made a cassette tape of someone else's music album?[63]

Record industry officials have spoken of "re-education" campaigns to teach young people about copyright laws. But to the average college student, these protestations sound as anachronistic as Chairman Mao's re-education campaigns during the heyday of the Red Guards.

Pitted against the communitarians, libertarians, and young people, of course, are the entrepreneurs, the publishers, the entertainment industry, the software industry, and business interests in general. These supporters of traditional copyright laws have typically come to the online world much more recently, and often with a conscious desire to make money, or at least to protect their perceived right to free and open commerce. The idea that copyright laws would no longer be valid in cyberspace strikes them as patently absurd. In their eyes, whatever the Internet might once have been is no longer relevant. Today, they argue, it is a bastion of commerce, and home to companies that have attracted large amounts of investor money. People are not playing games here anymore. What happens in the online world is central to the growth and development of the global economy in the twenty-first century.

Further complicating the debate is the extent to which some form of reproduction, distribution, or modification of copyrighted material actually occurs online from day-to-day. And this includes both copying *from* cyberspace and copying *to* cyberspace. At any given moment in the online world, people are engaging in the widespread and continuous downloading and uploading of text, graphics, audio, and video files without any sort of permission from copyright owners. They are also engaging in the unauthorized distribution of such files via e-mail, FTP, the Web, newsgroups, IRC, or innovative file sharing programs. And they may also be modifying existing works, raising issues of both attribution and integrity.[64] Advances in software development have not only made it easy for online users to change or delete the name of the original creator, but have enabled many to modify or even transform the nature of the works themselves.[65]

There are several key reasons why this activity is attractive to the average online user, and few reasons why it is not. Unlike other forms of copying, digital reproduction produces perfect copies without any loss of quality. Thus, as Goldman argues, there are no quality-related limits that inhibit persons "from making as many copies as they please, and recipients of these copies have no incentive to return to authorized sources to get another copy equal in quality to the original version."[66] In addition, the costs of reproduction and distribution in cyberspace are minimal. Once a user is online, copying and distributing are essentially free.

In addition, despite the efforts of those who would enforce traditional copyright doctrine in the online world, such enforcement has often been virtually nonexistent. Many Netizens skirt the limits of the law by posting copyrighted material online. And most day-to-day users continue to copy, distribute, and modify material from the Internet with impunity.

Both sides in this debate continue to view themselves as embattled. Copyright libertarians insist that any attempt to enforce outmoded rules goes against the very nature of cyberspace itself, while business and industry representatives reproduce charts and data projecting just how much money they stand to lose. Libertarians counter with an oft-heard admonition: If you don't like it, stay out of cyberspace. But business and industry may have no choice at this point in time. For one thing, copies of documents and products created at great cost by various companies are often posted online without permission, and, thus, the companies are "in" cyberspace whether they want to be or not. But even more important in this regard is the fact that the growth of e-commerce is transforming business practices to such an extent that establishing a presence in cyberspace is increasingly viewed as a necessity.

The MP3 controversy described in the introduction to this book exemplifies the ongoing tension. And the music industry has not been the only business enterprise impacted by Internet-related developments. The publishing industry, the software industry, and the film industry all find themselves on the front lines in digital copyright battles.

In spite of all the attention garnered by the music industry and its apparent failure to come to grips with the online world, it is the publishing industry that is perhaps more threatened by the emergence of today's Internet than any other major business enterprise. Not only has computer technology spawned the growth and development of an entirely new breed of "online publisher," but many experts have predicted that the print medium itself will ultimately be replaced by the digital medium.[67]

Certainly the problems of the publishing industry in this transition period go far beyond the copyright debate; nevertheless, industry leaders continue to view copyright issues as a central concern. While many publishing ventures—particularly newspapers and magazines—have already migrated to the Internet, most academic journals and traditional book publishers have kept their primary material offline.[68] For media publications that derive much of their income from advertising, the Internet can serve to increase profits—even if individual articles are downloaded and redistributed in great quantity. But for hardcover book publishers who rely on sales of the works themselves, the unresolved nature of copyright protection in cyberspace is a potential nightmare. And academic journals are confronting their own concerns regarding the possible loss of control over original materials.[69]

For the software industry, unauthorized copying has been an ongoing problem for several decades. And while the industry continues to be plagued by the manufacture and sale of counterfeit products in other countries, it has become increasingly apparent that the distribution of "pirated" software in the online world may become an even bigger problem. Unauthorized posting and downloading of applications, games, and other attractive software packages appear to have increased in cyberspace over the past several years. By the end of the 1990s, for example, industry experts had declared that the Internet had become "the primary delivery system for counterfeit games." The Interactive Digital Software Association (IDSA) estimated in early 1999 that there were literally "tens of thousands of sites offering illegal games." In addition, counterfeit PC and video games are apparently available for purchase at popular Internet auction sites as well.[70]

During the past decade, much of this unauthorized copying and distribution have taken place in university cyberspace. Many students who enter colleges and universities today are invariably technologically savvy. Most have grown up with computers, and see the online world as a natural component of their lives. For some students on tight budgets, the unauthorized distribution of software is viewed as a necessary service provided by their peers. For others, it is a form of protest. For many others, however, it can be characterized as little more than mischief, the same sort of mischief that has been part of campus life for centuries and is now occurring with increasing frequency on college and university servers.

Software companies in growing numbers are looking to the institutions of higher education to regulate student conduct and to monitor student behavior online. Yet colleges and universities are understandably hesitant to even attempt to police their students in this manner. An incident at the

University of Puget Sound several years ago exemplified the growing dilemma. In the spring of 1997, an employee of Emigre, Inc. discovered illegal copies of more than one hundred software programs posted on the Web page of a freshman at the university. Several of the programs had been created by Emigre itself. Following its normal procedures, Emigre notified the Software Publishing Association (SPA), which in turn notified the university. In response, Puget Sound officials shut down the site.

However, according to the *Chronicle of Higher Education,* the SPA decided to make an example of the student. They negotiated an agreement that required him to write a twenty-page paper about "computer piracy and copyright infringement" and to perform fifty hours of community service, helping to wire local schools for Internet access. If the student failed to perform these tasks, he would have been forced to pay a ten thousand dollar fine, and the association would *also* have been able to sue him for copyright infringement.[71]

Although no institution of higher education would defend a student who has posted illegal copies of software on its server, many college and university officials continue to feel that it is not their role to regulate student conduct either by monitoring student Internet use or collaborating with software publishers to discipline offenders.[72] Thus, the issue remains unresolved.

Similar problems may soon begin to plague the film industry as the quality of online "video" technology continues to improve. In the late 1990s, for example, Web sites offering movie fans the ability to watch excerpts or even full-length reproductions of their favorite films began to proliferate. At present, film requires far more memory and bandwidth to distribute than other forms of entertainment, but this is likely to change over the next few years, as capacity becomes more widely available and new technologies are developed to compress and distribute digital-movie files.

The *Wall Street Journal* reported in 1999 that "Hollywood studios are already racing to figure out how to take advantage of the technology without losing hard-won copyright protections for movies." Robert Daly, co-chair of Warner Brothers, stated at the time that the industry was not yet ready to post its own digital files until "the security issue" was resolved. "Nothing will be done until you have some sort of copyright protection," he said.[73] It is unclear, however, just what sort of "copyright protection" he was referring to, given that current copyright laws already set forth significant penalties for online infringement.

In the meantime, even though the quality of video distributed via cyberspace remained relatively poor in most cases, online users were increasingly drawn to the technology and the additional level of information it provided. Comparing these inadequacies to the poor reception of early television, one Net entrepreneur remarked, "It's about access, not about what the picture looks like. When you were young, didn't you watch cartoons, even though they were snowy?" The real point, he added, is that "the Internet is not . . . [just] . . . a print medium anymore, and the personal computer is becoming an entertainment device."[74]

Pornography in the Online World

By May 2001, pornography had become a $10 billion business in the United States alone—larger than all three major professional sports combined. And Internet pornography accounted for at least one-fifth of that business.[75] Yet while courts, legislative bodies, and policymakers around the world have wrestled extensively with this issue, we seem no closer to resolving the controversy today than we were in the mid-1990s.

At the outset, it must be recognized that there is a major difference between the terms *obscenity* and *pornography* under the law. *Obscenity* typically refers to illegal expression under the three-part *Miller* test discussed earlier. *Pornography* is a much larger universe and includes both legal and illegal expression.

Of course, as with other topic areas in category 3, there is major disagreement regarding the nature and extent of the problem; many believe that—outside of child pornography—there is no problem. After all, you do not have to go to the Internet "red-light district" if you do not want to. The U.S. Supreme Court itself said as much in *Reno v. ACLU*. The justices found in 1997 that although sexually explicit material was "widely available" online, "users seldom encounter such content accidentally."[76]

On a day-to-day basis, it may still be the case that little or no pornography is encountered in cyberspace by the average online user unless she actively chooses to conduct an online search in this area, go to a particular Web site, or access a particular newsgroup. Yet many would argue that circumstances have changed as the pornography industry continues to flourish in cyberspace and aggressive entrepreneurs seek to find ways to drum up more business.

Increasingly, it seems, people are finding that they arrive at a pornographic site by making a slight mistake when they enter a Web address. In 1998, for example, Netizens who had wanted to go to www.ucla.edu but had mistakenly typed in *www.ucla.com* found themselves accessing pornography rather than the Web site of the university.[77] In addition, once a Netizen arrives at a pornographic Web page, leaving often proves difficult. A growing number of sites have set up interconnecting URLs, so that if a person tries to return to a previously accessed nonpornographic site, he is transported instead to other pornographic pages from other sites.[78]

In addition, users often come across titles and descriptions of pornographic web pages when they enter relatively innocuous terms into search engines, only to find that the terms have been used as part of a creative title for a sex-related site. While it certainly can be argued that they do not have to "go there," the descriptions of the sites often contain sexually explicit language and may themselves be very offensive.

Finally, there is the ongoing issue of unsolicited e-mail, which can also be pornographic. And while it may be argued here too that a person does not have to go there but can choose instead not to open the message, some people may be offended by the actual subject descriptions themselves. And some e-mail messages may contain misleading titles that fool people into opening them.

Unsolicited pornography is only one of many concerns that persist in the area of obscenity. Some are bothered by the fact that pornography exists at all in cyberspace. Most are concerned, on some level, that young people may encounter obscenity years before they have the emotional maturity to deal with it. As the Internet becomes a central component of innovative education programs, more and more young people have access to the online world, and can easily find some of the most extreme pornography ever made available to the general public.

Understandably, people have looked to the legal system for solutions to these concerns, but, at this point, the law has arguably been even less successful in resolving these issues than it has been in the area of copyright. The definition of obscenity itself, for example, remains under fire, with many arguing, as did the defendants in *U.S. v. Thomas,* that a new definition of community standards must be set forth for the online world if obscenity laws are to have any impact in cyberspace. In the meantime, existing obscenity laws continue to be flouted or even ignored by many Netizens. And enforcement of these laws in cyberspace has proven extremely difficult.

Perhaps the most significant development in this area is the fact that the U.S. Congress has, thus far, been startlingly unsuccessful in its efforts to come up with viable legislation to regulate cyberspace in this context. Key portions of Congress' Communications Decency Act (1996) were ruled unconstitutional by the U.S. Supreme Court in 1997, and the Child Online Protection Act of 1998—a more modest statute that sought to address the concerns of that Court—has been blocked by subsequent litigation.[79]

At the end of the decade, the only viable option for the average online user who did not want to encounter obscenity in cyberspace was to try a software-based "architectural" solution of some sort. Internet filtering, for example, proliferated in the aftermath of the U.S. Supreme Court's *Reno* decision, bolstered by the majority opinion's clear suggestion that the control of pornography would be up to individual users.

Filtering software improved significantly, and many saw it as a viable option. But typical filtering systems continued to block many sites that could be important to access, depending on the nature of one's online use. And the legal system itself was sometimes employed as a barrier to prevent the use of filtering in publicly funded settings such as schools and libraries.[80]

Online Defamation

Like copyright infringement and obscene expression, defamation stands out as an example of behavior that has remained widespread in an online environment that many believe to be too free. While some continue to insist that this freedom is a breath of fresh air, others argue that all democracies have their limits and bemoan the apparent disappearance of these limits in the online world . . . where the rampant violation of copyright, obscenity, and defamation laws is not only tolerated but often encouraged.

At the heart of the matter in the defamation context is the often unrestrained dissemination of unsubstantiated allegations in cyberspace. Such activity not only includes defamatory statements by ordinary citizens, but also encompasses irresponsible and legally questionable remarks by a variety of persons and groups whose status enables them to attract large audiences to their Web addresses.

Indeed, in the eyes of many commentators, the Internet has turned into one vast gossip column. Particularly in the aftermath of the Clinton-Lewinsky scandal, which resulted in the controversial impeachment of the president, the Internet has come to be viewed by many as the seamier side of the national media. Of course, those who are familiar with cyberspace in this era are aware that the online world has become much too large and much too varied to be pigeonholed in this manner. Yet to the extent that a portion of the Internet may now, in fact, have truly become a part of the media, such allegations cannot necessarily be dismissed out of hand.

The media, in general, have been roundly criticized for their apparent role in the White House scandal, but some of the most scathing criticism has been reserved for so-called online media. It is highly significant that both the Lewinsky story and the reports of lead House prosecutor Henry Hyde's adultery were apparently not released by the mainstream media until they had first appeared on the Internet—in the Drudge Report and Salon, respectively. Both the online versions of mainstream newspapers and Internet publications such as Drudge have been taken to task for abandoning traditional canons of journalistic responsibility, including the basic principle of checking for corroboration before publishing accusations regarding the private lives of public servants. And in cyberspace such accusations by the online media have sometimes been only the tip of the proverbial iceberg, with posts by Netizens on mailing lists and discussion forums sometimes going far beyond the boundaries of basic civility.

For some commentators, the many egregious examples of unsubstantiated and often incorrect allegations within the context of the Starr investigation and the subsequent impeachment trial began to resemble the McCarthyism of 1950s America. Josh Getlin, for example, wrote that "[t]hen, as now, the press has played a critical role in reflecting and amplifying charges of misconduct, and its performance has come under heavy fire." Indeed, in that era, the media "routinely printed McCarthy's charges

. . . without verifying them." In cyberspace, when any Netizen can "print" charges, this sort of defamatory activity has increased incrementally.[81]

Allegations that are true at the time they are made cannot generally be defamatory under the law. But the online world on any given day is filled with absolute lies regarding persons, groups, and companies. Some of the worst allegations in recent years were reserved for President Clinton himself, with many of the accusers taking advantage of the technology to remain anonymous even as they spread rumor and innuendo across the globe.

In the early 1990s, online moderators often enforced a certain level of civility and ethical behavior on bulletin boards, discussion forums, and mailing lists. By the latter part of the decade, however, most of these moderators had disappeared.[82] The freewheeling nature of the current public discourse is seen as a right by the great majority of Netizens. But some are beginning to wonder about the possible negative consequences of such unrestrained openness as a large percentage of the population migrates to the online world.

As with other areas in category 3, the law has not always been particularly helpful here. Laws regarding defamation specifically and freedom of expression in general can vary tremendously from country to country, leading to some very difficult controversies in the areas of jurisdiction and enforcement. In the United States, the issue has arisen within the context of several trials addressing the liability of ISPs and content providers for defamatory acts, particularly as the courts attempt to interpret the provision in the Telecommunications Act of 1996 that insulates service providers from liability in particular situations.[83]

Section 230 of the act states: "No provider or user of an interactive computer service shall be treated as the publisher or speaker of any information provided by another information content provider."[84] The term "information content provider" is defined as "any person or entity that is responsible, in whole or in part, for the creation or development of information provided through the Internet or any other interactive computer service."[85]

Since the passage of the act, U.S. courts have had several opportunities to determine the scope of its protection for Internet service providers. In both *Zeran v. America Online*[86] and *Blumenthal v. Drudge and America*

Online,[87] the courts determined that AOL was, indeed, protected by Section 230, even though the commercial online service arguably could have done more to prevent the dissemination of the defamatory material.

The Drudge case was particularly troubling to some commentators. Drudge, who at the time was being paid three thousand dollars a month to post his "Drudge Report" on AOL, had allegedly set forth a series of defamatory remarks about White House aide Sidney Blumenthal. A lawsuit was brought by Blumenthal against both AOL and Drudge, but the court found that AOL was protected under the Telecommunications Act. It reasoned that according to the language set forth by Congress, AOL was indeed a "service provider" that could not be held liable for the defamatory remarks of "another information content provider," thus rejecting the plaintiff's claim that AOL was itself the content provider in this case. The court stated that Congress had provided immunity "even where the interactive service provider has an active, even aggressive role in making available content prepared by others."[88]

Thus, while the courts and the U.S. Congress have spent a great deal of time shoring up protections for Internet service providers in this context, they have arguably done nothing to address the larger question of what might be done to improve the quality of public discourse. Yet many believe that such questions go far beyond the scope of the role delegated to legislatures and judicial systems. Public discourse in the online world, the argument goes, is simply a reflection of the people who use the Internet and of the complex times in which we live. Libertarian Netizens insist that persons who are bothered by the freewheeling nature of the discourse can keep to the more sedate portions of cyberspace. After all, did not the U.S. Supreme Court itself endorse the "marketplace of ideas" nature of the Internet?

For many others, however, freewheeling and often mean-spirited discourse is simply another example of everything that is wrong with the online world. And some believe that it is appropriate to focus specifically on what may be an overly permissive law regarding defamation of public figures. Surely, they argue, persons can retain the freedom to question the policies of our political leaders without being given the right to accuse them of the most heinous crimes without any requirement of substantiation. According to this view, permissive laws are themselves the reason why cyberspace is out of control.

Inappropriate Conduct

The last major category of problematic conduct in cyberspace is comprised of behavior that most would label "inappropriate." It includes online harassment, hate-related activity, overly aggressive business promotions and practices, and other immoral or offensive acts that do not fit under any of the other areas described above. These acts—unlike those discussed in category 3—are typically neither anarchic nor unlawful, although some anarchic behavior may, in fact, occur in this area as well.

Given that the four categories in this chapter have been ordered according to degree of harm or threat, this last category includes activity that is likely to be considered less hazardous and troubling by the average person. But it must be emphasized that for many—particularly those who have been victimized by such behavior—these are not activities that can be taken lightly.

In this category, a consensus must be reached on not only whether particular activities are inappropriate, but whether they are *inappropriate enough* to try to control in some way. In this context, it is instructive to look at four specific types of activity: (1) discriminatory "hostile environment" harassment of individual persons, (2) extremist and hate-related websites, (3) inappropriate online activity in an educational setting, and (4) offensive or overly aggressive business practices.

Discriminatory "Hostile Environment" Harassment

The term "discriminatory harassment," as used in the legal community, refers generally to words or actions directed in a hostile and discriminatory manner against other persons. These words or actions typically "discriminate" on the basis of race, ethnicity, religion, sex, sexual orientation, and/or disability; although other similar categories have sometimes been included.[89] The exact definition of discriminatory harassment has itself been the subject of dispute, and many refer instead to a more specific subcategory, such as "hostile environment" sexual harassment, hate speech, or racial slurs.

On a day-to-day level, this type of conduct has proven extremely difficult to address, with disagreements regarding political correctness often obfuscating relevant issues. Yet few would deny that such behavior takes place in cyberspace all the time. Online "hostile environment" harassment can occur in a wide variety of contexts, ranging from e-mail to chat rooms to newsgroups. Individual persons who have been targeted in this offensive manner have reported verbal slurs, requests for sexual favors, and indeed an entire range of unwelcome online activity that often constitutes unwelcome intimidation, ridicule, or insult.

In the 1996 Communications Decency Act (CDA), the U.S. Congress sought to address at least some of this activity by extending certain protections against harassing behavior that were already on the books for telephone conversations to similar acts in cyberspace.[90] Even though this portion of the CDA was not struck down by the courts, online harassment does not seem to have abated at all since then.

In addition, it is unclear from the language of the statute precisely what sort of activity is allowed and what sort of activity is prohibited in cyberspace. Arguably, the online harassment prohibited by U.S. law is a very narrowly defined class of activity similar in nature to telephone harassment, and would not extend to the broader category of "hostile environment" harassment prohibited in the workplace or in federally funded educational programs. And since the courts—particularly in the campus-speech code cases of the late 1980s and early 1990s—did not look kindly on any efforts to expand the reach of "hostile environment" principles, it is very possible that the creation of a generic hostile environment in cyberspace would not be viewed as illegal under current law.

Still, it must be noted that many online users would certainly find hostile environment harassment inappropriate in cyberspace. In 1997, I gave a presentation on this topic at the Computers, Freedom and Privacy Conference in the San Francisco Bay Area, and asked the audience how many of them viewed online harassment as a significant problem that needed to be addressed by future laws. Even at this conference, which was attended by folks with a predominantly libertarian view of cyberspace, a good fifty percent of the audience saw the area as problematic and supported more aggressive regulatory efforts by law enforcement officials. But it must also be noted that the other fifty percent had reactions that ranged from a casual dismissal of the issue to outrage at the idea that anyone would seriously consider efforts to restrict online speech in this manner.

Over the past six to eight years, Internet service providers have themselves developed written policies prohibiting similar behavior. America Online's prohibitions in 1996 are particularly noteworthy in this regard.[91] These blanket prohibitions, however, are arguably as vague in some areas as the Communications Decency Act itself. And even if precise definitions could be set forth to identify the parameters of the prohibited behavior, enforcement remains a key challenge. If an ISP terminates a user's account for violating the rules, nothing prevents the person from then signing up with another company.

Extremist and Hate-Related Web Sites

Web sites espousing racism, hate, and hate-related violence raise many of same issues as acts of discriminatory harassment directed toward individual persons, but in a much more public way. A winter 1999 report by the highly respected Southern Poverty Law Center (SPLC) documented the nature and extent of this activity in the United States, and noted that many other sites with similar messages are posted on servers around the world.

The SPLC Report identified three types of problematic U.S. Web sites in this regard: militia sites, "racist thought" sites, and hate sites in general. Often masquerading as patriotic, academic, or religious in nature, the persons and groups that maintain such sites spread dangerous and divisive messages that often appeal to impressionable young people and to disenfranchised members of society. The "racist thought" sites, for example, include Future Generations (www.eugenics.net), a collection of writings by academics focusing on supposed race-based IQ differences and on eugenics—the "science of improving a race stock through selective breeding." They also include "David Duke's Race Information Library," a section of a huge site by the former Klansman that contains articles on alleged race-related differences.

The general hate sites are divided into subcategories representing the Ku Klux Klan, Neo-Nazis, Racist Skinheads, "Christian Identity" groups, Black Separatist groups, and others. They range from sites that are ostensibly informational in nature to web pages that actively promote hate. The inclusion of some groups is controversial, given that many do not view certain "white power" organizations or the Nation of Islam as hate groups.

The list also includes the American Knights of the Ku Klux Klan, the White Aryan Resistance, the National Socialist Hitler Youth of Amerika, and Racial Holy War.

The conventional wisdom among U.S. media, legal scholars, and others is that these Web pages—although highly offensive—are generally protected under the First Amendment; however, many others believe that such protections are improper, and point to other countries where this sort of expression is prohibited. The SPLC reports that many ISPs have taken the initiative to remove such sites from their servers. But Web site owners—like individuals who may have been terminated for engaging in harassing behavior—often find another ISP in a very short period of time.

The controversy continues. In the meantime, the number of hate sites on the Internet continues to increase. In 1998 alone, it reportedly increased by sixty percent. And that, the SPLC says, is only a conservative estimate.[92]

Inappropriate Online Activity in an Education Setting

As more and more education-related activity becomes part and parcel of the online world, traditional controversies regarding the free speech rights of students and educators have moved to cyberspace and have taken on the unique features that accompany such a move.

Free speech rights under the First Amendment include more than simply the right to speak. They also include the right not to speak, the right to receive speech, and the right not to receive speech. In an education setting, and particularly at the higher education level—where information technology plays an increasingly prominent role—disputes regarding the appropriateness of expression often impact several of these rights. Students and educators have been taken to task not only for the alleged inappropriateness of their own expression in cyberspace, but also for the alleged inappropriateness of material that they have accessed.

Three federal cases that have been decided in recent years reflect the parameters of these disputes: the *Jake Baker* case at the University of Michigan, the *Loving v. Boren* case at the University of Oklahoma, and the *Urofsky* case in Virginia.

In the first case, Michigan student Jake Baker was prosecuted by federal authorities after it was revealed that (1) he had posted a violent, sexually-related fantasy to a newsgroup regarding a woman who had been given the same name as a fellow student in his class, and (2) he had engaged in a series of e-mail conversations with a person in Canada regarding certain violent and depraved acts that they had thought about committing with young teenaged girls. In the end, he was prosecuted only for the e-mail exchange, but he was not convicted because the court found that his activity did not constitute a true threat. Judge Avern Cohn—the same judge who had struck down the University of Michigan's campus speech code in 1989—questioned the efficacy of prosecuting a student in a situation like this, and asserted that "the case would have been better handled as a disciplinary matter."[93]

The widely publicized Baker case not only left everyone unsatisfied but also left the larger issue unresolved. Free-speech advocates criticized the "persecution" of Jake Baker, who ultimately left the university after undergoing what amounted to a public humiliation. And university officials—justifiably concerned that expressions of intent to commit violent acts are often translated into reality—felt let down by the legal system.

Loving and *Urofsky* represent the other side of the coin because they both involved court approval of attempts to regulate arguably inappropriate conduct. In the Loving case, a journalism professor filed a First Amendment lawsuit challenging Oklahoma President David Boren's decision to restrict access to certain sexually-related newsgroups. Boren had apparently made this decision because he was concerned that the university might be violating a state law that made it a felony to "distribute . . . any obscene or indecent writing . . . [or] . . . photography" (21 O.S. 1021). After the lawsuit was filed but before the case went to trial, OU revised its newsgroup-access policy and set up a second on-campus "news server." The "A" server restricted access to those newsgroups "approved" by OU, while the "B" server allowed unrestricted access to all newsgroups on the Internet. Persons wishing to use the "B" server had to be over eighteen and had to certify that they were accessing the newsgroups "for academic and research purposes."[94]

At the trial, Professor Loving represented himself and argued that his rights had been violated because the university had acted to restrict access to a public forum. But Judge Wayne Alley rejected Loving's arguments, declaring that "[t]here was no evidence . . . that the facilities . . . [had] . . . ever been open to the general public or used for public communication. The state . . . has the right to preserve the property under its control for the use to which it is lawfully dedicated. In this case, the OU computer and Internet services are lawfully dedicated to academic and research uses."[95] Loving appealed the decision to the 10th Circuit Court of Appeals, but lost on procedural grounds.[96]

In the *Urofsky* case, professors at various Virginia state colleges and universities argued that a Virginia statute prohibiting state employees from accessing sexually explicit material online was violative of the First Amendment.[97] They alleged that the act unconstitutionally interfered with their research and teaching, and provided many examples for the court. Professor Urofsky argued that he had been reluctant to assign students online research assignments on "indecency" law because of the act. Professor Smith claimed that his Web site containing materials on gender roles and sexuality had been censored as a result of the act. Professor Meyers was concerned about his ability to access the Commonwealth's own database of sexually explicit poetry to continue his studies of certain Victorian poets. Professor Heller had stopped using the Internet to continue her research on lesbian and gay studies, and other professors were reluctant to use the Internet to continue their psychological research on human sexual experience.

Federal District Court Judge Leonie M. Brinkema ruled in favor of the professors. She declared that what is at issue here is a state employee's ability to "read, research, and discuss" sexually explicit topics. Among other things, the court determined that since sexually explicit online material may very well contain information that would benefit the public, it is entitled to constitutional protection.[98] But on appeal, the Fourth Circuit Court of Appeals disagreed, and reversed the decision because they found no First Amendment violation.[99]

At this point, courts in different parts of the country appear to be coming to different conclusions regarding university efforts to restrict what may be viewed as inappropriate online activity. Some believe that, ultimately, the U.S. Supreme Court will have to make a decision in this area, and contend that restrictions such as those upheld in the Oklahoma and Virginia cases run counter to the spirit of the Court's decision in *Reno v. ACLU*. Others argue, however, that the *Reno* decision dealt with a more narrow issue, and would not necessarily preclude the Court from upholding reasonable university regulations in this context. Yet it must also be pointed out that it could be many years before the Court agrees to hear such a case, and that the justices may ultimately decide to leave this sort of decision to local authorities. In the meantime, university officials must wrestle with contradictory signals regarding the parameters of First Amendment rights for students and educators in the online world.

Offensive or Overly Aggressive Business Practices

This area is yet another example of the fluid and elastic nature of these four categories, since there may be a fine line between business practices that are deceitful and business practices that are simply overly aggressive or offensive. But the key distinguishing feature is that the deceitful practices and promotions described under category 2 include dishonest behavior that negatively impacts the economic safety of Internet stakeholders and is often illegal. In contrast, the practices discussed here under category 4 are typically legal and not generally dishonest.

Examples of inappropriate conduct that have generated a great deal of attention in this context include day-to-day privacy infringements and overly aggressive advertising. E-mail privacy, for example, continues to be a major concern. Most people understand that their e-mail messages may be accessed under certain conditions by employers or law enforcement personnel if they are stored by either the sender or the receiver. But the lack of privacy in this context goes far beyond a user's inbox or outbox. Some e-mail systems transiently copy messages as they pass through, and other systems may automatically create back-up copies of new e-mail as it arrives on the servers. Thus, even erasing messages from inboxes and outboxes and "shredding" them with additional software does not typically delete e-mail, since it often remains on servers and backup media.[100] E-mail policies have justified such copying and back-up practices by citing concerns in the areas of security and system integrity, but, in at least some cases, these arguably inappropriate practices continue simply because the pattern has been in place from the beginning.

Influential commentators and organizations continue to insist that the privacy "problem" on the Internet is part and parcel of a much larger societal problem that has been ignored for too many years. With the development of increasingly sophisticated devices that can produce detailed records—including audio and visual documentation—of citizens' daily and weekly pursuits, many fear that on some level the classic dystopian visions of the future are close to being realized.[101] Such fears were only exacerbated by revelations in 1999 that both Microsoft and Intel had included new features in their latest products that would make it even easier to identify Netizens in cyberspace.

In light of discoveries by Cambridge software programmer Richard Smith, for example, it became apparent that Microsoft had not only included a unique identification feature in its Windows 98 operating system, but that it had designed Microsoft Office so that each document created would contain a serial number. Such a setup had enabled the company to create an extensive database of personal information regarding computer users. When registering their new computer operating systems with Microsoft, customers were told that they would be eligible for both support and updates. They were not told, however, that their Globally Unique Identifier was tied not only to their own name but also to identifying numbers on their computer hardware and even apparently to documents they might create in Word or Excel.

According to Smith, Microsoft was, in effect, establishing a "digital fingerprint" that could be used to match a document created by a word processing or spreadsheet program with a particular computer. Responding to the outcry that ensued, Microsoft promised to alter the way the registration program worked in future releases of Windows 98, and to "look through the company's databases and expunge information that had been improperly collected."[102] Microsoft subsequently issued a software utility program that enabled computer users to delete the numbering from their documents. Ironically, it was this very numbering system that enabled Smith to assist federal authorities in tracking down the alleged creator of the Internet virus "Melissa" a few weeks later.[103]

Early 1999 was a particularly busy time for privacy advocates, with the Microsoft revelations occurring soon after a major confrontation with Intel regarding the release of the Pentium III chip. In January 1999, Intel announced that it was planning to include a "unique Processor Serial

Number (PSN)" in every one of its new Pentium III microprocessors. According to Intel, this number would be used to identify users in e-commerce and other Internet-based applications. As envisioned by Intel executives, the PSN would facilitate security in chat rooms, online transactions, and a variety of other cyberspace activities. Unlike cookies, which are typically different for each Web site and can be deleted by users, the PSN would remain the same and could not be deleted or easily changed. It could be collected by many sites, indexed and accumulated, and tied to a person's real-world identity.[104]

While many stakeholders were pleased with the prospect of strengthening online security by limiting the impact of electronic anonymity, privacy advocates mounted a widely publicized boycott campaign. The boycott finally ended after Intel removed the feature from the chip's successor.[105]

A third privacy controversy also emerged in early 1999, but, compared to the Pentium III affair, it was relatively mild and most notable perhaps for a notorious quote by Sun Microsystems CEO Scott McNealy. Sun had recently announced the release of its newest software, known as "Jini," which was intended to interconnect virtually all types of electronic devices from computers to cameras. Privacy advocates argued that such software, which assigned an identification number to each device each time it connected to a network, "could be misused as networks envelop almost everyone in society in a dense web of devices that see, hear and monitor behavior and location." Dismissing the entire range of privacy concerns in a blatantly direct manner, McNealy's response was: "You already have zero privacy. Get over it."[106]

It is likely that McNealy, on some level, speaks for a sizable percentage of the stakeholders in the online world. To the extent that recent privacy debates reflect the age-old conflict between safety and privacy, it is very possible that a majority of online users would opt for safety over privacy. Libertarian Netizens may perhaps be more concerned about eroding privacy rights in cyberspace, but the more recent "settlers" and the entrepreneurial business interests are probably much more worried about hackers, scammers, and cyberstalkers than they are about Globally Unique Identifiers, Processor Serial Numbers, and Jini. Fortunately, there remains a very large and vocal portion of the online community that continues to monitor these issues, particularly within the larger context of the erosion of privacy rights across the board. Thus, here too, although many do not see privacy as a problem, the area remains substantially unregulated and the issues remain completely unresolved.

Advertising practices have also remained substantially unregulated, and here too there has been substantial disagreement regarding the extent to which the activities have constituted "problems." Online advertising has become increasingly aggressive, generating a variety of legal and policy questions. Typical practices include—but are not limited to—Web site ads, domain-name selection, and either targeted e-mails or mass e-mails.

In an unregulated and completely open commercial environment what is unacceptable for some is completely acceptable for others. While some are bothered by basic banner advertising on web pages, for example, most online users probably do not see the practice as a problem. Many others are bothered by the type of unsolicited bulk e-mail discussed earlier in this chapter—even if it complies with existing laws. But the reactions of those who receive spam can vary tremendously depending on the perspectives of the individual users and perhaps on the content of the messages themselves. Some see their e-mail inboxes as inviolable, and are offended by any unsolicited message. Many have come to view unsolicited e-mail as a customary practice in cyberspace, and find at least some of it interesting. Most, however, find large amounts of spam inappropriate and unacceptable—particularly if there is no recourse available under the law.

An analysis of the various disputes that have been documented in this chapter reveals a range of complex problems that remain unresolved. In some cases, the problems have not been addressed. In other cases, efforts to address them from either a legal or a policy perspective have been unsuccessful. Some of the problem areas reflect troubling behavior on the part of individual Netizens, whereas in other instances, it is the more powerful governmental and/or business interests that have caused the difficulties. In some cases, the law itself is arguably the problem.

At the same time, if a consensus can be reached on what sorts of harm should be prevented, some type of regulatory approach addressing this harm may be an appropriate next step. Indeed, parts 2 and 3 of this book focus on the nature of the regulatory options available and on their potential as problem-solving vehicles for representative problem areas. By dividing troubling online behavior into four categories, it becomes easier to identify common characteristics that can lead to a consensus among the various stakeholders. Building on such a consensus, it may then be possible to craft potential solutions based on the unique features of the different problematic activity.

But before the inquiry into the nature and extent of potential solutions can begin, it is important to address the limits of our legal system. As has been apparent from the beginning of this book, legal principles have been a central feature of cyberspace policy disputes. Whether stakeholders are trying to invoke the legal system, bypass the legal system, or change the legal system, one thing is certain: it cannot be ignored. Yet this system—which would-be regulators sometimes put so much faith in—has on many occasions over the centuries proven to be only marginally effective.

What *are* the limits of our legal system? In what ways has it worked? In what ways has it failed us? What lessons may be learned from history in this regard? We turn to these questions in chapter 4.

4

The Inherent Limits of Our Legal System

The more laws, the less justice.
—Cicero, *De Officiis,* Circa 44 B.C.

[For] too much law, more law will be the cure. If law makes blind, more law will make you see.
—Karl Llewellyn, "The Bramble Bush," Circa 1960

Anyone who believes that all laws should always be obeyed would have made a fine slave catcher. Anyone who believes that all laws are applied equally, despite race, religion, or economic status, is a fool.
—John J. Miller, "Jokertown Shuffle, Wild Cards IX"

If you've got a warrant, I guess you're gonna come in.
—The Grateful Dead, "Truckin'," Circa 1970

Generally, we are a law-abiding society. This is true not only in the United States, but also in most parts of the world at any given time. People may not know all the laws that might be applicable to their particular circumstances, but—often intuitively—they tend to comply with existing legal mandates and restrictions as a matter of course.

Yet our legal system does not always work. Sometimes existing laws are inadequate to address particular problems. Sometimes laws are overinclusive, and persons who were never intended to be impacted by particular restrictions end up in very difficult circumstances as a result. Sometimes, the laws themselves are just right, but the legal system may break down either at the jurisdiction level or the law enforcement level.

Difficulties arise in other contexts as well. For example, when people look to the legal system to sort out problems—either because they have been wronged or simply because things have become too complicated for them to sort out on their own—they may come away completely dissatisfied . . . or, even worse, irretrievably damaged by a process that has supposedly been designed to achieve justice.

A classic example of the inherent limits of our legal system in this regard is the case of *Jarndyce and Jarndyce,* which serves as the centerpiece for the Charles Dickens novel *Bleak House. Jarndyce* is the case that never ends, going on for decades and ensnaring just about everyone in its web. While the litigation may have made sense at some point in time, it eventually becomes impossible to understand, and the various procedural and transactional battles that seem to occur on a regular basis ultimately have little to do with the final outcome:

> This . . . suit has, in the course of time, become so complicated that no man alive knows what it means. The parties to it understand it least . . . Scores of people have deliriously found themselves made parties in *Jarndyce and Jarndyce,* without knowing how or why. Whole families have inherited legendary hatreds with the suit. . . .
>
> How many people . . . *Jarndyce and Jarndyce* has stretched forth its unwholesome hand to spoil and corrupt, would be a very wide question. From the master . . . down to the copying clerk . . . no man's nature has been made the better by it. In trickery, evasion, procrastination, spoilation, botheration, under false pretenses of all sorts, there are influences that can never come to good.[1]

Sometimes the legal system may break down in other contexts, such as when lawmakers try to legislate morality. While a determination as to what might constitute right and wrong is generally viewed as within the domain of religious authorities and therefore outside the control of the typical secular government, many modern statutory frameworks are shaped by both implicit and explicit moral imperatives. Commentators, for example, have consistently argued that jail sentences for so-called victimless crimes are examples of inappropriate and ineffective efforts by governmental authorities to define the boundaries of personal values and behavior.

Over the centuries, many people have analyzed the limits of our legal system, identifying conceptual frameworks and exploring major problem areas. Relevant schools of thought have been derived from the work of notable philosophers and political theorists such as Hobbes, Locke,

Rousseau, Beccaria, and Mill. Oliver Wendell Holmes, in an 1897 *Harvard Law Review* article entitled "The Path of the Law," discusses the limits of the law at some length, focusing, in particular, on the distinction between law and morality.[2]

In *The Limits of Law*—a 1974 collection of essays that has come to be viewed as something of a modern-day classic—twentieth-century scholars examine central features of this inquiry.[3] David Danelski, for example, suggests that an analysis might appropriately begin with the examination of two questions that would-be regulators continue to face today: how far *can* law go in fulfilling its functions and how far *should* it go. To answer the former question, he argues that it is necessary to consider the ethical dimensions of human behavior, while to answer the latter question, he contends that it is necessary to consider the possibility and probability of certain kinds of human behavior. Danelski discusses the empirical limits of the law at some length, and concludes that when these limits are reached, they stem from problems related to "(1) perception of officially sanctioned rules, (2) the development of a sense of obligation to obey them, and (3) their enforcement."[4]

In the same volume, Julius Cohen identifies a central but often overlooked limit of any law—its "side effects" or unintended consequences.[5] And Kent Greenwalt structures his own analysis of the area by setting forth three categories of limits. Under the first category, *limited effectiveness,* he discusses problems that may arise when people do not comply with laws, and he examines the resulting inability of legal systems to achieve certain goals. Under the second category, *practical limits,* he explores the costs to society of ascertaining observance and the difficulties that may arise in attempting to litigate cases when relevant facts may be uncertain. He also analyzes problems that may be linked to the nature of rules themselves. Under the third cateory, *moral limits,* Greenwalt argues that some areas of human behavior should not, from a moral perspective, be subject to legal control.[6]

In recent years, legal scholars have focused on specific areas of controversy within this broader context, examining the extent to which privacy regulation is limited by competing interests such as first amendment concerns,[7] the minimal successes of our criminal justice system in reducing crime,[8] the apparent inability of our legal system to resolve certain race-related issues in areas such as school desegregation and hate speech,[9] and the limits of the law as an instrument of social change in general.[10]

Analyzing the prospective role of our legal system in bioethical decision making, Roger Dworkin argues that law is not a collection of rules to govern human behavior, reasoning that if rules are directives that one can learn and follow, "many legal rules are not rules at all, because they are . . . [often] . . . created only after someone has acted." Even pre-existing rules, he explains, are "seldom clear" because "someone must interpret and apply them." Dworkin goes on to explore the ability of common law to address the problems of modern technology. Common law can be defined as the set of legal principles—typically found in case decisions—that have been developed "through the resolution of real, existing disputes." Dworkin contends that such a method may be inadequate because it fails to provide guidelines for problems that may arise in the future:

> [F]or common law to deal with a technology the technology must exist and have operated in a way that angered someone enough for that person to have claimed injury and sought legal redress. Thus, to the extent that a rapid response or a response in advance to a . . . [recent] . . . development is important, the common law cannot provide it. Common law is reactive, not proactive . . . . [In addition] . . . the real, existing disputes that the common law tackles one case at a time are decided largely through resort to analogy and precedent, . . . [and this means] . . . that the courts are seeking solutions to today's problems in yesterday's wisdom. As noted, there are good reasons for doing that. However, the backward-looking nature of the common law is . . . another reason to doubt . . . [its] . . . ability to deal with new problems posed by rapid changes in science and technology.[11]

Dworkin concludes by echoing the warning set forth by Cohen and many others over the centuries regarding the unintended negative consequences of lawmaking. He argues that "blind faith" in the law's ability to resolve problems or "unthinking acquiescence" in the dominant role of law would be unsound. "Attention to the costs of mistakes," he asserts, "counsels caution in resorting to the law at all." And he suggests that in most cases a low-level response—such as some administrative regulation or some noncriminal state legislation—might be best, "unless and until one is persuaded that a real and pressing need, which can only be met by extreme measures, exists, and that the costs of resorting to the extreme measures will not outweigh the gains."[12]

The wide-ranging scholarship in this area provides an important context for addressing the limits of our legal system in the online world. Indeed, an analysis of major research findings leads to the identification of four key principles that must inform any effort to control cyberspace by relying on the more traditional approaches to regulation:

1. On some level, our legal system is often based upon an implicit social contract;
2. The law works better in some areas than in others, and it is less effective in complex territory with many variables;
3. Laws are typically more effective where both the issues and the boundaries of control are localized; and
4. From an enforcement perspective, regulators must inevitably recognize the practical limits of any effort to bring everything and everyone under control.

The Implicit Social Contract

Social contract theory has not only influenced the founding of the United States and its Constitution, but has consistently played a role in the development of American jurisprudence. Rooted in the classic writings of noted social contractarian philosophers and reflected more recently in the work of John Rawls, social contract theory provides that "rational individuals will agree by contract, compact, or covenant to give up the condition of unregulated freedom in exchange for the security of a civil society governed by a just, binding rule of law."[13]

In 1999, Anita Allen examined the use of social contract theory in American case law since the late eighteenth century. Analyzing the results of an extensive computer-assisted study, she focused at great length on cases in which the courts use the concept of social contract implicitly or explicitly to justify a legal result.[14] Of particular interest are those cases where judges have characterized the entire legal systems of both the United States and other nations as social contracts.

In these cases, Allen finds some inconsistency regarding the parameters of the implicit social contract that may form the basis of our legal system. Some argue that the contract is "between the state and its citizens to preserve social order and . . . property."[15] Others argue, however, that the contract is a pact among individuals, "an agreement between members of society by which each member undertakes duties in consideration for the benefit received when all members fulfill similar duties."[16]

Whether the implicit social contract is characterized as an agreement between citizens and the state or as an agreement between citizens and other citizens, it is clear that this contract has broken down on several occasions in the twentieth century, when large numbers of people have decided for one reason or another to ignore or defy existing laws.

One example of such a breakdown cited by many commentators is prohibition. Over the centuries, the consumption of alcoholic beverages has been viewed with great ambivalence, and many societies have at one time or another instituted bans on its manufacture and sale. The American experience has certainly reflected this ambivalence. In the 1700s, a large number of people in both England and the American colonies believed that drunkenness was implicated in the rising incidence of crime, poverty, and violence. A movement to ban consumption of alcohol gathered steam in the late 1800s, and by 1900, millions of men and women were beginning to regard "the saloon" as the most dangerous social institution threatening the family.[17]

By 1916, many states closed their saloons and prohibited the manufacture of any alcoholic beverages. Finally, in 1919, the prohibition movement culminated with the ratification of the Eighteenth Amendment, which prohibited "the manufacture, sale, or transportation of intoxicating liquors." To enforce this amendment, Congress passed the Volstead Act, defining "intoxicating liquors" as those with an alcoholic content of more than 0.5 percent. Prohibition officially began in January 1920.[18]

From the beginning, the new law was defied, as large numbers of people expressed their resentment at what they perceived to be government intrusion into the private affairs of its citizens. Many felt that prohibition had become a classic example of a law with unintended negative consequences. Not only did it distort the role of alcohol in American life, causing people to drink more rather than less, but it actually promoted a disrespect for the law. In addition, as the implicit social contract continued to break down, prohibition generated a wave of organized criminal activity that included illegal sellers (bootleggers) and illegal saloons (speakeasies). At the height of prohibition, profits available to criminals from such activities corrupted almost every level of government.[19]

The U.S. ban on alcohol ended in 1933 with the passage of the Twenty-first Amendment, but there are those who believe that the same pattern of prohibition followed by defiance and a breakdown of the implicit social contract has continued—albeit to a lesser extent—with the current ban on recreational drugs. At one time, for example, marijuana, LSD, and cocaine were all legal in this country. Heightened concerns regarding the adverse effects of these substances on both individual users and society as a whole led to what some have characterized as a new prohibition, complete with disrespect for the law and unintended negative consequences.[20] And while few persons today would criticize the ban on LSD and cocaine or blame the legal system in any way for the relatively small number of people who use these drugs, the same cannot be said for marijuana.

Since the 1960s, the defiance of the marijuana laws, particularly by young people, has been a prime example of how the implicit social contract can break down in a particular area of our legal system. The first federal legislation prohibiting possession and use of marijuana was passed in 1937, and by 1956, mandatory prison sentences of two to ten years were required for those convicted of possessing even tiny amounts. Many state laws followed the federal model, but varied considerably in the severity of the penalties. Some actually mandated the death penalty for selling marijuana to minors.[21] In fact, federal and state marijuana violations were equated with murder, rape, and other serious offenses. Yet in spite of these stringent prohibitions, the use of the drug increased dramatically from 1964 to 1970.

In the United States as a whole, marijuana arrests doubled from 7,000 in 1964 to more than 15,000 in 1966.[22] In California, the number of marijuana arrests of juveniles increased 140 percent in 1966.[23] At the Mexican border, "well before the beginning of the federal government's campaign to cut off smuggling from Mexico, the number of marijuana plants seized . . . [by federal officials] . . . jumped from 72,772 to 1,327,260—an increase of over 1,500 percent" in one year (1967–1968). The amount of marijuana seized by border agents increased from 2,165 pounds in 1965 to 48,896 pounds in 1968.[24]

By the summer of 1967, health officials in Washington, D.C. estimated that 20 million Americans had tried marijuana, and that up to 4.5 million smoked it regularly. Campus surveys that same year at Princeton, Yale, and Caltech revealed that 25 percent of the student population had experimented with the drug.[25] In 1968, the *L.A. Times* reported that, according to some observers, local police were "no longer able to cope with pot smoking. . . . [I]f they went to some of the beaches on a weekend, it would take them all day to arrest all of the smokers . . . and when they got through they wouldn't have the jails to hold them." L.A. Police Chief Tom Reddin appeared to confirm these findings, and explained that "rather than try to make mass searches, we go for those openly and flagrantly abusing the law."[26] In 1969, a study by the Massachusetts Commission on Drug Abuse at four non-Ivy League colleges in the state found that "roughly half" of all the students smoked marijuana and that their grades were higher, on the average, than those of nonsmokers.[27]

By the 1970s, marijuana had become the recreational drug of choice for many persons across a wide spectrum of the population that included high school and college students, young professionals, and highly successful artists, authors, and entertainers.[28] In the larger U.S. urban centers, a great majority of people in their twenties and thirties had either known someone who used marijuana or had been exposed to marijuana at concerts or social events. Yet even as use of the drug became socially acceptable, many of the prohibitions remained in place, and simple possession in a good number of states still resulted in draconian penalties.[29] Efforts to lower penalties and, in fact, to decriminalize marijuana had some success in certain locations,[30] but a true disconnect remained between the laws on the books and the day-to-day acts of a large segment of society.

In the 1980s, marijuana use declined, as recreational drug users turned increasingly to alcohol. The 1990s, however, saw a new increase in the use of the drug, particularly among young people. At the K-12 level, for example, the 1998 National Household Survey on Drug Abuse conducted by the U.S. Department of Health and Human Services found that young people were using marijuana in growing numbers, and that the perceived risk of marijuana use among twelve- to seventeen-year-olds had continued to decline since 1991.[31] The National Center on Addiction and Substance Abuse at Columbia University found in its 1998 Back to School Teen Survey that, according to most teens, more than half of their fellow students in grades 9–12 had tried marijuana.[32] And at the college and university level, the *Chronicle of Higher Education*'s annual campus safety report in the spring of 1999 found that arrests for violation of drug laws on college campuses had doubled between 1996 and 1997. It also reported the results of a new study by the Harvard University School of Public Health, which concluded that there had been an increase in drug use by college students from 1993 to 1997. The survey showed that a large cohort of college students began using drugs in middle school and have continued doing so.[33]

By the end of the decade, legal issues had changed, as new controversies arose within the context of drug-testing programs and efforts to legalize marijuana for medical purposes. At some level, perhaps, there was an uneasy truce between casual marijuana users and the legal system. The fact remains, however, that marijuana use continues to be illegal in most parts of the world, even as people continue to break these laws with apparent impunity. And there is no resolution in sight. The persistence of marijuana use remains a prime example of how our legal system is based on an implicit social contract, and how the laws on the books can cease to matter when a large percentage of people decide they want to do something that may not be acceptable under the law.

The disturbances in Los Angeles in 1992 would qualify as yet another example of the breakdown of the social contract. These riots (or "rebellion," as some have called them) were triggered by a longstanding dissatisfaction with local law enforcement practices in many parts of the city over an extended period of time. When four white policemen who had been videotaped beating an African American suspect named Rodney King were acquitted by an all-white jury in an L.A. suburb on Wednesday afternoon, April 29, protests broke out in many parts of the city. Peaceful demonstrations soon grew violent, innocent people were beaten, and private property was damaged. Before long, fires had started, and by the afternoon of April 30, the city appeared to be literally out of control. Fires were spreading, looting was rampant, assaults on private citizens continued, and local incidents of vigilantism appeared to be on the rise. The national guard was called in, and a dusk-to-dawn curfew was ordered. By the end of the weekend, after many arrests, an uneasy semblance of order had been restored.

Those of us who experienced the L.A. Riots will never forget the images of lawlessness and the feeling that the social contract had indeed broken down on a large and frightening scale. Events that began with the exercise of the lawful right to freedom of speech soon degenerated into widespread violence, theft, and destruction, perpetrated by many who were simply taking advantage of the apparent failure of local law enforcement personnel to keep a lid on the protest activity. Did local law enforcement officials fail to maintain control, or was this a case where too many people decided too suddenly that the law did not matter? If, as many believe, the latter was indeed the case for a period of twenty-four to thirty-six hours, then the 1992 disturbances serve as a textbook example of the uneasy balance that exists in our society between the legal system and the desires of the people. When enough individuals decide, even for a brief period of time, that the social contract inherent in our legal system no longer yields the benefits of a civil and just society, anarchy necessarily follows. For some, this anarchy was based on the prevalent slogan of the time: "No justice, no peace." For others, however, slogans did not matter. Store doors were wide open, merchandise was readily available, and persons from all walks of life took advantage of the breakdown of law and order to fill their shopping bags, pickup trucks, and sport utility vehicles with stolen items of all kinds. And when no law enforcement officials were available to come to the rescue, shopkeepers sometimes took matters into their own hands.

Reflecting back on the events of those turbulent days in the spring of 1992, one can conclude that it is not our legal system or the day-to-day efforts of local law enforcement personnel that maintain law and order, but rather, the will and desire of the great majority of American citizens themselves. If too many suddenly decide, for whatever reason, to act differently, then the implicit social contract breaks down and only something resembling martial law can restore a degree of sanity.

Social contract theory is essential to an understanding of cyberspace by would-be regulators. Social contractarian philosophers such as Hobbes have maintained that a "state of nature"—defined as a condition of natural freedom and risk—exists prior to the formation of a civil society. The progression from a state of nature to a society based on an implicit social contract with evolving social norms follows a pattern that we have seen in both the settling of the American West and the early development of the online world. While it is clear that much about cyberspace is currently regulated and very much "under control," it is also apparent that a great deal of what occurs from day to day in the online world remains unregulated and based on an implicit social contract between online users. The acceptance of this implicit contract has been so widespread that jurists and political leaders at the highest levels continue to pay lip service to the view that the status quo must be maintained to the extent possible. Many have come to believe that the current social norms in cyberspace reflect the desires of the great majority of online users and should therefore not be altered.

Effectiveness of the Law in Complex Territory with Many Variables

A second principle that must inform any effort to regulate the online world is that the law works better in some areas than in others, and that—in particular—it is less effective in complex territory with many variables. Intellectually, this principle may seem so obvious that it is not necessary to even state it. Yet many recent attempts by attorneys, legislators and policymakers to address certain elaborate and multifaceted cyberspace issues have fallen short for the very reason that the law is, indeed, less effective in complex territory with a large number of variables. In retrospect, for a good number of issues, had this inherent limit of our legal system been recognized in advance, an approach less rooted in law might have been adopted and might have stood a better chance of succeeding.

Three problem areas are particularly instructive in this regard: attempts to equalize public-school funding, efforts to combat racism and hate crimes, and litigation in the area of toxic torts.

Fifteen years after *Brown v. Board of Education,* legal activists—frustrated by the slow pace of desegregation efforts and concerned about ongoing inequities in educational opportunities—turned to the area of school finance and the apparent inequitable allocation of resources in many parts of the country. The *Serrano v. Priest* litigation in California exemplified this focus. An analysis of California's school-finance structure in the late 1960s revealed that a system based primarily on local property taxes had resulted in significant funding disparities from school district to school district. For example, in the year 1968–1969, the amount spent by

Los Angeles County school districts to educate each of their students varied from $577.49 per pupil (in Baldwin Park) and $840.19 per pupil (in Pasadena) to $1,231.72 per pupil (in Beverly Hills). As the California Supreme Court indicated, "The source of these disparities is unmistakable: in Baldwin Park the assessed valuation per child totaled only $3,706; in Pasadena, assessed valuation was $13,706; while in Beverly Hills, the corresponding figure was $50,885—a ratio of 1 to 4 to 13."[34]

Litigation seeking to equalize per-pupil expenditures was an eminently logical approach to take. Novel legal theories based on an expansive view of equal protection were developed, and the lawsuit eventually succeeded in revamping California's inequitable school-finance structure. Yet, two decades later, significant disparities remain from school to school and from district to district. In addition, California public schools are often viewed as among the most troubled in the nation.

Why did an apparently successful lawsuit of such major proportions have so little positive impact in the end? The answer, for many, lies in the complex nature of public education in general and school finance in particular. The *Serrano* litigation and its implementing legislation only equalized per-pupil expenditures from the state's general fund. It did nothing to equalize district income from categorical funds, money that is tied to particular federal and state programs and can only be used for those programs. It also did nothing to equalize physical plants, instructional materials, and equipment. Thus, schools that started with better buildings and better equipment in the 1970s stayed in relatively good shape in this regard, while schools that started with run-down buildings and poor equipment remained behind. In addition, "booster clubs" have been allowed to raise supplementary money for local schools, and districts with wealthier populations have been more successful with these activities. Finally, most of the money from the general fund goes to teacher salaries, and increased expenditures for teacher salaries do not necessarily translate into better education. In fact, veteran teachers who command higher salaries may in certain instances be less effective than young, idealistic teachers at the bottom of the salary scale who may put more time, effort, and energy into their day-to-day classroom activities.

Efforts to combat racism have been met with similar frustrations, in spite of many apparent victories in the legal context. During the past fifty years, plaintiffs in race-related lawsuits have won a large number of significant battles, not only in discrimination cases, but also in areas such as school desegregation that include diversity as a central goal. In addition, federal and state statutes designed to prohibit discrimination and punish racist activity have been added to the law books in great quantity. And policies prohibiting discriminatory harassment in both the workplace and on colleges campuses have proliferated.

In spite of these changes in the law, many people believe that we are no closer to eradicating hatred and bigotry than we were fifty years ago. Overt acts of racism and discrimination are much rarer in the U.S. today, but racial stereotyping and resentment seem as prevalent as they were in 1950. For many, the hate-related Internet activity discussed in chapter 3 is further evidence of this fact.

Scholarly research in the area of race relations has proliferated, and the complexities of the issue across the country and around the world have been explored at great length. Although some believe that America has done much worse than other countries in this regard, others point to the racial, ethnic, and religious strife in such places as Latin America, the Balkans, Africa, and the Middle East, in support of the argument that America is neither less successful nor more successful than others have been in combating racism and eradicating prejudice. Most scholars, regardless of their perspectives on the efficacy of such efforts, appear to believe that we may have reached the limits of the law in this area. Race relations may simply be too complex, with too many conflicting variables at work, to hope for reasonable solutions via the legal system.

A third example of efforts to use the legal system to resolve complex social problems is the widely publicized class-action lawsuit by residents of Woburn, Massachusetts against two Fortune 500 companies—Beatrice Foods and W.R. Grace. As documented by Jonathan Harr in *A Civil Action,* this 1986 litigation represented the best efforts of private attorney Jan Schlichtmann and his legal team to win a large monetary award for the apparent victims of major toxic-waste pollution. In the mid-1980s, an unusually large number of Woburn residents—including many children—came down with leukemia at approximately the same time, and all these residents lived in a relatively secluded area not far from a Beatrice tannery and a W.R. Grace industrial plant. Extensive investigation by experts in the field appeared to yield compelling evidence of widespread and ongoing pollution of the area's water supply by Beatrice and Grace employees. All signs pointed toward a significant victory for the Woburn plaintiffs and a precedent-setting monetary award that would serve to punish and deter toxic-waste polluters once and for all.

Yet Schlichtmann, a relatively young but highly successful trial lawyer, clearly underestimated the resources of his corporate opponents and the ability of their high-powered law firms to employ a range of time-tested procedural strategies and ultimately derail his case. In the end, after having turned down fairly substantial settlement offers, Schlichtmann negotiated a small, almost-token award on behalf of his clients. But in the process of litigating the case, he incurred a range of insurmountable debts, and at several points in time, he appeared on the verge of losing his sanity as well. At the close of the final round of legal proceedings in 1990, owing his creditors $1,231,542 and being able to account for only $664 in assets, Schlichtmann filed for bankruptcy. He found himself unable to work on any more cases, and almost took his own life.

The Woburn litigation is a modern-day incarnation of the *Jarndyce and Jarndyce* case. Four-hundred cartons of documents were accumulated in the course of the proceedings. Attorneys for the defendants used literally every trick in the book to obfuscate the issues and delay the trial. They filed every possible motion, made every possible objection, and argued every possible point. They also succeeded in separating the trial into several parts, in essence keeping the jury from ever hearing the plaintiffs' own stories in a court of law.

Perhaps the most compelling example of the way in which complex litigation can spiral out of control is the series of questions that the jury was asked to resolve at the close of the trial's first phase:

> In truth, these questions were all but impossible to understand. An expert in semantics would have had a hard time finding his way through the thicket of words. But even worse, they asked for answers that were essentially unknowable. Science could not determine the moment when those chemicals had arrived at the wells with the sort of precision . . . [that was being demanded] . . . of the jurors."[35]

On one level, the Woburn case is a classic example of the limits of our adversarial system. But on another level, this may be yet another instance of a dispute with so many complex variables that the limits of our legal system were inevitably reached. As Jonathan Harr explains in discussing the unintelligible jury questions: "If these questions really were necessary to a just resolution of this case, then perhaps the case was one that the judicial system was not equipped to handle. Perhaps it should never have been brought to trial in the first place."[36]

For reasons such as those set forth in chapters 2 and 3, many people believe that cyberspace is just as complex as school finance, racism, and toxic waste. With its wide range of stakeholders, lack of national borders, large number of activities happening all at once, and the difficulty of ascertaining who might actually be in charge of a particular thing at a particular time, cyberspace has been viewed by both insiders and outsiders as a highly intricate maze of interconnecting realities with an unfathomable life of its own. Relying on our legal system to regulate certain problem areas in the online world may therefore prove as difficult as efforts to use legal strategies to equalize public education, combat bigotry, and put an end to the pollution of our natural resources.

The Boundaries of Local Control

Examining the history and development of our legal system, one is struck by the consistent difficulties that governing powers have experienced when trying to control persons and events from afar. Laws are invariably more effective when the issues addressed are local issues and governmental authorities are situated close by. Not only is there a much greater respect for the law when it is viewed as reflecting local realities and concerns, but local authorities who know and understand the local population have typically been able to work more effectively with their neighbors to maintain order and resolve conflicts.

When disputes have arisen between persons who do not live close by, or when authorities have sought to maintain control over persons and groups situated far away, the legal system has often broken down. Borders have a legal impact, and the reach of law across any border often becomes a matter of great controversy. Even in an era of instant global communication, geography continues to play a major role.

The difficulties involved in controlling persons and groups from afar are compounded in cyberspace by new realities that have changed the way in which we view space. A person, it can be said, may "arrive" at a Web site located halfway around the world without leaving the comfort of his own chair. From another perspective, however, we can say that it is a copy of the website that is coming through his computer in bright colors and sound; it may seem to be right there in front of him, but the original is actually located on a server halfway around the world.

No matter which conception of cyberspace one adopts, it must be recognized that, at least on some level, the online world crosses traditional geographical borders in new and different ways. Foreign users, for example, can send data through U.S. computers, and U.S. users can route their information through servers located overseas. Numerous countries over the years have routed nearly all their national data traffic through U.S. networks because of the capacity and speed of U.S. connections. The Peruvian government once engaged in a "computer war" with the Shining Path guerrillas, and both sides tried to wipe out data on their respective computers in Peru while using an Internet server in Brooklyn.[37] And Usenet discussion groups—where it has been possible to find much of the most extreme pornography available on the Internet—are clearly international in nature, consisting of "continuously changing messages that are routed from one network to another, with no centralized location at all."[38]

Not only are people crossing traditional borders effortlessly in cyberspace, but it may be nearly impossible in some cases to tell who they are and what they are doing. Messages may be sent using the latest encryption technology, and anonymous remailers can be used to hide identity. For some time now, through the cooperation of certain Internet service providers both in the U.S. and overseas, online users have been able to establish anonymity by routing all their activity through networks whose operators promise not to reveal or even inquire about who they really are.

An anonymous remailer is actually a technological buffer, a type of data-network relay that can be used to mask the origin of an e-mail message or the computer from which a person is browsing the Web. The remailer does this by stripping off identifying information and substituting an anonymous code number or term. In late 1999, there were about forty anonymous remail services worldwide. The more sophisticated remailers, such as nym.alias.net at MIT, also route messages through many different relay computers around the world, leaving no record of the path that a message may have traveled after leaving the remailer.[39] At the Thirty-fifth Anniversary Conference of the MIT Laboratory for Computer Science, David Mazieres explained that nym.alias.net owners on the MIT server were completely anonymous, and that even people who administered the MIT system did not know the true identities of the users. The service had been open to the public since June 1996, and throughout its existence, there were about two thousand to three thousand active accounts at any given time.[40]

The interrelated issues of hidden activity and the boundaries of local control have led to an extensive analysis of questions relating to jurisdiction in the online world. As discussed in chapter 2, novel inquiries have emerged, and not only has it been uncertain which entity might have jurisdiction over a particular dispute, but it is not clear whose rules might apply, and in what context. Johnson and Post—who take the view that the online world is, indeed, a different place—argue that because cyberspace "undermines the relationship between legally significant phenomena and physical location," it "radically subverts the system of rule-making based on borders between physical spaces." They insist that basing jurisdiction on where a server might actually be located makes no sense because, for example, a Web site "physically located in Brazil . . . has no more of an effect on individuals in Brazil than does a Web site physically located in Belgium or Belize that is accessible in Brazil." Yet they also contend that jurisdiction based on where digital information is accessed is equally illogical because under such a jurisdictional framework any state or any country could regulate the cyberspace activities of any other state or country. All Internet-related activity would, therefore, be subject simultaneously to the inconsistent laws of all territorial sovereigns.[41]

Jack Goldsmith, who subscribes to the more traditional view that cyberspace is not that different, still concedes that the problems raised by Johnson and Post reflect the limits inherent in our legal system's structure of basing jurisdiction primarily on traditional geographical borders. Goldsmith argues that transnational choice-of-law options developed over the past several decades to address similar problems outside of cyberspace can be employed to help resolve online issues, but he explains at some length how challenging such an approach might be. Our legal system has currently evolved to the point where customary international law permits a nation to apply its law to extraterritorial behavior with substantial local effects. A transaction "can legitimately be regulated by the jurisdiction where the transaction occurs, the jurisdictions where significant effects of the transaction are felt, and the jurisdictions where the parties burdened by the regulation are from." Yet the rules regarding which jurisdiction's laws might be applicable in a particular dispute may vary from country to country, and the spillover effects of one nation's court decision in this regard may very well affect individual behavior and regulatory efforts in other countries. Such spillover effects, according to Goldsmith, remain "the central problem of modern conflict of laws."[42] The basic principle that our legal system works best where both the issues and the boundaries of control are localized continues to apply:

> Short of . . . [developments in public or private international coordination or technological innovation] . . . transnational transactions in cyberspace, like transnational transactions mediated by telephone and mail, will continue to give rise to disputes that present challenging choice-of-law issues. For example: "Whose substantive legal rules apply to a defamatory message that is written by someone in Mexico . . . [and] . . . read by someone in Israel by means of an Internet server located in the Unites States, injuring the reputation of a Norwegian?"[43]

Although scholars such as Post and Goldsmith may not be that far apart regarding the characterization of jurisdictional problems that have emerged with the growth and development of cyberspace, there has been significant disagreement over the location of real or imagined borders. Goldsmith and other traditionalists insist that cyberspace transactions are no different than "real-space" transactions, and that "there is no general normative argument that supports the immunization of cyberspace activities from territorial regulation."[44] Johnson and Post argue, however, that a new border has effectively been drawn around the online world, and that the old rules do not necessarily apply in this new place. According to this view, a map of cyberspace can be drawn, and its borders not only cross over traditional national and international boundaries, but include additional borders within borders that may reflect the jurisdictional boundaries of individual networks.[45] Some believe that if cyberspace is indeed a different place, then perhaps the relevant boundaries are the overlapping areas of the online world that are controlled by the various systems operators and Internet service providers. Accordingly, the America Online network might be viewed as one sovereign territory, the EarthLink network as a second, the AT&T network as a third, and so on. Effective local control could thus continue in cyberspace, and in fact many believe that this is exactly what has been happening in recent years.

Lawmakers, however, continue to subscribe to the view that local Internet-related activity can be regulated in a traditional manner at the local level. Not only are nations promulgating a range of contradictory laws in this regard, but individual states and even local municipalities are seeking to regulate what they view as their portion of the online world. In recent years, some of the inevitable disputes in this area have reached the U.S. courts, and judges have moved toward a series of rules that can help address questions regarding which state's laws might apply in what context. A 1997 federal district court decision in Pennsylvania synthesized court rulings in several recent disputes and concluded that web jurisdiction cases are appropriately analyzed according to whether (1) substantial business, such as contracts or sales, is conducted in a particular state via the Web, (2) the site is simply interactive, or (3) the site is purely passive, serving only as an advertisement.[46] Under this analysis, which has apparently been adopted by several other courts—including the Ninth Circuit Court of Appeals[47]—any state can assert jurisdiction over a Web site owner conducting substantial business in that state through the Web site, but cannot assert jurisdiction over the owner of a purely passive site. The simply interactive site, however, remains a gray area, and no hard-and-fast rules typically apply.

This threefold typology appears to be an appropriate starting point, but it must be recognized that it appears to work best in an e-commerce setting and may apply only to Web sites and not to other Internet-related activity. The lack of concrete rules for interactive sites that do not serve as conduits for substantial business leaves a significant gap in the law at this point in time. Many sites fall into this second category, and more guidance will be needed as more day-to-day activity moves to the online world. In addition, no similar rules have been generated on an international level, and there is a danger that cases such as the prosecution of CompuServe Deutschland's

Felix Somm in Munich under local German law will proliferate as more nations attempt to assert local jurisdiction over the flow of information in their part of the world.

The Practical Limits of Law Enforcement

In the scholarly literature regarding the inherent limits of our legal system, much has been written about the practical limits of any effort to bring everything and everyone under control. Commentators and indeed regulators themselves have recognized that in a democracy, even under optimal conditions—a strong and effective social contract, a simplified problem area, and clearly defined boundaries of local control—there is only so much that can be done to enforce existing statutes and regulations.

Under typical criminal laws, for example, authorities certainly cannot prosecute or punish everyone. It is always the case that certain suspects end up serving as examples. Under the range of civil laws, the situation is even more complicated, given that rules are not generally enforced unless and until a wronged party sends a threatening letter, files a lawsuit, and either prevails at trial or wins a favorable settlement. And when court orders, consent decrees, or administrative regulations are set up to provide regulatory structures for civil statutes, case decisions, or settlement agreements, the compliance monitoring that accompanies such a structure is limited by its own individual set of realities.

Literature that focuses on the limits of law enforcement in our criminal justice system typically reflects the prevailing view. Hans Zeisel, for example, in *The Limits of Law Enforcement* (1982), argues that law enforcement officials too often fail to make a dent in the crime rate because of the practical limits they face. These limits include very low rates of victim reporting, arrest, conviction, and sentencing for felonies committed, as well as a consistent relationship between crime rates and adverse social and economic conditions.[48]

Copyright enforcement is another example of these practical limits. Although both criminal and civil copyright laws are violated daily in great number, very few cases are prosecuted, and a relatively small number of civil infringement lawsuits go to trial. In the criminal area, there are simply not enough federal prosecutors, and the more extreme crimes such as murder and large-scale drug trafficking tend to take precedence over copyright cases. In the civil area, copyright owners may not ever know that their rights have been violated, but even if they become aware of violations, they may decide that the expense of a civil trial is not worth the gamble, given that success is never assured in a court of law. If copyright owners are successful at all in the legal system on a day-to-day basis, it is usually when they hire attorneys to send threatening letters that eventually convince the infringer to stop. But even if this occurs, any damage from previous infringing activity is typically written off.

The K-12 public-school classroom is another representative example of the limits of law enforcement. A range of laws may be on the books, but when a teacher closes the classroom door, he or she is alone with the students and—as long as no one complains—many of the statutes debated by legislators and many of the lawsuits won at great cost will end up having little or no practical impact. In fact, teachers may not even know that a statute is on the books or that a particular case decision has been reached. And on the few occasions when the typical principal may actually visit the classroom, the visitation agenda is usually given over to a series of basic curricular and management-based observations that have little to do with any sort of "law enforcement."

To address this problem, administrative regulations, court orders, and consent decrees often build on compliance-review mechanisms. But even these structures have their limits. I have personally served as the California State Consent Decree Monitor for the desegregation of the San Francisco Public Schools, and under that decree, I am required to submit an annual report to the federal district court. This report is expected to provide a paragraph-by-paragraph analysis of school-district compliance with the terms and conditions of the Consent Decree. Yet no built-in mechanism is in place to enforce compliance should the district fail to abide by any of its requirements. Individual parties to the original lawsuit may choose to go to court to enforce a provision, but such a process is lengthy and complicated, and no easy victory is assured. Thus, I have tried to share my findings with district officials immediately, as they arise throughout the year, and have worked to build a collaborative relationship so that everyone is working toward the same goals and no one gets caught up in a law enforcement situation that may not resolve anything in the end.

Similar patterns arise in cyberspace. Goldsmith, for example, identifies the interrelationship between jurisdiction and enforcement, and then outlines the limits of enforcement within that framework. He explains that a nation typically can only enforce its rules against (1) persons with a presence or assets in its territory, (2) persons over whom a nation can obtain personal jurisdiction and enforce a default judgment against, and (3) persons who can be successfully extradited. And he goes on to point out that because a defendant's physical presence or assets within the territory remain the primary basis for a nation to enforce its laws, such a structure may be particularly problematic in cyberspace. Countries may be able to regulate the service providers and users who have established a physical presence within their borders, but there will invariably be a large number of online users who lack a physical presence in the regulating jurisdiction.[49]

Legislators and policymakers who seek to rely on our legal system to control the online world must, therefore, be cognizant of a range of important considerations. History teaches that laws must be established with great care, taking into account not only the nature and extent of the general limits of law identified in the scholarly literature over the centuries, but also the basic principles directly applicable to cyberspace. Authorities also cannot lose sight of the importance of the implicit social contract, the relative ineffectiveness of the legal system in areas of great complexity, the boundaries of local control, and the practical limits of law enforcement in both the criminal and civil areas.

As the analysis in part I has shown, would-be regulators of the online world face many challenges, but some regulation in this context is clearly inevitable. The average online user may feel relatively free in cyberspace, and may sense that other persons and groups are operating in an unrestricted fashion. In actuality, however, numerous traditional laws have governed the online world from the beginning, and—particularly in the United States—a large variety of Internet-related cases, statutes, and administrative regulations have been decided, and numerous statutes have been created over the past six to eight years to address a range of online activity. In addition, at the individual network level, acceptable-use policies have been developed that set forth additional rules for individual subscribers. To the extent that much freedom remains, it has often been the result of a conscious choice on the part of various governing bodies to maintain a level of independence and autonomy for Netizens.

Although it may have once made sense to address the regulation question in an all-or-nothing fashion, such an analysis at this point in time is anachronistic. The question is no longer whether cyberspace as a whole can or should be regulated, but whether and to what extent individual problem areas within particular cyber spaces can or should be addressed via regulation. In proposing a range of strategies for selected problem areas, we will build on the analysis in part 1 by emphasizing the importance of seeking to reach a consensus not only on the harm we wish to prevent, but also on any new approaches to jurisdiction and enforcement that we might wish to adopt. Only through such a consensus can the barriers to regulation inherent in both the limits of our legal system and in the complexity of cyberspace itself be appropriately addressed.

Part II

5

The Traditional Regulation Model: Applying Existing Rules and Developing New Legal Frameworks at the Individual Country Level

A society in which men recognize no check upon their freedom soon becomes a society where freedom is in the possession of only a savage few. . . . The spirit of liberty is the spirit which is not too sure that it is right; the spirit of liberty is the spirit which seeks to understand the minds of other men and women; the spirit of liberty is the spirit which weighs their interests alongside its own without bias.

—Judge Learned Hand, U.S. Court of Appeals, 2d Circuit, 1944

The law is conservative in the same way in which language is conservative. It seeks to assimilate everything that happens to that which has happened. It seeks to relate any new phenomenon to what has already been categorized and dealt with.

—Robert Wasserstrom, "Postscripts, Lawyers and Revolution," Circa 1968

Our vision of an uncensored Internet was clearly shared by the U.S. Supreme Court when it struck down the 1996 Communications Decency Act (CDA). . . . [T]he Court declared the Internet to be a free speech zone, deserving of at least as much First Amendment protection as that afforded to books, newspapers and magazines. The government, the Court said, can no more restrict a person's access to words or images on the Internet than it could be allowed to snatch a book out of a reader's hands in the library, or cover over a statue of a nude in a museum.

—Censorship in a Box, Cyber-Liberties: ACLU Freedom Network, Circa 1998

In the early 1990s, cyberspace was known as a place where online users took care of their own problems. When troubling issues arose, typically within the context of speech that did not fit the social norms of virtual communities, they were generally resolved through intervention by other online users and systems operators. Most of the time, all it took was "additional speech" to put an end to disputes in a setting where free and open dialogue was the prevailing norm. Few even thought of getting the government involved in any way.

Although it may once have been possible for persons and groups to resolve most of their Internet-related problems by relying on the power of social norms and on such community-based strategies as private monitoring and increased communication, the online world today has simply grown too large and unwieldy for this type of resolution to work across the board. In particular, the commercial nature of cyberspace has now made it extremely difficult for individuals or even corporate entities to resolve disputes in the way they once did.

Commentators and in fact many companies continue to argue that self-regulation remains the most appropriate strategy, and it may be that in certain cases and particularly in certain industries, this sort of free market, libertarian approach to day-to-day affairs in cyberspace would work best. Some industry leaders, for example, have been able to design self-policing guidelines that address problematic aspects of previous practices. But it must be noted that self-regulation in the online world has already run into some of the same constraints that we have seen within the context of deregulation or self-regulation efforts in the offline world. If people and groups have the same priorities and are working toward similar goals, then self-regulation often works well. In recent years, however, it has become apparent that persons and groups who populate today's Internet sometimes have conflicting priorities and dissimilar goals. In such instances, certain problems can be resolved—and, in fact, avoided altogether—by relying on one or more of three basic regulatory models: (1) legal frameworks within individual countries, (2) international cooperation, and (3) changes in the architecture of the Internet itself.

This chapter addresses the first of these models, and it does so by focusing on U.S. law as an example of how this model may operate. Arguably, the principles discussed in this chapter are applicable to any country, although variations are inevitable depending on the country, its size, and its system of government.

At first glance, resolving problems through existing legal systems may appear to be the simplest model to pursue. Clearly defined avenues are available for those who would seek changes in the law or some form of redress under the law. Yet it must be recognized that the aforementioned issues of jurisdiction, enforcement, and boundaries of local control are inevitably implicated under this model. Indeed, the entire discussion in chapter 4 regarding the inherent limits of our legal system is directly applicable to any analysis of this model's potential effectiveness in cyberspace.

Before proceeding with this discussion, however, it is important to note that some people believe the Internet is not truly a global medium at all, but simply an extension of the United States. According to this view, cyberspace is international to the extent that it is accessible internationally and can be used to maximize global communication, but certain components of the Internet—and particularly the World Wide Web—are seen as vehicles for extending America's influence around the world in an unprecedented fashion. After all, the argument goes, the Internet from the beginning was an American project, online access is typically dependent on one or more American companies, and to the extent that international representatives have been involved in cyberspace policy issues on a global level, they have participated on America's terms. In addition, the great majority of Web sites accessible online are U.S. Web sites. The language of the Internet is overwhelmingly English, and the culture of the Internet is predominantly American at this point in time.

While such a perspective may provide additional support for commentators across the globe who criticize alleged "Yankee imperialism" and argue against alleged "American hegemony," it may have little practical impact on our inquiry, particularly if "cyberspace as an extension of the United States" is seen simply as a metaphor reflecting a particular worldview. From a legal perspective, however, there may be a more precise set of facts at work here. If the great majority of persons and groups in charge (as described in chapter 1) are American, and the great majority of online users at this point in time are American, then U.S. law will inevitably play a much greater role in resolving online disputes under any view of existing legal systems. In this context, it can be argued that under any proposed regulatory structure for cyberspace, the online world cannot and should not be seen as directly analogous across the board to older forms of international communication such as the telephone and telegraph. It may be analogous to these forms of communication with regard to person-to-person interaction via e-mail, for example, but the existence of the World Wide Web arguably calls for a different construct. Persons and groups accessing the Web or even establishing a Web presence at this point in time may need to begin from the perspective that U.S. law is likely to have a significant impact on the result of a particular dispute that may arise.

A related issue is the ability of a particular government to literally shut down the Internet. During the NATO war against Serbia in 1999, there were those who feared that the United States was about to shut down Yugoslavia's Internet connection. This shutdown might have occurred not just through targeted bombing, but via an executive order by President Clinton "prohibiting the delivery of any services by a U.S. entity into [Yugoslavia]." An investigation by the Electronic Frontier Foundation and subsequent follow-up reports by *The Scotsman,* the *Christian Science Monitor,* and the *International Herald Tribune* revealed that the four largest Internet providers in Yugoslavia were linked to the outside world by three fiber-optic cables and one satellite channel. All four connections were overloaded during the latter days of the NATO bombing, and experts believed that the breakdown of any one of them could have led to the others collapsing as well. In particular, the reports focused on U.S. satellite company Loral Orion, which supplied the Internet satellite feed to Yugoslavia and which had announced that it would have to follow the executive order.[1]

The potential extent of the U.S. government's day-to-day control over the online world is unclear at this point in time. For most of us, the government is little more than a benign presence, encouraging the use of a technology it created and helping to facilitate networking capabilities worldwide. But if in fact the U.S. can shut down Internet connections, then American law may ultimately play an even greater role in online disputes than many might have initially thought.

We will proceed, however, as we have thus far, under the more traditional assumption that cyberspace is indeed international in nature, recognizing that there are unresolved questions regarding the dominant role of the U.S. government that cannot be completely discounted from an international perspective.

A key question underlying the inquiry in this chapter is whether cyberspace actually needs any more *new* legal frameworks. As we saw in earlier chapters, there are those who feel that cyberspace is not all that different and that existing laws can simply be applied to the Internet as they might have been applied to earlier technological advancements. Yet most legislative bodies across the country and around the world have apparently decided otherwise . . . generating an increasingly large body of high profile legislation aimed specifically at regulating the online world in key ways. Particularly for certain specific issues at certain specific times, most legislators have come to agree that although there may very well be a place for the application of existing laws, cyberspace is different enough to merit a range of new legal frameworks.

As a starting point, it should be noted that there are five basic sources of U.S. "law": (1) constitutional provisions, (2) statutes, (3) case decisions, (4) administrative regulations, and (5) policies. All the rules or decisions set forth by government officials under these categories have the force of law. The list is also a hierarchy, and in the event that there are conflicts between rules from one category and rules from another, the higher category prevails. Thus, for example, if there is a direct conflict between a statute and a constitutional provision, the constitution—as the supreme law of the land—will prevail, and we will say that the statute is unconstitutional.

As a practical matter, there are actually two major vehicles available to those who seek to restructure national law—legislation and litigation. Legislation is more direct, and typically spawns both administrative regulations and implementing policies. But activists in certain areas of the law have found over the years that they may have more success changing the law by bypassing the legislature and pursuing litigation aimed at winning declarations of rights ("declaratory relief") or court orders that force people and companies either to start doing something or stop doing something ("mandatory or prohibitory injunctive relief"). Such litigation strategies, pursued at times with particular effectiveness in such areas as civil rights and education, have not only an immediate, short-term effect, but also the long-term effect of changing case law so that courts in subsequent disputes must follow the same rules.

With regard to cyberspace, most of the changes in the law thus far have been the result of legislation. A set of emerging legal principles can be discerned from case decisions (a.k.a. "common law") in recent years,[2] as Internet-related disputes continue to be decided by the courts. But common law is slow to change, and clearly the most dramatic developments in this context have taken place in the legislative arena.

It is instructive to examine some of these major federal legislative packages . . . in order to determine how this regulatory model can work and what pitfalls need to be recognized. We will examine the Communications Decency Act, the Child Online Protection Act (COPA), the "No Electronic Theft" Act, and the Internet Tax Freedom Act. We will also analyze related efforts to regulate the Internet at the state level, and the extent to which these developments further complicate an already tangled set of legal principles.

The "Decency" Legislation of 1996 and 1998

Even before the 1990s, there were already laws on the books prohibiting the transmission of obscene material. The Thomases, for example, as discussed in chapter 2, were convicted under a statute originally passed by Congress in 1955 (Title 18 of the U.S. Code, Section 1465), which prohibits knowingly using and causing to be used a facility and means of interstate commerce for the purpose of transporting obscene materials in interstate commerce. And many defendants have been convicted under child pornography statutes originally dating back to 1978. Precise definitions of obscenity and child pornography have been identified over the years, and laws restricting these types of expression have been deemed constitutional in the highest courts of the land.

Still, the U.S. Congress—recognizing that these laws had not been effective in preventing the proliferation of online pornography—tried on two different occasions in the late 1990s to protect children by attempting to further regulate this area. In 1996, it included the highly publicized Communications Decency Act in its omnibus Telecommunications Reform Bill, and in 1998, it passed the Child Online Protection Act. Both the "under 18" provisions of the CDA and the basic text of COPA started from the position that much of the distasteful material in cyberspace did not constitute obscenity or child pornography under previous laws, and that only through new prohibitions could the dissemination of such material be criminalized. Thus the two acts added additional prohibitions—and additional penalties—for the transmission of certain inappropriate material.

As we saw in chapter 3, the attempts by Congress to add these additional prohibitions are generally regarded as failures because the statutes were successfully challenged in the courts. Many commentators have analyzed these court battles, and while some argue that the results were inevitable, others contend that things did not have to turn out the way they did and that we can ultimately do better.

The Communications Decency Act and Subsequent Lawsuits

The Communications Decency Act contained a series of interrelated provisions set forth within the larger framework of a wide-ranging telecommunications-reform bill. Although the publicity surrounding the *Reno v. ACLU* case led many to an initial conclusion that the entire CDA was invalidated by the courts, this was not the case. In fact, only two disputed provisions were struck down, and other provisions not only remain on the books, but have been viewed as significant new rules governing behavior in the online world.[3] These rules range from additional prohibitions regarding certain types of offensive speech to provisions that can effectively insulate ISP from both criminal and civil liability if their subscribers violate obscenity and defamation laws.[4]

In this context, it is instructive to examine the course of events following the passage of the CDA and some of the thinking underlying the subsequent lawsuits themselves. As the CDA worked its way through Congress in 1995 and early 1996, a powerful grassroots campaign of opposition emerged in the online world. The act was seen by the great majority of Netizens as a dangerous attempt by the government to "censor" the Internet by setting forth general prohibitions that, under the guise of protecting children, would inevitably restrict the communication of every person in cyberspace. When the legislation passed, many Web site owners, including fledgling companies that were maintaining popular search engines and Web portals, displayed their screens in black as part of an organized protest against this congressional action.

Reno v. ACLU Immediately after President Clinton signed the Telecommunications Reform Bill into law on February 8, 1996, a coalition led by the ACLU appeared in federal court and was able to temporarily halt the implementation of the bill's "decency provisions."[5] For plaintiffs, the most problematic sections of the CDA were those that set forth criminal penalties for certain communications sent to or received by persons under the age of eighteen that might be considered "indecent" or "patently offensive."[6]

In late February 1996, a coalition led by the American Library Association and the newly formed Citizens Internet Empowerment Coalition filed a second lawsuit challenging the constitutionality of the CDA.[7] On February 27, 1996, the ACLU and ALA cases were officially consolidated, and plaintiffs' attorneys worked together from that point on. In their briefs, the plaintiffs continued their efforts to challenge all the "indecency" and "patent offensiveness" provisions of the act.[8] They set forth a series of First Amendment arguments rooted in basic principles prohibiting vagueness and overbreadth.

On March 21, 1996, the cyberlaw "Trial of the Century," as it has been called, began in the federal district court in Philadelphia. A notable feature of these proceedings was the installation of a T-1 circuit and a small local area network in the Ceremonial Room of the Philadelphia court that enabled judges, attorneys, and witnesses to access the Internet together. Courtroom observers believed this was the first time in history that a federal courtroom had been wired to the Internet for the purposes of a trial.

Among the witnesses appearing for the plaintiffs were Vanderbilt Professor Donna Hoffman, a marketing expert who testified that many mom-and-pop Web sites might be forced to close down because of uncertainty about indecency penalties; Kiyoshi Kuromiya, an anti-AIDS activist who testified that his site might be implicated by the new law because it provides crucial, sexually explicit information on safer sex practices for teens around the world; and Howard Rheingold, an author and cyberspace expert who testified to the difficulties inherent in attempting to define "community standards" for a worldwide network.

According to trial updates provided on the Internet by the Electronic Privacy Information Center, witnesses presented conflicting testimony regarding both the state of technology in general and strategies that might be available for prohibiting indecent and offensive material. Special Agent Howard A. Schmidt, testifying on behalf of the government, acknowledged under cross-examination that the majority of sexually explicit sites he had come across in his investigation would have been off-limits had he been running a software program such as SurfWatch. The final plaintiffs' witness, Dr. Albert Vezza of the MIT Laboratory of Computer Sciences, told the court about Platform for Internet Content Selection—the new system designed to allow parents to control children's access to the Internet according to their own values or via a rating system devised by a trusted organization.

The final government witness, Dr. Dan Olsen of Brigham Young University, testified that the best way to comply with the new laws would be to block all words and images that might be deemed "indecent" until the "questionable" material could be reviewed and labeled for adult consumption. Olsen explained that he had created the "-L18" system, which would enable content creators to determine whether their words or images were "indecent" or "patently offensive." An electronic "-L18" label would then be attached to all such sites. Several judges questioned Dr. Olsen on this system, and wondered how "-L18" might apply to e-mail or to chat rooms.[9]

On June 11, 1996, the three-judge panel in *ACLU v. Reno I* ruled unanimously that the disputed portions of the CDA were unconstitutionally vague and overbroad. A preliminary injunction preventing authorities from enforcing these provisions was entered.[10] Each of the three judges wrote separate opinions that emphasized various aspects of their findings.

Chief Justice Sloviter, for example, wrote that the statute "sweeps more broadly than necessary and thereby chills the expression of adults." She found that the terms *patently offensive* and *indecent* were "inherently vague," and she rejected the value of the affirmative defenses built into the CDA.[11] Judge Buckwalter added that the unique nature of the Internet aggravated the vagueness of the statute.[12] And Judge Dalzell reviewed at length the "special attributes of Internet communication," finding in the end that the CDA would abridge significant protected speech, particularly by noncommercial speakers, while "perversely, commercial pornographers would remain relatively unaffected." As "the most participatory form of mass speech yet developed," the Internet, he concluded, is entitled to "the highest protection from governmental intrusion."[13]

After losing at trial, the Justice Department decided to appeal. Such an appeal was not a foregone conclusion, given that key people in the Clinton Administration apparently felt that an appeal would be fruitless. Indeed, many wondered why the leadership in Washington D.C. even backed a statutory scheme that most legal experts had deemed unconstitutional in advance. Some speculated that the proponents of the bill expected the statute to be overruled in the courts, but felt that it was politically important to back a highly publicized effort to protect young people.

The case moved forward on the fast track to the U.S. Supreme Court,[14] and oral argument took place in front of the nine justices on March 19, 1997. As discussed in chapter 2, not only did the government argue that the trial court incorrectly found the CDA vague and overbroad, but it predicated much of its argument on the fact that the Internet should be viewed as akin to broadcast media and should, therefore, be subject to the more stringent restrictions upheld by previous courts under the First Amendment. Plaintiffs' attorney Bruce Ennis rejected these contentions, stating that the strongest argument *against* the CDA was that it would have "the unconstitutional effect of banning indecent speech from adults in all of cyberspace": "For forty years," he explained, "this Court has repeatedly and unanimously ruled that Government cannot constitutionally reduce the adult population to reading and viewing only what is appropriate for children. That is what this law does."[15]

Ennis's argument carried the day, and on June 26, 1997, the Supreme Court ruled 7–2 in favor of the plaintiffs.[16] Justice Stevens's majority opinion was a ringing endorsement of the Internet as a "dramatic" and "unique" "marketplace of ideas." The justices found that although sexually explicit material was "widely available" online, "users seldom encounter such content accidentally." And in his First Amendment analysis, Justice Stevens found that the lower court in this case "was correct to conclude that the CDA effectively resembles the ban on 'dial-a-porn'" invalidated in an earlier decision.[17] Finally, examining the issue of whether the rights of adults should be compromised in order to protect children, the justices declared that "in order to deny minors access to potentially harmful speech, the CDA effectively suppresses a large amount of speech that adults have a constitutional right to receive and to address to one another. . . . [W]hile we have repeatedly recognized the governmental interest in protecting children from harmful materials, . . . that interest does not justify an unnecessarily broad suppression of speech addressed to adults." The disputed provisions of the Communications Decency Act were therefore declared unconstitutional.

ApolloMedia Corp. v. Reno While most Netizens cheered the result in *Reno v. ACLU,* it soon became clear that other CDA prohibitions retained the force of law. Particularly noteworthy were the provisions prohibiting communication with the "intent to annoy, abuse, threaten, or harass another person."[18] Those who thought they had achieved an ultimate victory over the "forces of censorship" realized that it may not have been a complete victory after all.

In 1997, ApolloMedia filed a constitutional challenge to the "intent to annoy" portion of the CDA in federal district court, arguing that the language was similar to wording that had been struck down in *Reno.* The company asked that it also be deemed vague and overbroad under traditional First Amendment law.

ApolloMedia had maintained a Web site entitled "annoy.com" through which persons might "communicate strong views." At the time, the site was organized into four separate sections—heckle, gibe, censure, and CDA. The "heckle" section contained articles by authors who might "take strong, provocative positions on various issues." The site allowed visitors "to construct, from a preselected list of options, anonymous e-mail to public officials or figures named in the articles." Another section, entitled "gibe," was a "threaded message board" that allowed visitors to read previously posted messages and add uncensored messages of their own. The "censure" section enabled visitors to send digital postcards to intended recipients through the Web site. And the "CDA" (Created and Designed to Annoy) section consisted of several pages of commentary and visual images.[19]

The company contended that the CDA could directly implicate its basic activity because it prohibited "[using] a 'telecommunications device' to engage in 'indecent' communications with an 'intent to annoy.'" It asserted that its clients and site visitors should be free under the First Amendment "to be able to criticize public officials and public figures by using whatever language or imagery that seems to them appropriate to the occasion and, whenever they wish, to 'annoy' such persons by getting their attention, upsetting them and making them understand the depth of displeasure with their acts or political positions."

In 1998, however, a panel of federal judges in San Francisco ruled 2–1 against ApolloMedia. The panel agreed with the government position that the string of words in the challenged statute—"obscene, lewd, lascivious, filthy, or indecent"—could simply be interpreted as variations on the word *obscene,* a word that has been precisely defined under U.S. law. Thus, the court reasoned, these provisions were only prohibiting the use of obscene communication with the intent to annoy, abuse, threaten, or harass another person. Such a prohibition would be constitutional.[20]

ApolloMedia appealed directly to the U.S. Supreme Court, but in early 1999, the Court declined to hear the case, and let the lower court decision in *ApolloMedia v. Reno* stand.

Zeran v. America Online A third lawsuit focusing on the Communications Decency Act did not actually challenge the constitutionality of provisions in the CDA, but simply sought to hold American Online liable for the allegedly defamatory acts of a subscriber. It was AOL—the defendant—that brought the CDA into the picture by using Section 230 of the Act as a defense.

Kenneth Zeran's lawsuit stemmed from a series of posts by an unidentified subscriber on an AOL discussion forum, and the subsequent failure of AOL officials to intervene.[21]

The subscriber used the screen name "KenZZ03,"[22] and posted a message that set in motion a nightmarish series of events in Mr. Zeran's life. The message appeared less than a week after the April 1995 bombing of the Alfred P. Murrah Federal Building in Oklahoma City, a tragic event that killed 168 Americans and injured hundreds more. It advertised "Naughty Oklahoma T-Shirts," and featured offensive and tasteless slogans relating to the event . . . such as "Visit Oklahoma. . . . It's a BLAST!!!" "Putting the kids to bed . . . Oklahoma 1995," and "McVeigh for President 1996."[23] Those interested in purchasing the shirts were instructed to call "Ken" at Zeran's home phone number in Seattle, Washington.[24]

As might be expected, Zeran soon received a high volume of calls, comprised primarily of angry and derogatory messages, but also including death threats. He called AOL and informed a company representative of his predicament, but received little in the way of immediate help. The employee assured Zeran that the posting would be removed from AOL's bulletin board at some point but explained that, as a matter of policy, AOL would not post a retraction.[25] The next day, an unknown person using a slightly modified screen name (KenZZ033) posted another message advertising additional shirts with new tasteless slogans related to the bombing. These included: "Forget the rescue, let the maggots take over—Oklahoma 1995," and "Finally a day care center that keeps the kids quiet—Oklahoma 1995." Again, interested buyers were told to call Zeran, . . . and to "please call back if busy" due to high demand. The angry, threatening phone calls intensified.

Over the next four days, the unidentified person continued to post messages on AOL's bulletin board, advertising additional items, including bumper stickers and key chains, with still more offensive slogans. Apparently, only one person was posting these messages, and, arguably, impersonating the plaintiff as well, . . . but Zeran was allegedly never able to discover his or her identity. During these difficult days, Zeran repeatedly called AOL and was told by company representatives that the individual account from which the messages were posted would soon be closed. He also reported his case to Seattle FBI agents. Six days after the original post, Zeran was receiving an abusive phone call approximately every two minutes. To make matters even worse, an announcer for Oklahoma City radio station KRXO received a copy of the first AOL posting, read the message's contents on the air, attributed them to "Ken" at Zeran's phone number, and urged the listening audience to call the number. After this radio broadcast, Zeran was inundated with death threats and other violent calls from Oklahoma City residents. Over the next few days, Zeran talked to both KRXO and AOL representatives. He also spoke to his local police, who subsequently surveilled his home to protect his safety. Only after an Oklahoma City newspaper published a story exposing the shirt advertisements as a hoax and after KRXO made an on-air apology did the number of calls to Zeran's residence finally subside.

Zeran sought to hold AOL liable for defamatory speech initiated by the subscriber. He argued to the district court that "once he notified AOL of the perpetrator's hoax, AOL had a duty to remove the defamatory posting promptly, notify its subscribers of the message's false nature, and effectively screen future defamatory material."[26] AOL countered by arguing that Section 230 of the CDA protected them from any such claims.[27] Both the federal district court and the Fourth Circuit Court of Appeals agreed with the defendant, finding that "[b]y its plain language, § 230 creates a federal immunity to any cause of action that would make service providers liable for information originating with a third-party user of the service."[28]

The ironic result of this litigation was that a key provision of the CDA was actually strengthened only a few months after the U.S. Supreme Court invalidated other provisions of the same act. The Fourth Circuit's characterization of the CDA in the Zeran opinion only reinforced this irony. Congress' purpose in passing Section 230, in the court's view, was tied to the recognition that "tort-based lawsuits" pose a "threat to . . . freedom of speech in the new and burgeoning Internet medium. The imposition of tort liability on service providers for the communications of others represented, for Congress, simply another form of intrusive government regulation of speech. Section 230 was enacted, in part, to maintain the robust nature of Internet communication and, accordingly, to keep government interference in the medium to a minimum."[29] Thus, while the U.S. Supreme Court was almost ridiculing Congress for passing an act containing vague and overbroad language that would intrusively regulate speech, the Fourth Circuit was congratulating Congress for passing an act that would serve to prevent intrusive regulation of speech!

The Child Online Protection Act of 1998

While the annoy.com case and the AOL case—both focusing on the CDA—were also decided in 1997, the story of the CDA for most people that year was the story of the U.S. Supreme Court's decision invalidating provisions aimed at "cleaning up" cyberspace. Following this defeat, members of the Congress went back to the drawing board, attempting to craft a second statute that would serve to protect children from obscene and pornographic material in cyberspace. Labeled "Son of CDA" or "CDA II" by many commentators, this statute—The Child Online Protection Act—was passed and signed into law by President Clinton in 1998.

The congressional team that worked on the Child Online Protection Act knew that the Court in *Reno v. ACLU* had identified three basic structural flaws in the provisions of the Communications Decency Act that were ultimately struck down: (1) the prohibitions were too broad, (2) key terms were vague and undefined, and (3) the steps potential defendants might take to avoid prosecution and conviction may not have been technologically feasible at the time.[30] Congress sought to respond to the ruling by crafting a much narrower statute aimed at commercial activity directed toward young people. It only addressed the World Wide Web, and only prohibited material "harmful to minors." Under the terms of the act, both civil and criminal penalties were mandated for persons who "knowingly and with knowledge of the character of the material, in interstate or foreign commerce by means of the World Wide Web, [make] any communication for commercial purposes that is available to any minor and that includes any material that is harmful to minors."[31]

By using the term "harmful to minors" and defining it precisely, Congress hoped to avoid the problems that had arisen in *Reno I* because of such vague and indeterminate terms as *indecent*. Under the act, a minor was defined as a person under the age of seventeen,[32] and "material that is harmful to minors" was defined as:

> any communication, picture, image, graphic image file, article, recording, writing, or other matter of any kind that is obscene or that
>
> (a) the average person, applying contemporary community standards, would find, taking the material as a whole and with respect to minors, is designed to appeal to, or is designed to pander to, the prurient interest;
>
> (b) depicts, describes, or represents, in a manner patently offensive with respect to minors, an actual or simulated sexual act or sexual contact, an actual or simulated normal or perverted sexual act, or a lewd exhibition of the genitals or post-pubescent female breast; and
>
> (c) taken as a whole, lacks serious literary, artistic, political, or scientific value for minors.[33]

It is important to note that other statutes prohibiting material that is "harmful to minors" are on the books at the state level, and a similar prohibition focusing entirely on the offline world had already been deemed constitutional in a 1968 U.S. Supreme Court decision.[34]

Given the apparent precision of the Child Online Protection Act and the fact that it appeared to target commercial pornographers, there was much less concern in the online community that these prohibitions might actually have a negative impact on the day-to-day activities of the average online user. Indeed, compared to the outcry that greeted the passage of the CDA, the reaction to the COPA was relatively muted. And the coalition of plaintiffs assembled by the ACLU to challenge the act was significantly smaller than the coalition that had challenged the CDA. Notably absent from the list were *Reno I* plaintiffs such as the American Library

Association, American Online, and Microsoft, but plaintiffs did include the Electronic Frontier Foundation, the Electronic Privacy Information Center, selected bookstores, online-publishing ventures, and the Internet Content Coalition, whose members at the time included CBS New Media, Time Inc., The New York Times Electronic Media Company, C/Net, Warner Bros. Online, MSNBC, Playboy Enterprises, Sony Online, and ZDNet.[35]

From these plaintiffs, and from others who filed friend-of-the-court briefs, the arguments set forth against COPA often mirrored the criticisms of the government that had been set forth in the *Reno I* briefs. For example, the U.S. Chamber of Commerce and the Internet Education Foundation criticized COPA in very strong terms, asserting that the legislation "threatens to turn . . . [the Internet] . . . into a child-proof medium whose 'level of discourse' would be reduced to that 'suitable for a sandbox.'"

Beyond the rhetoric, plaintiffs in *ACLU v. Reno II* actually put together some very cogent legal arguments under the First Amendment. In particular, they asserted that the implementation of the act would unconstitutionally burden the speech of adults. Analyzing the act under traditional First Amendment principles, the trial court determined that any assessment of burden placed on protected speech by COPA must "take into consideration the unique factors that affect communication in the new and technology-laden medium of the Web." In particular, the court found that "the nature of the Web and the Internet is such that Web site operators and content providers cannot know who is accessing their sites, or from where, or how old the users are, unless they take affirmative steps to gather information from the user and the user is willing to give them truthful responses." Thus, Web site owners and content providers who think they may be displaying material harmful to minors must construct barriers to the material that adults must cross as well.[36]

The trial court agreed with the plaintiffs that "the implementation of credit card or adult verification screens in front of material that is harmful to minors may deter users from accessing such materials and that the loss of users of such material may affect the [site owner's] ability to provide such communications." The U.S. Government had argued that the statute targeted only commercial pornographers, but the court agreed with the plaintiffs that many "respectable" sites might be implicated as well.[37]

Indeed, the trial court questioned whether the statute could "efficaciously meet its goal" at all, given that minors could still gain access to 'harmful to minors' materials via overseas sites, noncommercial sites, and online "protocols other than http." Moreover, minors could "legitimately possess a credit or debit card and access 'harmful to minors' material despite . . . [the existence of] . . . screening mechanisms." Echoing the U.S. Supreme Court's conclusions in *Reno I,* the court declared that a more effective and "less restrictive means to shield minors from harmful materials is to rely upon filtering and blocking technology."[38]

Not only did the trial court rule for the plaintiffs, but the decision was upheld by the Third Circuit Court of Appeals in the summer of 2000. Central to the appellate court's reasoning was the determination that key differences exist between the World Wide Web and other forms of communication. In language reflecting the view that cyberspace is at times unique enough to merit significantly different legal approaches and conclusions,[39] the court of appeals declared:

> [E]ach medium of expression must be assessed for First Amendment purposes by standards suited to it, for each may present its own problems. In considering "the unique factors that affect communication in the new and technology-laden medium of the Web," we are convinced that there are crucial differences between a "brick and mortar outlet" and the online Web that dramatically affect a First Amendment analysis.[40]

Reno II, now re-named *Ashcroft v. ACLU*, will be heard by the U.S. Supreme Court in 2001–2002. But no matter what the courts ultimately decide in this case, there are some very important lessons that can be learned from the CDA, COPA, and their respective legal challenges. First and foremost, any new government restriction on expression in the online world must pass First Amendment scrutiny, and it is clear that the state of U.S. First Amendment jurisprudence is such that this type of scrutiny constitutes a formidable hurdle. Second, it is likely that if the U.S. Congress keeps trying, some type of narrow prohibition of "harmful to minors" speech may be upheld in the end, but it is questionable whether such a law would have more than just a symbolic effect. Third, while regulations such as COPA that are aimed solely at the World Wide Web may ultimately be more likely to pass constitutional muster, such regulations fail to address the range of questionable activity that takes place in the online world every day via e-mail, newsgroups, IRC, and Napster-like file-sharing software.

Fourth, any legal restrictions prohibiting obscenity that are explicitly geared to a traditional "contemporary community standards" approach will inevitably run into the same problem noted earlier in our analysis of the *Thomas* case; that is, what is obscene in one part of the country may not be obscene in another. Finally, even if new, relatively broad laws designed to protect our children are upheld, they are likely to generate the same types of problems regarding the limits of the law that we have seen with previous statutory frameworks in this area.

The legal limits documented in chapter 4 are particularly relevant here. As we have seen, sometimes existing laws are inadequate to address particular problems. This may be especially true with regard to expression in the online world, given the nature and extent of the unfettered interaction that currently takes place. Attempting to restrict expression in cyberspace by passing more laws may have the same effect as attempting to restrict what people say in private telephone conversations.

We have also seen that sometimes the legal system breaks down when lawmakers try to legislate morality. For some commentators, this principle is especially relevant to an analysis of the CDA and COPA, legislation that has been driven at least in part by conservative, religious, and family-oriented groups. However, it must be noted that for many others, the CDA and COPA are not about morality but simply about restricting the access of children to age-appropriate material.

The principle of unintended consequences may also be relevant in this area, since many have expressed concern that while the CDA and COPA are intended to protect children, they may have the unintended result of limiting the free exchange of information and thought in a medium that the U.S. Supreme Court has called a dramatic and unique marketplace of ideas.

Other principles identified in chapter 4 are relevant as well. Our legal system is often based upon an implicit social contract, and it is clear that in the area of online expression a different set of social norms has emerged for a large number of Netizens, making behavior that much harder to change. Given that laws are typically more effective when the boundaries of control are localized, online speech thus presents a particular problem. In addition, there are always practical limits to the law that must be recognized from an enforcement perspective, and the content of expression in cyberspace is clearly not an area that traditional law enforcement agencies are equipped to address across the board. Even with the increased monitoring of the online world in recent years, federal authorities are simply not able to keep track of even a small fraction of the speech that takes place in cyberspace today.

The "No Electronic Theft" Act of 1997

The NET Act was probably the first major federal legislative package designed to regulate the online world that was *not* challenged in the courts. In this respect, the story of the NET Act is very different than that of the CDA and COPA. There are, however, a number of unresolved issues regarding this legislation that include some striking parallels to the decency acts of 1996 and 1998.

Congress essentially began from a similar perspective in both the decency and the copyright infringement contexts. As with online expression, there was already an established legal framework in place addressing the behavior in question.

Under U.S. law, for example, the general rule has long been that people who *willfully* copy the works of others face criminal penalties *if they have a discernible profit motive.*[41] The term "willfully" has been defined by the courts to mean more than simple intent alone. The copyright infringement must be committed "(1) voluntarily, (2) with knowledge that it was prohibited by law, and (3) with the purpose of violating the law, and not by mistake, accident or in good faith."[42] Although relatively few persons have been prosecuted under this law over the years, its mere existence has arguably had a deterrent effect.

Concerns regarding the widespread copying of digital works led to several changes in 1992, when the felony copyright statute—17 U.S. Code Section 506 (a)—was updated so that it no longer prohibited infringement for only certain specific types of work. A particular concern at the time was software piracy, and thus the specific categories in the old statute such as sound recordings, motion pictures, and audiovisual works were replaced by a more generic and all-encompassing prohibition.

The failed attempt to prosecute MIT student David LaMacchia in the early 1990s made it clear to many that the old rules were not sufficient to address the new realities of cyberspace. LaMacchia—a modern-day Robin Hood—encouraged others to upload lawful copies of computer games to a BBS, and then transferred the copies to another BBS where users with passwords could download them without charge for personal use. Since LaMacchia had no discernible profit motive and indeed did not benefit financially in any way, he could not, in the end, be convicted.

Anyone familiar with Net culture at the time knew that LaMacchia's actions were not an aberration. More often than not, the average Netizen in those days viewed the online world as an "open range" where traditional offline restrictions on the transfer of data did not apply. These Netizens often took a very dim view of any government attempt to restrict the flow of information by tightening up on the laws governing freedom of expression either under First Amendment doctrine or under intellectual property doctrine.[43]

Since LaMacchia's actions did not fit within any existing federal criminal statutes, and since software industry representatives in particular continued to raise the specter of widespread anarchy if such actions went unpunished, the U.S. Congress went ahead and passed the "No Electronic Theft" Act of 1997.

The NET Act modified the traditional U.S. rule for the online world in several ways, clearly taking into account the potential threat that online behavior by other "Robin Hoods" might have in the business and economic sector. The longstanding definition of "financial gain" under Section 101, Title 17 of the U.S. Code, was adjusted to include "receipt, *or expectation of receipt,* of anything of value, including the receipt of other copyrighted works."[44] And the definition of criminal infringement itself was changed so that it is now a crime to infringe a copyright willfully, either

> (1) for purposes of commercial advantage or private financial gain, or (2) by the reproduction or distribution, including by electronic means, during any 180-day period, of 1 or more copies or phonorecords of 1 or more copyrighted works, which have a total retail value of more than $1,000.[45]

By broadening the scope of copyright protection in certain areas and, at the same time, criminalizing behavior by Netizens that had previously not been considered a crime, the NET Act generated considerable debate. Understandably, it was strongly backed by the software and entertainment industries but opposed by science and academic groups.

It is important to note that both misdemeanor provisions and felony provisions are included in the act. "Willful" infringement,[46] either (a) for purposes of commercial advantage or private financial gain or (b) by reproduction or distribution of one or more copyrighted works with a total retail value of more than $1,000 within a 180-day period, constitutes a misdemeanor, with a one-year maximum sentence and a fine of up to $100,000. The willful reproduction or distribution of at least ten copies of one or more copyrighted works with a total retail value of more than $2,500 within a 180-day period constitutes a felony, with a maximum sentence of three years' imprisonment and a fine of $250,000. If the defendant also acted for purposes of commercial advantage or private financial gain, the maximum felony sentence can rise to five years.[47]

The legislative history of the act reveals a clear intent to close a loophole in the law that had been highlighted by the LaMacchia case. But in a speech delivered for the *Congressional Record,* Senator Hatch declared that this law would still exempt "innocent infringers" under the copyright fair-use doctrine. In particular, he emphasized that the "willful" requirement would exclude an educator who, in good faith, believes that she is engaging in fair use of copyrighted material.[48]

Although relevant stakeholders paid a great deal of attention to this new statute, there was little if any outcry from online users after its passage. No web displays were blackened, no online protests were organized, and no legal challenges were forthcoming. Months turned into years, and nothing new or different happened in relation to this act or under this act. Electronic theft, or *alleged* electronic theft—depending on one's perspective—continued unabated. It was during this time, for example, that the MP3 "revolution" described in the introduction to this book came to the forefront.[49]

In May 1999, eighteen months after President Clinton signed the NET Act into law, the House Courts and Intellectual Property Subcommittee held a hearing to investigate why the Department of Justice had "failed to enforce" the act. Congressman Bob Goodlatte, who had originally sponsored the Act, set the tone for the hearing by declaring that he was "not only unaware of any efforts by the Department of Justice or the FBI to apply resources to address theft of software on the Internet," but that "letters inquiring as to the status of these efforts have gone unanswered." "I think," he said, "that that is totally irresponsible." Congressman Bob Coble added that he was very troubled by the lack of action in this area. "According to U.S. intellectual property-based industries," he said, "there is no shortage of potential prosecutions that could be pursued under the Act."

The subcommittee heard from representatives of the software and entertainment industries, who complained about the ongoing "pirating" of their products.

Batur Oktay, an attorney for Adobe Systems, testified on behalf of the Business Software Alliance (BSA) and expressed his disappointment that "despite much good work on the part of both the private sector and the law enforcement agencies, there have been no NET Act prosecutions. Left unprosecuted, these types of Web sites—which are brazen about their own illegality—send the message that Internet pirates can operate with impunity, that there is no effective enforcement, that intellectual property protection on the Internet is unavailable. More domestic enforcement activity would also better position the U.S. to exercise leadership in advocating stronger protections for intellectual property overseas."

Appearing on behalf of the U.S. Justice Department, Kevin DiGregory, Deputy Assistant Attorney General for the Computer Crimes Division, agreed that "even a handful of appropriate and well-publicized prosecutions under the NET Act . . . [are] . . . likely to have a strong deterrent impact, particularly because the crime in question is a hobby, and not a means to make a living. If these prosecutions are accompanied by a vigorous anti-piracy educational campaign sponsored by industry, and by technological advances designed to make illegal copying more difficult, we are hopeful that a real dent can be made in the practice of digital piracy."

"We are continually fine-tuning this initiative," DiGregory explained, "to ensure that investigations are handled as quickly and efficiently as possible." He suggested that there were several reasons for failing to bring any prosecutions: (1) Not enough FBI and Department of Justice personnel "possess special technical skills," (2) "Those agents who are technically adept are in high demand to fight the growing incidence of attacks on the confidentiality, integrity and availability of computers and networks, leaving few to focus on digital piracy," and (3) the difficulty of identifying violators.[50]

Perhaps in response to this hearing, the Department of Justice announced two months later that a new interagency "Intellectual Property Rights Initiative"—involving Justice, the FBI, and U.S. Customs—would focus on "the wide range of copyright and trademark law violations." And, three months later—in August 1999—the first prosecution under the "No Electronic Theft" Act resulted in the conviction of twenty-two-year-old University of Oregon student Jeffrey Levy, who pleaded guilty in federal district court to one count of felony criminal copyright infringement.

Levy had actually been arrested in February—three months before the House subcommittee hearing—for allegedly violating the NET Act. Another modern-day Robin Hood following in the footsteps of David LaMacchia, he had apparently been distributing illegal copies of software programs, movies, and MP3 files without any discernible profit motive. Joanne Hugi, director of the university's Computing Center, said she noticed an unusual amount of traffic on Levy's Web site, and she subsequently notified both "administrative officials and federal law enforcement" agents. The FBI soon discovered that Levy was operating what has come to be known as a "warez" site.

After the prosecution was announced, government and industry officials were quick to emphasize that, in their view, it was important to make an example of Levy and send a message to the "millions" of young people worldwide who operate such sites. "There is a cultural phenomenon here that this is not stealing, and it is particularly prevalent among young people," said Roslyn Mazer, special counsel for intellectual property in the criminal division of the U.S. Department of Justice. "We hope this case will fire a shot across the bow."

In a news release, James K. Robinson, assistant attorney general for the criminal division, went even further. "Mr. Levy's case," he said, "should serve as a notice that the Justice Department has made prosecution of Internet piracy one of its priorities. Those who engage in this activity, whether or not for profit, should take heed that we will bring federal resources to bear to prosecute these cases. This is theft, pure and simple."[51]

When compared with the attempts documented above to restrict expression by passing decency legislation, the NET Act appears to be a much more realistic approach. It does not attempt to go beyond existing laws, but simply expands the basic rules of criminal copyright infringement to encompass what many believe to be a common practice in cyberspace—distribution of illegal copies without any discernible profit motive. Thus, it has apparently managed to avoid the sort of ongoing court battles that can take the life out of a statute. In addition, by not targeting run-of-the-mill copying but instead focusing only on large-scale copying, it arguably represents a much more realistic effort to take social norms into account. The CDA had focused on all forms of "indecency," and even COPA targets all Web speech of a commercial nature that may be "harmful to minors." In contrast, the NET Act only appears to target Robin Hoods such as LaMacchia and Levy who illegally post copies of software and multimedia files in great quantity.

It remains to be seen what effect the Levy case will have on those who distribute illegal digital copies online. From an enforcement perspective, it is clear that the U.S. Department of Justice does not have the resources to prosecute more than a handful of violators. And many wonder whether the Justice Department should be expending valuable resources on this area. For, as discussed in chapter 3, it remains unclear whether and to what extent such highly profitable businesses as the software industry and the entertainment industry are really losing much money as a result of the inconsistent and arguably playful efforts of otherwise law-abiding college students. On some level, too, this may be yet another effort to legislate morality that may be doomed to fail because of the nature of Internet architecture and the prevailing social norms in the online world. Many Netizens, it must be noted, see nothing wrong with what LaMacchia and Levy did.

Other issues are bound to arise within the context of the principle that laws are typically more effective where the boundaries of control are localized. Many warez sites are located on overseas servers, and much of the "inappropriate" speech targeted by the decency legislation may originate in other countries. The U.S. Congress and the Business Software Alliance may have determined that they could have a significant impact on current practice simply by focusing on U.S. universities. But targeting the universities raises an entirely different set of issues.

For years, many American university officials have chafed at the idea that they might be viewed as policemen in this context. And many members of university communities were shocked by the revelation that a University of Oregon official had actually turned Jeffrey Levy in to the federal authorities.

As a general rule, campus policies do not say anything definitive about the nature and extent of the interface between internal campus enforcement and external law enforcement agencies. Certainly, external law enforcement agencies are brought in when students commit violent crimes, such as kidnapping or murder. But in the more typical, mischief-related campus-crime scenario, university officials often handle these matters internally. Campus conduct "codes of procedures" are generally the foundational documents for any disciplinary actions against students.

It is probably safe to say that many universities would not view LaMacchia's activity as the sort of thing that would or should require them to notify external law enforcement officials immediately. As a practical matter, campus network administrators are aware of unusual traffic on computers hooked to their networks, and they do monitor and oversee such use, albeit without regard to the content. But without explicit campus directives to the contrary, the average university official would probably view turning a student like Levy into the FBI as a draconian act that strays far from campus norms. The more typical intervention would involve an initial warning to the student, urging him to discontinue the site.

Yet others have criticized universities in this context, arguing that the "folk model" of the university as a sovereign zone reflects an outmoded view of the campus as a "halfway house" somewhere between childhood and adulthood. And certainly the record industry, the film industry, and the software industry would like the universities to stop "coddling" their students.

Clearly, the actions contemplated by industry officials would be a transformation of the status quo in most places. But is this what the public as a whole would want? When we send our young people away to college, on some level, do we not want the university to take care of them? Indeed, the concept of *in loco parentis*—that school officials act "in the place of the parent"—appears to have made a significant comeback in recent years, even after many people had argued in the late 1960s and early 1970s that such a view of the university had become anachronistic. By explicitly targeting the LaMacchia exception in its "No Electronic Theft" Act, Congress has raised a very serious policy question within the larger framework of university-community relations—a question that has been further highlighted by the events surrounding the arrest and prosecution of Jeffrey Levy at the University of Oregon.

The Internet Tax Freedom Act of 1998

The Internet Tax Freedom Act (ITFA) was a very different type of legislative enactment than either the decency legislation or the NET Act. For one thing, it focused on the activities of the government rather than the activities of Netizens. For another, it appeared to set forth a very simple mandate—a three-year moratorium on any new state or local taxes targeting Internet access or Internet commerce. No law enforcement activity was contemplated, and thus, no issues of jurisdiction or enforcement were triggered. No constitutional challenges were filed because no constitutional rights issues were raised. The U.S. government has been given the right to determine when and under what circumstances taxes may be levied. And this—essentially—is all that it did in the ITFA, with Section 1101 of the Act providing:

> (a) Moratorium.—No State or political subdivision thereof shall impose any of the following taxes during the period beginning on October 1, 1998, and ending 3 years after the date of the enactment of this Act—
> (1) taxes on Internet access, unless such tax was generally imposed and actually enforced prior to October 1, 1998; and
> (2) multiple or discriminatory taxes on electronic commerce.

The ITFA therefore addressed a major issue in the growth and development of e-commerce by postponing a decision on whether states would be able to charge new taxes intended specifically to tap the Internet. Up until the late 1990s, with rare exception, most online purchases were viewed as analogous to mail order/catalogue sales, and typically, businesses were not required to collect sales tax for such transactions when conducted across state lines. But with Internet-based commerce increasing dramatically in both size and scope, many states expressed an interest in changing the law and tightening the regulatory structure in this context. Not only did state governments wish to take advantage of the growth of the online world, but they feared that as more and more business transactions moved to cyberspace, their sales-tax income would dwindle accordingly. Thus, while the heart of the ITFA was very simple, the underlying issues were, of course, very complicated, and raised all sorts of volatile questions regarding federalism in general and the e-commerce marketplace in particular.

In addition to establishing a three-year moratorium, the Act accomplished two other things that extended both its scope and its potential long-term impact. First, it set forth several "Sense of the Congress" declarations. Second, it established an Advisory Commission on Electronic Commerce that was required to report back no later than eighteen months after the passage of the act in October 1998.

The declarations were notable for their broad policy imperatives. Section 1201 was entitled "Declaration that Internet Should Be Free of New Federal Taxes," and read, "It is the sense of Congress that no new Federal taxes . . . should be enacted with respect to the Internet and Internet access during the moratorium." Section 1203 was entitled "Declaration That the Internet Should Be Free of Foreign Tariffs, Trade Barriers, and Other Restrictions," and read:

> It is the sense of Congress that the President should seek bilateral, regional, and multilateral agreements to remove barriers to global electronic commerce through the World Trade Organization, the Organization for Economic Cooperation and Development, the Trans-Atlantic Economic Partnership, the Asia Pacific Economic Cooperation forum, the Free Trade Area of the America, the North American Free Trade Agreement, and other appropriate venues.

In addition, the declaration went on to actually set forth negotiating objectives for the United States: (1) "To assure that electronic commerce is free from . . . tariff and nontarrif barriers, *burdensome and discriminatory regulation* and standards, and discriminatory taxation," and (2) "to accelerate the growth of electronic commerce" by expanding various market-access opportunities.[52]

It is clear, therefore, that the ITFA represents a major policy statement from the U.S. government on Internet commerce and the free market. Consistent with the Clinton administration's July 1997 Framework for Global Electronic Commerce,[53] the act appears to contemplate an online world that would remain substantially unregulated, at least with regard to conducting business in cyberspace. However, whether e-commerce can remain substantially unregulated—while rules are tightened in other areas such as content expression and copyright—is still an unresolved question at this point in time. FTC regulatory activity, for example, increased significantly in the area of online consumer fraud between 1997 and 2000, after the agency had determined that self regulation was not effective enough.[54] And in fact many have argued that other aspects of e-commerce must ultimately be regulated, not only to protect consumers but to protect businesses against the range of possible fraudulent activity. Given the likelihood that everything will eventually become so interconnected that the lines between offline commerce and online commerce will be virtually indistinguishable, commentators argue that such regulation is not only inevitable, but that it will invariably extend to the widespread taxation of Internet-related transactions.

"Sense of Congress" resolutions and declarations of legislative purpose do not have the force of law in and of themselves, and they come into play as a general rule only when courts and regulatory agencies seek to interpret and apply statutes. Thus, no one was obligated by law to comply with the antitaxation thrust of the statute after the three-year moratorium ended. On the other hand, given the strong current of support among both consumers and businesses for a tax-free Internet, the underlying statements of purpose in the act could not be ignored either.

Such complex questions were at the heart of the inquiry when the advisory commission on electronic commerce mandated by the act met to determine its recommendations. Under Section 1102, the commission was expected to consider such questions as: (1) how e-commerce barriers imposed in foreign markets might affect U.S. consumers and businesses, (2) how "consumption taxes on electronic commerce" work and how they might work in the United States and abroad, (3) how "model state legislation" might impact e-commerce, (4) how taxation—including the absence of taxation—might affect interstate sales transactions, and (5) how to simplify "Federal and State and local taxes imposed on the provision of telecommunications services."

It is instructive to compare the aftermath of the act with the events that followed the other statutes addressed in this chapter. While the decency legislation triggered lawsuits and the NET Act generated prosecutions and an ongoing debate about the efficacy of further federal law enforcement activity, the ITFA led to the formation of a high-powered commission and a series of policy-making deliberations over time.[55]

In the end, the commission could not agree. Governor Gilmore delivered a report to Congress in April 2000 that endorsed a five-year extension of the Internet tax moratorium, called on states to simplify their sales-tax structures, and supported a sales-tax exemption for products delivered digitally and their physical equivalents, like books and compact discs. But the 10–8 commission vote fell short of the "super majority" of thirteen votes required by Congress for a formal "recommendation" under the act.

Newspaper accounts indicated that although commission members argued frequently during the proceedings, the group apparently came "close to consensus on many principles . . . including tax simplification and bans on new taxes that would put Internet sales at a disadvantage . . . [vis-à-vis] . . . other kinds of retail transactions." But disagreements over details such as an adjustment of the definition for *nexus*—the legal term for whether a company has a physical presence in a state that would justify the collection of sales taxes from that state's residents—could not be resolved. The business caucus sought a definition that would relax current nexus rules, but opponents said that the move could mean the death of sales taxes nationwide.[56]

The report was seen as a victory for America Online and other antitax businesses on the commission that drafted the plan. Members voting against the report, led by Utah Governor Mike Leavitt, released a statement calling "both the report and the process that fostered it . . . seriously flawed."[57] And less than two weeks later, more than two-thirds of the nation's fifty governors sent Congress a scathing letter accusing the Internet tax commission of ignoring its mandate and instead pursuing special-interest tax breaks. The letter, signed by nineteen Republicans, fifteen Democrats, and two independents, argued that the most important reason to oppose the commission's report "is that it would substantially interfere with state sovereignty."[58]

A month later, on May 10, 2000, the House of Representatives surprised many observers by voting overwhelmingly (352-75) to extend the moratorium until 2006. But the legislation faced a more uncertain future in the Senate.[59]

In the short term, the Internet sales-tax debate apparently remains unresolved. It is important to note, however, that according to most estimates, the amount of money at issue is significantly lower than many people believe it to be. E-commerce in late 2000 still accounted for only a very small fraction of all sales transactions occurring across the country and around the world. Indeed, the *Wall Street Journal* reported at the time that "Internet purchases represent less than 1% of overall retail sales, according to Jupiter Communications, a New York market-research firm." And an April 2000 study by two University of Tennessee economists estimated that if online sales were to balloon so that total state losses on sales taxes swelled to $10.8 billion in 2003, that amount would still represent, on average, less than 2 percent of total state sales-tax revenue for the year.[60]

While state officials insist that sales-tax losses totaling in the millions cannot easily be ignored, others continue to emphasize the fragile nature of Internet commerce and the importance of fostering its growth in the aftermath of the major shakeout that occurred in the year 2000. In the end, most commentators believe that at some point down the road, a workable compromise can and will be devised. But few deny the challenges inherent in a status quo that includes approximately seven thousand tax jurisdictions in the United States alone, with each jurisdiction seeking to tax different things to different degrees.[61] And even though software could logically be devised that would enable e-commerce sites to adjust their tax collection for these differences, political interests at the individual state level may continue to work against the radical simplification that most agree is necessary before a consensus can be reached.

Related Efforts to Regulate Content at the State Level

To make matters even more complicated, individual states in recent years have also sought to regulate online content. Instead of taking a cue from the Internet sales-tax debate and recognizing the inherent value of national standards for basic online activity, state legislatures have gone ahead and passed numerous Internet-related laws.

For those familiar with the American system of federalism and the plethora of "duplicate" laws governing offline activity at both the federal and state levels, such legislative activism in state capitals comes as no surprise. Criminals, for example, can be charged under both federal law and state law. And plaintiffs can often choose between state court and federal court. Indeed, an ongoing tension between the power of the states and the power of the federal government is built into the U.S. system.

But with regard to cyberspace, some believe that all bets are off in this context. It is difficult enough to address issues relating to jurisdiction and enforcement when one country attempts to regulate the online world, but when individual states start getting involved, then arguably things get completely out of hand very quickly.

In the late 1990s, New York, Georgia, Virginia, Michigan, and New Mexico were in the forefront of a state-by-state effort to regulate online content by passing restrictive Internet-based laws. Each statute was challenged in federal court under a variety of legal theories, however, and thus far only one has been able to withstand judicial scrutiny. The New York law, for example, was overturned in the 1997 case of *American Library Association v. Pataki.*[62] The court in that case ruled that the law prohibiting "indecent" online communication violated the commerce clause of the U.S. Constitution, which essentially prohibits one state from regulating the commercial activity of other states.

While the *Pataki* case was not appealed,[63] other rulings invalidating state laws have been taken to higher courts. Yet only the Virginia case—which held that a statute prohibiting state employees from accessing sexually explicit material online was violative of the First Amendment—was reversed at the appellate level.[64]

Both the New Mexico and the Michigan laws were put on hold by federal district courts after being challenged under both the First Amendment and the Commerce Clause of the U.S. Constitution. Particularly noteworthy in both the lower-court New Mexico decision (*ACLU v. Johnson*)[65] and the lower-court Michigan decision (*Cyberspace Communications v. Engler*)[66] was the emphasis on the futility of any one state trying to control the online world. In the *Cyberspace Communications* decision, for example, the court addressed the interstate nature of online activity at length, and found the following to be true in 1999:

- The Internet is wholly insensitive to geographic distinctions, and Internet protocols were designed to ignore rather than document geographic location.
- While computers on the network do have "addresses," they are digital addresses on the network rather than geographic addresses in real space. The majority of Internet addresses contain no geographic indicators. . . .

• No aspect of the Internet can feasibly be closed to users from another state. There is no way to stop or bar speech at . . . [a state's] . . . border.

• An Internet user who posts a Web page cannot prevent Michiganians or Oklahomans or Iowans from accessing that page. They will not even know the state residency of any visitors to that site, unless the information is voluntarily (and accurately) given by the visitor.

• Participants in chat rooms and online discussion groups also have no way of knowing when participants from a particular state have joined the conversation.

• Because most e-mail accounts allow users to download their mail from anywhere, it is impossible for someone who sends an e-mail to know with certainty where the recipient is located geographically.

• In addition, the Internet is a redundant series of linked computers over which information often travels randomly. Thus, a message from an Internet user sitting at a computer in New York may travel via one or more other states—including Michigan —before reaching a recipient who is also sitting at a computer in New York.

• There is no way for an Internet user to prevent his or her message from reaching residents of any particular state. Similarly, "once a provider posts its content on the Internet, it cannot prevent that content from entering any community."[67]

Such findings are highly significant, because they indicate that the courts have begun to recognize the inappropriateness of many state efforts to regulate Internet content. With federal courts in New York, New Mexico, and Michigan all making similar determinations, it may be that over time, individual states will put their legislative energy elsewhere.

Under U.S. law, even though there is a built-in tension between federal power and state power, it has long been recognized that certain areas of regulation are the domain of the federal government and certain other areas are regulated primarily by the states. Such a determination often stems from explicit language in the U.S. Constitution or from specific acts by Congress indicating an intent to "occupy the field." But court decisions can play a part as well. Certainly the Internet—as a recognized instrument of interstate commerce—would appropriately qualify as an area that could eventually be viewed as outside the domain of an individual state's power to regulate.

Many continue to view national legal systems as the best option for the regulation of the online world. But an analysis of recent Internet-related developments in this context reveals a rocky terrain with no guarantees of success. Indeed, a determination of the success or failure of the legislation discussed in this chapter may vary significantly depending on the perspective one takes.

From the perspective of lawmakers, for example, the Internet Tax Freedom Act would clearly be viewed as the most successful, given that it did what it intended to do—establish a three-year moratorium on new Internet taxation. The "No Electronic Theft" Act would be viewed as somewhat successful, given that the statute is now on the books and people can no longer claim that the uploading or downloading of valuable digital files is legal as long as you do not intend to make a profit from it. But lawmakers remain concerned over the small number of prosecutions under this act, the resources available in the U.S. Attorney's offices, the prevailing social norms in cyberspace, and the prospects for any long-term changes in behavior. The federal "decency" legislation, up to this point, would be viewed as fairly unsuccessful, with portions of the CDA and all of COPA running into major First Amendment challenges. And state content-based legislation may prove to be even less successful in the end.

From the perspective of Netizens and other stakeholders, however, the picture is somewhat different. Many would agree, for example, that both the passage of the ITFA and the failure of certain states to prevail in court against challenges to their content-based regulations are examples of the law working for the good of the online world. With regard to the decency legislation and the NET Act, however, there may be little consensus at this point in time regarding recent legal developments, since many do not believe that there are enough problems to warrant intrusive government regulation. Indeed, many libertarian Netizens are very happy about the minimal impact these laws have had, and view the results as a vindication of their original positions.

Overall, it is clear that there are both advantages and disadvantages to relying on a traditional legal system for the purpose of establishing an appropriate level of control over the online world. Particularly in a free society, these advantages include a process that is participatory, with checks and balances at every level. And precise, realistic rules targeting specific persons or groups in ways that reflect a broad consensus have a very good chance of succeeding. It is no accident, for example, that the most successful federal legislation discussed in this chapter—the ITFA moratorium—targeted the acts of the government rather than the acts of Netizens, and was a highly popular move at the time, reflecting agreement among most of the relevant stakeholders.

On the other hand, the events surrounding the legislation in this chapter reflect some of the pitfalls of a regulatory approach under a democratic legal system. The story of the decency legislation, for example, shows how statutes may be challenged, held up, eviscerated, or struck down in a lengthy and sometimes divisive process that may lead everyone back to square one, or may even result in additional barriers to future legislation in the same area. The story of the NET Act shows that getting a law on the books is only a first step, and that enforcement is invariably an issue in cyberspace. The story of the ITFA commission's deliberations shows how difficult it can be to find consensus among stakeholders for long-range policy decisions in controversial areas. And the inherent limits of our legal system continue to reveal themselves in all these cases, making things that much more difficult for all concerned.

Addressing online problems by relying upon and restructuring national law is one viable approach, and it clearly works better in some cases than in others. But it is not the only approach. International agreement and changing the architecture of cyberspace are two other approaches that may be equally valid, and in some cases, significantly more effective. In chapter 6, then, we turn to an analysis of international agreement and how such a strategy might play out in the online world.

6

International Models of Agreement and Cooperation

[P]eace, commerce, and honest friendship with all nations—entangling alliances with none . . . these principles form the bright constellation which has gone before us, and guided our steps through an age of revolution and reformation.

—Thomas Jefferson, First Inaugural Address, March 1801

Modern judicial systems must, under any democratic theory, rest on a basis of complex legislation derived from competing social inputs. . . . [T]he WTO lacks such a basis, [but it] . . . nevertheless continues to move forward on an ambitious route towards global economic integration. It is a matter for urgent academic consideration that no mechanism exists for measuring the desirability among national voters of this newly strengthened global legal system.

—Sara Dillon, *Minnesota Journal of Global Trade,* Summer 1999

Electric circuitry has overthrown the regime of "time" and "space" and pours upon us instantly and continuously the concerns of all other men. It has reconstituted dialogue on a global scale. Its message is Total Change, ending psychic, social, economic, and political parochialism.

—Marshall McLuhan and Quentin Fiore, *The Medium Is the Massage,* Circa 1967

Global agreements and other methods of international cooperation together form a second broad approach to cyberspace regulation. Unlike the regulatory model discussed in chapter 5, which relies on traditional legal systems country-by-country, this model is based on the collaborative efforts of every nation that might have access to the online world.

At the simplest level, international law enforcement cooperation, such as the Internet "sweeps" described in part 1, can serve as an example of global agreement in this context. But the model described in this chapter can conceivably extend far beyond what may be a de facto agreement that is limited to specific operations at particular times.

The idea that every nation might work together to build and maintain an orderly, problem-free cyberspace is very attractive at first glance. International rules, particularly in the areas of jurisdiction and enforcement, can help avoid many of the complexities that may arise when individual states and nations create their own separate bodies of law for this global medium. Yet there is no reason to think that such a model would be any less complicated than the model set forth in chapter 5. Indeed, most of the sticking points addressed in that chapter regarding the limits of our legal system would also be applicable in a global context, because international law is often based on the rules of individual countries and therefore faces many of the same inherent limitations.

Moreover, those who attempt to build international agreements face a range of additional challenges that often prove insurmountable. It can be extremely difficult, for example, to transcend national interests and conclude treaties between individual countries. And even if treaties are finalized, the ratification process often proves to be an impossible hurdle as individual legislatures and parliaments confront their decisions within the context of their own nations' political realities.[1]

Despite the existence of so many hurdles and complications, the international agreement model merits further exploration. Breakthroughs in this context are invariably more far-reaching and complete than those that might be attained through any individual nation's legal system, and as a result, the problem-solving potential of any such regulatory approach is arguably much greater.

International Law in General

Whether the goal is to generate new global agreements that redefine the parameters of international cooperation in this area or simply to build on existing international legal principles and current organizational frameworks, it is instructive to begin by analyzing the nature of international law as it has evolved over the centuries.

Commentators sometimes scoff at the notion of international law, questioning whether an international legal system can truly be said to exist. In support of this position, they argue that individual nations tend to do what they can get away with, and that ultimately the only controlling forces on a global level are the military and economic superpowers . . . who can and do dictate the rules after they have established their preeminence in a given era.

But such a position ignores a "law of the nations" literature that goes back at least to the time of Ancient Rome, if not earlier. In the second century, for example, Gaius identified a *jus gentium* (law of nations) common to all men—a universal law that could be applied by Roman courts to citizens of other states when the specific laws of their own nations were unknown and when Roman law was inappropriate.[2] In the Italian city-states of the eleventh and twelfth centuries, a *lex mercatoria* (law merchant) was developed, consisting of customary legal rules that were used in international commercial transactions to supplement the often-incomplete commercial laws of individual nations.[3] Five hundred years later, in the classic *Law of War and Peace* (1625), Grotius argued that the law of nations established legal rules binding the sovereign states of Europe.[4] And in 1789, Jeremy Bentham declared that this law of nations constituted an "international law."[5]

In addition, despite the unsettled nature of international relations over time, nations almost always try to act in a lawful manner if they can. Indeed, recent history is filled with examples of nations invoking legal principles and purporting to follow accepted legal processes when they have taken forceful and controversial action against other nations. Germany's invasion of Poland in 1939, for example, was accompanied by its official withdrawal from the Geneva Conventions in place at the time. The U.S. blockade of Cuba in 1962 was labeled a quarantine by American officials, relying on the fact that under international law a "blockade" was considered an act of war, while a "quarantine" arguably had no legal significance. Similarly, Israel's apparently preemptive air strike against Egypt in 1967 was justified by Israeli officials under the doctrine of "anticipatory self-defense."[6] The Soviet Union's use of force in Czechoslovakia during the Cold War and the U.S. involvement in Vietnam were also justified by the respective governments under a series of agreements, conventions, and international law doctrines.[7]

Beyond these recent examples, Mark Janis argues that international law's vitality rests on its continuing practical utility in a number of broad, general circumstances. It is often useful, for example, for different states to follow similar rules or apply like standards in their domestic legal systems with regard to international commercial transactions. In addition, it may make sense for sovereign states to limit their own liberties in exchange for reciprocal limitations on the part of other states. Finally, states have found international law helpful as a means of achieving common international goals. Thus, although international law—like any legal system—is not always respected, Janis concludes that "there is more international law today than ever before, and the role it plays in world affairs—political, economic, social, and humanitarian—has never been greater."[8]

Commentators in this era typically identify four broad sources of international law: explicit agreements, customary practices, rules of law common to most if not all nations, and international organizations.

Explicit International Agreements

Explicit agreements under international law may include treaties, conventions, or other contract-like arrangements such as pacts, protocols, and accords. Treaties arguably carry the most weight, and an entire "law of treaties" exists under both international law and the laws of individual nations.

At the international level, rules governing treaties have been derived from customary practice over the centuries. The Vienna Convention on the Law of Treaties—sometimes called the Treaty on Treaties—brought together and clarified these rules in one document. It was adopted in 1969, ratified in 1980, and is now seen as the formal source of international rules in this area. The provisions of the Vienna Convention are often elaborate, and address everything from the effect of treaties to amendment, invalidity, and termination. Among the most noteworthy of these provisions are those addressing the adoption and ratification process. After treaties are signed, this process typically shifts to individual states, which must determine that the text is satisfactory before it can be adopted. If the text has been concluded at an international conference, "a vote of two-thirds or another mutually agreed-upon fraction of the states present and voting" is generally viewed as sufficient for ratification.[9]

At the individual nation level, technical rules regarding treaties are usually incorporated into basic legal documents. In the United States, for example, key principles governing treaties are written into the Constitution.

The president is granted the power to make treaties, with the advice and consent of the Senate. Two thirds of the Senate must concur for the treaty to be ratified by the U.S. If ratified by the requisite number of nations, the treaty then becomes "the supreme law of the land." In practice, however, it may not ultimately be "supreme." Federal statutes and treaties are seen as virtually equivalent, and rules have been developed to address potential conflicts in this regard. Generally, if no reconciliation is possible, the most recent in time typically controls.[10]

A central feature of treaties, and indeed of all international agreements, is that the nations involved take upon themselves the obligation to act in good faith. Throughout history, of course, treaties have been violated or broken, and in these instances the process may break down completely because there is typically no external enforcement mechanism.

Customary Practices

Custom, the second major source of international law, is a much less precise area of analysis. Instead of looking at a specific written document such as a treaty, we examine "certain maxims and customs . . . observed by nations in their mutual intercourse with each other as a kind of law."[11] While customary practices may often be difficult to discern, their potential as a source of rules and regulations in a global medium such as cyberspace cannot be discounted. Indeed, as discussed in other sections of this book, commentators, legislators and jurists have already begun to identify certain implicit rules in the online world that have emerged as a result of customary practice and attendant social norms.

Up until the twentieth century, custom was often viewed as the principal source of international law. And even today, since treaties leave many international topics untouched and most nations are not party to most treaties, custom remains a significant source of traditional rules in certain areas.

Customary practice, of course, does not become a "universal law of society" right away. Instead, it must be determined that the practice has become more or less uniform over time. The practice should be consistent, although it need not be unanimous. It need not be an ancient practice either. Fairly recent custom may ripen into law as long as the practice is "both extensive and virtually uniform." In addition, it must be apparent on some level that states are acting in a consistent manner out of a sense of legal obligation.[12]

Rules of Law and General Principles Common to Most, If Not All Nations

The third major source of international law, unlike treaties and customary practice, is not based on any sort of explicit or implicit agreement. Instead, this "nonconsensual" category of rules has evolved over the centuries from the national laws of individual countries and from a generic body of principles grouped under such terms as natural law, *jus cogens,* and equity.

Rules in this category have typically been viewed as supplemental to any agreements and customary practices that might exist. There have been times, however, when some of these generic principles have been found to be so basic and so compelling that they must necessarily override prior agreements. For example, the right to be free from official torture—a "peremptory norm" under the doctrine of *jus cogens*—was viewed by the Nuremberg tribunals as so fundamental and universal that it was deemed to "transcend the consent of the states."[13]

The most useful and precise source of these supplementary rules is the body of laws that are common to most, if not all, of the individual countries. The basic notion is that certain propositions of law are so fundamental that they will be found in virtually every legal system. Beyond these specific laws, persons empowered to resolve international disputes may turn to other general principles that are often grouped under the labels of *natural law, jus cogens,* or *equity.*

Natural law is seen, ultimately, as rooted in the law of nature itself. The concept of natural law is derived from the view that "there is a law so natural that it is to be found in any community, including the community of states." One of the most persistent and prevalent rules of natural law was identified by Montesquieu in 1748:

> The law of nations is naturally founded on the principle that the many nations ought to do to each other, in times of peace the most good, and in times of war the least bad, that is possible without injuring their genuine interests.[14]

Jus cogens is often viewed as a modern form of natural law that consists of certain peremptory norms which are so fundamental to the international community of states as a whole that they constitute the basis of entire legal systems. Thus, the central guarantee of the sovereignty of states is seen as a rule of *jus cogens*. Certain principles of human rights are also typically added to the list.

Finally, basic "equitable" principles applied by tribunals over the centuries are sometimes employed to supplement these other sources of international law. Aristotle defined equity as the "corrective of what is legally just,"[15] and in practice, courts over the centuries have "adjusted" the rights of the various parties to a dispute by referencing not merely the "strict law," but a general analysis of what might be considered fair under the circumstances.

International Organizations

At this point in time, international organizations together comprise a fourth broad source of international law. The concept of a modern international organization dates back to the mid-nineteenth century when the International Telegraphic Union (1865) and the Universal Postal Union (1874) were established. Today, there are international organizations for practically every field of human endeavor, but the central organization remains the United Nations, which was established in 1945.[16]

Conceptually, the influence and power of the major international organizations are typically derived from treaties spelling out the designated functions that individual states have delegated. In addition to the United Nations, some regional international organizations are particularly powerful. One notable example, of course, is the European Union, which in 1993, became the accepted designation for a grouping formerly known as the "European Communities" and included the European Coal and Steel Community, the European Economic Community (also known as the "Common Market") and the European Atomic Energy Community.[17]

The League of Nations was the first "universal" international organization. Established in 1919 by the Treaty of Versailles, it built upon intellectual and moral principles articulated by a range of philosophers over the centuries, including Zeno, Marcus Aurelius, Erasmus, Sir Thomas More, Grotius, Rousseau, and Kant. Neither the United States nor the Soviet Union ever joined the League, and its failure to prevent World War II resulted in its dissolution, in spite of the significant contributions that it had made during its first ten years in the areas of international law, world health, the protection of minorities, and the settlement of global disputes.[18]

Hoping to build on the successes of the League and learn from its mistakes, four major allies—the United States, the Soviet Union, Great Britain, and China—began negotiations during World War II. In 1944, representatives met at Dumbarton Oaks in order to set out the basic configuration of a new organization. In 1945, fifty states met in San Francisco to agree on the definite terms of the United Nations and to sign its charter.

The UN was initially organized into six principal organs—the General Assembly, the Security Council, the Economic and Social Council, the Trusteeship Council, the International Court of Justice, and the Secretariat. Today, the UN includes a wide range of organs and committees, and employs over fifty thousand people.[19]

International Agreements Focusing on Cyberspace: WIPO and ICANN as Early Examples

By the end of the twentieth century, two highly publicized agreements focusing on cyberspace in a global context had been concluded: The World Intellectual Property Organization (WIPO) Copyright Treaty (December 1996) and the Memorandum of Understanding between the U.S. Department of Commerce and the Internet Corporation for Assigned Names & Numbers (November 1998). Both agreements recognized the international nature of the online world, and both sought to break new ground within the larger framework of international law discussed above. Yet it should be noted at the outset that while the WIPO Copyright Treaty was a true international agreement within a global framework, ICANN can arguably be characterized as simply a U.S. creation—a delegation of authority to the private sector that may require the participation of representatives from other countries but does not represent a true model of international cooperation in the traditional sense.

The WIPO Copyright Treaty

WIPO, a specialized arm of the United Nations, is charged with administering the Berne Convention, which has served as *the* major international copyright agreement since the formation of the International Union for the Protection of Literary & Artistic Works (Berne Union) in 1886. In late 1996, WIPO delegates met in Geneva to consider, among other things, the draft of a copyright treaty that was intended to supplement the Berne Convention. Given the active role that the United States played in Geneva, it is interesting to note that until its adherence to the Berne Convention in 1989, the United States was the only western country that had not signed on to the Berne Union.

Initially, the Clinton administration's agenda in Geneva included attempts to formalize a series of new regulations that would have strengthened the rights of copyright owners and limited the rights of users of protected works. In this manner, according to many commentators, it sought to accomplish at WIPO what it had not been able to accomplish in the U.S. Congress, that is, to implement a "highly protectionist" agenda that would have resulted in unprecedented changes inconsistent with traditional copyright principles.[20] In the end, however, the fifty-one nations that signed the treaty agreed to a much more balanced set of provisions.

Pamela Samuelson, who closely monitored both the events leading up to the WIPO conference and the negotiations at the conference itself, concluded that the democratic process triumphed and that efforts both within the U.S. and at Geneva led ultimately to a positive result. In a 1997 law review article, Samuelson documented both the nature of the WIPO debates and the modifications in the copyright treaty draft. Comparing the final treaty with the original Clinton administration agenda, she described a resolution that reflected significant compromise and gain.

For example, Samuelson noted that U.S. efforts to implement its "maximalist" agenda in certain controversial areas did not succeed. The conference rejected proposals that would have (1) treated temporary copies of protected works in the random-access memory of computers as copyright violations, (2) deemed all transmissions of protected digital works to be "distributions" in violation of copyright laws, (3) cut back on existing fair use rights of individuals under their own nations' laws, (4) attached copyright-management information to digital copies of works, and (5) created a unique and aggressive form of database protection.

In other areas, however, the U.S. digital agenda arguably had considerable success. Among other things, Samuelson explained:

It is now clear that copyright law applies in the digital environment, and that storage of protected works is a reproduction that can be controlled by copyright owners. The treaty also protects copyright owners from digital transmissions insofar as they constitute communications to the public. It also requires states to have adequate protection and effective remedies against circumvention technologies and services.[21]

On balance, Samuelson applauded the end result, but warned that just because these even-handed principles found their way into the WIPO treaty "does not mean that there will cease to be pressure to grant more extensive protection to copyright owners." Even if the treaty is ratified by the requisite number of nations and becomes part of the Berne Convention, this convention, after all, only establishes minimum rules for national laws. Countries may individually choose to go beyond these basic rules.[22]

Two years after the conclusion of the Geneva agreement, the U.S. Congress passed the Digital Millennium Copyright Act, which served to implement the WIPO Copyright Treaty in the United States.[23] But by the end of the 1990s, the U.S. remained one of only nine countries—and the only highly industrialized nation—to have ratified the document. Canada, France, Germany, and the United Kingdom were among the forty-two other signatories whose parliaments had still not ratified the treaty, and at least twenty-one nations must do so if the treaty is ever going to take effect on an international level.[24]

The ICANN Memorandum of Understanding

In 1998, a second major agreement focusing on cyberspace in a global context was concluded. President Clinton, acting within the context of the 1997 Framework for Global Electronic Commerce, directed the Secretary of Commerce to privatize the management of the domain name system (DNS)[25] in a manner that increased competition and facilitated international participation in its management. To that end, the Commerce Department drafted a Memorandum of Understanding formalizing this delegation of tasks to the new "not-for-profit entity" that had been chosen for this purpose—the Internet Corporation for Assigned Names and Numbers:

This Agreement promotes the technical management of the DNS in a manner that reflects the global and functional diversity of Internet users and their needs. This Agreement is intended to promote the design, development, and testing of mechanisms to solicit public input, both domestic and international, into a private-sector decision making process. These mechanisms will promote the flexibility needed to adapt to changes in the composition of the Internet user community and their needs.[26]

According to this Memorandum of Understanding, ICANN had demonstrated to the government that it could "accommodate the broad and diverse interest groups that make up the Internet community." It would initially work in concert with the Commerce Department on the "DNS Project," jointly designing, developing, and testing "the mechanisms, methods, and procedures to carry out (a) the establishment of policy for the allocation of IP number blocks; (b) oversight of the operation of the authoritative root-server system; (c) oversight of the policy for determining the circumstances under which new top-level domains would be added to the root system; (d) coordination of the assignment of other Internet technical parameters as needed to maintain universal connectivity on the Internet; and (e) other activities necessary to coordinate the specified DNS management functions, as agreed by the Parties."

The parties agreed to work together on facilitating the transition to the new oversight system without disrupting the functional operation of the Internet. Among other things, ICANN also agreed to collaborate on the design, development, and testing of both a plan for the introduction of competition in domain-name registration services and a plan for creating a process that would consider the possible expansion of the number of top-level domains. The Memorandum of Understanding specified that the design process for possible expansion of top level domains "should consider and take into account . . . recommendations made by WIPO . . . regarding trademark/domain name policies, including the development of a uniform approach to resolving trademark/domain name disputes involving cyberpiracy, a process for protecting famous trademarks in the generic top level domains, and the effects of adding new . . . [top level domains] . . . and related dispute resolution procedures on trademark and intellectual property holders."[27]

Once the temporary ICANN board was chosen and the nonprofit corporation began meeting in various locations to address this highly technical and seemingly innocuous set of tasks, its actions generated a tremendous amount of controversy across the globe. Critics focused on everything from the general accountability of ICANN to issues of representation, jurisdiction, and alleged hidden agendas.

Representation in particular was a central issue from the beginning. Not only was the composition of the governing board and the method of choosing the directors criticized as undemocratic, but some questioned whether ICANN was truly international in nature. For example, in order to "ensure broad international representation" on the 19-member board of directors, specific seats were designated as representing certain geographic regions . . . and those seats had to be filled by representatives of those regions. This initial formula was criticized by commentators who determined that even with these alleged safeguards, most of the persons on the board could end up being Americans, and that even if ICANN continued to meet in different cities across the globe, it could remain essentially a private entity created by the United States and consisting primarily of U.S. members.

In July 1999, hearings focusing on ICANN were held in Washington, D.C. by the House Commerce Committee (Subcommittee on Oversight and Investigations) and the House Judiciary Committee (Subcommittee on Courts & Intellectual Property). Subsequently, ICANN announced a series of initiatives aiming to convince the public that its process was indeed democratic.[28] And changes were made in both the original Memorandum of Understanding and the original bylaws.

By mid 2001, ICANN could point to concrete achievements in the area of arbitration for disputes regarding domain names. The organization developed a Uniform Dispute Resolution Policy, which contained a series of rules governing the process.[29] And it approved four arbitration and mediation centers, which handled over 1,000 cases in less than a year.[30] But critics continued to question both the process itself and the ultimate authority of ICANN. Indeed—as highlighted by the respective congressional testimony of former ICANN official Michael Roberts and Internet law scholar Michael Froomkin in early 2001—many key issues remain unresolved in this context.[31]

ICANN-related developments have been complex and indeterminate, but no one doubts the importance of its work. And debates focusing on both the organization's obligations and the extent to which it can be held accountable will no doubt continue for some time to come.[32]

Other Models of International Cooperation with Potential Applicability for Cyberspace

The WIPO Copyright Treaty and the formation of ICANN have both been controversial from the beginning, and it remains to be seen whether and to what extent these developments will be viewed as notable instances of successful international cooperation with regard to cyberspace. But even if they both prove successful, these agreements will only have addressed certain aspects of cyberspace on a global level. Assuming that some degree of international regulation is appropriate on a broader scale, we will examine three broad-based models of global cooperation and their potential applicability to the online world—legal regimes focusing on analogous international "territory," global adjudication via international tribunals, and the law of international commerce and trade.

Legal Regimes Regulating International "Territory"

The word *regime* in French law means "a system of rules and regulations." In international law, the term *international regime* refers to a system of rules set by custom or treaty that cover territories governed by some form of international jurisdiction. The key feature of an international regime is that the rules give all states similar rights and duties over these territories.[33]

The sea, airspace, and outer space are all viewed as controlled on some level by international regimes. And, at first glance, all three can be viewed as analogous to cyberspace. After all, they all qualify—at least in part—as international territory, and to the extent that the nations of the world have been successful in devising rules to regulate this territory, these rules might arguably prove useful for the regulation of the online world.

The Law of the Sea Like cyberspace, the sea has typically been viewed as an international resource open to all. Almost all nations do in fact have access to it, although from time to time certain nations seek to extend their own jurisdiction over certain parts of it.

Over time, a law of the sea has emerged through a combination of customary practice and international agreement. Indeed, although it has not been without its share of problems, the development and continuing vitality of the law of the sea is almost universally viewed as a positive model of international cooperation, and as concrete evidence that the nations of the world can indeed come up with rules that address a common global resource.

Dating back to the days of ancient maritime codes, the law of the sea was recognized by Grotius in 1608 as rooted in the fundamental principle that the high seas should be open to the ships of all states. This principle, he explained, was based on "the most specific and unimpeachable axiom of the Law of Nations . . . [that] . . . every nation is free to travel to every other nation, and to trade with it."[34] By the nineteenth century, it was generally accepted that the territory of coastal states could extend three miles from shore, but that beyond three miles vessels were deemed to be on the high seas, and thus subject only to legal rules by the vessels' flag states and by the law of nations.

In the twentieth century, this body of customary international law threatened to unravel as individual nation-states sought to enlarge their own maritime jurisdictions for economic reasons. When it became clear that the natural resources of the sea included not only fish but also oil, gas, and hard minerals, nations began to compete for control of these resources. In 1945, for example, the United States issued the Truman Proclamation, asserting its sovereign jurisdiction over the oil and gas beneath its offshore "continental shelf"—an underwater plateau sometimes extending hundreds of miles out to sea—while emphasizing that these national claims to mineral resources would in no way impact freedoms of the high sea recognized under international law. It was not long before other nations began to lay claim to their own expanded maritime zones. The 1958 Geneva Law of the Sea Conference resulted in four international agreements that codified a range of customary practices in this area, but the nations failed to reach a consensus on issues relating to territorial waters. In addition, the discovery of manganese modules on the ocean floor led to an entirely new controversy focusing on the mining of the deep seabed.

Calls for an international legal structure to govern the deep seabed led to the establishment of a UN Seabed Committee and to a new UN Conference on the Law of the Sea. After hundreds of meetings throughout the 1970s and early 1980s, an agreement on a new UN Convention was reached in 1982. This Convention on the Law of the Sea entered into force on November 1994, after its ratification by sixty nations. Agreement was reached on the limits of the territorial sea, the parameters of sovereignty over "exclusive economic zones" extending up to two hundred nautical miles, and the establishment of an International Tribunal for the Law of the Sea that would have exclusive jurisdiction over deep-seabed mining disputes.[35] The convention, however, has still not been ratified by the United States—a fact that casts doubt on the efficacy of such a model for the regulation of the online world.

It is instructive to examine the reasons for the failure of the United States to ratify the convention. U.S. representatives, of course, participated in all the meetings leading up to the 1982 agreement. Indeed, until 1981, the U.S. government had generally supported the concept of a new and comprehensive law of the sea treaty. Reagan administration officials, however, took a different position and opposed the idea. With regard to navigation rights, they believed that customary international law provided sufficient protection for all countries without the need for a new treaty. And they were especially opposed to the establishment of a new international seabed organization with any real power.[36]

By 1992, fifty-one states had ratified the Convention, but the list did not include any Western industrialized nations with the exception of Iceland. In addition, virtually none of the Eastern European or Southeast Asian nations had ratified the treaty either. Issues relating to the international seabed remained at the center of the disagreements. But in 1994, these issues were resolved—with heavy input from the United States—by a new Deep Seabed Mining Agreement. By 2000, more than 130 countries had become parties to the convention. The list included the United Kingdom, China, Japan, France, and Germany—but still did not include the United States. In fact, the U.S. Senate apparently would not even schedule the hearings needed to review the convention.[37] The United States adhered to the convention, but only voluntarily, and without being a formal party to this notable example of global cooperation.

The Law of Aviation Space In the twentieth century, airspace emerged as a second major international regime. The development of recognized laws and practices in both aviation space and outer space has been viewed by many as parallel to the law of the sea, although commentators have noted that the skies may not be directly analogous to bodies of water.

Still, the emergence of treaties, conventions, and interstate cooperation in this area has been particularly noteworthy. The Chicago Convention of 1944, for example, established basic rules regarding civil aircraft and territorial airspace. Under the convention, each state has complete sovereignty over the airspace above its land areas as well as the airspace above the territorial waters under its control. This sovereignty includes the right of nonscheduled flight, and the right to control which nations—if any—may schedule flights across the airspace. In addition, the convention recognizes that aircraft take on the nationality of the state in which they are registered.

Over the years, however, other issues have emerged. One area of disagreement concerns the height of national airspace. Nations have agreed that national sovereignty stops at some point above the earth, but different governments have disagreed over the exact height at which territorial airspace ends. Other areas of disagreement have included the concept of "entry in distress." Unlike the law of the sea, such entry has generally been prohibited by individual nations unless a treaty has been concluded. Governments have also disagreed over claims beyond airspace, with different nations establishing a variety of requirements regarding the point at which another country's civil aircraft must identify itself. Such requirements may also change depending on the state of international relations at the time and the latest developments in technology.

The Law of Outer Space Outer space law has developed differently, and may be viewed as more directly analogous to the law of the sea. In this regard, then, it may also be seen as a more appropriate model for the regulation of cyberspace. Outer space emerged as a disputed "entity" in the 1950s and 1960s as technological advances enabled human beings to pursue space exploration for the first time. As with cyberspace, new issues regarding access and control quickly came to the forefront, and it became clear that they needed to be addressed. Unlike cyberspace, however, access to outer space has been limited only to a handful of nations that have been able to develop space exploration programs. Thus outer space law developed within the context of the ongoing cold war rivalry between the United States and the Soviet Union. Cyberspace regulation issues have emerged in a much broader context, since ostensibly every nation and potentially every human being can access the online world.

Despite the clear differences between outer space and cyberspace, there may be enough similarities between them to build on the successes that have been achieved in the area of outer space regulation. And these successes cannot be discounted. During a particularly difficult period of time—with Cold War tensions very high, a traumatic war in the Middle East, the Vietnam War raging out of control, and the cultural revolution in full force in China—nations were still able to conclude the landmark Outer Space Treaty of 1967.

The basic overarching principle of the Outer Space Treaty was that outer space is and should remain open to all. Article I provides that "the exploration and use of outer space shall be carried out for the benefit and in the interests of all countries . . . and shall be the province of all mankind." It emphasizes that "outer space shall be free for exploration and use by all States," and that individual countries shall facilitate and encourage international cooperation in scientific investigation. Article II provides that outer space is "not subject to national appropriation by claim of sovereignty, by means of use or occupation, or by any other means."[38]

In determining the applicability of these "regimes" to the regulation of the online world, a number of considerations are apparent. On the positive side of the ledger, the laws of the sea, aviation space, and outer space certainly reflect the ability of nations to work together and come up with rules to govern a physical space that no one country controls. In particular, the 1982 Law of the Sea Convention—representing customary practice over time as well as agreement on a range of new issues peculiar to the twentieth century—can be viewed on some level as one of the finest examples of global cooperation to be found in the annals of international law.

Yet these legal regimes also reflect the limits of international cooperation. Apart from the susceptibility of these frameworks to violent acts by terrorists and rogue nations, it is clear that for a variety of reasons, ranging from domestic political considerations to hidden global agendas, not all nations will agree to a legal regime.

In addition, each of these regimes is rooted in legal structures that may make them inapplicable to cyberspace. The law of the sea, for instance, is rooted in customary practice that has developed over hundreds, if not thousands, of years. Recent social norms and customary practices, as we noted in earlier chapters, have already had an impact on the development of U.S. common law in the Internet speech and copyright areas, but customary practice on an international level typically takes much longer than five to ten years or even a few decades to ripen into well-settled international doctrine. And since 1918 international law has developed primarily via treaty, with little or no reliance on any new twentieth-century customary practices that might have been identified.

The laws of aviation space and outer space may not rely on customary practice, but they have their own limitations. Aviation law relies primarily on the legal systems and territorial regulations of individual countries, and as a result, some argue that it is not really an example of an international regime at all, but simply "a field of extensive inter-state cooperation."[39] Outer space law, on the other hand, has only addressed a handful of issues thus far, and, as discussed earlier, may only apply as a practical matter to the handful of nations that have undertaken space exploration.

Formal International Adjudication

A second broad-based area of global cooperation is the international adjudication model, where nations submit voluntarily to some form of judicial deliberation or arbitration.[40] Public international arbitration dates from the earliest times of recorded history, but it was not until 1899 that nations actually came together and established a Permanent Court of Arbitration (PCA). The PCA convention was ultimately ratified or adhered to by 44 states, and by 1914, more than 120 arbitration agreements had been concluded. Over time, however, the PCA was eclipsed, first by the Permanent Court of International Justice (under the League of Nations) and then by the International Court of Justice (ICJ) (under the UN).[41]

The International Court of Justice is the principal judicial organ of the United Nations. Known as the "World Court," it is located in The Hague and operates under a statute which is an integral part of the UN Charter. The Court has been empowered "to settle in accordance with international law the legal disputes submitted to it by States, and to give advisory opinions on legal questions referred to it by . . . authorized international organs and agencies." It is composed of fifteen judges elected to nine-year terms of office by the General Assembly and the Security Council. Elections are held every three years for one-third of the seats, and no more than one judge of any nationality may be elected. The judges "must possess the qualifications required in their respective countries for appointment to the highest judicial offices, or be jurists of recognized competence in international law."

At this point in time, only nations—and not individual parties—may appear before the ICJ. These nations may include both UN member states and other states that become party to the Court's statute. Judicial proceedings include a written phase, where the parties file documents and exchange pleadings, and an oral phase consisting of public hearings. All judgments of the Court are final, and no appeals are allowed. Decisions are made "in accordance with international treaties and conventions in force, international custom, the general principles of law and, as subsidiary means, judicial decisions and teachings of the most highly qualified publicists."[42]

Between 1946 and 1999, the ICJ delivered sixty-eight judgments on disputes concerning land frontiers, maritime boundaries, territorial sovereignty, the use of force, interference in the internal affairs of states, diplomatic relations, hostage-taking, the right of asylum, nationality, guardianship, rights of passage and economic rights.[43] In recent years, the Court has become an especially popular forum for nations that have war-related grievances. In 1999 alone, Croatia sued Yugoslavia for genocide during the 1991–1995 war, Yugoslavia sued ten NATO countries for aggression and genocide, and the Congo sued Burundi, Rwanda, and Uganda for aggression and violations of human rights.[44]

Although there is much to admire in the history and development of the World Court over the past one hundred years, any analysis of this model's potential applicability to cyberspace-related disputes must also focus on two persistent problems that have dogged the ICJ and its predecessors from the start—jurisdiction and enforcement.

In essence, no nation can be forced to appear before the ICJ unless it agrees to accept the Court's jurisdiction. Such acceptance can occur only if (1) nations conclude a special agreement to submit a dispute to the Court, (2) nations are parties to a treaty that contains their explicit consent to the Court's jurisdiction if a particular dispute takes place, or (3) a nation signs on with the Court to accept its "compulsory jurisdiction" in general if any dispute arises with any other nation that has also signed on. Over sixty nations have agreed to this "compulsory jurisdiction," but a number of them have specifically excluded certain types of disputes.[45] Even more problematic is the issue of enforcement. The Court has no enforcement powers per se, but rather it is dependent on the good faith and good will of the participating member states.

Given that these limitations have been the basis of much criticism over the years, with commentators often questioning the value of the ICJ itself, it may be that the ICJ is not a particularly effective model for the online world. The advantages of a "world court" model, however, cannot be ignored. Douglas Cassel notes that even with all its flaws, the ICJ can facilitate negotiations, help clarify rules, and strengthen a nation's hand in economic negotiations. Each case may pave the way for the next, and the cumulative effect may sometimes constrain, shortcut, or even compensate for "evils" that one nation may perpetrate upon another.[46]

Ultimately, questions regarding the efficacy of the "world court" model reflect analogous issues that were raised in chapter 4. Indeed, the same limits of the law that were discussed on a national level are equally applicable in this context on an international level.

The Law of International Commerce and International Trade Generally

Perhaps the most compelling example of international agreement and cooperation over time can be found in the principles that have been developed to govern global commerce and trade. Such principles can be found not only in modern international commercial law generally, but also in the rules and procedures developed by the World Trade Organization (WTO), the International Monetary Fund (IMF), and the International Bank for Reconstruction & Development (World Bank). Like the legal regimes and the frameworks for international adjudication referenced in this section, the principles governing international commerce and trade might arguably serve as models for the global regulation of cyberspace.

But the law of international commerce and international trade differs from the other models discussed above because their impact on cyberspace is not speculative. Particularly in relevant areas of e-commerce, for example, it can be argued that on a global level these international rules and procedures already do control certain types of online transactions.

International commercial law evolved over time and was originally derived from the *lex mercatoria,* a medieval body of customary rules that was used in certain places to supplement the often incomplete rules of individual nation states. Today, for example, common international terms have been identified that may be incorporated into international sales contracts. These terms include *CIF* (cost, insurance and freight) and *FOB* (free on board), which are designed to mean the same thing even in different countries with differing local rules. Other uniform terms and even model international sales contracts have been developed by various trade associations. In addition, uniform laws and conventions addressing global trade have been developed under the auspices of the UN.[47]

Arguably the single most important development in this area over the past ten years has been the emergence of the World Trade Organization as a major international body with broad regulatory powers over international trade.

The Growing Impact of the World Trade Organization (WTO)

The WTO was formerly known as *GATT,* which began in 1947 under the General Agreement on Trade and Tariffs and eventually emerged as an organization defined by a complex set of more than one hundred agreements. These agreements were revised on a periodic basis with the purpose of "moderating" the foreign trade policies of individual countries so that international commerce could flow in a free and unencumbered manner.

Organization, Goals, and Achievements of the WTO As the only international organization devoted exclusively to global rules of trade between nations, the WTO was established to ensure that trade flows "smoothly, freely, fairly, and predictably." According to the WTO's official Web site, "trade friction is channeled into the WTO's dispute settlement process . . . [avoiding] . . . the risk of disputes spilling over into political or military conflict. By lowering trade barriers, the WTO's system also breaks down other barriers between peoples and nations." The result of its efforts, the WTO claims, is "a more prosperous, peaceful and accountable economic world."[48]

The WTO is designed to meet its goals by administering trade agreements, acting as a forum for trade negotiations, settling trade disputes, reviewing national trade policies, assisting developing countries in trade policy issues, and cooperating with other international organizations. By the year 2000, the WTO had more than 130 members, accounting for over 90 percent of world trade.[49]

From a cyberspace perspective—both in terms of a model with potentially broad applicability and in terms of the development of rules that may themselves have a direct impact on Internet-related activities—the two most important initial contributions of the WTO have been an aggressive dispute resolution process with "teeth" and the Agreement on Trade Related Aspects of Intellectual Property Rights (TRIPS).

Dispute Resolution under the WTO Framework The WTO dispute resolution process that emerged in the mid-1990s was intended to be the first with the ability to make its findings stick. Agreeing to participate in this process and accept its jurisdiction is a key requirement of membership in the WTO. Dispute resolution decisions are made by three-member panels, consisting primarily of politicians, economists, lawyers, and professors. Once the decisions are made, they can actually be enforced through sanctions of various types. And, in a sharp departure from the previous approach under GATT, losing parties no longer have the right to block rulings—including any financial sanctions—unless they are joined by a consensus of WTO members, which is extremely difficult if not impossible to achieve under the circumstances.

American leaders apparently assumed that the relatively open U.S. economy would prosper in such a system, and that the United States would lodge grievances much more often than it would be named in other countries' complaints. Indeed, the United States has employed the WTO dispute resolution process more vigorously than any other country. By early 2000, it had lodged sixty complaints of unfair trade against its trading partners; the EU came in second with forty-seven complaints. Of the complaints that have been resolved, the United States has won twenty-two and lost two. Separately, the United States has been named the defendant fourteen times, leading to five U.S. losses and nine settlements. While some view this as a strong track record, others argue that the lost cases are more significant than those won. For example, Kodak's loss to Fuji could cost American firms more than two billion dollars in tax benefits. And environmentalists continue to criticize the process by noting that the United States has had to cut back on its environmental regulations as a result of a loss at the WTO.[50]

Clearly, the WTO has provided a viable international framework for negotiating agreements and resolving disputes in the area of international trade. Yet it is this very dispute resolution structure that has been the subject of vehement criticism in recent years. Sara Dillon, for example, recently documented the changes brought about by the emergence of the WTO. Arguing that these changes have been characterized by an "enormous proliferation in causes of action"—legal vehicles that enable nations to challenge other nations in a dispute resolution process that resembles an international court—the Dublin professor declared that the WTO dispute resolution panel decisions have been "unabashedly expansionist," and that "they have shown little concern for domestic regulations."

Dillon explained that before 1995, the old GATT system "was not designed to impose an absolute will on participating states through orders and sanctions. States could block panel decisions unfavorable to themselves." But under the Uruguay Round of agreements, she contended, there was a "decisive shift . . . away from a diplomatic approach to international trade rules and dispute resolution," a shift that has arguably resulted in "the startling power of WTO law over national regulation." Particularly troubling to her was what she described as the "greatly enhanced powers of genuine enforcement for WTO panel decisions."[51]

These characteristics are exactly what many supporters of the WTO believe to be its strongest suit. They note that WTO ministerial decisions "are made by the entire membership," typically by consensus, and that "all WTO agreements have been ratified in all members' parliaments."[52] They also argue that it is appropriate, in this era of shrinking distances and effortless border crossings, both online and offline, to rely more on a global system of democracy and less on the laws and policies of individual nations, at least with regard to international commerce and trade.

Agreement on Trade-Related Aspects of Intellectual Property Rights

When the document establishing the WTO was concluded in 1994, the Agreement on Trade-Related Aspects of Intellectual Property Rights was added on as an annex. TRIPS resembles earlier international intellectual property treaties such as the Berne Convention in that it establishes minimum standards for the laws of individual nations that all members must adhere to. Pamela Samuelson notes, however, that it goes beyond earlier treaties in several important ways, including its insistence on "adequacy and effectiveness of remedies and enforcement practices when intellectual property rights have been violated," its dispute resolution mechanism with "meaningful sanctions" for countries in the area of intellectual property protection, and its placing of a "trade spin on intellectual property rules that have in the past been guided by a host of other principles."[53]

Commentators have identified several interrelated explicit and implicit goals in the TRIPS agreement. One goal, clearly, is to stop nations from adopting blatantly protectionist intellectual property rules that serve as barriers to free trade. A second goal is to address the piracy of intellectual property products in the global marketplace. And a third goal, in the eyes of many, is the harmonization of national intellectual property laws over and above the basic minimum guidelines that TRIPS establishes.

In addition to the more consistent rules that the WTO dispute resolution panel decisions are likely to trigger, a more important source of harmonization may be the Council for TRIPS, which provides oversight of the intellectual property laws of member nations. WTO members must report to the council on a regular basis regarding their intellectual property laws and enforcement practices.[54]

Criticism of the WTO from the Left and the Right The turn of the century has been seen by many as a golden age of "globalization," with successful business transactions being conducted on an international level and a significant degree of cooperation between the world's great economic powers. This globalization has come to be symbolized by the WTO and its far-reaching agreements. And while some view globalization as a catalyst for greater prosperity across the board and the beginning of global unity on a scale that may not have been imaginable in another era, others believe that the version of transnational economic cooperation that emerged by the year 2000 leaves many persons and nations behind. This feeling of being left behind has been at the heart of the criticisms that have been leveled at the WTO from both the left and the right.

The massive street demonstrations that took place in Seattle at the WTO Ministerial Conference of November 1999 and apparently helped contribute to deadlocked negotiating sessions were generally seen as reflecting the unhappiness of the left with the progress of globalization. Indeed, labor relations and environmental concerns were at the forefront of the agendas set forth by many of the liberal activist groups that traveled to Seattle in great numbers and held rallies throughout the week.[55]

Other demonstrators—both advocates and anarchists—included persons and groups focusing on food safety, affordable medicine, human rights, and native cultures. All were united by a belief that the agents and purveyors of global commerce, represented by the WTO, have shoved aside social priorities in a "relentless quest for profits."[56] And their activism was fueled by commentators who argued that the WTO has become the virtual antithesis of democracy because of its apparent ability to overrule inconsistent laws of individual member states. One U.S. commentator, for example, referred to these developments as a "stealth coup," and declared that the WTO has essentially become a new branch of the government, "in many ways more powerful than Congress and the President."[57]

A different perspective on globalization has emerged on the right, especially among the neo-fascist and neo-Nazi parties that have gained ground in many countries. According to a recent report submitted by the special rapporteur of the UN Commission on Human Rights, the increase in power of the extreme right-wing parties, particularly in Europe, has taken place in "an economic and social climate characterized by fear and despair." These political movements have been fueled by concern over immigration, the Euro, the apparent blurring of indigenous differences, and new information technologies. All of these manifestations are viewed by the extreme right as part and parcel of globalization.

The populist backlash against globalization is reflected in rhetoric that is not only anti-immigrant in nature but critical of the European Union and the recent introduction of a single currency. The European Monetary Union is seen in this context as an attempt by Europe's big business interests to adapt to the needs of "the new global economic order." In addition to capitalizing on the anguish in certain quarters over the decision to relinquish authority over key fiscal matters to "unelected central bankers in

Frankfurt," the far right has warned against the loss of cultural and national identities. And the new information technologies are seen not as an opportunity but as a tool of the key players in the global economy—the multinational corporations, transnational lobbies, and elite trade associations—rather than popularly elected officials. In the end, Martin Lee points out, "as economic globalization has accelerated, so, too, has the momentum of neo-fascist and right-wing extremist organizations." He also contends that "European integration is likely to foster the continued growth of radical right-wing parties," and that in this way "unfettered globalization—accompanied by social injustice—will continue to breed the very monstrosities it purports to oppose."[58]

The events in Seattle—in particular, the images of street demonstrators battling police, breaking windows, and rallying against globalization—led to a great deal of instant analysis regarding the failures of international cooperation. Others were more sanguine. They pointed out that not only did the elaborate WTO network of agreements, negotiating frameworks, and dispute resolution procedures remain in place, but that the events of the week drove home the importance of opening up the WTO process. Indeed, trade representatives seemed to view Seattle as a watershed event that would inevitably lead to a more open and collaborative approach. Such openness could conceivably help blunt the criticisms and address the concerns of those who warn of future unrest on both ends of the political spectrum.

The WTO, E-Commerce, and Cyberspace The WTO framework, we would emphasize again, may be applicable to the online world not only as a model of international cooperation in general, but also as a vehicle for the promulgation of specific rules governing e-commerce. TRIPS certainly qualifies as an example of such Internet-related rule-making; other regulatory issues considered by WTO officials in late 1999 may ultimately qualify as well.

The e-commerce questions that WTO delegates hoped to address at the November 1999 ministerial conference reflected the nature of the growing impact the organization could have on the global regulation of the online world. At the outset, U.S. officials went in hoping to use the new round of trade talks to achieve four goals in the area of e-commerce: (1) declare a moratorium on Internet tariffs, parallel to the moratorium on taxes within the United States; (2) establish some basic rules for e-commerce trade, similar to the WTO rules that exist for other sorts of trade, assuring that foreign firms are not discriminated against; (3) reach an agreement that members of the WTO will refrain from unnecessary measures that restrain e-commerce; and (4) agree on the principle of technological neutrality; that is, products traded in the electronic world should be treated in the same way as those traded in the real world.[59]

Developing countries were wary of these efforts and concerned about the alleged "sacrifices" they were being called upon to make. The United States was criticized by those who feared that "U.S. moves are very much designed to make the world safe for Microsoft and Oracle and companies like that." At the very least, developing countries planned to oppose efforts to establish a permanent ban on tariffs for digital transactions.

In a related controversy, developing nations hoped to press for an extension of a deadline requiring them to establish laws and set forth enforcement plans that would protect software, music, and other copyrighted material.

WTO negotiators were also faced with tricky questions over how to classify goods and services delivered over the Internet. The temporary moratorium on customs duties, in place since a May 1998 WTO agreement, applied only to goods and services transmitted electronically such as software, digital books, and music. But a dispute developed between the United States and the European Union over whether to classify such transactions as goods or services, with experts projecting that it could take years to resolve. Under WTO rules, software at the time was treated as goods, and was therefore taxed according to the minimal value of its medium, such as a blank compact disk. If, however, electronically transmitted software and other products were instead treated as a service, countries could become liable for duties and other restrictions under a separate WTO regime. U.S. officials and technology companies apparently feared that such a development could open the door to inconsistent taxation of digital transactions from country to country.[60]

The massive demonstrations and the breakdown in trade negotiations across the board led to little in the way of concrete developments during the week in Seattle. But because Internet-related matters were not at the heart of contentious issues raised by protesters in the streets and developing nations in the meetings themselves, many viewed this policy area as one that would be ripe for further negotiations in the near future. Indeed, a spokesperson for the U.S. Business Software Alliance insisted that the events in Seattle were not a defeat in any way, shape, or form: "The status quo on high-tech industries works fine for us," she said. "We already enjoy strong copyright protection for software in the TRIPS agreement . . . and there was general consensus . . . [on many e-commerce related issues]." Especially when compared with other issues that had been raised during the week, e-commerce was, in the end, one of the less controversial issues."[61] In the aftermath of the events in Seattle, commentators appeared to view the extension of the three-year global moratorium on tariffs for international sales conducted over the Internet as not only desirable but also doable.[62]

In general, it is likely that the debate regarding the emerging power of the WTO and its impact on the decision-making power of individual nations will continue for some time to come. Assuming, however, that the WTO retains a certain level of influence and authority, it is bound to have a significant impact on the regulation of e-commerce in the future. And its legal structure could emerge as one of the most important models of international agreement with regard to the resolution of other online problems down the road.[63]

International Models of Agreement and the Prospective Regulation of Cyberspace: Analysis and Prognosis

The nations of the world have not only generated a body of rules over time but have developed a range of viable working models for the resolution of disputes and the facilitation of international cooperation across the board. Although these models may not always work as planned, and although issues relating to both the limits of legal systems in general and the politics of international relations in particular come up over and over again, there is much that would-be regulators of cyberspace can learn from them.

In reflecting on both the global rules currently in place and the sources of future international regulation in this area, it is important to note that the treaty—and not customary practice—is likely to be the basic foundation of any prospective Internet-related rule-making. The foundation of international law is state consent, and it is always easier to accomplish consent via treaty rather than through the evolution of customary practice over time. Since 1918, almost all new international law has been promulgated by treaty.

Rules that emerge from customary practice remain controversial in any sense, and with regard to the online world, there has simply not been enough time for customary practice and social norms to "harden" into settled international doctrine. The law of the sea, for example, evolved through over five hundred years of customary practice, during which time states in general were not interested in reaching broad agreement on issues relating to international waters. Social norms and customary practices in cyberspace have emerged only over a decade or two, and unlike the sea, the Internet is "territory" that nations are very interested in addressing right now, rather than waiting to see what might develop over the next five hundred years. Some might argue that Internet time operates differently, and that events in this area move so quickly that a decade in cyberspace may be equivalent to five hundred years on the sea. But most international regulators are not likely to be persuaded by this metaphysical approach.

This is not to say that the customary practices and social norms referenced throughout this book would not be applicable in any new rule-making process that might be developed on an international level. New treaties or decisions by an international tribunal must necessarily be informed by the commonly accepted practices that have emerged over time—in the same way that national common law must take note of these practices. But customary practice in and of itself is not likely to be viewed as the equivalent of new law in the complex arena of international cyberspace regulation at the present time.

Once a consensus is reached on the need for international regulation with regard to a particular problem area in cyberspace, and after the relevant questions relating to prospective solutions are sorted out and agreed upon, a key inquiry would focus on what regulatory forum is most appropriate for this purpose and what sort of adjudication and compliance process might be put into place.

Examples of regulatory forums that have been discussed thus far include WIPO and the WTO. It may be that the WTO model is most appropriate for the e-commerce problems that may arise in cyberspace because, unlike the other models, nations signing on *must* agree to both the jurisdiction of the organization and the unique enforcement mechanisms that accompany the dispute resolution process.

In addition, the WTO may be an appropriate forum for the resolution of Internet disputes because so many of the emerging problems in cyberspace are trade-related on some level and have already been discussed or even addressed in the WTO. These include intellectual property controversies, the exchange of goods and services, export controls, tariffs, and encryption issues across the board.

Yet the emergence of the WTO as both a major international forum and as a central vehicle for the growth and development of globalization has resulted in an inevitable backlash, and those who wish to further expand its powers must certainly consider these criticisms and address the "bad trade-offs" and issues of secrecy that have concerned so many persons and groups in recent years. Instead of choosing to work within the WTO, nations seeking a model of global dispute resolution and enforcement for cyberspace may wish to consider forming a new international organization devoted solely to Internet-related issues. Such an organization would necessarily be informed not only by the legal principles and historical developments documented in this chapter, but also by the emerging theoretical literature on international cooperation.[64]

International models of agreement and cooperation have the potential to play a central role in the resolution of many Internet-related problems.[65] Before we consider the prospective applicability of these models, however, a third broad approach to cyberspace regulation must be examined. In the next chapter, then, we address this approach, which some have described as "code-based" rule-making and others have characterized as nothing less than the changing of the architecture of the Internet.

7

Changing the Architecture of the Internet: Code-Based Regulation and Its Implications

Out there on the electronic frontier, code is the law. The rules governing any computer-constructed microworld . . . are precisely and rigorously defined in the text of the program that constructs it on your screen. . . . For citizens of cyberspace, computer code—arcane text in a highly formalized language, typically accessible to only a few privileged high-priests—is the medium in which intentions are enacted and designs are realized, and it is becoming a crucial focus of political contest. Who shall write the software that increasingly structures our daily lives? What shall that software allow and proscribe? Who shall be privileged by it and who marginalized? How shall the writers of the rules be answerable?"

—William J. Mitchell, *City of Bits: Space, Place, and the Infobahn,* Circa 1995

Regulation need not be perfect to be effective . . . regulation works through transaction cost rather than hermetic seal.

—Timothy Wu, "Application-Centered Internet Analysis," Circa 1999

We should have Departments of Offense, not Defense. Society uses new technologies, but continues to think and operate in old ways. Society is always surprisedpuzzleddisturbed by the sweeping impact of these technologies.

—R. Buckminster Fuller, *I Seem to Be a Verb,* 1970

The third major model of online regulation that we examine in part II reflects what can be done or indeed what already has been done by software architects to change the nature of cyberspace itself. It recognizes that the way cyberspace "feels" now is based on protocols and standards that can be adjusted or even transformed, and that the ability of individuals and groups to go online and operate in certain ways is a function of the software code currently built into the architecture of the online world at various points.

While regulators may choose to apply this model in concert with one or more of the traditional, law-based approaches discussed in the previous two chapters,[1] it must be emphasized that code-based regulation can take place completely apart from any legal regulation on either a national or an international level. In fact, more often than not, code-based regulation today occurs as a result of independent decision-making on the part of various private or quasi-private entities, at different stages of the technical structure and hierarchy.[2] It can also take place on an individual level, as persons and groups take advantage of the many so-called software solutions that have emerged to counter both real and perceived problems in cyberspace.

No one has been more influential in identifying this model of regulation, establishing many of its parameters, and emphasizing its importance than Internet law scholar Lawrence Lessig. In legal articles dating back to the mid-1990s[3] and in his recent *Code and Other Laws of Cyberspace* (1999), Lessig argues that code-based regulation is the most effective way to approach certain cyberspace-related issues, given that architectural changes in many instances can effect an immediate, final, and complete transformation. In this context, Lessig warns that cyberspace as we know it—or, in fact, as we once knew it—should not be taken for granted, because in his view market-based forces are inevitably moving the online world in the direction of tighter controls through more restrictive software code.[4]

The relatively free and open online world that early Netizens experienced was based on a carefully constructed series of protocols and open standards that enabled the growth and development of that place that many found so similar to the archetypal American West. And the somewhat more restrictive, persistently multi-dimensional, and often highly "built-up" cyberspace that we experience today continues to reflect an emerging world, Lessig argues, that "is being remade to fit the demands of commerce," where "architectures are being added to make it serve commerce more efficiently." Thus, just as the development of a tighter infrastructure in the Old West—including better roads, expanding rail transportation, and a range of new services for citizens—was often fueled by a growth in commerce and typically enabled the authorities to exercise a greater degree of control over inhabitants, so too in cyberspace, Lessig contends, "regulability will by a byproduct of these changes."[6]

To demonstrate the different ways that code might enable or disable certain ways of life in cyberspace, Lessig compares the architecture and subsequent development of four different online communities—an open discussion forum tied to a particular law school class, LambdaMOO (a text-based virtual reality), Counsel Connect (a subscriber-based, online lawyers' cooperative), and America Online.

It is quickly apparent in each case that the architecture of these spaces determines the level of access, the type of interaction, and the nature of the community. In the law school forum, for example, the professor employs software that enables students to engage in online inquiry and also allows any person from the outside to join in. LambdaMOO's software provides a similar level of open access, but is designed to facilitate the building of online characters and the creation of elements for the purpose of participating in virtual games. In Counsel Connect, the software code enables interaction as well, but only among "pre-approved" attorneys and only through a moderator. And the code restricts access to those who sign up, meet certain requirements, pay a fee, and agree to use only their real name online.

As a result of the software architecture, community is a central feature in each of the first three examples. But the nuances of community vary significantly depending on the level of freedom of each person to determine the nature of the communication. In some cases, social norms may play a key role in the regulation of these online spaces.

In contrast, Lessig notes, certain features of the AOL architecture combine to set it apart from the other three communities, namely a member's "power of pseudonymity" as reflected in the ability to go by one or more of five possible screen names, the limit of twenty-three persons to any chat room, and the ability of AOL to monitor and trace the behavior of its members online. It is the software code, Lessig points out, that has given AOL these unique features. AOL is a classic example of how code can be used to structure an online reality in such a manner that at least some types of regulation are easily facilitated.[7]

To ascertain the nuances of code-based regulation, it is instructive to examine the technical history and architectural structure of today's online world. At the outset, it must be recognized that the Internet is not a single physical or tangible entity, but rather a complex series of interconnected computer networks forming a widespread information infrastructure, or a "network of networks." These networks are connected in a manner that permits each computer in any network to communicate with computers in any other network in the system by using the nonproprietary[8] Internet protocol (IP), a set of rules for exchanging data. As referenced in earlier chapters of this book, the computers and computer networks that make up the Internet may be owned by governmental and public institutions, nonprofit organizations, or private corporations. Thus, according to the 1996 findings of fact by the panel in *ACLU v. Reno I,* "the resulting whole is a decentralized, global medium of communications–or 'cyberspace'—that links people, institutions, corporations, and governments around the world."[9]

Most people agree that the origins of the Internet can be traced back to the development of ARPANET, a 1969 experimental project of the U.S. Department of Defense's Advanced Research Project Agency (ARPA). ARPANET originally linked together only computers and computer networks owned by the military, defense contractors, and university laboratories conducting defense-related research. As ARPANET grew during the 1970s and early 1980s, several similar networks were established, primarily between universities.

According to noted Internet pioneers who co-authored a classic online history of this process, the Internet was based on the idea that there would be multiple independent networks of rather arbitrary design, beginning with the ARPANET as the pioneering "packet-switched" network, but soon to include packet satellite networks, ground-based packet radio networks and other networks. A key underlying technical concept for the Internet was "open architecture networking," where individual networks could be separately designed and developed and each could have its own unique interface that it might then offer to users and other providers.[10] From the beginning, the Internet was designed "to be a decentralized, self-maintaining series of redundant links between computers and computer networks, capable of rapidly transmitting communications without direct human involvement or control, and with the automatic ability to reroute communications if one or more individual links were damaged or otherwise unavailable."[11]

Building on the system it had developed for the reliable transfer of information over a computer network, ARPA began to support the development of communications protocols for transferring data and electronic mail between different types of computer networks. Many universities, research facilities, and commercial entities soon recognized the value of such computer networking, and began to develop and link together their own networks implementing these protocols. For example, the U.S. Department of Energy established MFENET for its researchers in Magnetic Fusion Energy, NASA Space Physicists established SPAN, and several individuals established CSNET for the (academic and industrial) computer science community with an initial grant from the NSF. In addition, AT&T disseminated the UNIX computer operating system, which gave rise to USENET and the BITNET, which linked academic mainframe computers in an effective e-mail system.[12]

At first, many of these initial networks—with the exception of BITNET and USENET—were intended for, and largely restricted to, closed communities of scholars and researchers in particular scientific and academic areas. Thus, there was little pressure for the individual networks to be compatible with one another. However, the growing use of these networks over time led to the implementation of a recognized standard of communication in cyberspace—the Transmission Control Protocol/Internet Protocol (TCP/IP).[13]

TCP/IP is not a computer language, but a standard for providing "all the facilities for two computer systems to exchange information, interpret it properly, and present it in a format which can be understood by the local machine and its users." This format is generally described as being divided between four layers: the data link, network, transport, and application layers.[14]

Richard Vermut explains that when information is sent across the Internet, it begins at the "application level" and is first categorized by the application for which it is being used, since each application has a unique protocol for completing its task. For example, when file transfers are being performed, TCP/IP's file transfer protocol application is used. When logging on to a remote computer, TCP/IP's Telnet application is used. When sending e-mail, the application is the simple mail transfer protocol

(SMTP). When sending information over the World Wide Web, hypertext transfer protocol is used.[15]

Michael Froomkin argues that TCP/IP is one of three technologies that underlie the Internet's resistance to control.[16] He notes at the outset that each of the millions of computers connected by the Internet is "independently managed by persons who have chosen to adhere to common communications standards, particularly . . . [the] . . . fundamental standard known as TCP/IP, which makes it practical for computers adhering to the standard to share data even if they are far apart and have no direct line of communication." He also emphasizes that there is no single program one uses to gain access to the Internet; rather, there are "a plethora of programs" that adhere to Internet Protocols. Indeed, he claims, "it is the TCP/IP standard that makes the Internet possible."

It is generally agreed that the most important feature of TCP/IP is that "it defines a packet switching network, a method by which data can be broken up into standardized packets which are then routed to their destinations via an indeterminate number of intermediaries." Froomkin explains that "under TCP/IP, as each intermediary receives data intended for a party further away, the data are forwarded along whatever route is most convenient at the nanosecond the data arrives. Neither sender nor receiver need know or care about the route that their data takes and there is no particular reason to expect that data will follow the same route twice."[17]

Vermut clarifies from a technical standpoint how packet-switching works for e-mail under TCP/IP's various "layers" via the simple mail transfer protocol application:

> To send a mail message . . . TCP/IP must first take the message and place it in a format that is standardized for the sending and receiving of e-mail. . . . TCP/IP handles this at the top layer known as the application layer. This layer is responsible for providing all the information and formatting so that the message can be interpreted by the application layer at the receiving end. The format includes addressing the mail with a header providing information about the sender and receiver. Next, the e-mail message is converted into a format which can be sent over the network. This is handled by the network layer. This layer takes the message and divides it into smaller chunks called packets. . . . The network layer also orders the packets so that the receiving end will know how to reassemble them.
>
> Once the packets are created, each one must be addressed to the destination. The network layer . . . [also] . . . handles this responsibility. The packets are inserted

with the necessary internet protocol address to reach their destination. The lowest layer, the data-link layer, handles all the hardware details and the transmission of the packets across the cabling. The data-link layer converts the packets into electrical impulses that travel along the physical cables.[18]

Froomkin notes that during this packet-switching process, computers in the network all communicate without knowing anything about the network technology carrying their messages. Ultimately, he points out, it is this "decentralized, anarchic, method of sending information . . . [that] . . . appealed to the Internet's early sponsor, the Defense Department, which was intrigued by a communications network that could continue to function even if a major catastrophe . . . destroyed a large fraction of the system."[19]

Consistent with the online world's decentralized, anarchic structure, architecture-based regulation can occur at various points in the system, and just about anyone from the powers-that-be to individual users can help set it in motion. Not only is architecture-based regulation potentially the most effective form of regulation currently available, but—to the extent that it can be accomplished by bypassing the legal system—it may also very well be the easiest to set in motion. Thus, otherwise libertarian commentators who typically argue that the government should stay out of cyberspace are finding that they are actually looking to the government to establish limits on what persons and groups might be able to accomplish through it.

Although, in theory, code-based changes serving to regulate the online world can occur in any segment of the Internet's architecture or at any stage of communication between computers in this networked environment, most agree that the basic "Internet plumbing" consisting of the TCP/IP protocols and the data link, network, and transport layers is likely to continue in its present form for the foreseeable future.[20] But it is possible to identify four broad types of code-based changes that can conceivably lead to significant modifications in the control of cyberspace. These changes might occur at the root server level of the domain name system, at the application layer of TCP/IP, on individual users' hard drives, or in the design of digital products that may be sold or distributed either online or offline.

Code-Based Changes at the Root Server Level of the Domain Name System

As noted, the architecture of today's Internet includes a domain name "addressing system" distributed across the network and designed to correspond to the numerical IP addresses. In cyberspace, all that is needed by *computers* to send and receive information is the Internet Protocol (IP) address consisting solely of numbers. But a second addressing scheme—the domain name system—has been created for *humans* based on characters and words. Persons, groups, and companies apply for and register their own unique domain names, which are then used by the domain name system to identify the relevant computers connected to the network. Domain names are a series of characters or words separated by periods, with the word at the right end known as the top-level domain name.[21]

Thus, on the World Wide Web, when a user types in the characters and words constituting a "Web site address," the request is initially passed along to the user's Internet service provider. When the ISP receives the request, it first searches its own servers for the corresponding IP number. Most large ISPs actually have their own "name servers" that contain IP numbers for many commonly accessed Internet domains. If the IP number is located, the site is contacted and sends back a page that is displayed on the user's screen, a process that usually takes less than a second. If the IP number for the site is not stored on the ISP's servers, the ISP then queries one of the "root servers," which have authoritative lists of domain names and their corresponding IP numbers. Once the number is found, the site is accessed.[22]

The root server, then, plays a crucial role in the day-to-day operations of cyberspace, serving as *the* "electronic directory" for the online world. As of early 2001, there were thirteen root servers on the Internet, located in different parts of the network. Ten were operating in the U.S., and three others in London, Stockholm, and Tokyo, respectively. Only one server—Root Server A—serves as the main computer holding the address database, but the system is set up to provide redundancy in case any individual system should fail. The database is updated daily, at which point the twelve secondary servers receive the new information. Without these updates, some e-mail would disappear, and certain newly posted pages on the World Wide Web would not show up.[23]

In light of the fact that the root server system—and particularly Root Server A—is the closest thing to a centralized nerve center in a decentralized network of networks, some have expressed concern that root servers are the Achilles heel of the Internet and have argued that this segment of the architecture should therefore be redesigned. They point to an incident in 1997, when employees of Network Solutions, Inc. (NSI)—the company that was delegated with the task of controlling Root Server A throughout most of the 1990s—accidentally wiped out the critical "address book." The mistake was caught within half an hour, but by then it had spread across the network, eventually affecting thirty-five percent of the computers on the Internet for hours. Among other things, all e-mail traffic to .com and .net domains in Europe broke down.[24]

In addition, with the increased focus on cyberterrorism at the turn of the century, some have questioned the level of security employed to maintain this loosely coupled system. Two of the root servers—including Root Server A—were managed in the late 1990s by the Network Information Center of the U.S. Defense Department in Vienna, Virginia, and the Army Resource Laboratory in Aberdeen, Maryland, with the military rotating the servers among undisclosed locations.[25] But the other eleven were run largely by volunteers at universities and other organizations worldwide.[26]

Beyond concerns regarding security and the fact that perhaps the root server system does not reflect the same level of independent routing capability as the other components of the online world, others have expressed concern about just who should control this Archimedean point on which the architecture of the domain name system turns, and in what manner this control should be effectuated.[27] For a long time, Saskia Sassen explains, "the power to control the root servers was not formalized, in good part because its origins lie in the first phase of the Internet." Instead, it was "the power held by the group of computer scientists who invented the communication protocols and agreed on the standards that make the Internet work today. They worked at debugging the systems over the last twenty years and did so not necessarily under contract by any agency in particular."[28]

On some ultimate level, however, the U.S. government was also operating the root server, working in concert with the Internet Assigned Numbering Authority (IANA), a group of engineers led by the late Jon Postel, to organize the necessary data and to see that the various domain servers were being properly managed. And in 1992, the government also engaged a private firm, Network Solutions, to manage and maintain the databases and servers.[29] As discussed previously, things changed significantly in the late 1990s when the government decided to delegate control of assigned names and numbers—including the operation of the root server system—to the newly formed, nonprofit, Internet Corporation for Assigned Names and Numbers.[30]

With the emergence of ICANN as the designated body in charge of working with the Department of Commerce to develop policy and ultimately assume "oversight of the operation of the authoritative root server system,"[31] the range of controversies that were inevitably generated focused as much on governance issues as they did on the technical aspects of potential code-based changes and their implications. And an examination of DNS governance quickly revealed an interconnecting structure that reflected in a classical manner the decentralized and anarchic nature of the Internet itself. As Marshall Leaffer pointed out in 1998, for example, Network Solutions at that time operated the "A" root server and other organizations operated the remaining twelve, but the U.S. government was also *involved* in operating about half of them. Leaffer describes a partnership on some level between NSI, other organizations, and the government—with the parameters of the partnership remaining imprecise and ultimately undefined.[32] Some have argued that the formation of ICANN, based as it was on a Memorandum of Understanding between the U.S. government and the new nonprofit corporation, has kept the government involved on a similar, ultimately undefined level.

In addition, another important nuance of root server management and control should be noted. As Joseph Liu has explained, no matter who is allegedly overseeing the operation of the authoritative root server, "no legal obligations require Internet hosts to consider . . . Root Server A . . . as authoritative." In fact, all of the computers on the Internet could decide to accept as authoritative a different root directory set up by another person or entity. While in practice such a result is unlikely—given the difficult task of coordinating so many computers—it must be emphasized that "the key characteristic of the entire domain name system is that it is largely legally voluntary; there exist few lines of binding legal authority."[33]

With the overwhelming majority of the online world voluntarily adhering to the current domain name system, the root server remains at the heart of the Internet architecture. As ICANN began focusing on the domain name system in its early deliberations, concerns regarding possible changes in this architecture came to the forefront. Crystallizing these concerns, David Post argued in mid-1999 that whoever has control over the operation of the root server not only has the power to determine who gets an address in any of the domains, but can also require domain server operators to comply with certain conditions:

> You can require that all domain server operators pay you a certain fee, or provide you with particular kinds of information about the people to whom they have handed out specific names and addresses, or only allow transmission of files in a specified format, or abide by a particular set of laws or rules or regulations. And you can demand that they "flow through" these conditions (or others) to anyone whom they list in their authoritative databases, that they revoke any name given to anyone who does not pay the required fee, or provide the required information, or use the specified file format, or comply with the specified rules and regulations.
>
> This is quite literally a kind of life-or-death power over the global network itself, because presence in (or absence from) this chain of interlocking servers and databases is a matter of [network] life or death: If your name and address cannot be found on the "authoritative" server, you simply do not exist—at least, not on the Internet. Eliminate the entry for xyz.com from the COM domain server and xyz.com vanishes entirely from cyberspace; designate as the new COM domain server a machine that does not have an entry for xyz.com in its database, and you have imposed the electronic equivalent of the death penalty on xyz.com.

ICANN's stormy first year ended with an agreement between the new corporation, Network Solutions, and the U.S. Department of Commerce. Noteworthy features of this agreement included formal recognition by NSI of ICANN's authority in certain areas, the licensing of companies other than NSI for the purpose of registering domain names, and the approval of procedures for handling domain name disputes.[34] But in light of the analysis set forth above, perhaps the most important development to come out of this process by the end of 1999 was the agreement to maintain something of a status quo regarding the management of the authoritative root server, and the announced intention of the Commerce Department to retain "policy authority" over the DNS root indefinitely.[35]

Code-Based Changes at the Application Layer of TCP/IP

Unlike the prospective code-based changes at the root server level described above, architecture-based regulation at the application layer of TCP/IP appears almost too easy to implement. An analysis of possible root server adjustments inevitably focuses on the complexities inherent in any attempt at Internet governance, and ultimately leads to the conclusion that the domain name system may not be very easy to modify. But an exploration of the potential for code-based changes at the application layer reveals an entirely different picture. In fact, while the domain name system has continued to operate in its same basic form, the application layer—by its very nature—continues to reflect a range of ongoing changes.

Individual portions of the application layer are so easy to change because, as Barbara Esbin explains, TCP/IP has been designed to enable those providing Internet services—as well as Netizens receiving Internet services—to operate independently and exercise their own level of free will. The routing mechanisms of TCP/IP do not define the actual services provided through the Internet to end users. Internet services depend on higher-level applications protocols, such as hypertext transport protocol (HTTP); file transfer protocol (FTP); network news transport protocol (NNTP), and simple mail transfer protocol (SMTP), which are independent of the basic Internet "plumbing" operating at the lower levels of TCP/IP. Thus, from a technical perspective, "a new application layer protocol can be operated over the Internet through as little as one server computer that transmits the data in the proper format, and one client computer that can receive and interpret the data." As Timothy Wu explains it, "coding power" in the Internet structure has therefore been delegated to the designers of applications, who have been granted "the maximum possible autonomy . . . to achieve . . . goals in whatever manner they see fit, and innovate whenever and however they like."[36]

What all this means, according to scholars who have examined the issue, is that the "application space" is where code-based regulation can occur with relative ease. This "regulation" can be achieved on either an ad hoc or a systematic basis by the powers-that-be—institutions, private companies, ISPs, etc.—and might take place on web servers, browsers, operating systems, encryption modules, Java, and e-mail systems.[37] Specific examples of code-based regulation in this context include architectures of identification, content filtering at the server or browser level, and copyright management systems.

Architectures of Identification in Cyberspace

Other than such things as static IP addresses and Pentium III serial numbers, there are generally three code-based techniques that may be used to identify a person in the relatively anonymous online world: passwords, cookies, and digital signatures. All Internet users today are familiar with passwords, which verify that the person using the system or accessing information is authorized to do so. Such verification typically occurs at the server level, when a person signs on to an ISP network, an e-mail system, or a particular Web site.[38]

Unlike passwords, cookies are code-based entries that are placed in a web browser's "cookie file" when an online user interacts with a site in a certain way. Registering at a site, purchasing goods, or configuring a web portal to deliver chosen content will all typically generate the placement of cookies directly on a person's hard drive. These cookies might include basic information that the person has provided plus other data regarding the nature and extent of previous interaction. When the person types in the Web site address at a later time, his or her browser automatically sends the cookie along with the request for that site, and the server can then set preferences according to the individual's account. The verification is seamless, and has proven quite effective over time. Persons troubled by the potential invasions of privacy in this context can instruct their browsers to accept no cookies, but they will then be prevented from accessing top sites, making online purchases, or configuring the delivery of content on Web portals.

Digital signatures are an even more elaborate and secure method of establishing identity in cyberspace. Relying on encryption technology, digital signatures enable digital certificates, which serve as a kind of passport in the online world. Digital certificates, under some designs, can reside on a user's computer, and a server might automatically check the certificate and authenticate the information after unlocking a pass phrase or biometric device as the user enters a site. If and only if the computer holds the right certificate, that user would be let in, and the server would then know all the facts that are stored on the certificate.[39]

Content Filtering by Organizations or Entities

A second major type of code-based control at the application layer of TCP/IP is content filtering. Although generally occurring at the server level, the filtering may also be enabled or adjusted at the browser level by individual users who take advantage of a system that has been set up for them on one or more servers. Content filtering systems at the turn of the century were typically created and installed by private companies, institutions, and organizations.

Filtered Access Provided by ISPs One example of such architecture-based regulation by private entities is the filtered access to cyberspace offered by certain Internet service providers. While filtering at the ISP level is not new, the practice has proliferated in recent years as legislative efforts to control online content, such as those described in chapter 5, have proven unsuccessful. Indeed, for many online users, it has become clear that affirmative steps must be taken to filter content at the individual and group level, particularly for the purpose of protecting young people. And such steps have not only been encouraged by the judiciary, but have been considered in a variety of instances by local and national legislators.

Examples of ISPs that have provided all-filtered content all the time include Integrity Online and Rated-G Online, which cater to a largely Christian market and have been operating since 1996. Others that have offered similar services include this.com, FamilyClick.com, and MayberryUSA. This.com, launched in late 1999, had an advisory board that included former U.S. Education Secretary William Bennett, former Christian Coalition Head Ralph Reed, and Wiesenthal Center Rabbi Abraham Cooper. FamilyClick.com was created by Tim Robertson, former chief of the Family Channel and son of televangelist Pat Robertson. MayberryUSA was reportedly designed for persons who want the Internet to be a little bit more like the small-town America they remember from 1960s TV. "We have everything the Net has to offer—except the smut, the hate groups, the profanity, the bomb-making and the deviant behavior," said MayberryUSA founder Richie Martin, who has advertised extensively on Christian-targeted shows.[40]

A notable force in this area has been N2H2, a company which was founded by two Seattle parents in 1995, and which originally focused primarily on the school market. By the late 1990s, its server-based filter was used in seven hundred school districts and had been sold to two hundred ISPs. The company expanded its operations significantly at the turn of the century, going public on the NASDAQ and being selected by British Telecom to provide Internet filtering services for businesses and consumers in the United Kingdom.[41]

The material that is blocked by server-based filtering services will vary, but it typically includes sex, violence, hate and illegal activity.[42] None of these services are one hundred percent effective, particularly in light of the fact that new Web sites are being created every day. But providers try to maximize their effectiveness by using lists from several companies, and some also use "intelligent" software that blocks pages on the fly—based on text or, for images, a high percentage of flesh tones. ISPs also rely on users to notify them of additional pages that should be blocked but are not.[43]

PICS Another example of content filtering at this level is the ratings protocol called the Platform for Internet Content Selection, which has been far more controversial than the ISP-based systems described above. As referenced in chapter 3, PICS is an "open platform" system that can be employed by using controls built into web browsers to allow access only to sites that have voluntarily agreed to rate their content. The system, developed by MIT's World Wide Web Consortium, was designed to be content neutral, providing online users and Web site owners with a tool to configure access based on their own specified preferences. Any group is free to design its own ratings based on PICS. Thus, an individual user might be able to configure his or her browser to access only those sites that have met the requirements of, say, a coin-collecting group, a sports station, a church organization, or even a pornography club.

From a technical perspective, PICS is nothing more than a series of standards that anyone can use as labels on content. Organizations and groups that choose to establish PICS-based rating systems can ask website authors to fill out questionnaires establishing their eligibility for a particular rating, and then send these authors sets of HTML labels, or tags. Authors can put these tags into their HTML documents, which can then be read by network computers, which process the labels in the background and either automatically shield users from undesirable material or direct their attention to sites of particular interest.[44]

This seemingly innocuous set of standards at the application layer of TCP/IP was the subject of much criticism, particularly at the beginning. Critics argued that any sort of "built-in" content control that could easily be configured at the browser level would inevitably lead to a more fragmented and less open online world.[45] Indeed, it was the "built-in" nature of the PICS system that troubled many people. Unlike ISPs that persons may sign up with for the purpose of filtering content all the time, PICS systems already came on a person's hard drive as part of the Internet browser. This, in the eyes of critics, amounted to a permanent change in the architecture of cyberspace for everyone.[46]

By 2001, PICS had not really caught on. Three PICS-based systems were being used—RSACi (sponsored by the Recreational Software Advisory Council and incorporated into Microsoft's Internet Explorer browser), SafeSurf (developed by a group of concerned parents), and NetShepherd. RSACi and SafeSurf relied on self-ratings by website authors, and NetShepherd conducted its own ratings. Each system set up categories that a user could choose to restrict—such as violence, nudity, profanity, drug use, intolerance, and gambling—and a ratings scale, usually from one to five.[47] But only a small handful of Web site owners chose to participate in these ratings system, and thus, a PICS system user seeking to restrict access to a specified category ended up with an extremely limited World Wide Web, since all the sites that chose not to participate were automatically restricted as well.

Copyright Management Systems

A third type of "fence-building" in cyberspace at the application layer of TCP/IP is the "copy management" or copyright management system. "Trusted" systems of this type continue to be developed, and some have been deployed in the online world to protect posted digital content from widespread copying and distribution. Copyright owners may choose to strengthen their control by employing such systems in concert with one or more of the architectures of identification described above.[48]

Mark Stefik, principal scientist at the Xerox Palo Alto Research Center, has played a major role both in developing and in disseminating information about trusted systems. Stefik explains that a trusted system "is a system that can be relied on to follow certain rules. In the context of digital works, a trusted system follows rules governing the terms, conditions and fees for using digital works." Thus, if a person does not have the right to copy a digital work, such a system will not allow him or her to do so. Instead, the system might provide the opportunity for the person to purchase a copy.

Purchasing a digital work via a trusted system might typically begin with the use of a network browser to select the digital work from an online distributor. At this point, the two systems—the consumer's system and the distributor's system—would need to (a) establish that they are both trusted systems and (b) determine their security levels and billing methods. Stefik writes that one way to do this is with a challenge-response protocol, which is "similar to what you might imagine in a 'spy versus spy' scenario when two secret agents who are strangers to one another first meet."[49] Such communication may be secured in a variety of ways via encryption. Once the distributor's system determines through the use of a particular application that a consumer qualifies for a copy of the digital work, it enables the requested copying.[50]

But Stefik emphasizes that even trusted systems cannot prevent all unauthorized copying. If you can print a digital page, for example, you can then photocopy or scan it. Thus, he argues, trusted systems can be strengthened by embedding digital watermarks, hidden or visible, in renderings. These watermarks may be used "as social warnings, to carry information, and to leave digital fingerprints for detecting and tracing unauthorized copying."[51]

Commentators continue to warn that copyright management systems—like architectures of identification and built-in filtering systems such as PICS—pose a great danger to the free flow of information and ideas in the online world. Internet law scholar Julie Cohen, one of the most vocal early critics of this development, rejects "the possibility that the impending digital copyright management regime constitutes no more than legitimate private ordering regarding the terms and conditions of access to copyrighted works." Exploring both the sources and justifications for an "individual right to read anonymously," she has argued that "reading is so intimately connected with speech and freedom of thought that the First Amendment should be understood to guarantee such a right." And she has suggested that proposed federal protection for digital copyright management technologies might be unconstitutional to the extent that it penalizes individuals who seek only to exercise their rights to read anonymously, or to enable others to do so. Finally, she has written that "rather than seeking to enshrine a set of practices designed to negate reader anonymity, Congress should, instead, adopt comprehensive legislation designed to shield individual reading habits from scrutiny."[52] The U.S. Congress, however, chose to follow a different direction, establishing extensive rules prohibiting online users from employing "anti-circumvention" code to get around copyright management systems that may have been set up. These prohibitions—originally included in the WIPO Agreement of 1996—are now part of the U.S. Digital Millennium Copyright Act of 1998.

Still, by the turn of the century, fears regarding the "perfect control" of online content were far from being realized. While filtering systems (particularly at the server level) have become more effective, and trusted systems (reinforced by the anticircumvention provisions of the DMCA) can provide formidable protection against unauthorized access and copying of digital works, cyberspace has, nevertheless, remained relatively free and open. Unfiltered access to the Internet is still the norm rather than the exception, and a tremendous amount of valuable content is not only still free for the taking but increases in volume on a daily basis. Yet many remain fearful that this could change significantly over time, and that code-based regulation is the perfect vehicle for ultimately perfect control.

Code-Based Changes on Individual Users' Hard Drives

In addition to code-based changes that might occur at the root server level and at the application layer of TCP/IP, architectural adjustments can take place on individual hard drives, which may have the similar effect of changing the nature of cyberspace for users. Such changes typically occur as a result of decisions by individuals or groups to pursue "self-help" remedies built into software packages that may either be downloaded online or purchased offline.

Two noteworthy examples of such self-help remedies are filtering devices that may be installed on one's personal computer and surveillance devices that law enforcement officials employ to monitor activity on the computers of particular suspects.

Filtering software is perhaps the most well-known of all the code-based strategies for changing the architecture of the Internet on an individual level. Individual software packages such as Net Nanny, CyberPatrol, and CyberSitter are becoming increasingly effective at performing a variety of tasks. Such software can block access to certain sites, filter sites containing certain keywords, prevent certain information from being sent out over the Internet by children, and track online usage by children. Although not nearly as effective as ISPs that filter content at the server level, these software packages are increasingly popular because they afford individual users the opportunity to customize and adjust code-based changes in light of personal preferences and needs.[53]

Code-based surveillance devices, on the other hand, are not nearly as well-known. Indeed, only a comparatively small number of Netizens may actually realize that the software to perform such tasks has actually existed for some time now. The monitoring devices can be e-mailed as attachments to an individual person's computer, and—if opened—may then sit on a person's hard drive and provide an "observer" with a range of information regarding both the user's online activity and the content of a user's files.

DIRT, developed by former New York City detective Frank Jones, is an example of such monitoring software. The acronym stands for Data Interception by Remote Transmission and was originally created by Jones as a tool to help catch online child pornographers. But DIRT has been used to battle hacker groups and to trap terrorists, drug dealers, money launderers, and spies. It is sold only to government and law enforcement agencies by Codex Data Systems, and enables officials to monitor and intercept data from any Windows PC in the world.[54]

The "client side" version of DIRT is less than 20KB in size and is typically installed on a target PC using a Trojan horse program, which is a set of instructions hidden inside a legitimate program. The DIRT program may be sneaked inside an e-mail attachment, a macro, or a workable program that a targeted user is enticed to download.

It appears that the most difficult challenge for those who use DIRT is luring owners of targeted computers to download and unzip the programs. Once inside a target Windows computer, however, the program is not detectable by virus scanning software and apparently gives law enforcement complete control of a hard drive without the user's knowledge. For example, DIRT starts off by secretly recording every keystroke the user makes. The next time the user goes online, DIRT transmits a log for analysis. As time passes, law enforcement officials can upload and download files to the PC without the user ever being aware that anything is taking place. In fact, government agencies have even managed to open encrypted files by obtaining password locks in this manner.[55]

Criticism of these self-help products has of course proliferated over the years. Filtering and blocking software has been mocked by libertarian Netizens as hopelessly ineffective, with commentators citing countless examples of valuable content that has been unintentionally filtered out and of Net savvy teenagers who are invariably able to bypass the code-based controls. Such criticism, however, has become more muted over time, as the software increases in popularity and as Internet content continues to proliferate in a relatively free and open fashion despite the use of content filters. And any remaining criticism has focused not on the individual user but on efforts to mandate the use of such software in schools, libraries, and workplaces.[56]

As might be expected, however, criticism of devices such as DIRT has not been as muted by those who discover its functions and become aware of its increasingly widespread use by law enforcement officials. DIRT cannot be used indiscriminately, and agencies must first obtain a wiretap search warrant, but libertarian Netizen groups such as the Electronic Frontier Foundation (EFF) have argued that this type of electronic surveillance "goes far beyond wiretap warrants because DIRT allows authorities to invisibly snoop inside a targeted PC's entire hard drive—not just monitor electronic communications." EFF spokesperson Shari Steele has insisted that unless appropriate checks and balances are in place, "DIRT can quickly go from being an effective crime-fighting tool to a privacy activist's worst nightmare." And Barry Steinhardt, associate director of the ACLU, warns that "clandestine searches like these are the worst kind . . . This is exactly the kind of search the Fourth Amendment is designed to protect us from."[57]

Code-Based Changes in the Design of Digital Products

A fourth type of change in software code that may serve a regulatory function in cyberspace is the adjustment in the design of certain digital products. Such an adjustment offline can sometimes play an indirect but significant role in the control of certain activity online.

Perhaps the most notable example of this type of code-based change in recent years is the record industry's Secure Digital Music Initiative (SDMI). As conceived by industry officials, SDMI is an attempt to control the distribution of digital music in the online world and limit the unauthorized uploading and downloading of MP3 music files.

While some in the music industry have focused on developing and marketing other file formats that would limit the transfer of digital music but would still be attractive to online users because the sound quality is better and the file size smaller, many others have determined that the best approach is to accept the fact that MP3 is the file format of the moment and to develop viable code-based solutions that work within the MP3 technology.

Thus, the SDMI plan announced at the end of 1999 sought to change the code on compact disks and other forms of digital music that were sold or distributed legally in record stores and on allegedly legal Web sites. Such a code-based change in these products was designed "to develop a secure format that would facilitate the sale and distribution of digital music while protecting the rights of the copyright owner." This protection would be accomplished by encoding digital music files in such a way that would restrict the ability of consumers to make digital copies of their music. The SDMI framework at the time was projected to be "sufficiently flexible" to permit music owners to establish differing levels of permissible usage. One copyright owner might choose to allow unrestricted use and copying, while others could set the number of permissible copies for an established price.[58]

The SDMI "specification" discussed at the time was to be implemented in two phases, with the first phase focusing on the development of portable MP3 players that would be SDMI compliant. The second phase, as envisioned at the time, would include a "check in/check out process" by which consumers could maintain a library of "protected content" on their personal computers and then "check them out" on an ongoing basis. In addition, Netizens would still be able to "rip" songs from their own CDs and transfer them onto their PCs or their portable MP3 players, but they might be limited to a certain number of copies each time a CD was inserted. Apparently, the goal of the initiative at the time was not to completely eradicate personal copying of MP3 files, but merely to "hamper" copying in such a way as to make larger-scale piracy unprofitable.[59]

While many welcomed the potential inherent in the SDMI, others—ranging from those within the music industry to those within the "MP3 community"—expressed doubt on a variety of levels. Some focused their criticism on the projected architectural changes themselves, which apparently included restrictions on the ability to play single copies on multiple machines. Others wondered why SDMI was needed, given the fact that so many MP3 collectors and traders do not seek to make a profit. Still others, concerned about the loss of profits and apparent delays in progress, jumped ship and formed splinter groups to seek code-based solutions in different ways. Many speculated on how the problem would play out in the end, with critics generating a range of pessimistic, dystopian scenarios.

Reactions to SDMI and the prospective scenarios outlined by commentators lead to the identification of key inherent restrictions in code-based regulation generally. Changes in architecture at either the powers-that-be level or the self-help level may at first glance appear to be the equivalent of perfect—or at least substantial—control, but the impact of such changes may be significantly limited by (a) the development of other code to counter the effort, and (b) conflicts with current or future laws.

In many, if not most, cases, code-based changes can be countered by other code-based changes that bypass, break through, or otherwise circumvent the new controls. These circumvention efforts may range from finding a way to turn off a feature in an application to developing new software to counter the effects of other software to elaborate forms of hacking and cracking at the national or international level. Anticircumvention rules are, of course, built into the 1996 WIPO treaty and the 1998 U.S. Digital Millennium Copyright Act, but these rules themselves may be subject to significant modification over time as courts hear lawsuits focusing on fleshing out the parameters of the statutory scheme. And even if the anticircumvention rules are upheld, there may be significant problems at the enforcement level. As described in other sections of this book, it has been extremely difficult to enforce basic copyright rules in cyberspace. Why should anticircumvention rules be any easier to enforce?

Beyond the likelihood of ongoing "code wars," with new code constantly being developed to counter other new code, certain architectural changes will undoubtedly trigger lawsuits, and some may prove to be violative of basic legal rights. The SDMI, for example, may ultimately be limited by potential conflicts with the fair use doctrine and with the rights of purchasers to use products in a particular way. New legislation may be triggered as well. Legislators analyzing the potential implications of code-based changes in selected areas may very well decide to heed the warnings of commentators and head off unintended consequences by passing laws limiting the implementation of certain architectural adjustments.

Particularly for certain problem areas, the model described in this chapter has the potential for profound and perhaps permanent transformation. Whether implemented solely by the private sector, the government, or individual users, code-based change offers the promise of both flexibility and security for stakeholders in the online world. It is, on many levels, a logical and intuitive approach—using technology to effect change in a technological environment. And it can be employed in a variety of creative ways, ranging from private sector action in a free market to architectural adjustments that are either mandated by law or are designed to work in concert with legal systems or governance plans.[60]

An analysis of the various code-based changes discussed above reveals just how wide-ranging and precise this model can be. Explorations of possible adjustments to the root server system, for example, directly address a central problem in cyberspace regulation—the inability to find a control point. Architectural changes at the application layer of TCP/IP can conceivably limit both anonymity and the free flow of content, two central barriers to regulation of the online world. Self-help measures at the hard drive level address major concerns of individual users and law enforcement officials by empowering them with tools to take control of those portions of cyberspace that they view as problematic. And SDMI might ultimately serve as an example of a technological breakthrough that enables the music industry to take back control of its product distribution.

In addition, while code-based changes may not succeed in controlling every person and every illicit activity in the online world, such a level of control may not be necessary. Several commentators have argued that "regulation need not be perfect to be effective." Lessig, for example, identifies an important distinction between "perfect control" and "effective control." "Just because perfect control is not possible," he writes, "does not mean that effective control is not possible."[61] And Wu draws an analogy between architecture-based regulation and door locks. A lock may be picked, he notes, but that does not mean that a lock cannot serve any regulating function:

> [Those who] . . . have the Internet skills equivalent to the real-space locksmith generalize from their own experience to conclude that no regulation of Cyberspace is possible. But neither the theory nor the results are convincing—if regulation is impossible, then what are criminal hackers doing in prison?[62]

Yet the prospective advantages of this model may in many cases be outweighed by its limitations and its potentially negative effects. The principle of unintended consequences, for example, certainly comes into play in this context. Building too many fences in cyberspace may not only have a negative impact on the nature of cyberspace from a free speech and privacy perspective, but it may also limit the growth of e-commerce. Proponents of commercial activity in cyberspace continually emphasize the convenience. At a certain point, however, a combination of identity verification, trusted systems, online monitoring, and offline encoding might very well drive consumers away. Local shopping malls and neighborhood stores could suddenly begin to appear much more attractive in comparison. Extensive code-based changes may ultimately backfire.

Finally, to the extent that "code is the law" and is expected to operate as law, many of the same limitations inherent in our legal system may operate in this context as well. While enforcement might at first glance be less of a problem if the architectural changes succeed in locking the digital door, there is no guarantee that this door will remain locked. Indeed, Wu's locksmith analogy may not apply in this context. Unlike the offline world, where very few people may have the tools or the wherewithal to pick locks and commit burglary, technological innovations may offer an entirely different set of circumstances. Not only might lock-picking tools become easily available to a widespread population, but social norms in the online world might operate to encourage the breaking down of digital doors.

Part II identified three basic approaches to the regulation of the online world. In some cases, these approaches have already been tried, with varying degrees of success. In many other instances, however, the prospective applicability of the three models remains speculative at best.

The inquiry at this point has revealed key advantages and disadvantages of the different regulatory approaches, and no one model has emerged as the preferred vehicle. Thus, it is important to compare and contrast the models and determine the efficacy of each one. Yet such an analysis cannot take place in a vacuum. It is only through an exploration of the potential applicability of each model to selected problems identified in part I that concrete conclusions can be drawn regarding their prospective effectiveness. We turn, in part III, to such an exploration, focusing on how these models might be employed in the future to resolve some of the major legal and policy disputes of our era.

Part III

8

Charting a Roadmap for Prospective Regulation

We are finding that both our substantive laws and procedural tools are not always adequate to keep pace with the rapid changes in technology.

—Attorney General Janet Reno, Testimony before U.S. Senate Committee, February 1999

In considering "the unique factors that affect communication in the new and technology-laden medium of the Web," we are convinced that there are crucial differences between a "brick and mortar outlet" and the online Web that dramatically affect a First Amendment analysis.

—Judge Leonard I. Garth, U.S. Court of Appeals for the Third Circuit, *ACLU v. Reno,* July 2000

At this point, we have identified a range of controversial and problematic activity in cyberspace, and we have explored three basic models that can help address the controversies and resolve the problems. In these final chapters, we focus on how the models might be used and on what conclusions can be drawn from such an analysis.

The three models—traditional national law, international agreement, and code-based regulation—are potentially very powerful, and their capacity to transform today's Internet in dramatic and far-reaching ways should not be underestimated. For example, the U.S. Congress—seeking to increase online safety, protect Netizens, and enhance e-commerce—could require driver's licenses for the Information Superhighway. Legislation would mandate the creation of a National Internet Clearinghouse, akin to a nationwide Department of Motor Vehicles, which would issue such licenses. Access to the Internet in the United States could then be limited to those who do not have a criminal record and who pass a written test regarding a new, international "acceptable use policy." The license would need to be renewed every four years, and could be revoked if an Internet-related crime is committed. The latest in voiceprint and fingerprint technology would be used to make sure that when a person logs on, his or her license number is correctly identified.

Such an approach would take advantage of features from each of the three models. There would be a national law component, an international agreement component, and code-based changes to seal the Internet off from those who do not have a "driver's license." As a result of this strategy, the online world would change in significant ways. Not only would anonymity decrease, but the powers-that-be (such as they are) would make it clear that the use of the information superhighway is a privilege and not a right. Many people concerned about issues of safety and about the integrity of e-commerce would support this far-reaching legislation.

Of course, barring any unforeseen changes in the status quo that existed at the beginning of 2001, this transformative combination of legislation, international agreement, and architectural change is highly unlikely. Given the decentralized and anarchic nature of today's Internet, and the fact that things generally seem to be working well in cyberspace on a day-to-day level, most people will probably continue to gravitate toward a position of comfort with things as they are. Thus, at the national law level, the recent U.S. combination of occasional legislation focusing on specific but limited target areas and an emerging common law based on court decisions in recent Internet-related disputes appears to be consistent with the comfort level of most Internet stakeholders.[1] At the international level, de facto agreements in the area of law enforcement and occasional formal agreements in the areas of e-commerce and intellectual property seem to be generally acceptable.[2] And at the architectural level, code-based adjustments that empower individual users but leave the basic Internet architecture alone will undoubtedly continue to be favored by the majority of persons and groups involved.[3]

Still, many people are of two minds. When asked how they feel about changes in broad regulatory patterns, they are likely to start from the position that the status quo should not be changed. But should stakeholders consider themselves impacted by a particular problem area, they will certainly support more aggressive regulatory approaches—by the government or by any of the other powers-that-be. Thus, for example, while both the information technology industry and cyberlibertarians have continued to pay lip service to the myth that the Internet is unregulated and should remain so, many within each group have supported specific regulatory measures aimed at particular problem areas. The IT industry backed the highly regulatory U.S. legislation of 1997 and 1998 aimed at tightening copyright restrictions in cyberspace,[4] while cyber-libertarians continue to argue for government action to restrict corporate practices that may impact individual privacy rights online.[5]

A snapshot in time from early 2000 may shed light on who might be the most powerful regulators in this context—both the powers-that-be as well as those who, separately or together, may have the ability to change the architecture of the online world. After a series of denial-of-service attacks on major e-commerce sites in February of that year, the White House convened an Internet security summit with high-tech leaders to plan a response. Those invited to meet with President Clinton, Attorney General Janet Reno, Commerce Secretary William Daley, and National Security Adviser Samuel E. Berger included not only several companies who had been victimized by the attacks—such as Yahoo and eBay—but also such IT industry leaders as IBM, Microsoft, and Cisco. In addition, invitations went out to major ISPs such as AOL and MCI WorldCom.[6]

A close examination of this list reveals that those invited included only key U.S. government officials and certain major IT industry representatives who have the ability to effect major code-based changes in the online world. Interestingly, the list included no volunteer Internet organizations, no legislators, no Net advocacy groups, and no representatives of other nations. Assuming for the sake of argument that the invitees were those who should be at such a meeting, and that the Clinton administration did not inadvertently leave anyone out, then the persons in the room on that day were arguably *the* regulators, *the* primary powers-that-be, *the* individuals in charge of the Internet at that moment in time. Such a conclusion is consistent with the analysis set forth above, although the failure to include other governments raises questions yet again regarding whether the Internet is truly a global medium or really just the province of the United States. Although it can be argued that the February 2000 denial-of-service attacks were only a U.S. problem, since they targeted only U.S. companies, most viewed the events as significant enough to impact the operation of the Internet as a whole. If other countries were not invited, it can be argued that their presence would not have made any difference. And if their presence would not have made any difference, then perhaps their influence is much more limited than many would believe.

Indeed, it is rare for commentators in the recent scholarly literature on cyberspace regulation to focus on any set of circumstances that does not include either the role of the United States government or the role of those who can implement code-based changes in the Internet architecture on some level.[7] This, too, is consistent with the view that those invited to the summit were, in fact, those who should have been invited.

One of the most relevant scholarly inquiries in this area focuses on the issue of private ordering in cyberspace.[8] At the heart of the topic is the ongoing tension between traditional, centralized public control and decentralized, anarchic private control of cyberspace. In particular, such tension is reflected in the IT industry's relatively consistent position that, for the most part, the government should stay away from the Internet and leave things to the companies that allegedly "understand" cyberspace and know what to do to take care of it.[9] Beyond this basic ongoing controversy, however, one of the most interesting aspects of the "public versus private ordering" debate is the analysis of the extent to which private networks have taken control of the Internet.[10]

Internet law scholar Joel Reidenberg was one of the first to point out that not only have Internet service providers and network administrators established a significant level of decentralized control over cyberspace, but that a viable model of Internet governance could very well be based on such control, with each network operating as something akin to a separate and independent state.[11] Indeed, it is through individual ISPs that people and groups typically access the Internet, and it is the network administrators who may be performing the most consistent and regular monitoring of online activity throughout cyberspace on a day-to-day level. ISPs generate their own rules through acceptable use policies (AUPs), and those who do not follow these rules can be removed from the network. While not all networks are privately owned and operated—since, for example, public colleges and universities may also serve as ISPs—the great majority of online users are signed up with private companies.

As acceptable use policies become more elaborate and as more laws are passed granting ISPs a greater level of freedom to operate without fear of liability, the ability of individual networks to control online activity has arguably increased. Many continue to believe that this is a good thing, since ISPs and, in particular, network administrators are especially well situated to address day-to-day problems online. The fight against unsolicited bulk e-mail (a.k.a. spam), for example, has been facilitated by network administrators whose AUPs increasingly warn that sending spam will result in termination of user privileges. Thus, many networks can now set up abuse desks, where users of the network who receive spam can file complaints. These complaints are forwarded to the originating ISP, where network administrators—although not legally obligated in most cases to do anything—increasingly do take action against the spammer.

On the other hand, many commentators have questioned the efficacy of a regulatory approach that relies heavily on private ordering. Some point out that those removed from one network can always sign up with another. Others have focused on particular terms of certain AUPs, and have argued for greater government control over what might be included in these policies. Some have questioned, for example, whether certain policies provide too much protection for copyrighted works by requiring that users agree to extensive and far-reaching limits on their ability to make copies. Niva Elkin-Koren has focused on information content providers in this context, questioning practices that essentially force users into private contractual agreements that may have a significant negative impact on fair use rights in the online world.[12] Elkin-Koren's analysis of content provider practices may be equally applicable within the larger universe of ISPs, especially since more than one content provider is also an ISP.

In addition to the private ordering controversy, another relevant issue for the purposes of our inquiry is the question of where and how private networks fit under the three models we identified in part II. On one level, the issues raised by the type of ISP activity described above may fit under one or more of the three models depending on the activity in question. For example, the controversy over AUPs that may limit fair use can be addressed under either the national law or international agreement models. And an examination of the role that individual networks can play in any architectural adjustment of cyberspace fits cleanly under the code-based regulation model.

A more complicated question, however, is whether ISPs at this point should be viewed as one of the powers-that-be, or simply as members of the Internet "community." If they are now considered one of the powers-that-be, and evidence increasingly points in that direction, then an argument can be made that, as a matter of policy, they are de facto agents of the state operating in an environment that should be considered, at least on some level, as public. Taking this view, some have insisted that not only should they be subject to the sort of additional restrictions that Elkin-Koren supports, but they should be obligated to maximize freedom of expression by following the basic tenets of the First Amendment.[13]

On the other hand, if networks and network administrators continue to be seen—as they have been by many—as members of the online community, then their actions might be examined through an entirely different lens. Any steps they take to limit their subscribers' rights would be viewed as no more than self-regulation, or perhaps not as regulation at all, but simply an allowable form of activity in a free and open online environment. Since many ISPs are now extremely large and profitable companies, it has become increasingly difficult to view them as community and not as powers-that-be. Yet they continue in many cases to be free to ignore such basic protections as the First and Fourth Amendments, since the Bill of Rights does not generally apply in the private sector.[14]

As the various nuances of these controversies continue to be debated in the scholarly literature, some might contend that private ordering could stand alone as a fourth model of regulation for the online world. This book, however, takes the position that a regulatory model must be all-encompassing, with the potential to address almost every controversy in cyberspace. Although private ordering can be applicable in certain situations, it may be irrelevant in many other instances. And private ordering often does not have the same implicit and explicit power that our three basic regulatory models reflect.

It is useful, then, within the context of our analysis, to identify two types of private ordering. One type, private code-based regulation, can serve a *protective* function against unlawful or inappropriate activity, and an analysis of its prospective impact fits most directly under the "architectural change" model. The other type—private rule-making by networks, content providers, institutions, and others—often attempts to *dictate* what others can and cannot do. This second type of private ordering would typically fit under self-regulation—a default position outside the three models we documented in part II and will apply in part III.

In examining how the three models—national law, international agreement, and code-based changes—might be applied in specific situations, we begin of course with the premise that not every situation in cyberspace needs to be regulated. With the Internet in general working quite well, many things should simply be left alone. But certain persistent problems have arisen that are not easily resolved. In addition, as the online world continues to change, new problematic activity will undoubtedly become apparent. In such instances, a roadmap for prospective regulation can be of great benefit to all concerned.

This roadmap—informed by the analysis in the previous chapters—begins with an inquiry into the potential for consensus through an examination of the type of problem that may exist. It continues with an exploration of just how different the setting and the activity might be from similar settings and activities offline, and concludes with a determination of the potential applicability of the three regulatory models.

Potential for Consensus The analysis in this book has been based on the premise that problems in cyberspace are most easily and effectively resolved when there is a consensus among relevant stakeholders regarding both the severity of the harm and the appropriateness of the regulatory approach. The book has recognized from the beginning that the online world is no longer free and open terrain, but rather is increasingly subject to a number of powerful entities that can be viewed as directly or indirectly in charge. It has also recognized that because of the decentralized, anarchic nature of Internet architecture and the resulting diffusion of the locus of control, the social contract is particularly important in cyberspace, and the wishes of online communities cannot be ignored. Finally, it has recognized that although some networked environments and some of the interaction that takes place in the online world may be no different than anything that exists or takes place offline, other online settings and cyberspace activities may be different enough to merit new regulatory approaches or so different as to constitute separate and unique virtual realities.

Identifying the relevant stakeholders at both the powers-that-be level and the constituency level is not always a simple task in an information technology environment that is growing and changing in unprecedented fashion. New players are continually emerging, new alliances being formed, and online constituencies shifting and regrouping in response to these changes. In the early twenty-first century, however, a representative list of such stakeholders at the powers-that-be level would include national governments (particularly lawmakers, courts, and those units with jurisdiction over certain online activity), international organizations (especially those with stakes in individual online issues and problems), national and international Internet organizations, large private companies such as Microsoft, AOL Time Warner, and Network Solutions with key stakes in online activities because of their business interests or online presence, the omnipresent Internet service providers, and other individuals and companies that develop and manufacture software.

Key constituencies include educational institutions, old media companies that have moved online, new media/entertainment industry companies, online businesses engaged in e-commerce, national and international organizations that have a vested interest in cyberspace, online-user activist groups, and other consumer groups. At some point, of course, it may be unclear which persons and groups are part of a constituency and which persons and groups constitute the powers-that-be. It may also be unclear on some level what the difference is between a constituency and a power, since both arguably have a great degree of control. In addition, given the protean nature of this environment, a group may be a constituency in the morning and one of the powers-that-be by the afternoon. The key, however, is that regulation may not be either effective or appropriate unless a consensus can be reached among these stakeholders. Otherwise, as has been evident throughout the past decade, those who feel disenfranchised will often find a way around the rules—and new problems may then emerge.

Relevant Categories of Problematic Conduct Consensus begins with agreement on the severity of the harm, because if persons and groups cannot agree that certain activity is particularly harmful or problematic, they will not support efforts to bring it under control. Thus, the categories of problems in chapter 3 were designed to provide a framework for this analysis. They were organized in a sliding scale fashion, based on the nature and extent of the harm, the likelihood that most would agree on whether the behavior should be regulated, and the prospects for consensus on a particular regulatory approach: (1) dangerous conduct, (2) fraudulent conduct, (3) unlawful anarchic conduct, and (4) inappropriate conduct.

As noted in chapter 3, the activities described in the first category would be viewed as more harmful than those in the latter categories and would certainly be more likely to generate agreement regarding both the need for regulation in general and the efficacy of possible approaches to resolving the problems. Activity described in the fourth category, however, would be expected to generate little consensus, with many stakeholders not viewing the conduct as problematic at all.

Once the category is identified and it can be ascertained what degree of consensus might be possible, we can then focus on how different the problematic setting and activity are when compared with analogous circumstances and conduct offline. As we concluded in chapter 2, such a focus will inevitably help determine which regulatory approach or combination of approaches might be most effective.[15]

Differences between Online and Offline Settings and Activities If the circumstances and acts are not radically new or different, we have argued, then traditional approaches and existing laws are likely to work best. There would typically be no need to risk unintended negative consequences by developing new regulatory approaches for alleged problems of this sort. It is clear, at this point, from our exploration of the inherent limits of our legal system that would-be regulators must proceed with caution before enacting any new laws. For settings and behaviors that are not particularly unique, responses should inevitably be limited and informed by knowledge of prior strategies that may have been successful in analogous situations.

If the circumstances and the acts are not very new or different, but there are novel jurisdiction or enforcement issues, then the traditional approaches and existing laws would only constitute part of the regulatory approach. Many people within the legal community have been wrestling extensively with cyberjurisdiction and cyber-enforcement questions, looking initially to analogous problems in the offline world. On a national level, for example, many believe that the U.S. courts are developing a viable legal framework to address jurisdiction disputes in cyberspace.[16] On a global level, commentators have identified prospective strategies for both jurisdiction and enforcement under an international model of agreement and cooperation.[17] New, code-based solutions may also be considered here, separately or in combination with other approaches.

If the setting and the behavior are significantly different, then no one formula is appropriate. Alleged problems must be examined on a case-by-case basis, and potentially unique regulatory solutions may be apparent under one or more of the three models. For some of these situations, however, there may, in fact, be no apparent solution. In such cases, it may be appropriate to allow individual users, local networks, and relevant institutions to develop strategies based on their own unique circumstances. Finally, it is important to note that a given problem may not fall cleanly under any one of these three alternatives.

To summarize, a five-step framework for analysis has emerged in this book over the course of the first eight chapters. In determining what regulatory approaches, if any, might help us address a particular problem in cyberspace, we first identify the category of allegedly problematic conduct from the list of four broad areas documented in chapter 3, and determine through this identification, certain representative characteristics of the problem. Next, we explore the potential for consensus among the various stakeholders regarding both the nature and extent of the problem and the prospects for *any* sort of regulatory solution. Then we examine just how uniquely cyber this problem might be, and analyze the extent to which such a determination might help answer the question of *how* we might regulate the problem area. Informed by the analysis in the first three steps, we continue by exploring in detail the potential applicability of each of the three basic regulatory models identified in part 2. After going through all these steps, we seek to identify a synthesis, pointing whenever possible toward a combination of realistic approaches while trying in general to avoid major changes in the current regulatory structure.

In the remainder of the book, we will employ the roadmap we have outlined to analyze four major representative problem areas. In chapters 9 and 10, we examine how conduct considered dangerous or fraudulent can effectively be regulated in cyberspace. In chapters 11 and 12, we turn to the even more complicated question of how to regulate activity in areas that many do not think of as problems. Building on the blueprint identified thus far, we point toward generating a list of relevant principles that can help guide the regulatory process across the board.

9

Combating Dangerous Conduct in Cyberspace: A Focus on Cyberterrorism

While we see no electronic disaster around the corner, this is no basis for complacency. We did find widespread capability to exploit infrastructure vulnerabilities. The capability to do harm—particularly through information networks—is real; it is growing at an alarming rate; and we have little defense against it.

—The Report of the President's Commission on Critical Infrastructure Protection, October 1997

Damage from the "Love Bug" virus and variants has already reached about $5 billion and could amount to *ten billion dollars* . . . [It] . . . is the most virulent computer bug ever created. When a person opens the infected attachment using Microsoft software such as the Outlook e-mail program, the virus sends a copy of itself to everyone in that person's address book and seeks to destroy a variety of files throughout a computer network, including picture and music files.

—"'Love Bug' Suspect Freed Pending More Evidence," Reuters: Special to CNET News.com, May 2000

The fact that I authored these tools does . . . [not] . . . mean that I condone their active use.

—Mixter, alleged author of Tribal Flood Network (TFN) software, February 2000

In the early and mid-1990s, safety-related issues often took a back seat to the free speech controversies that were at the forefront of many Internet-related inquiries. Indeed, most of the legal and policy scholarship in the years after the commercialization of NSFNET focused on questions related to expression and reflected the debates in the interrelated areas of First Amendment law, copyright law, and encryption policy. But as more and more day-to-day activity moved online—activity that included government operations, e-commerce, and interpersonal communication in general—dangerous conduct began to be part of the picture.

In chapter 3, dangerous conduct was defined as "acts and behaviors that may impact physical or national safety." Examples discussed at length included (1) threatening behavior, (2) creating and trafficking in child pornography, (3) unlicensed online health care, and (4) certain types of hacking activity that may be considered *cyberterrorism* or acts of *cyberwar*. We focus in this chapter on cyberterrorism, and we treat the February 2000 "distributed denial-of-service" attacks against major Web portals and e-commerce sites as a representative case study of problematic behavior under this category.

Denial-of-Service Attacks

Denial-of-service (DoS) attacks—at their simplest, nontechnical level—are nothing more than giant streams of useless data directed toward particular network locations. Once a network location is saturated in this manner, it gets overloaded and may have to shut down for a period of time.

Any Web site can be vulnerable to DoS attacks, which require little technical skill and were once viewed as no more than the electronic equivalent of adolescent pranks. On some level, in fact, DoS attacks may be seen as much more innocuous than other forms of electronic intrusion. They are typically masked to appear as requests for information, and—unlike computer viruses—they do not cause damage to files. In addition, unlike traditional hacking into sites, they do not change information. But large-scale DoS attacks can have a devastating effect because of their ability to close down network operations.

An earlier type of DoS attack, employed by perpetrators since 1997, decreased over time when defenses against it became well-known.[1] By late 1999, however, a much more virulent type of attack had been developed as several new software programs were created to take advantage of the open and distributed nature of the Internet. Posted online so that they were free for the taking, these programs—called "TRIN00" and "Tribal Flood Network"—enabled anonymous perpetrators to take over other computers and then use the machines as unknowing agents in distributed DoS attacks. The programs were designed to act as amplifiers and create hundreds of copies of mock requests.

According to an advisory released by the Computer Incident Advisory Capability (CIAC) of the Lawrence Livermore National Laboratory on December 21, 1999, the new DoS attacks employing TRIN00 and TFN were far more dangerous than anything that had come before:

> In the past, these attacks came from a single location and were easy to detect. TRIN00 and TFN are distributed system intruder tools. These tools launch DoS attacks from multiple computer systems at a target system simultaneously. This makes the assault hard to detect and almost impossible to track to the original attacker. Because these attacks can be launched from hundreds of computers under the command of a single attacker, they are far more dangerous than any DoS attack launched from a single location. . . . The target system can . . . be of any type because the attack is based on the TCP/IP architecture, not a flaw in any particular operating system. CIAC considers the risks presented by these DoS tools to be high. . . ."[2]

Perpetrators of distributed DoS attacks relied on the use of non-secure computers that belonged to others, planting software that essentially commandeered them for use in the operations. Typically, they would first send out probes to ascertain if particular computers were, in fact, nonsecure. These probes—the equivalent of trying an electronic doorknob to see if it is locked—reportedly happened continuously on major networks throughout early 2000. A probe does not mean that someone is looking into files or actually planting programs on hard drives, but it does indicate that an effort is being made to identify machines and possibly look for security holes. Most individual users do not even know that this is going on. Once security flaws are discovered, perpetrators attempt to transfer TRIN00 or TFN "daemons" to the unwitting computer's hard drive. If these daemons are successfully transferred, the machine can be used at a later date in coordinated attacks against other machines.

February 2000: The Internet "Under Siege"

In early February 2000, during a period of two to three days, several of the Internet's most visited sites were hit with distributed DoS attacks. Yahoo was hit first, suffering a three-hour outage on February 7. Company officials described it as a "a coordinated attack designed to take down the site." Indeed, at one point, the mock requests to access Yahoo's network came at a rate of one gigabyte—one million bits of information—per second, about what some sites handled in an entire week during this era.

Because Yahoo had been using advanced encryption technology to protect its databases, the only route for attackers was this indirect approach in this manner. "If you can't get a bomb into the building," one Internet security consultant said, "you create traffic jams in roads leading to the building." Yahoo had apparently relied on an outside firm called GlobalCenter to host its servers and take precautions to circumvent such attacks, but a company spokeswoman said that the perpetrating requests to the Yahoo servers appeared to be normal requests from regular users, and that it was therefore difficult to assess who and where the attackers were. Still, she emphasized that the attackers had not changed any information on Yahoo's sites.

Yahoo spokespersons said that the planned attack had come from more than fifty different Internet addresses and had created such a demand in a short period of time that the company was unable to serve all the Web pages that were requested. They reported that most of Yahoo's core services had been backed up, however, and that not all of the company's service was completely shut down. Unaffected sites, for example, included the free e-mail service, the e-commerce store, and the GeoCities Web site hosting service. Company engineers apparently worked quickly to identify the problem and install a system of filters that could distinguish between real requests for information and fake requests.[3]

By Wednesday morning, February 9, attacks had also impacted the operations of Amazon, eBay, CNN, eTrade, ZDNet, and Datek. Networks were snarled, and millions of legitimate visitors were thwarted. The *Wall Street Journal* reported that "almost half of the Internet's top stops" had been affected in some manner.[4] While smaller sites had been hit in this manner in the past, this was the first time that top-tier sites had been impacted by distributed DoS attacks. It was unclear whether one person or group was responsible for all the attacks, or whether the latter incidents were copycat attacks. Some speculated that the rapid succession of disruptions on a massive scale suggested that the same group was behind all of the attacks, since it would arguably be very difficult to assemble this level of attack quickly. Such a high level of traffic clearly required a large number of machines working together.

The distributed DoS attacks garnered the top headlines across the country and around the world, with journalists proclaiming that the Internet was "under siege." Commentators agreed that the attacks constituted the "largest malicious assault in the history of the Net."

While the media was quick to proclaim the attacks to be the work of "hackers," others were not so sure. In addition, it was unclear whether the attacks had been coordinated within the United States or from overseas, and what the ultimate motives of the perpetrator(s) might have been.[5]

Run-of-the-Mill Hacking or Cyberterrorism?

A threshold question under this inquiry is whether these distributed DoS attacks truly constitute cyberterrorism. Certainly, by process of elimination, such attacks go beyond anything that can be considered either inappropriate (category 4) or simply unlawful and anarchic (category 3). But might these incidents be viewed within the framework of category 2, potentially impacting economic safety but not rising to the level of danger required under category 1?

Terrorism has been defined as "the systematic use of violence as a means to intimidate or coerce societies or governments."[6] Under this traditional definition, distributed DoS attacks may not fit. There was no evidence, at least initially, of any attempt to intimidate or coerce, and the attacks were arguably not "violent."

Yet it may be appropriate to define the term *cyberterrorism* a bit differently. Behaviors other than acts of intimidation or coercion might be included in such a definition. Synonyms for *terrorism* include *anarchy, disorder, chaos, disturbance, discord, contention, lawlessness,* and *conflict.* And, in fact, certain recent types of terrorism may be described more directly by one or more of these synonyms than they would be by the terms *intimidation* or *coercion.*

In addition, it can be argued that the word *violence* in an online setting might mean something different than it does offline. *Black's Law Dictionary,* for example, defines *violent* acts as those "characterized by physical force." But it defines the word differently in other contexts. *Violent* speech, for example is defined as "vehement" or "passionate" speech. And *violent* can also mean "displaying or proceeding from extreme or intense force; caused by unexpected unnatural causes." Under such broader definitions of the term, distributed DoS attacks can arguably be viewed as violent. To the extent that they constitute speech, the speech is unquestionably vehement. And it could certainly be said that the directing of one gigabyte worth of data to a site every second amounted—in the year 2000—to "extreme or intense force caused by unexpected unnatural causes."

Thus, a new definition of *cyberterrorism* might read something like this:

> Extreme or intense force in an online setting, causing unexpected or unnatural results, and used for purposes of intimidating, coercing, or creating an atmosphere of anarchy, disorder, or chaos in a networked environment.

This definition is certainly consistent with similar uses of the term in other contexts over the past five to ten years. Media pieces, for example, have at times used the word *cyberterrorism* to refer to "hackers and attackers getting into vital portions of the nation's infrastructure," but at other times have simply equated it with the term "information warfare," which can include a wide range of online activity.[7] Others have adopted even narrower definitions. Attorney James Pooley, for example, defined *cyberterrorism* in late 1999 as "the improper posting of information on the Internet."[8]

The various examples of alleged cyberterrorism discussed in chapter 3 would also fit under such a reasonable definition of the term. In that chapter, we documented a range of prospective acts that might ultimately cripple or even shut down a nation's communication system. Such acts could conceivably cause chaos or disorder, without necessarily being used for purposes of coercion or intimidation.

Comments by Mixter—the alleged author of software that may have been used in the wave of distributed DoS attacks against top Internet sites—further reinforce the view that this conduct in fact constituted a form of cyberterrorism. In a *Los Angeles Times* interview, Mixter identified himself as a twenty-year-old male living in Germany and initially insisted that he had done nothing wrong because under relevant laws merely writing and distributing potentially harmful computer code is not illegal.

At first glance, the interview placed the events within a relatively benign context. Mixter's motivation in creating and posting the TFN software was twofold, he said. He "considered it . . . interesting from a technical perspective," and he published a working version "to make the information public and generate awareness." It turns out that Mixter had finished school about six months before these events unfolded, had been getting "some offers from security companies," and would "probably be going to work in the area of source code security auditing." In addition, long before the February 2000 attacks, he had posted copies of the program to a number of security professionals' Web sites, including a September 1999 posting to a site operated by Packet Storm, a Palo Alto-based security firm.

Upon further examination, however, the line between innocuous conduct and dangerous behavior becomes blurred. In a highly ironic revelation, for example, Packet Storm revealed that Mixter won $10,000 from the company in a recent security contest. His winning entry was "a lengthy treatise that described 'step by step' how to protect large networks against the type of attacks" that actually ended up taking place. And commentators familiar with such practices contend that folks like Mixter occupy the "murkiest territory" in the morally ambiguous world of the computer underground. "Enablers and defenders, they often insist that their work benefits the security community even as they arm its enemies."

Mixter's own reactions to the events of February 2000 also indicated that he was troubled by how things ultimately unfolded. He concluded that he had nothing but negative feelings regarding the attacks, conceding that he certainly should have expected some misuse of the software and declaring that the programs were used in this case for "overly idiotic and hysteria-generating purposes." His ultimate reaction was one of concern regarding "pretty clueless people who misuse powerful resources."[9]

In the end, the picture presented by the Mixter interview and by others who commented on the implications of the attacks was that the perpetrator's conduct had indeed risen to the level of dangerous conduct that threatens a nation's communication system. Shutting down or attempting to shut down major sites that are used by citizens of an entire country to accomplish essential tasks goes beyond simple threats to economic safety and becomes a danger to national security. This danger exists even if there is no evidence of any attempt at coercion or intimidation.

Indeed, the U.S. government, in perhaps its earliest public reaction to the new types of DoS attacks, issued warnings to the Internet community that placed this type of behavior squarely within the context of a national security threat. On December 6, 1999, for example, the FBI's National Infrastructure Protection Center issued a "security alert" that reported earlier incidents of distributed DoS attacks on "different civilian, university, and U.S. government systems." The NIPC expressed concern "about the scale and significance of these incidents" because—among other things—they represented "a possibly significant threat to Internet traffic." And the alert warned that "possible motives for this malicious activity range from exploit demonstration, to exploration or reconnaissance, to preparation for widespread denial of service attacks."[10]

Less-publicized attacks preceding the events of early February 2000 had, in fact, included efforts to disable communication systems . One incident, for example, was synchronized with the World Trade Organization summit in Seattle and succeeded in shutting down the WTO's web server computers.[11] Other incidents were reported at major universities nationwide. At UCLA, according to a campus bulletin issued in late January 2000, "an unknown assailant launched a very high bandwidth denial of service attack at a computer on a UCLA department network. This resulted in UCLA's T3 connection from the Internet becoming saturated and created a denial of service situation for the entire campus," which persisted for about two hours, until technicians succeeded in rerouting the "offending inbound traffic."[12] On February 8, during the period of widespread attacks on major Internet sites, UCLA was hit again.[13]

In the aftermath of the February attacks, the Clinton administration made it clear that it continued to view these events within the context of national security. The U.S. cybersecurity summit, convened to discuss the implications of these attacks, included both Attorney General Janet Reno and National Security Council Director Sandy Berger on the invitiation list. And just a few weeks later, a leading U.S. cyberwar expert told the Joint Economic Committee that "the very same means" that the perpetrators used in the distributed DoS attacks "could also be used on a much more massive scale at the nation-state level to generate truly damaging interruptions" to both the national economy and the nation's infrastructure.[14]

Protecting Against Cyberterrorism: An Initial Assessment of Regulatory Options

To determine what proactive regulatory approaches—if any—might help address the problem of cyberterrorism, we analyze the potential for consensus and explore the ways in which distributed denial-of-service attacks in cyberspace are different from analogous activities and settings in the offline world. Based on these initial findings, we then focus on the potential applicability of one or more of the three regulatory models.

Consensus For the problems in categories 1 and 2, consensus is not typically an issue, since the categories were organized in part by the likelihood that some degree of consensus could be reached in advance. Cyberterrorism as exemplified by distributed DoS attacks fits right in here. Most—if not all—stakeholders would agree that such attacks are indeed a problem, and that something more must be done from a regulatory perspective to address the problem in the future. The unresolved question, in this case, is twofold—what should be done to counter cyberterrorism, and who should do it.

In seeking an answer to this two-part question, we examine the appropriateness of particular problem-solving approaches. And, as we concluded in earlier chapters, such an examination is typically a function of how unique the setting and the activity might be.

Uniqueness of Conduct and Setting In some ways, distributed denial-of-service attacks are very similar to certain types of criminal conduct that take place offline. Although not directly analogous to specific offline crimes, the attacks embody features of activity that is certainly not atypical in a criminal law setting. Such activity involves the intentional use of force, directed without consent toward particular individuals or groups, and resulting in some degree of injury.

But while the *conduct* in this case may be fairly similar to criminal activity that has taken place from time immemorial, the online *setting* embodies features that create a certain degree of uniqueness. Commentators have noted, for example, the relative ease with which such crimes are committed in cyberspace, and how effortless it is to impact large numbers of people. In addition, cyberspace offers criminals a greater opportunity to remain anonymous. These features not only affect law enforcement operations, but they make such attacks more difficult to prevent. On the other hand, the unique availability of code as a potential controlling force in cyberspace may operate to the benefit of regulators in this setting.

It appears, then, that no one model or approach in and of itself is effective in countering cyberterrorism. Traditional strategies based on analogous laws are a good starting point, but they arguably need to be supplemented by code-based regulations. In addition, from an enforcement perspective, there is a need for an international regulation strategy as well. It is appropriate, therefore, to examine the potential ways that all three regulatory models might be employed to address the problem of distributed denial-of-service attacks.

Traditional Regulation under National Law

Overview of Applicable U.S. Law

In analyzing what might be done under traditional national law, we start with the fact that, in general, such activity is already prohibited in the United States. Under the Computer Fraud and Abuse Act, for example, it is a federal crime to knowingly access computers without authorization, obtain unauthorized information with intent to defraud, or "cause damage" to "protected computers" in one of three ways:

> (a) knowingly . . . [causing] . . . the transmission of a program, information, code, or command, and as a result of such conduct, intentionally . . . [causing] . . . damage without authorization, to a protected computer;
> (b) intentionally . . . [accessing] . . . a protected computer without authorization, and as a result of such conduct, recklessly . . . [causing] . . . damage; or
> (c) intentionally . . . [accessing] . . . a protected computer without authorization, and as a result of such conduct, . . . [causing] . . . damage;

A "protected computer" is defined as one that is used exclusively either for "a financial institution or the United States Government," or "in interstate or foreign commerce or communication." "Damage" is defined as "any impairment to the integrity or availability of data, a program, a system, or information, that

> (a) causes loss aggregating at least $5,000 in value during any 1-year period to one or more individuals;
> (b) modifies or impairs, or potentially modifies or impairs, the medical examination, diagnosis, treatment, or care of one or more individuals;
> (c) causes physical injury to any person; or
> (d) threatens public health or safety;[15]

Punishment for perpetrators who have been identified and caught will vary under this act, but can include a substantial fine and a jail term of up to five to ten years for first-time offenders, depending on which subsection has been violated. The criminals would face civil penalties as well.

In addition to federal law, certain state laws might conceivably be employed by law enforcement officials. These may include both specific statutes aimed at computer-related fraud or abuse in a networked environment and general laws prohibiting trespass to property. An example of the former is California Penal Code Section 502, a provision of the state's "crimes against property" laws. The section prohibits "unauthorized access to computers, computer systems and computer data," and under Paragraph (c)(5), a person can be prosecuted if he or she "knowingly and without permission disrupts or causes the disruption of computer services or denies or causes the denial of computer services to an authorized user of a computer, computer system or computer network." Such a statute could conceivably enable California state officials to prosecute any California residents who might have engineered the denial-of-service attack against Yahoo, a California corporation.

For states that do not currently have such specific laws, generic laws establishing criminal penalties for trespass may also be applicable. The penalties are typically not as severe, but they arguably provide law enforcement officials with yet another legal "hook."[16]

Finally, it should be noted that perpetrators could be subject to *civil* liability under a variety of legal theories. *Trespass to chattels,* for example, has already been successfully employed as a relevant legal doctrine by CompuServe, a large ISP and content provider, in a major 1997 lawsuit focusing on spam. Under the doctrine of trespass to chattels, a plaintiff must show either that the defendant has taken possession of the plaintiff's personal property or that the defendant used or intermeddled with the plaintiff's personal property. In the lawsuit, CompuServe sued Cyber Promotions, a company that had been sending large amounts of unsolicited commercial e-mail advertisements to unwilling recipients. CompuServe asked the company to stop sending 'spam' to its subscribers, but Cyber Promotions ignored the request, and instead began disguising the origins of its e-mail messages to prevent CompuServe from blocking them.

The court ordered Cyber Promotions to stop sending spam to any e-mail address maintained by CompuServe. It also held that the act of sending these messages constituted a common-law trespass to chattels. Judge James L. Graham, a federal district court judge in Ohio, found that because an inordinate amount of space was used to store the unwanted messages and because computer time was used up by attempts to reply to messages with forged origins, the act of sending unwanted e-mails to

CompuServe customers interfered with its ability to use its computers for their intended purposes.[17]

Prospective plaintiffs suing perpetrators of denial-of-service attacks could certainly argue that not only is the trespass to chattels doctrine applicable in general to this type of situation, but that the DoS attacks are actually analogous to spam in that they also involve the transmission of unwanted data to a particular network location. If spam can be countered by lawsuits under the trespass to chattels doctrine, then it would seem to follow that DoS attacks could be countered in the same way. Such a conclusion would be bolstered by recent scholarship documenting the potential applicability of the trespass to chattels doctrine to counter other similar Internet-related activity at both the criminal and the civil levels.[18]

Thus, it is apparent that there are already a range of laws addressing acts that might be considered cyberterrorism. Some were written specifically to address computer network activity, while others are rooted in the common law and go back many centuries. Most people do not have a problem with such laws. Indeed, it is highly unlikely that any law-abiding citizen would criticize statutes and case-law doctrine prohibiting either computer fraud and abuse or trespass to personal property in general.

Yet whenever existing laws apply to cyberspace—even if they are relatively popular—it is appropriate to ask whether any additions or modifications might be necessary in light of changing circumstances. Due to the fact that new technology is continually emerging and new code-based adjustments are constantly being implemented, existing legal principles may not be sufficient. In fact, the Computer Fraud and Abuse Act itself, originally promulgated in 1984, was amended for these very reasons in 1986, 1988, 1989, 1990, 1994, and 1996.

Assuming that the current laws are an appropriate baseline, two questions might be asked: (1) should additional amendments to the Computer Fraud and Abuse Act be adopted, and (2) should any new laws be passed in this area?

Modifying or Beefing Up Existing Laws

U.S. Attorney General Janet Reno, testifying before a Senate Subcommittee in the week after the February 2000 distributed DoS attacks, addressed these very questions. Discussing what she called "the challenge of fighting cybercrime," she declared that "the challenges come in many forms: technical problems in tracing criminals online, resource issues facing federal, state, and local law enforcement in being able to undertake online criminal investigations and obtain evidence stored in computers, and *legal deficiencies caused by changes in technology.*" She went on to say that legal issues were "critical," and that "both our substantive laws and procedural tools are not always adequate to keep pace" with these rapid changes.

Reno suggested to the senate panel that the United States may need to "strengthen" the Computer Fraud and Abuse Act by "closing a loophole that allows computer hackers who have caused a large amount of damage to a network of computers to escape punishment if no individual computer sustained over $5,000 worth of damage." She also argued that it may be necessary to update what she called the "trap and trace laws," under which law enforcement officials "are able to identify the origin and destination of telephone calls and computer messages." Under current U.S. law, it is sometimes necessary to obtain court orders in multiple jurisdictions to trace a single communication. "It might be extremely helpful," Reno said, "to provide nationwide effect for trap and trace orders."[19]

In particular, as the types of cybercrimes change, some believe that the scope of the Computer Fraud and Abuse Act may need to be expanded to incorporate behavior that would be enabled by technological advances. Other suggestions for possible adjustments to the act include greater penalties—particularly for acts that may reasonably be construed as cyberterrorism. The act already mandates twice as much jail time for obtaining information requiring protection against "unauthorized disclosure for reasons of national defense or foreign relations . . . with reason to believe that such information so obtained could be used to the injury of the United States, or to the advantage of any foreign nation." Other similarly egregious activity that may directly or indirectly impact national security should arguably have the same level of punishment—either in the same act or in a new act specifically addressing cyberterrorism. Such additions would be consistent with offline penalties for terrorism that currently exist.

Developing New Laws to Counter Cyberterrorism and Address Counteroffensive Activity

Another possible change would be to mandate penalties for those who probe computers to see if they are secure. This digital equivalent of "trying a door to see if it is locked" is currently viewed by network administrators as an essentially legal activity, and most are at a loss as to what should be done about it. In early 2000, for example, probes of computers on college campus networks continued to take place on a regular basis, and some of the computers that were found to be nonsecure ended up being used in distributed DoS attacks. The traditional rules of trespass might be useful here, since a probe—like unsolicited bulk e-mail—can be considered a form of trespass to private property. But it may be more appropriate simply to prohibit the conduct explicitly.

Lawmakers may also wish to consider addressing the volatile issue of retaliatory, counteroffensive activity in this context. Such behavior, which some justify as "self-defense" and others decry as "cybervigilantism," has apparently proliferated on the Internet in recent years. Private companies have increasingly turned to private security agents, who have assisted them in developing measures that are not just defensive, but also include counteroffensive acts designed to punish and deter perpetrators who have been identified.[20]

Corporations and organizations that have resorted to such measures either do not trust law enforcement officials or have become frustrated by what they view as the inability of state and federal agencies to stop cybercrime. Increasingly emboldened, these persons and groups are striking back against network attacks that may range from simple hacking and cracking to elaborate instances of cyberterrorism. Retaliation is often accomplished "with military efficiency and intensity,"[21] and has fueled a debate regarding the nature and extent of a company's right to defend itself.

Perhaps the most extreme reported example of such corporate vigilantism was documented in a January 1999 *Network World* piece. According to an anonymous "senior security manager at one of the country's largest financial institutions," his group had management approval to do "whatever it takes" to protect the firm's corporate network and its assets. "We have actually gotten on a plane," he declared, "and visited the physical location where the attacks began. We've broken in, stolen the computers and left a note: 'See how it feels?'" On one occasion, he added, "we had to resort to baseball bats. That's what these punks will understand. Then word gets around, and we're left alone. That's all we want, to be left alone."

Such offline retaliatory activity, however, is viewed as an aberration. Most of the companies that engage in counteroffensive measures limit their acts to cyberspace. And the number appears to be growing. A late 1990s study conducted by an intelligence firm in Annapolis indicated that thirty-two percent of the 320 Fortune 500 companies it surveyed had installed counteroffensive software.[22] These companies are motivated by the view that particularly on the Internet, people must be willing to take matters into their own hands. They recognize that purely defensive measures such as firewalls, passwords, and access control lists may not always be sufficient. In addition, many believe that law enforcement officials are simply not up to the task of protecting them in cyberspace. Complaints regarding law enforcement from top firms in the United States refer to lack of staff, lack of funding, courts overcrowded with cases, and the "snail-like" speed at which typical law enforcement investigations run. And some companies are also fearful of what might happen if they do bring in law enforcement officials. Many distrust the FBI, and worry that sensitive corporate information will not be protected.

Counteroffensive online measures might be as simple as sending strongly worded messages to the source IP address or to an ISP in the path. But retaliatory acts often go far beyond simple messages. "Strike-back" software has been around for some time now, and new products are being developed every day. Sidewinder, for example, is a novel firewall with strike-back capabilities. If it senses an attack, it launches a daemon that will trigger the offensive techniques of your choice. Other examples include counterattacks via massive e-mail spamming, the so-called Ping of Death,[23] and hostile Java applets. The Pentagon itself defended its Web site in this manner against the Electronic Disturbance Theater, a group of activists that practiced cyber civil disobedience. When the group launched a denial-of-service attack against the Pentagon site in late 1998, the Pentagon responded by redirecting the requests to a Java applet programmed to issue a counteroffensive. The applet flooded the browsers used to launch the attack with graphics and messages, causing them to crash.[24]

While no one disputes the legality of purely defensive software that is the functional equivalent of building a wall around one's property, many have raised questions regarding whether counteroffensive measures such as those described above can or should be justified as a type of self-defense under national law. As a practical matter, this issue can either be left to the courts to flesh out over time under common law, or to legislators who might wish to address the question by putting together a relevant statute.

Common law is the default approach. If nothing is done by the powers-that-be to change the status quo, then cases of cyber self-defense will inevitably be brought to trial, and U.S. courts can tap into the large body of common law that already exists to address offline self-defense in both the criminal and the civil context.[25]

Under common law, four separate but related doctrines have emerged in this area over the centuries: self-defense, defense of others, defense of habitation, and defense of property. Aggressive defensive or counteroffensive measures such as the ones described above may qualify under either the "defense of habitation" or the "defense of property" doctrine. The distinction is important because persons are generally given much more leeway to defend their dwelling than other property.

Companies seeking the protection of the "habitation" rule would start by attempting to establish the principle that defending a business would be akin to defending a dwelling. They would note that in many prior cases the traditional doctrine of "defense of habitation" has been held to include the defense of a store, office, or other place of business.[26] Under this view, they would contend, defending a business presence in cyberspace would be analogous to defending a place of business offline. Prosecutors or plaintiffs would counter that a Web site does not automatically qualify as a place of business. They would explain, for example, that many company sites are relatively passive, with no business actually being conducted there. And even if business is conducted there, an interactive Web site may be seen by the courts as different from a tangible business location. The whole idea behind the "defense of habitation" rule is that a person's home is viewed as his or her "castle," and thus, he or she is entitled to protect it by using reasonable force. Establishing an analogy between an online Web site and an offline castle might be viewed as too much of a stretch.

Still, if a defendant company somehow succeeds in getting a court to recognize this analogy, then it could invoke the rule that a "dweller" (or in this case a business owner) is allowed to use reasonable *nondeadly* force to save the dwelling/business site from damage or destruction, or to preserve its character by preventing unlawful intrusion. And he or she would even be allowed to use *deadly* force against an intruder who the business owner reasonably believes intended to conduct a malicious attack that might destroy the dwelling/site by fire, explosion, or in some other manner.

A next step under a common law analysis is to determine whether the force used to counter cyberattacks in a given situation should actually be considered "deadly" or "nondeadly." The law is much kinder to those who use nondeadly force in self-defense and, understandably, much less tolerant of those who kill or attempt to kill in self-defense. Deadly force has been defined as "force intended or likely to cause death or great bodily harm." Could counteroffensive activity in cyberspace such as the behavior described above ever be considered analogous to deadly force? It might actually be argued that counteroffensive activity that succeeds in completely shutting down a perpetrator's operations or removes a perpetrator from the Internet might be viewed as the cyberequivalent of deadly force. But the more likely view is that deadly force under this doctrine only addresses physical attacks against individuals, and thus, the only time the doctrine would apply is if a cyber-vigilante attacked a perpetrator offline with a baseball bat or similar dangerous weapon. In all other cases, we would probably be talking about nondeadly force.

Finally, the courts would need to determine whether even nondeadly force is justified in cyberspace under the "defense of habitation" rule, and this is likely to depend on the nature of the counteroffensive attack. The rule appears to contemplate protection for defendants when an immediate response is necessary to repel an imminent attack. Thus, any responses that are generated after the attack has already happened would probably not be justified. Some sort of counteroffensive measure once the imminence of the attack is known might be allowed, but with attacks such as this happening so quickly in cyberspace, it may not be possible to head them off. Defendants might argue that a counteroffensive act should be justified under this rule as a preemptive measure to protect against the next attack, but absent concrete knowledge that another attack is forthcoming, it is not likely that the courts would rule for the defendants. And if the courts do not rule for the defendants under the "defense of habitation" rule, they are certainly not likely to rule for them under the lesser protection of the "defense of property" doctrine.

One other set of common law principles should be noted here. Over time, there have been a good number of criminal and civil cases involving the use of such "automatic" devices as spring guns, traps, and vicious dogs to defend property. Certain types of counteroffensive software used in cyberspace might be viewed as analogous to these types of offline measures; however, defendants are not likely to gain anything by having the courts recognize this analogy. Offline defendants using spring guns, traps, and vicious dogs to defend their property are held to the same standards that would apply if they themselves had engaged in similar activity. Thus, if a spring gun had gone off and maimed an intruder who had broken down a door, the owner of the property would be absolved of any criminal or civil responsibility only if he or she would have been justified in maiming the intruder had he or she been standing there under the same circumstances.

Perhaps the only way defenders employing counteroffensive measures might prevail in a common law setting would be if they could somehow be granted the greater protection the law affords to those who defend *themselves* rather than their dwelling or property. The law recognizes that once an intruder actually enters a person's home, the liberal rules of self-defense replace the more stringent rules governing defense of a dwelling. A person defending himself or herself may use such force as reasonably appears to be necessary to protect against the imminent use of unlawful force. Defendants might succeed in getting a court to recognize that any extreme counteroffensive measures are justified in a cyberspace setting because the cyberattacks amounted to an actual intrusion rather than simply the threat of intrusion. But again, the defendants would be limited by the requirement of imminence. Under common law, once the initial intrusion and accompanying threat is over, defendants are not justified in conducting any sort of counteroffensive or retaliatory attack.

As can be seen from the above analysis, common law is a complex and elaborate process. Cases often take a great deal of time before they come to trial, and at trial members of the legal community are faced with a range of intricate legal principles derived from thousands of prior cases that may or may not be viewed as directly applicable to an online setting. For this reason, as discussed in earlier chapters, many believe that simply allowing common law to take its course is inappropriate for Internet-related issues.

Unlike the common law, legislation addressing such issues can cut to the chase, zeroing in on the exact type of new behavior that has generated concern. Congress, for example, may decide to grant defenders of cyberattacks additional new rights above and beyond those that may exist in an offline setting. Or they may decide to expressly prohibit the more extreme types of countermeasures discussed above. In either case, the rules would be clarified, and some semblance of order brought to an area that some think may spiral out of control.

It should be noted once again, however, that legislation is not necessarily a panacea. History is filled with instances of laws passed by Congress that prove ineffective for one reason or another. The story in chapter 5 of failed congressional efforts to protect children from obscenity and pornography is a perfect example of the challenges regulators face. And lawmakers must continually beware of any unintended consequences that might flow from additional legislation. Especially given the fact result the Internet is a relatively recent creation that no one may completely understand—and a medium that could change drastically over time—many commentators continue to argue that great caution should be exercised before *any* new Internet-related laws are passed.

Finally, it must be emphasized that neither the existing legal principles nor any proposed legislative changes will be particularly effective if cybercriminals cannot be identified. Any law, of course, creates some level of deterrent effect just by being on the books. But if it becomes clear that it is easy to avoid prosecution simply by avoiding detection, then a law can quickly become irrelevant. Particularly in the aftermath of the February 2000 distributed DoS attacks, when no one seemed to be able to identify the perpetrators, such questions came to the forefront. Everyone agrees that it is impossible to catch every criminal. But if major, high-profile cybercrimes remain unsolved because law enforcement officials cannot even determine who the attackers are, then additional lawless behavior can certainly be expected. Such behavior only perpetuates the image of cyberspace as a lawless frontier that remains out of control, with continued negative consequences for all major stakeholders in the online world.

Strengthening Law Enforcement Efforts

At the turn of the century, federal law enforcement efforts in cyberspace appeared to be undergoing a period of significant transition. President Clinton had asked Congress for a substantial amount of money to increase both the amount and the scope of crime-fighting operations in the online world, and this budget request resulted in a great deal of reflection on both the effectiveness of previous efforts and the prospects for greater success in the future.

In her February 2000 testimony before a Congressional subcommittee, Attorney General Reno addressed the law enforcement issue from several perspectives, focusing on challenges at both the national and the international levels. In addition to arguing for "more robust procedural tools to allow state authorities to more easily gather evidence located outside their jurisdictions," she emphasized the need for increased law enforcement efforts across the board.

Reno noted that several federal agencies were beginning to devote significant resources to cyberterrorism and cybercrime. She explained that computer crime investigators in a number of FBI field offices had been coordinating information with the National Infrastructure Protection Center (NIPC), and that the agents were also working closely with the Justice Department's network of "specially trained computer crime prosecutors who were available 24 hours a day/7 days a week to provide legal advice and obtain whatever court orders are necessary."

In the testimony, the emerging role of these specially trained attorneys—who comprised the Criminal Division's Computer Crime and Intellectual Property Section (CCIPS)—was given particular emphasis. According to Reno, these attorneys constituted "the cornerstone" of the Justice Department's "cybercrime program," and were "experts in the legal, technological, and practical challenges involved in investigating and prosecuting cybercrime."[27]

CCIPS responsibilities in early 2000 included criminal prosecutions in general, taking a lead role in certain computer crime and intellectual property investigations, and a coordinating role in national investigations such as the one focusing on the February DoS attacks. CCIPS was also described as "a central point of contact for investigators and prosecutors who confront investigative problems with emerging technologies."[28]

Reno pointed proudly to specific CCIPS accomplishments, which included working with U.S. Attorneys, the FBI, and state law enforcement officials to help "ensure that David Smith, the creator of the Melissa virus, pled guilty to a violation of the computer fraud statute and admitted to causing damages in excess of $80 million." She also praised the efforts of the Computer and Telecommunications Coordinators, who, in her words, were "responsible for the prosecution of computer crimes across the country, including the prosecution of . . . Kevin Mitnick in Los Angeles, the prosecution of the hacker group 'Global Hell' in Dallas, and the prosecution of White House web page hacker, Eric Burns, in Alexandria, Virginia."[29]

Reno concluded her extensive testimony by emphasizing that the U.S. Justice Department "had the prosecutorial infrastructure in place to combat cybercrime," but that they needed additional resources "to keep pace with the growing problem." This testimony has certainly been reinforced by mounting evidence that, at least in certain areas, national law enforcement officials have been unable to bring things under control.

Clearly, a strengthening of law enforcement resources—with or without the passage of any new legislation in this area—will help U.S. officials stay abreast of the problem. But efforts under the national law model may not be sufficient, given the global nature of the medium and the rapid changes in technology. It is necessary to explore what might also be done to counter cyberterrorism under both the international cooperation model and the code-based regulation model.

Additional Regulation under the International Cooperation Model

Even though the distributed DoS attacks we have analyzed were directed only toward U.S. sites, most would agree that on some level cyberterrorism is not simply a U.S. concern, but a problem that may impact all Netizens and every entity with an online presence across the globe. Given this level of agreement, it is likely that a consensus can be reached not only on a national level but an international level as well regarding the need to take more affirmative and aggressive steps to counter this threat.[30]

Under traditional principles of international law common to most if not all nations, cyber-attacks—a type of unprovoked and unjustified use of force directed toward person or property—will undoubtedly be viewed as unacceptable, as they would be under any set of generic principles, whether these principles are labeled "natural law," "*jus cogens,*" or "equity." Indeed, the right to be free from the unprovoked and unjustified use of force is likely to be viewed as "so fundamental and universal that it is deemed to transcend the consent of the states."[31] In addition, the laws of many nations explicitly outlaw various forms of terrorism, including the type of online activity described above, and there are innumerable treaties that commit states to fight terrorism no matter where it might occur. Yet the basic underlying problem in international law, as discussed in chapter 6, is that it typically relies on the good faith of individual nations. Enforcement is almost always an issue.

Attorney General Reno addressed international aspects of cybercrime in her early 2000 congressional testimony. On several occasions, she referred to "the borderless nature of computer crime," and emphasized "the importance of cooperation and sharing with state and local law enforcement *and our international counterparts.*"[32] She urged Congress to consider the technical challenges created by "a global medium that does not recognize physical and jurisdictional boundaries." "A hacker," she said, "armed with no more than a computer and modem, can access computers anywhere around the globe. They need no passports and pass no checkpoints as they commit their crimes."

Reno explained that while the United States was working with "our counterparts in other countries to develop an international response, we must recognize that not all countries are as concerned about computer threats as we are. Indeed, some countries have weak laws, or no laws, against computer crimes, creating a major obstacle to solving and to prosecuting computer crimes." She was "quite concerned that one or more nations will become 'safe havens' for cyber-criminals."

In the end, Reno declared that "we need to develop effective partnerships with other nations to encourage them to enact laws that adequately address cybercrime and to provide assistance in cybercrime investigations.

A balanced international strategy for combating cybercrime should be at the top of our national security agenda."

The U.S. Attorney General's testimony was revealing, focusing as it did on both jurisdiction and enforcement problems in an international context. It is clear that, at least from the Justice Department's perspective, the United States cannot go at it alone in this area. International cooperation is essential if the problem of cyberterrorism is to be adequately addressed.[33]

As discussed, many nations already work together in a variety of ways to track down criminals, facilitate extradition, and combat lawlessness across the globe. This cooperation might be expanded by establishing consistent cybercrime prohibitions from country to country, perhaps through the development of a new international convention that most nations would agree to adopt. Such a strategy might be built on the model of international agreement adopted by the UN's World Intellectual Property Organization, which administers the Berne Convention. Another model might be the world community's approach to countering offline terrorism, given that many countries work together very closely in this regard.

Yet another approach would be to establish a new international agency to address Internet security issues. Such an agency might be formed under the auspices of an existing organization, such as the UN or the WTO. Alternatively, it could be completely separate and independent. The agency might focus on everything from the development of model penal code statutes and the identification of common standards and protocols for security to the establishment of an international tribunal with jurisdiction and enforcement powers over cyberterrorists.

The potential effectiveness of consistent laws, mutually agreed-upon standards, and some sort of international adjudicatory body cannot be discounted. In chapter 6, for example, we discussed at length the potential advantages of an international court, and examined the typical hurdles that have prevented the "World Court" from having much of an impact. We also noted, however, that the WTO has been able to overcome these hurdles, providing a viable framework for negotiating agreements and resolving disputes in the area of international trade. The key, of course, is that not only must members agree to participate in this process and accept the jurisdiction of the agency over its citizens, but that all are subject to the greatly enhanced powers of genuine enforcement for panel decisions.[34]

Not all nations, of course, will agree to participate in such arrangements. As with offline terrorism, there may always be rogue states who for one reason or another try to operate outside of any international constraints. In addition, politically motivated cyber-attacks will inevitably be complicated by the state of international relations at the time. For example, a cyberwar of sorts developed between hackers from Taiwan and the People's Republic of China in July 1999, after Taiwan President Lee Teng-hui called for bilateral ties to be conducted on a "special state-to-state" basis. By March 2000, with elections approaching, Taiwan's military reportedly set up Internet defenses after allegedly discovering more than seven thousand attempts by Chinese hackers to enter the country's security and military systems through Internet Web sites. A Taiwan government spokesperson also reported concerns regarding possible interference with online vote tabulation networks through the swamping of government Web sites "with huge megabytes of electronic mail or e-mail bombs."[35]

International tensions and geopolitical realities will always impact efforts to expand international cooperation. But, as with the offline world, the more nations that can agree, the greater the potential for effective measures in this context. And such measures can be reinforced by efforts of organizations such as Interpol.[36] Proposals have surfaced to develop similar private global security agencies for the online world, or to expand the scope of Interpol's own international activities so that they might include cyberspace.[37]

While the development and implementation of any new international law enforcement mechanism is a challenging task, such a task might be much easier in an era of increasing globalization, with so many nations working together on so many fronts. The Internet has already served as a major unifying force in this context, and a new international agency designed to strengthen cyber-security and expand the effectiveness of online communication and global e-commerce may prove to be an idea whose time has come.

Changing Internet Architecture to Maximize Security

Many believe that code-based architectural adjustments constitute the most realistic and practical approach to the problem of cyberterrorism. They point out that in the offline world, we do not simply rely on law enforcement officials to combat crime. We also lock our doors, install security alarms, and buy high-tech devices such as lo-jack to deter auto theft. Code-based adjustments would constitute the online equivalent of such crime-fighting efforts. Particularly in the aftermath of the February 2000 distributed DoS attacks, industry spokespersons consistently referred to this model as the logical centerpiece of any effort to counter such activity. At the same time, software developers and Internet security experts outlined the variety of code-based tools that could be employed by both the powers-that-be and individual online users.

By mid-2000, there were a range of viable strategies available, including filters and related defensive procedures to protect the sites themselves, security measures to prevent computers from being used as unwitting agents in distributed attacks, and software that could reroute attacks either to standby computers or back against the perpetrators. In addition, analysts identified a number of possible initiatives that could lead to wide-ranging architectural changes across-the-board. These initiatives included the introduction of a new IETF standard that would limit anonymity, proposals to redesign computer operating systems, and suggestions for changing Internet communications protocols across the board. Finally, security experts insisted that the entire online world could become much safer if software developers stopped marketing "flawed products" that "boosted the Internet's vulnerability to rapidly evolving forms of cyber-attack."[38]

Filtering Software and Related Defensive Measures

The simplest code-based strategy available to Web site owners in the year 2000 was to rely on defensive software. Several products of this type were readily available, either as built-in features of existing routers or as separate and independent products. Cisco, for example, a company that has played a central role as the "traffic cop" of the Internet backbone, reported in early 2000 that it had designed its products to include a variety of built-in filtering tools and other defensive measures. Indeed, given the fact that almost all Internet traffic apparently moves through Cisco's equipment at some point, the company has increasingly urged online businesses to "take a proactive approach to Internet security." Such an approach includes activating the tools it provides, "with the goal of developing an intelligent, self-defending network."[39]

Cisco's router-based defensive measures include devices that limit the amount and type of data that could be directed at a host computer in a DoS attack.[40] They also include "reverse-address lookup," where the routers at the edge of a company's network check outgoing traffic to make sure that it legitimately originates from their network, and "intrusion detection" software, which passively monitors all the traffic moving through a network segment and raises a red flag or sends an alert if traffic patterns resemble suspicious activity. Another type of defensive software, designed as an independent filtering device, protects Web sites by distinguishing between real requests for information and fake requests. Yahoo itself directed company engineers to install such a system of filters once the attack on its site had been reported.[41]

As might be expected, security experts have warned against assuming that all defensive tools of this type are equally effective against DoS attacks. Some have noted, for example, that proxy and packet filter firewalls are archaic technologies with rudimentary security features that anybody with the right software can bypass. Modern "packet inspection technologies," on the other hand, have been praised for providing the best all-round security, customization and speed.

In addition, red flags have been raised regarding security holes resulting from the use of a network by portable machines. Even if servers are "secured" with a decent firewall, experts note, the defensive measures may fail because some company users may have laptop computers linked to networks via analogue or ISDN modem cards. These computers can themselves become possible entry points for perpetrators of cyber-attacks.[42]

Preventing Computers from Being Used as Unwitting Agents

A second major software-based strategy that can be used to protect against cyber-attacks focuses on computers enlisted as unwitting agents. In comparison to the defensive measures described above, solutions available to counter the commandeering of individual computers are relatively simple, and constitute the equivalent of turning off the car, taking out the keys, and locking the door.

A distributed DoS attack takes advantage of the open nature of the Internet, probing computers for security flaws and then essentially taking them over for use in criminal activity. If these computers are secured, they cannot be hijacked in this fashion. Software solutions that can help prevent such activity typically enable a computer owner to determine whether his computer is vulnerable to being taken over, or indeed, whether the attacking software has already been planted on his hard drive. The U.S. government posted free software of this type on its NIPC Web site in late December 1999. The software application, which the NIPC developed, could be used by system administrators to scan their computer systems and determine whether they contain the "TRIN00" or "TFN" tools that might be used as part of a distributed DoS attack. In early 2000, the latest version of this detection software could be downloaded from the NIPC Internet Web site.[43]

Several commercial products were also available by mid-2000 for individual Netizens to use on both their home desktop computers and their laptops. These products not only help prevent individual computers—particularly those connected to the Internet all the time—from being used as unwitting agents in attacks, but they also serve to help plug holes in network security systems across the board. As noted above, a company might have server-side security measures in place, but mobile workers accessing the Internet from home or from a hotel room can easily compromise those measures.

Most of the newer tools of this type can be divided roughly into two categories—intrusion detection and personal firewalls. Intrusion detection systems monitor the packets on the network for telltale signs of a break-in or a denial-of-service attack. Like an antivirus program, an intrusion detection system compares activity with signatures of known intrusions to detect an attack. The best known product of this type at the time was Network Ice Corporation's Blackice Defender. A relatively inexpensive program that works on Windows machines, it scans all traffic between the individual PC and the Internet and blocks intruders. The program also contains alert features that indicate if someone is trying to get in, and keeps a log so that persons can find out if anyone has tried to break in when the user was away from the computer.

Personal firewalls, on the other hand, are designed to corral inbound and outbound network traffic to a single point of entry that can be controlled by the user, based on rules that the user has specified. Until recently, firewalls were too difficult for average users to install and configure, but several personal firewall products have emerged in recent years. Symantec, for example, developed Norton Internet Security, a program designed to shield a PC from invaders by blocking unauthorized attempts to get into a user's system.[44]

In the end, because it is apparently so easy to "lock the door" and prevent both network computers and individual desktops and laptops from being used in distributed DoS attacks, some have actually suggested that owners who do not secure their machines in this manner should be held negligent if the computers are ultimately used as unwitting agents in future attacks.[45]

Rerouting DoS Attacks

A third code-based method that could help counter cyberterrorism in this context would rely on software that reroutes attempted DoS attacks. In the aftermath of the February 2000 incidents, for example, a team of engineers at BMC Software looked into the possibility of enhancing the company's Web site–monitoring software so that it would include rerouting capabilities. The engineers speculated that a program could be designed that would "reroute the attack to a standby computer where the source of the attack could be isolated and studied, saving the main site from being overwhelmed." Conceivably, switches such as those that distribute traffic from a clogged computer server to another with more available space could be used in such a setup. Practical considerations, however, may limit the potential of such an approach. Before Web site operators can redirect traffic to other computers in this manner, they would have to install those additional computers, duplicate their content, and pay for additional network connections. Many companies might not be eager to take all these steps.[46]

A second possible rerouting approach would be to develop a counteroffensive measure similar to the ones described earlier in this chapter, where software automatically turns the attack back on the perpetrators. The main problem with such a strategy, however, is that to accomplish the task a perpetrator must be identified. And with distributed DoS attacks, not only are the primary perpetrators difficult to pinpoint, but the attack comes from many unwitting computers all at once.

Still, RSA Security announced after the February 2000 attacks that it had actually identified a method to counter distributed DoS attacks by rerouting the "requests for information" back toward the perpetrators.

RSA, which provides the encryption technology used by most companies to secure communications and identities on the Internet, said that it had devised a cryptographic measure that would automatically respond to requests for information by sending out cryptographic puzzles that would themselves require a response. In essence, then, the tables would be turned on the attacking computers, which would be quickly overwhelmed by the return "questions."

RSA presented a very optimistic picture in its February announcement, declaring that its scientists had been working on such a concept for two years, and that it hoped to have a software product available for sale during the second half of the year 2000. Such a result was clearly not guaranteed, and many wondered whether Web site owners would be willing to add any security measure of this type that might slow down their systems, even by a fraction of a second.[47]

Initiatives Focusing on Widespread Architectural Changes

Other code-based strategies suggested by security experts and policymakers in the aftermath of the DoS attacks included ideas for changing the architecture of the Internet across the board. One of these strategies, for example, would rely on a new fundamental communications protocol developed by the Internet Engineering Task Force that would strengthen security by cutting back on anonymity. The protocol in use during the year 2000, called "Internet Protocol Version 4" (IPv4), essentially allowed online users to create fake return addresses on data packets, thus making it more difficult to trace DoS attacks. By mid-2000, however, the IETF has already approved a new communications protocol known as "IPv6." This protocol would apparently mark each packet with an encryption key that could not be faked by hackers, and that would securely identify the packet's origin. This would not make DoS attacks impossible, but it would make it much harder for the perpetrators to remain anonymous.[48]

There was little apparent urgency for Internet stakeholders to move to Ipv6. Free speech activists continued to express ongoing concerns about any attempt to limit anonymity,[49] and IT industry leaders noted that such a conversion would be an expensive task. Widespread adoption would require software vendors and makers of operating systems to rewrite their code so that they could take advantage of several advanced IPv6 features.

Others have argued that operating systems themselves need to be redesigned. Many people familiar with these issues have contended for some time now that typical operating systems are filled with security holes because the companies designing them have not felt the need to do things any differently. Bill Hancock, the author of twenty-five books on information security, for example, believes that operating systems could be rewritten to prevent machines from performing some tasks involved in denial-of-service attacks, such as disguising the source of Internet traffic sent from a machine. "Not one operating system on the market has network-access controls built in as part of the design," Hancock declared. He insisted that changing this design would "kill off" many of these attacks.

Finally, there are those who contend that the biggest problem with current cyberspace architecture is that the Internet's fundamental communication protocols, *including* IPv6, are still designed for "best case" assumptions—"not taking into account the possibility that someone will try to abuse them." Unless this architecture is changed, these critics warn, security problems will only continue.[50]

Demanding Change in Software Industry Practices

In the same vein, commentators have criticized the software industry in general. Soon after the rash of DoS attacks hit top Web sites, for example, top U.S. cyberspace security experts asserted in Congressional testimony that software developers were marketing "flawed products" that "boosted the Internet's vulnerability to rapidly evolving forms of cyber-attack." Some argued that the security features of most products had not improved in recent years, and that "developers are not devoting sufficient effort to apply[ing] lessons learned about the sources of vulnerabilities." Others declared that the problem was not isolated, but rather 'universal' throughout the industry. A common complaint in this regard was that the rush to meet the demand for constant upgrades "has resulted in software that is increasingly supportive of subversion, computer viruses, and other malicious acts." And these experts believe that the prevalence of software with security holes was unlikely to change until customers demanded it.[51]

All in all, code-based adjustments in Internet architecture by both the powers-that-be and individual users can go a long way toward countering cyberterrorism. Each approach that has been identified can help in potentially significant ways, but there are inevitable hurdles that must be overcome and major trade-offs that must be addressed. Many defensive tools are not attractive to businesses because they may tend to slow down web operations. Individual computers can only be secured if persons and groups at every level of a network become aware that it is only through a series of affirmative steps that this will happen. Rerouting strategies, particularly those of a counteroffensive nature, are still untested. Absent unforeseen developments, new protocols that limit anonymity in any way are not likely to be adopted without a protracted legal and policy battle ensuing. And there is currently no financial incentive for software companies to develop products that are more secure.

Some have suggested that since these strategies are typically dependent upon the individual initiative of persons and entities, code-based approaches to countering cyberterrorism will succeed across the board only if they are mandated by law. Legislators must proceed very carefully in this area, however, because—as discussed at length in chapter 7—widespread architectural changes could have a significant negative impact on the Internet as we know it. In addition, even if narrow, targeted changes are deemed appropriate after extensive analysis, none of these code-based strategies in and of themselves can provide airtight protection against distributed DoS attacks. And even the most effective systems today can become outmoded tomorrow as perpetrators continue to develop new methods of circumventing or breaking through code-based lines of defense.

Yet it must be emphasized that Internet stakeholders are not helpless in the face of cyberterrorism. Many potentially effective strategies can be identified under all three regulatory models. Strong laws already exist to counter criminal activity in this area, and precise, carefully crafted legislation might conceivably add to this body of law in a positive way. The potential for international cooperation in the law enforcement context is promising, and the opportunity exists for nations to come together and develop creative new vehicles for fighting cybercrime. Code-based adjustments—particularly those that constitute the cyber-equivalent of locking the door and installing alarms—can play a major role in this regard as well.

Crime fighting, as we have seen over the centuries in the offline world, is never completely successful. Some conduct goes undetected, and some criminals are never apprehended. But a combination of thoughtful laws, international cooperation when appropriate, and strategies that law-abiding citizens can themselves undertake will inevitably result in a safer and more secure environment. Cyberterrorism is a challenge, but it is not unresolvable. There is already a tremendous amount that can be done, even within existing legal and technological frameworks. And creative, carefully thought-out modifications of the status quo, including innovative combinations of all three regulatory models, can only make things better. Overall, there is reason for great optimism.

10

Combating Fraudulent Conduct in Cyberspace: A Focus on Consumer Rights

Much of the opportunity for honest Internet entrepreneurs . . . may be lost if consumers fear commerce on the Internet due to fraud. It is in all our interests—business, government, and consumers—to place a high priority on preserving the safety of the Internet.

—*Fighting Consumer Fraud: New Tools of the Trade,* FTC Report, April 1998

The Federal Trade Commission, long a sleepy regulatory agency, is emerging as the chief enforcer of the Internet, and Web companies are starting to warn that its crackdown could affect their businesses.

—Glenn R. Simpson, The *Wall Street Journal,* February 2000

Pagejacking, mousetrapping and disabling people's browsers are not even identified as criminal offenses. The rules of business on the Net remain vague, and the authorities are scrambling to catch up. . . . If people choose to cruise the Internet, it's a free-for-all territory at the moment. It's not really governed by anything . . . it's the Wild West. And if people can take advantage of the Wild West, then let them. That's what I believe.

—Greg Lasrado (Australian entrepreneur, originally implicated in *FTC v. Pereira*), *The Times* (London), September 2000

Fraudulent conduct—the second category of problematic behavior we have identified—is comprised of behavior that may impact the *economic safety* of persons, businesses, institutions, and governments. As discussed in chapter 3, the generic term *fraudulent* can refer to a wide-ranging universe of generally dishonest activity, which might include hacking that poses the threat of financial loss, identity theft, auction fraud, and securities fraud.

In this chapter, we focus on consumer fraud in general as a representative problem under this category. As cyberspace continues to be viewed as a place of significant opportunity for financial gain, the average online user is confronted on a daily basis with numerous offers to purchase goods and services. Many of these offers are made by legitimate businesses with only the most honest of intentions, but others represent schemes for defrauding unsuspecting citizens. If we look at cyberspace in this context, online users often play the role of consumers, whether or not they actually intend to engage in e-commerce at the time.

The U.S. Federal Trade Commission, with an ongoing mandate to protect consumers in interstate commerce, has adopted an increasingly expansive definition of the term *consumer*. According to this definition, a consumer is not just a shopper, patron, or client, but also an Internet user who might be impacted directly or indirectly by a range of online practices and policies. Even the issue of privacy infringement, which many view as a separate matter entirely, has been added to the list of conduct affecting consumers that FTC officials may view as fraudulent.[1]

Following the roadmap identified in chapter 8, we begin our inquiry into possible regulatory approaches by analyzing the potential for consensus and exploring the ways in which consumer fraud in cyberspace might be different from analogous activities and settings in the offline world.

Consensus As discussed, consensus is not typically an issue for alleged problems identified under categories 1 and 2. Most would agree, for example, that the defrauding of consumers is a problem in cyberspace, and that something must be done to address it. It is clear, however, that not everyone agrees on how to define the term *consumer fraud*. A narrow definition limits the term to the sort of traditional, run-of-the-mill fraud that is characterized by dishonest, manipulative, and misrepresentative activity, but a broad definition such as that adopted by the FTC appears to include activity that is troubling to many Netizens but does not necessarily constitute fraud under the original common law definition. By defining the term so broadly, the FTC is able to bring a much wider range of conduct under its scrutiny. And some persons with substantial business interests in cyberspace believe that this U.S. regulatory agency may have gone too far in that regard.

The controversy regarding the collection of data on consumer online shopping practices (aka "data mining") is an example of this disagreement. Many welcomed the FTC's aggressive posture here, but others feared that these developments reflect a "rapidly evolving and uncertain regulatory environment . . . [which] . . . make it difficult to ensure compliance with the law." Several companies actually filed statements with the FTC in early 2000 claiming that such agency moves could directly affect the way they do business or could "create uncertainty in the marketplace."[2]

This potential lack of consensus for certain types of alleged problems raises a red flag that impacts the prospective effectiveness of the traditional national law model in this context. As we have seen in earlier chapters, the social contract is particularly important in the online world because of the decentralized, anarchic nature of Internet architecture and the resulting diffusion of the locus of control. Companies who disagree with the FTC's approach, for example, may seek to find a way around any guidelines that are identified. Such actions not only impede efforts to reach a consensus, but may even create new problems.

Uniqueness of Conduct and Setting Online consumer fraud is probably more similar to analogous offline conduct than any other representative problem area that we discuss. Whether the problem is generally dishonest behavior resulting in economic harm or specific acts that qualify as fraud under well-settled legal doctrine, such activity tends to be no different in cyberspace than it is in person or via other forms of communication. In these types of situations, one person or entity operating in bad faith is generally seeking to gain economic advantage by fooling another person or entity.

The online setting typically does not make a difference. Unlike cyberterrorism—which takes advantage of major differences in setting—there is little evidence that cyberspace operates to the benefit of criminals in most run-of-the-mill online fraud. What criminals do on the Internet is typically what they have done in the past on the phone, through letters, or in person. According to FTC attorney Paul Luehr, the great majority of online consumer fraud cases are very traditional in nature, and include pyramid schemes, credit repair scams, and fraudulent investment opportunities. Some have an Internet twist, but only a handful of the defendants have taken unique advantage of cyberspace in their attempts to defraud Netizens.[3]

From an enforcement perspective, the Internet may actually work against those who attempt to defraud others. While many offline schemes are not in writing and thus can be very difficult to verify, online perpetrators may leave all sorts of digital footprints—including written communication—that can make their activity easier to track down and easier to prove in a court of law.

An initial assessment of regulatory strategies would seem to indicate that the national law model is potentially the most effective approach to combat consumer fraud in cyberspace. Given the fact that in most cases of online consumer fraud, the circumstances and the acts are not radically new or different, traditional legal approaches and existing laws are likely to work best. For settings and conduct that are not particularly unique, regulatory responses should inevitably be limited and informed by knowledge of prior strategies that may have been successful in analogous situations.[4]

International agreement may also be relevant in consumer fraud cases where the perpetrator is based in another country, but unlike cyberterrorism—which often reflects a more global focus—the international role in combating fraudulent activity may prove much more limited. And potential adjustments in Internet architecture may be less relevant for this problem area as well. Most protective software, for example, is generally designed to counter problems such as those we have seen under the other three problem categories.[5] In the most typical fact pattern, consumer fraud cannot happen unless the victim responds affirmatively in some fashion. Software is likely to be of limited assistance in these situations.

Traditional Regulation of Consumer Fraud under National Law

At the outset, an overview of relevant law reveals the same range of applicable legal principles that we saw in our analysis of distributed denial-of-service attacks. There are already a significant number of laws in the U.S. that address fraudulent activity directly or indirectly, and the area of consumer fraud in particular has become highly regulated. In fact, all signs point toward increased momentum that may lead to even stronger protection for consumers.

Applicable Laws in General

Under U.S. law, a variety of federal and state statutes address fraudulent conduct impacting consumers, and case decisions are filled with evolving common law principles that shape much of the recent thinking in this area. Criminal penalties are mandated for much of the activity defined as fraudulent, and aggrieved plaintiffs can also prevail in many types of civil cases.

The federal Computer Fraud and Abuse Act, for example, discussed above within the context of cyberterrorism, is also directly applicable in the area of online consumer rights. The act provides criminal penalties for those who obtain information for fraudulent purposes through a computer or a computer network. Persons implicated by the statute include those who intentionally access a computer without authorization—or exceed authorized access—and

- obtain "information contained in a financial record of a financial institution, or of a card issuer, or contained in a file of a consumer reporting agency on a consumer, as such terms are defined in the Fair Credit Reporting Act," or
- "knowingly and with intent to defraud" actually "further the intended fraud" and "obtain anything of value."

In addition, persons who "knowingly and with intent to defraud . . . [traffic] . . . in any password or similar information through which a computer may be accessed without authorization" can be convicted under this act, if "such trafficking affects interstate or foreign commerce."[6]

Other federal statutes also provide direct or indirect protection for consumers in cyberspace. These include the Fair Packaging and Labeling Act (designed to prevent consumer deception), the Consumer Credit Protection Act (addressing a range of banking and credit reporting activity that may negatively impact consumers), the Magnuson Moss Warranty-Federal Trade Commission Improvement Act (establishing remedies for breach of warranty or service contract obligations), the Hobby Protection Act (regulating the manufacturing and importing of certain imitation collectible items), and the Children's Online Privacy Protection Act (regulating unfair and deceptive acts and practices in connection with the collection and use of personal information from and about children on the Internet).[7]

As discussed in chapter 3, common law principles in this area are also very highly developed. They include well-recognized rules prohibiting *intentional misrepresentation,* which has been defined as the "false representation of a material fact or opinion" by someone who either knows it to be false or makes it with reckless disregard for the truth, and intends to induce reliance on the representation.[8] And they also include common law definitions of crimes that may contain an element of fraud, such as *larceny* (if the property is taken through consent obtained by fraud), *embezzlement* (intent to defraud required), and *false pretenses* (intent to defraud also required).[9]

The Legal Authority of the U.S. Federal Trade Commission

Perhaps reflecting the range of activity that can constitute consumer fraud, it is clear that even more laws may be applicable in this area than in the area of cyberterrorism. In addition, the Federal Trade Commission Act gives the FTC wide-ranging jurisdiction over consumer-rights issues across the board.

Under this act, the FTC is empowered, among other things, to (1) prevent unfair methods of competition, and unfair or deceptive acts or practices in or affecting commerce; (2) seek monetary compensation and other relief for conduct injurious to consumers; (3) prescribe trade regulation rules that specifically identify acts or practices which are unfair or deceptive, and establish requirements designed to prevent such acts or practices; (4) conduct investigations relating to the organization, business, practices, and management of entities engaged in commerce; and (5) make reports and legislative recommendations to Congress.[10]

In its ongoing effort to pursue this agenda, the FTC has set forth a wide-ranging statement of its vision, mission, and goals. According to the June 1999 version of this statement, the FTC

- enforces a *variety* of federal antitrust and consumer protection laws;
- seeks to ensure that the nation's markets function competitively, and are vigorous, efficient, and free of undue restrictions; and
- works to enhance the smooth operation of the marketplace by eliminating acts or practices that are unfair or deceptive.

The commission emphasizes that its efforts "are directed toward stopping actions that threaten consumers' opportunities to exercise informed choice."[11]

The FTC's Aggressive Consumer Rights Agenda in Cyberspace

For some time now, the FTC has pursued an aggressive agenda in cyberspace, interpreting the term *consumer rights* broadly and targeting fraudulent behavior in a commercial context. Historically, this century-old, independent government agency has been viewed in many quarters as the Justice Department's "poor regulatory cousin." Both have been asked to police U.S. commerce, but traditionally Justice would take on the "big crooks" while the FTC went after the "fraudsters and petty cons."

On the Internet, however, the FTC has played a prominent role long before other agencies, such as Justice and the SEC, became involved. And by the year 2000, the FTC had expanded its role to such a degree that it was viewed in most quarters as the government's de facto regulator of Internet commerce. Its Consumer Protection Division had been increased fivefold, new investigations continued to be announced, and lawsuits filed by the agency continued to proliferate. FTC Chair Robert Pitofsky confirmed in an early 2000 interview that Internet commerce was the commission's "No. 1 issue."[12]

As far back as the fall of 1995, the commission held extensive hearings on the implications of globalization and technological innovation for both competition and consumer protection. Testimony from members of the information industry, the online business community, privacy and consumer advocates, government representatives, and experts in interactive technology led to an apparent consensus on several broad issues:

1. Basic consumer protection principles should apply in the "electronic marketplace";
2. Government should tailor its efforts to avoid undue burdens on business and technology;
3. Effective self-regulation should be encouraged; and
4. The public and private sectors should work together where possible.[13]

In light of these principles, the major policy goal of the FTC has been to identify and stop wrongdoers before they harm individual consumers and undermine confidence in the electronic marketplace. Many thought that this goal would be accomplished with significant assistance from online businesses. But when it became apparent that in many cases companies were paying lip service to the idea of self-regulation but were not following through with their own measures, the FTC became more and more aggressive in its regulatory role.[14]

By the year 2000, the FTC was also using technology as a tool in its efforts to stop fraud, deception, and unfair conduct in cyberspace. The philosophy of the agency was that any attempts by criminals to use the Internet to their advantage should be countered by aggressive, high-tech monitoring practices that would enable its officials to identify the fraudulent behavior and put an immediate stop to it.

In 1997, for example, the commission established *Consumer Sentinel,* a consumer fraud complaint database available online to law enforcement officials across the U.S. and Canada. Through a secure Web site, law enforcement officials could access data that provide information about particular wrongdoers and show trends at the local, national, and international levels. According to the FTC, *Consumer Sentinel* was the largest North American consumer fraud database in existence at the turn of the century. And during the first nine months of 1999, the number of complaints in the database increased on average by six thousand a month. Most of the fraud data in *Consumer Sentinel* is supplied by consumers who call the FTC's toll-free telephone number or use its online complaint form, and by law enforcement agencies and consumer organizations.[15]

The FTC contends that *Consumer Sentinel* is an example of how Internet technology is changing the way law enforcement operates by enabling "a fast and well-coordinated response to the most serious fraud problems across North America." It points to the apparent success of the Internet Fraud Rapid Response Team, which monitors the *Consumer Sentinel* complaint database, spots emerging frauds, and puts matters on a fast track for litigation or settlement. In *FTC v. Benoit,* the team's first case, the FTC obtained an injunction to stop a scheme dealing with deceptive spam within three weeks of identifying it on the Internet.

Another FTC initiative in the area of online monitoring has been the Internet "Surf Day." Since 1996, this has been a popular tool for the commission and other agencies to identify online scams of all kinds. Between 1997 and 2000, the FTC participated in some 20 Surf Days with over 150 agencies in the U.S. and 25 other countries, identifying thousands of commercial Web sites that had been making apparently false or misleading claims. Questionable activity uncovered by these initiatives included the marketing of products to treat major diseases, the advertising of pyramid schemes, and the promotion of spurious business and investment opportunities.

Surf Days enable law enforcement officials to learn more about online practices and also provide the FTC with an opportunity to alert Web site operators that their sites appear to violate the law in some way. E-mail messages are sent to Web site operators explaining why a law may have been violated and providing a link to the FTC Web site, where more information is available. Follow-up visits are subsequently made to the sites, and Web site operators who continue questionable practices may become the subjects of FTC law enforcement efforts.[16]

Combating Consumer Fraud via Litigation

From 1994 to 2000, the FTC used its law enforcement authority to successfully litigate over one hundred Internet-related cases. Not only were assets sometimes recovered to compensate consumer for their losses, but *every case* filed by the agency in this context ultimately resulted in an end to the illegal conduct.

To stop scams before they can spread, the FTC will often immediately seek to obtain a temporary restraining order (TRO). The TRO freezes the company's assets and appoints a receiver to temporarily take over the business. As the case proceeds, the commission will then seek preliminary and permanent injunctions that bar the challenged practices and may require refunds to consumers injured by defendants. Many of these cases are settled early in the litigation. Other cases—where an immediate stop to the activities is not necessarily in order—may simply result in an investigation. FTC staff in these instances typically establish contact, obtain further information, and often attempt to settle the case before issuing a formal administrative complaint.

The FTC's Internet-related cases thus provide excellent examples of how the traditional national law model can be employed to successfully combat fraudulent conduct under category 2. An examination of individual cases is particularly instructive in this context. Cases targeting deceptive unsolicited commercial e-mail, for example, include several major instances of misrepresentation. In *FTC v. Benoit,* defendants sent consumers e-mails stating that their "order" had been received, even though no order had ever been made. Consumers were also told that their credit card had been charged \$250 to \$899, and that to cancel the order they could call a specified international number. The operation was designed to trick consumers into making an expensive international call, and also to provide perpetrators with a kickback in each case. The FTC obtained an asset freeze to stop any flow of money to defendants through the telephone payment system, even as the commission's investigation continued.

In *FTC v. Internet Business Broadcasting* and *FTC v. Dixie Cooley,* defendants used spam to sell phony work-at-home schemes, business opportunity schemes, and services that would allegedly repair credit reports. The commission obtained orders to stop the practices and provide compensation for defrauded consumers.

Other cases targeted both the practice of billing for unauthorized Internet-related services and the promotion of widespread pyramid schemes. The FTC has been especially active in working with individual states to crack down on pyramid schemes. In *FTC v. Fortuna Alliance,* for example, defendants used a high-tech chain letter scheme to recruit at least 25,000 consumers around the world. The FTC obtained an order for \$5.5 million in refunds for over 15,500 consumers in the United States and seventy foreign countries. In *FTC v. Nia Cano,* defendants used live sales presentations to recruit new members, who, in turn, used the Internet to try to recruit other members. The FTC successfully obtained an order requiring the company to spend \$2 million to compensate consumers. In *FTC v. Equinox International* and *FTC v. Five Star Auto Club,* two cases involving multimillion-dollar pyramid operations, the courts ordered preliminary relief with asset freezes and appointment of receivers pending trial.

To counter credit scams, the FTC had already filed over twenty-five lawsuits by early 2000. These included *FTC v. Corizine,* the commission's first

Internet case, which was filed in 1994 and targeted a defendant who promoted credit repair kits online. The commission obtained an order stopping the practice and providing consumer compensation. In addition, the FTC led the *Operation New ID/Bad Idea I & II* law enforcement sweeps, which involved more than a dozen federal, state, and local law enforcement agencies and produced fifty-nine cases involving false claims that consumers could clean up their credit histories by obtaining new identification numbers.

Online auction fraud has continued to be a major area of activity as well. Most complaints received by the FTC involve failure to deliver the merchandise. Consumers "win" the auction, send their money, but never receive the goods from sellers, who are often individuals or small operators located across the country. In *FTC v. Hare,* a defendant used various Internet auction houses to sell computers and computer-related equipment that he did not have. The commission obtained an order barring the defendant from selling online and referred the case to the U.S. Department of Justice for criminal prosecution. The defendant pled guilty to wire fraud, was sentenced, and has been ordered to pay "consumer redress." And in *Operation Safebid,* the Commission initiated a law enforcement program with local, state, and federal agencies to prosecute Internet auction fraud where the wrongdoers are located. By the year 2000, these efforts had resulted in two civil and three criminal prosecutions, with a number of other cases under investigation.

Cases targeting business and investment opportunity scams have also been wide-ranging. In *FTC v. Intellicom Services,* for example, the Commission charged twenty-seven defendants with deceptively promoting partnership interests in high-tech ventures involving Internet access and Internet shopping malls. Settlements included over $24 million in monetary judgments. In *Project NetOpp,* the FTC brought five lawsuits involving false earnings claims in selling business opportunities for high-tech products and services such as computer kiosks, website design and development, and Internet access. The cases resulted in over $3.5 million in redress, and many of the defendants were banned from marketing any business opportunities in the future or required to post substantial bonds before doing so.

Online health-related cases have proliferated as Netizens increasingly head to cyberspace for medical information and health-care opportunities. The FTC has apparently made the burgeoning number of false or unsubstantiated health claims online a law enforcement priority. In *Operation Cure.All,* four cases were filed against the marketers of products such as magnetic therapy devices, shark cartilage, and CMO (cetymyristoleate) for their claims that these products could cure a host of serious diseases, including cancer, HIV/AIDS, multiple sclerosis, and arthritis. All the companies, which used Web sites to market the products and recruit distributors, entered into settlements with the Commission. In *FTC v. Slim America, Inc.,* defendants were charged with falsely advertising that their product would produce dramatic weight loss. After a trial, the court ordered defendants to pay $8.3 million in consumer redress and to post multimillion-dollar bonds before engaging in the marketing of any products and services. And in *FTC v. American Urological Clinic,* the defendants touted "Vaegra" (a sham Viagra) and other impotence treatment products, claiming that the products had been developed by legitimate medical enterprises and proven effective. The FTC obtained an $18.5 million judgment that required the defendants to post a $6 million bond before they promote any impotence treatment in the future.

Advertising cases brought by the FTC also reflect the view that traditional consumer protection law applies in cyberspace. These cases involve an array of practices, including the deceptive promotion of online services, hidden contract terms, and deception in the collection and use of personal information. In 1997, for example, the commission brought lawsuits against AOL, CompuServe, and Prodigy for using misleading promotions to recruit online consumers. Among the practices alleged were the deceptive use of the term "free trial," inadequate disclosures about cancellations, and the unauthorized debiting of consumer accounts. The companies agreed to consent orders that prohibit misrepresentations about the terms of trial offers and require clear disclosures about electronic fund transfers from consumers' accounts. And in 1999, the FTC filed cases against Dell Computer and Micron Electronics, arguing that in advertising their computer leasing plans online, these companies placed important information about cost in inconspicuous areas, or omitted the information altogether. The commission obtained consent orders requiring the companies to clearly and conspicuously disclose all material leasing terms in their advertising.

Two privacy-related cases were also brought in this context. In the *GeoCities* case, the FTC charged the company with misrepresenting the purpose for which it was collecting information from children and adults. Under a settlement, the company agreed to post a prominent privacy notice and obtain parental consent before collecting information from children under age thirteen. And in the *Liberty Financial* case, the company was charged with falsely representing that personal information collected from children on its Young Investor Web Site would be maintained anonymously. Under a settlement, the company agreed to post a privacy policy on its Web sites and get verifiable parental consent before collecting information from children under age thirteen.[17]

A review of the FTC's online consumer rights activity between 1994 and 2000 reveals the extent of the U.S. government's regulatory activity in this area. This activity flies in the face of the myths we have referenced throughout this book regarding online regulation. Clearly, in certain key portions of cyberspace, the national law model is being used to effect significant change in day-to-day behavior. And its use demonstrates just how effective traditional law can be in the right hands.

The "Moldovan Modem" and "Pagejacking-Mousetrapping" Cases

Three adult entertainment cases filed by the FTC are unique in several important ways, and thus qualify for discussion in a separate section. These legal actions—known in the FTC community as the "Moldovan Modem" and "Pagejacking-Mousetrapping" cases—represent aspects of both the traditional national law model and the international agreement model. In addition, both cases involve defendants who, unlike those in most of the other FTC lawsuits described above, took special advantage of certain unique aspects of cyberspace to defraud consumers.

FTC v. Audiotex Connection and *FTC v. Beylen Telecom*

Both the *Audiotex* case and *Beylen Telecom* case had very similar fact patterns. In *Audiotex,* defendants maintained adult entertainment sites at <www.beavisbutthead.com>, <www.sexygirls.com>, and <www.1adult.

com>. The FTC presented evidence that online users who visited one of these sites were encouraged to download a free viewer program (david.exe) in order to view free images. Once downloaded and executed, however, the program took over the user's modem. It disconnected the user's computer from his or her own ISP, turned off the user's modem speakers, dialed an international telephone number, and reconnected the computer to a remote foreign site. Charges kept accruing until the user shut down the computer entirely, and the users were billed for calls purportedly made to Moldova, even though the calls actually went only as far as Canada. In *Beylen Telecom,* the facts were the same, except that the sites from which the activity was generated included www.erotic 2000.com and www.erotica2000.com. In both cases, defendants made their money by receiving kickbacks from foreign telephone companies.

The FTC's primary goals in all consumer fraud cases are to put a stop to fraudulent activity and return money to victims. It did so in the Moldovan modem cases by working closely with certain telephone companies. FTC investigators actually learned about the Audiotex and Beylen activity when they were informed by AT&T security. The commission subsequently worked closely with both AT&T and MCI to identify and freeze assets still within the elaborate payment system that exists between national and international telephone companies.

The cases were ultimately resolved in the federal courts. The Eastern District of New York issued a temporary restraining order in *Audiotex,* followed by a preliminary injunction, which required defendants to cease these activities and place one million dollars in escrow for potential consumer redress. In late 1997, a final settlement agreement was reached. Defendants were barred from claiming that consumers could use certain software to view computer images for free, from offering calls connected through the Internet without posting specific disclosures, and from causing consumers to be billed for calls to destinations other than those listed on their telephone bills. In addition, most of the consumers impacted by this activity would receive telephone credits through AT&T and MCI. The *Beylen Telecom* case was concluded in a similar manner in early 1998.[18]

FTC v. Carlos Pereira

In the *Pereira* case, the FTC presented evidence that the defendants engaged in unique, code-based tactics to drive unsuspecting online users to adult Web sites and hold them there. According to the FTC, defendants set the process in motion by first making "counterfeit" copies of over twenty-five million Web pages. They then inserted a hidden "redirect" command in these cloned pages and placed them online. As a result, when Netizens used a search engine to look up certain information, they sometimes pulled up listings for defendants' counterfeit sites. Thus, even though the search engine results might have displayed links to ostensibly innocuous sites addressing such everyday matters as recipes, children's games, or automobiles, a user clicking on a counterfeit site link was taken instead to a sexually explicit site operated by the defendant. This code-based control of a person's online activities by the adult site owners has come to be known as "pagejacking." Reports in the national media indicated that Netizens searching for everything from the *Harvard Law Review* to "Oklahoma tornadoes" to "Paine Webber" had been pagejacked in this manner.

To make matters even worse, once the unwitting online user arrived at the sexually explicit site, he or she could not easily leave. Defendants had apparently designed the process to disable a person's normal browser functions. Someone trying to escape by hitting either the "back" button or the "close it" button on his or her Web browser would either not be taken anywhere or would be taken to a different adult site with even more explicit content. This set of circumstances has come to be known as "mousetrapping."[19]

According to FTC investigators, defendants stood to make money from the scheme in three ways: by selling advertising on the adult sites based on the amount of traffic recorded, by offering viewers the chance to see more Web sites by paying for them, and by inflating the value of their domain names so that they could be auctioned off at hundreds of times their original cost. The FTC brought the case to federal court, arguing that defendants had deceived consumers by pagejacking Web sites and misleading them about where they were going. In addition, the agency contended that defendants had engaged in illegal and unfair practices when they mousetrapped consumers and prevented them from leaving defendants' sites.

As we have seen, the typical FTC lawsuit in this context asks the court both to put a stop to the fraudulent activity and order defendants to refund money to the defrauded consumers. In this case, since no money was actually being taken directly from the pagejacked and mousetrapped Netizens, the FTC sought a unique remedy for a unique set of circumstances. It asked the court to order the defendants off the Internet. This order could be accomplished simply by directing Network Solutions to suspend the defendants' registration, so that their domain-name addresses no longer existed. The Eastern District of Virginia granted the FTC's request in its entirety, issuing a TRO and then a preliminary injunction.[20]

Although trademark cases typically result in one party's domain name being suspended, the FTC's victory in the *Pereira* case appears to be the first instance where a defendant was actually ordered off the Internet in this way. The potential for using this online "death penalty" in future cases cannot be discounted. Combining a court order to stop activity with the actual removal of a lawbreaker from cyberspace may prove to be one of the most effective vehicles available under the traditional national law model to ensure that such activity will not continue.

Combating Consumer Fraud under the International Agreement Model

While the traditional national law model clearly plays a dominant role in this area, international agreement can and should be an important part of the picture in relevant instances. International law enforcement cooperation, for example, can be essential when perpetrators are based in another country. In the Moldovan modem and pagejacking-mousetrapping cases, legal action could not have been possible without such cooperation. And the analysis in chapter 9 of the international law enforcement role in countering cyberterrorism is also applicable in the area of consumer fraud. The global role may be more limited here, since most fraudulent activity today appears to have occurred between citizens of the same country, but circumstances may change over time.

Recognizing the need for such global cooperation, the FTC has begun to share information from its database when requested by enforcement officials around the world. It is the commission's view that this type of information-sharing among countries is essential to the success of coordinated law enforcement efforts. In addition, a number of the FTC strategies for gathering data—including international Surf Days—are based on the global cooperation model.

Over time, there may also be a role for the sort of international adjudication referenced in chapter 6 and the discussion of cyberterrorism. Since the WTO dispute resolution model is designed to facilitate global commerce, such a structure may be especially applicable in a consumer fraud context. Member nations could be required under that model to establish consistent standards of consumer protection. Yet there are those who fear that the WTO process may lead to the opposite conclusion. When global commerce is primary in importance, consumer rights—in the event of a conflict—may take a back seat to the smooth and efficient functioning of international business.

Employing Code-Based Regulation to Combat Consumer Fraud

Architectural changes may be particularly important in combating cyberterrorism, but they appear to be much less essential in the area of consumer fraud. The basic traditional national law model is not effective in countering cyberterrorist activity today unless it is supplemented by both international cooperation and the extensive use of protective software code. But while the national law model as employed by the FTC to combat consumer fraud may benefit from global assistance, it does not appear to require the assistance of any code-based adjustments.

There are still some potential roles, however, for code in this context. As referenced earlier in this section, law enforcement officials may benefit from the ability to identify the digital footprints of perpetrators through the use of code-based forensic techniques. In addition, code-based strategies may be employed to protect against tampering with consumer records that could lead to billing fraud, identity theft, and falsified credit reports.

But for the generic types of online scams that the FTC has been fighting via traditional litigation, software code may be of limited assistance. Architectural adjustments at either the powers-that-be level or the individual consumer level may serve to limit contact with "strangers" who might be likely to attempt fraudulent activity. This strategy, however, would run counter to what cyberspace is all about. People typically go online to meet others and to interact with others. They are not seeking to limit human contact, but to maximize it. Filtering e-mail messages may play some role here, but it has proven very difficult for online users to limit potentially fraudulent offers from coming through on e-mail without also limiting legitimate messages that may be of interest to them. In the end, consumers must remain alert and vigilant in cyberspace to protect themselves against being taken in by fraudulent conduct, just as they have needed to remain alert and vigilant in the offline world from time immemorial. Software is not yet at the point where it can do a lot in this regard, unless draconian measures such as Internet driver's licenses are implemented. And barring unforeseen developments, the public is not ready to endorse such widespread architectural changes.

There may still be a role in this context, however, for code-based strategies designed to counter specialized types of fraudulent behavior. In the case of pagejacking and mousetrapping, for example, the FTC has succeeded in stopping the identified defendants, but it has not succeeded in stopping the activity across the board. Netizens continue to report numerous instances of being hijacked to other pornography sites and being mousetrapped there. Code-based protection can be devised to prevent such intrusive and fraudulent conduct.

Finally, it should be noted that the discussion in the cyberterrorism section regarding the importance of tightening the design of software in general is equally applicable here. Operating systems and basic everyday software continue to be released with extensive security flaws that require ongoing patches and upgrades. Although no software can be designed to protect against all possible security breaches, most commentators and security experts agree that the software companies can and must do a much better job than they have been doing.

Regulating Online Consumer Fraud: Assessment and Prognosis

At this point in time, online consumer fraud appears to be a problem that is being addressed in a relatively effective manner. While consumer fraud persists in cyberspace, it is closely monitored by a responsive government agency that clearly follows up on reports of questionable activity. Less uniquely "cyber" than most of the other problem areas identified in this book, consumer fraud can be regulated by employing many of the same traditional law enforcement strategies that have worked in the offline world. In addition, consumer fraud is typically much less controversial than most of the other problem areas; accordingly, stakeholders have found it easier to agree on both the nature and extent of the problem and on appropriate regulatory approaches.

We have spent much time in this chapter examining the role of the U.S. Federal Trade Commission under the traditional national law model. In many ways, it is a definite success story. Building on approaches that have worked in the offline world, and reflecting a stated determination to stop wrongdoers and maintain confidence in the electronic marketplace, the FTC's aggressive litigation strategy has already had an impact on both day-to-day online activity and public policy in general. The success of the FTC flies in the face of a myth that continues to be perpetuated in certain quarters, namely, that cyberspace is not regulated and cannot be regulated. Clearly, cyberspace has been regulated in a very stringent fashion by the FTC, and consumer protection law is working here.

As we have shown in this chapter, the traditional national law model can appropriately be supplemented by international cooperation and code-based adjustments in certain instances, but the latter two models are—at this point in time—much less relevant here than they might be for other problem areas. This may change over time, as new technological developments emerge and the nature of online global communication changes. But as of 2001, traditional law is working here and existing principles can be relied upon to maintain a lively and productive status quo in the online world.

That is not to say that the picture is totally positive. Online fraud continues to proliferate, as it does in the offline world, since law enforcement officials can never stop everyone. And the omnipresent issue of privacy infringement, which at this point appears to have become a part of almost every major area of controversy in cyberspace, remains very much unresolved. Internet advocacy groups, the FTC, and Congress have all played a part in placing privacy issues squarely within the context of consumer rights.

As noted in chapter 3, the recent DoubleClick controversy exemplifies the ongoing consumer privacy debate. The Electronic Privacy Information Center complaint argued that DoubleClick's data mining activities and future plans constituted unfair and deceptive activity within the meaning of the FTC Act.[21] Others, however, argued that the company's plans were consistent with similar commercial activity that has been occurring in the offline world for some time and is not considered illegal in any way.

Still, the public outcry was so great and the fear of a continued backlash so significant within the e-commerce industry that any data collection and tracking that matched anonymous data mining with actual names and addresses appeared to be on hold until some sort of consensus could be reached from both a legal and a policy perspective. A key concern among prominent stakeholders was the issue of trust. Many angry consumers, for example, would concede that such data collection was not dishonest in and of itself, but the same consumers feared that the personal information—once obtained—might be used in a deceptive, abusive, or fraudulent manner.

While consumer privacy issues remain unresolved, there is much reason for continued optimism—not only in the fight against consumer fraud but in the ongoing effort to combat fraudulent conduct in cyberspace across the board. Even the privacy debates in this context can be seen as adding a positive note, since controversies such as the DoubleClick data collection plans may very well lead to clarification of privacy interests under both national and international law.[22]

As we have seen in our analysis of strategies to combat consumer fraud and cyberterrorism, a consensus is emerging in this area, unique features of the territory have been mapped out, and much positive work is already being done. While the fight against fraudulent conduct may be much farther along at this point than the battle against cyberterrorism, regulatory directions in both cases are very clear. Law enforcement officials are operating in cyberspace, but in most cases, they have remained relatively unobtrusive, and have avoided tampering with or changing the basic nature of the Internet. Indeed, the FTC's policy imperative of maintaining a vibrant status quo and preserving confidence in the electronic marketplace can serve as a positive model for law enforcement officials everywhere.

Unfortunately, this level of optimism may not be warranted for anarchic and inappropriate conduct that is more uniquely cyber in nature. Consensus in these areas is much harder to establish, and a myriad of issues remain both persistent and unresolved. Yet it may still be possible to identify strategies under one or more of the regulatory models—or under some form of self-regulation—that might be employed to address representative questions and bring about some degree of order. In chapter 11, we begin such an analysis by focusing on private personal digital copying.

11

Coming to Terms with Unlawful Anarchic Conduct in Cyberspace: A Focus on Private Digital Copying by the Average Netizen

The limited scope of the copyright holder's statutory monopoly, like the limited copyright duration required by the Constitution, reflects a balance of competing claims upon the public interest: Creative work is to be encouraged and rewarded, but private motivation must ultimately serve the cause of promoting broad public availability of literature, music, and the other arts.

—Justice Potter Stewart, U.S. Supreme Court, Circa 1975

Although the courts have considered and ruled upon the fair use doctrine over and over again, no real definition of the concept has ever emerged.

—U.S. Congress—House, Committee Report on Fair Use, H. R. Rep. No. 94–1476, at 65–66, Circa 1975

I look at Napster as being a very, very new form of radio . . . as the connection between file sharing and downloadable distribution, and as the power going back to the people. . . .

[B]ack in 1967 when FM radio came about, there was this big outcry that . . . it was going to take away from the artists' sales. When cassette recorders came in, it was "They're gonna rob us, they're gonna take away from our sales." As a matter of fact, these things have been a turbo boost to the music industry.

—Chuck D, PBS Debate with Lars Ulrich of Metallica, Spring 2000

Gnutella is a tool for general peer-to-peer file sharing. It can be used to share spreadsheets, source code, design documents, really any file on your computer. Yes, it is possible to exchange illegal files. This is entirely the choice of the people sharing them. . . . We do not condone or endorse the exchange and transfer of such files, and would like to point out that doing so is entirely at your own risk.

—Frequently Asked Questions, http://gnutella.wego.com, Spring 2000

Moving on to the last two categories of allegedly problematic behavior, we turn to the volatile area of private personal copying as a representative controversy under *unlawful anarchic conduct*. Not only has this area garnered a tremendous amount of attention in recent years, but it has become perhaps the most contentious of all the alleged Internet-related problems.

While the dangerous and fraudulent conduct discussed in chapters 9 and 10 is typically more egregious, issues raised under anarchic and inappropriate conduct have proven significantly more troublesome from a problem-solving perspective. Not only has it been difficult to reach any sort of consensus in these last two areas, but the problems defy easy solutions under traditional models because they are often so uniquely cyber in nature.

In addition, it is not clear under these last two categories which "side" the would-be-regulators should protect. While both the powers-that-be and private individuals, for example, would unquestionably seek to restrict dangerous activity across the board, we cannot automatically assume that a similarly restrictive regulatory approach would be the best way to address unlawful anarchic conduct or inappropriate conduct. There are major libertarian interests in maintaining a greater level of freedom in cyberspace, interests that may be consistent with the intent of the American founding fathers and the thrust of basic common law principles. Intellectual property law and U.S. First Amendment law have both proven to be major battlegrounds in this regard in recent years.

The Dilemma of Private Personal Copying: From Xerox Machines to MP3

Online copyright issues at the intersection of law and policy are wide-ranging and extremely complicated, reflecting both a highly complex legal system and a technical arena that is changing by the minute. Unresolved controversies in this area have been documented at great length by top legal scholars,[1] and new developments continue to generate both legislative proposals and a growing number of lawsuits. A complete analysis of this territory alone would require at least several volumes the size of this book.

Yet it is still possible, by focusing briefly on one aspect of this area—the day-to-day, private copying by the average Netizen—to explore the range of regulatory issues that exist under this broad topic and determine how the framework developed in this book might serve to help map out appropriate directions and goals. Most online users are copying digital files allegedly belonging to others all the time, and the controversy regarding whether and to what extent these activities can or should be controlled has continued unabated. In addition, the digital tools that have been developed to facilitate the electronic transfer of valuable multimedia files by average Netizens have not only served to crystallize the recurring issues but have succeeded in triggering a host of new questions as well.

In part I, we determined that category 3 of alleged Internet-related problems would appropriately include digital copying, pornographic expression, and online defamation. We noted that this category, in fact, focused to a great extent on the acts of individual Netizens, and we identified the following distinguishing features: (1) acts in this category often violate the law as it currently exists but are not necessarily criminal, (2) the behavior is not generally fraudulent or dishonest, (3) there is no danger to physical safety or national security, (4) the potential impact on the economic well-being of other persons and groups may not be very clear, and (5) the behavior exemplifies the anarchic image of the online world.

For some commentators who bemoan the lawlessness of cyberspace, the areas of conduct in this category are consistently cited as examples of a medium that is out of control. For others, including many stakeholders, there may indeed be problems here, but these problems are instead viewed as the direct result of an inconsistent, overbearing, and anachronistic legal system. Less regulation is often seen as a panacea.

Private day-to-day copying without "permission" is an ideal representative topic area under this category. As we have documented in earlier portions of this book, no area of controversy in cyberspace law has been more emotional and more difficult to resolve. Individual Netizens are consistently being taken to task for their allegedly irresponsible and unethical behavior, while content providers and IT industry leaders are castigated for their alleged refusal to look beyond profit motives and their consistent push for even more restrictive rules. Scholarship in this area has been unusually rich and fruitful,[2] with commentators sometimes going so far as to place intellectual property disputes at the very center of the inquiry regarding the role of law in the online world.[3]

It is important at the outset to identify the different levels of copying, distributing, and displaying that may occur without permission in cyberspace and are often illegal under typical statutory schemes of large industrial nations. In general, there are two broad types of behavior at issue here: (1) downloading, copying, or forwarding material that can already be found online, and (2) uploading, posting, displaying, or distributing material "to the world" for the first time.

Under each of these broad areas, there are several variables that may determine just how egregious someone's conduct might be. They include (a) whether the copying is for private, noncommercial purposes or for widespread, business-oriented purposes; (b) whether the copied documents, picture files, multimedia files, or software are of much value, some value, or little or no monetary value; (c) whether large amounts of material are being copied and distributed on a regular basis, or only small amounts on occasion; (d) how the original material came into the possession of the copier or distributor; and (e) whether the original material before copied or distributed included any warnings or any notices requesting that they not be reproduced, displayed, or distributed.[4]

Thus it is possible to set forth an accurate and explicit list of typical online conduct in this area—ranging from limited, private downloading and printing for noncommercial purposes to widespread, business-oriented uploading and distributing—that would reflect most of the generic copyright infringement that occurs in cyberspace. Such a list might enable would-be regulators to develop a precise and realistic model for addressing what some call "intellectual property theft" and others label "the free flow of information."

Consensus Problem areas under categories 3 and 4 have thus far been noteworthy for their lack of consensus, and online copyright issues have been particularly challenging in this regard. Not only has it been extremely difficult to reach agreement on what, if anything, is the problem, but it has been just as difficult to reach a consensus on whether *any* new regulatory approach should be adopted.

If pressed, most stakeholders could identify at least one problem in this area. For those who would like to see greater control, the major problem is the ease with which perfect copies are reproduced and distributed in cyberspace. For others, inadequate legal systems are the problem. Still others believe that we have satisfactory laws, but bemoan what they perceive to be shoddy or nonexistent law enforcement efforts. And there are those who characterize the problem as simply one of too much anarchic activity triggering widespread industry damage.

On the other side, for those who would like to see even less restriction on day-to-day activities, the problem is that public access to information in this wonderful new medium is in great danger of being limited. Others add that current legal systems are too restrictive and are tilted in favor of content providers, new media companies, and the IT industry in general. Still others argue that we must worry about widespread code-based changes such as architectures of identification and trusted systems that could establish perfect control over online information to the detriment of society as a whole.

Yet a close examination of these positions regarding the nature of the alleged problem reveals that they are not necessarily mutually exclusive. Both sides are dissatisfied with current legal systems, and many on either side can agree that public access to information is important, that certain industries are in fact in danger of being hurt by current practices, and that architectural changes pose a danger to the Internet as we know it in the early twenty-first century. In addition, most people would agree that this is a particularly important time in the growth and development of the online world, and that structures put in place during this era may be with us for some time to come. Finally, all agree that technology continues to change rapidly, and that any long-range plan must take into account the fact that certain things may be very different before too long.

In the late 1990s, an impressive group of business leaders, academics, and policymakers representing many of the stakeholders in cyberspace came together under the umbrella of the National Research Council (NRC) to address "the digital dilemma" in the area of copyright law. Their findings, released in final form in early 2000, were tempered by the revelation that they *could not* reach a consensus on what to do about these issues. The NRC Committee on Intellectual Property Rights and the Emerging Information Infrastructure did, however, reach agreement on a number of signposts, and these signposts can prove very helpful as we seek to build on their findings.[5]

The committee determined that the problem could best be characterized as simply a question of what to do about the respective rights of creators and the public in a digital environment. Inherent in such a characterization is the recognition that both groups believe the other side currently has too much going in its favor.[6]

But then it must also be recognized that many people may end up being both creators and members of the larger public at different times for these purposes, and that there is a great advantage to the idea of reaching a reasonable balance of interests here. U.S. copyright law, for example, was designed to reach just this sort of balance of interests. Under Article I, Section 8, Clause 8 of the U.S. Constitution, Congress shall have the power "[t]o promote the Progress of Science and useful Arts, by securing for limited Times to Authors and Inventors the exclusive Right to their respective Writings and Discoveries."

The U.S. Supreme Court has characterized the copyright protections granted to creators as a "monopoly privilege," and it has explained that this privilege is "neither unlimited nor primarily designed to provide a special private benefit." It is, the Court determined, "a means by which an important *public purpose* may be achieved." Thus, unlike the laws of many other countries, copyright law in the United States is not—as many people incorrectly believe—an absolute protection of the creator's work. In fact, the law "makes reward to the owner a secondary consideration," and the "granting of such exclusive rights" to the creator has been viewed as conferring "a benefit upon the public that outweighs the evils of the temporary monopoly."[7]

Copyright law is thus perceived as actually embodying the tension between the interests of an individual creator and the interests of the public as a whole. Creators may have individual property rights in their works, but only for the ultimate purpose of benefiting the public by encouraging the creation of more works.[8] When enacting a copyright law, Congress must consider two questions: "First, how much will the legislation stimulate the producer and so benefit the public; and, second, how much will the monopoly granted be detrimental to the public?"[9] This task, the U.S. Supreme Court has said, involves:

> a difficult balance between the interests of authors and inventors in the control and exploitation of their writings and discoveries on the one hand, and society's competing interest in the free flow of ideas, information, and commerce on the other hand.

Agreeing that it is essential to maintain this balance may therefore be an important additional step toward reaching the sort of consensus necessary to move forward in this area.

Uniqueness Throughout this book, we have documented examples of the various ways that online copying issues are particularly different. In fact, copyright issues are consistently viewed as reflecting the most unique aspects of cyberspace, including speed, scale, and the ability to make perfect digital copies. Today's PC is also a copy machine, and so much of what the typical online user does from day to day constitutes copying under traditional legal doctrine.[10] A new reality has thus emerged that simply did not exist before the age of cyberspace. Although there were copyright enforcement problems in the offline world before the 1990s, and although many parallels to the current situation can be discerned in some of the issues raised by the introduction of xerox machines, audiotaping, and videotaping, the speed, scale, and perfect quality of the digital reproduction has generated a set of circumstances that can truly be described as uniquely cyber.

In addition, the rapid development of new technologies has led to circumstances unlike anything that has been seen before. Distance education and the ongoing battle over MP3 music files are two prominent examples of such realities. As discussed, new legal issues have been raised in these unique cases, and many commentators have questioned the prospective ability of traditional legal structures to adequately address the emerging disputes.

The MP3 controversy, in particular, has continued to exemplify the unique nature of private, day-to-day copying issues in cyberspace. Much has been written about music industry issues, for example, but no one person or group has been able—as of 2001—to come up with a viable solution.[11] Indeed, the unprecedented ability of individual Netizens to avoid easy detection as they exchange perfect copies of digital data rapidly and simultaneously has made it almost impossible for record industry officials to bring these practices under control.

Not that the record industry has not tried. As we have seen, the RIAA has been aggressive on every possible front, using full-time staffers to seek out major MP3 sites, enlisting the help of ISPs and educational institutions to remove offending files, employing attorneys to file strategic lawsuits, and attempting to fashion code-based solutions at the product manufacturing end. Yet despite a series of small ongoing victories in these areas, the larger problem remained completely unresolved by 2001, as Netizens continued to find other ways of sharing MP3 music files without being caught.

A noteworthy example was the emergence of Napster. Even as popular Web sites, FTP sites, and Usenet groups were being eviscerated by the RIAA, Napster came out of nowhere to occupy a central position in this ongoing controversy.

Napster began as a file-sharing program, enabling persons to access a very large and constantly changing collection of MP3 music files by searching the hard drives of other Napster users who may have been connected at any given moment. Unlike the more traditional sharing of MP3 files that emerged in the late 1990s, the Napster process did not depend on persons uploading files to Web sites, FTP sites, or newsgroups. Instead, it helped maximize the ability of individual Netizens to share files that they already possessed on their own computers.

Persons wishing to participate in Napster's free service could go to www.napster.com and download the complimentary software. When installing the software, they would be asked a key question: did they want their own digital music files (if any) to be accessible to other Napster users? Most people apparently said yes, because research in late 2000 and early 2001 revealed that a wide and extensive range of music files showed up in Napster search results. Yet even those who chose not to share their own files could still use Napster to search other users' computers and download MP3s.[12]

Commentators have suggested that Napster technology—which enables users to swap files on an automated, decentralized, and distributed network—may come to be viewed as "a computing breakthrough on the level of the World Wide Web" itself. Napster was perhaps the first widespread use of a peer-to-peer system on the Web, with individual users' computers directly linked to each other without a "client server" in between.[13] Tristan Louis, for example, declared in his online newsletter that Napster has created "a true hybrid computing environment. For the first time since the creation of the Web, you have an application that allows for the widespread distribution of files across a network. It could allow for a new set of cooperative tools" in a variety of online environments.[14]

A company spokesperson has in fact asserted that Shawn Fanning—who first conceived of Napster when he was a college freshman—had cooperative work tools in mind from the start. "Collaborative communities of users sharing content is exactly what we're about," the spokesperson explained. Apparently, Fanning was "enamored with the distributed nature of the Internet Relay Chat peer-to-peer communication paradigm" that allowed for chat and file sharing, but which lacked the effective indexed search capabilities of a Web search engine." Internet technology expert Karen Heyman agreed, declaring that Napster "made it easier by orders of magnitude to transfer entire files from one computer to another."

Dr. Lincoln Stein, a participant in the Human Genome Project at the Cold Spring Harbor Laboratory in New York, argues that we were "stuck in a client-server paradigm for many, many years," and that people who wanted to share digital data faced many technical hurdles. The beauty of the Napster system, according to Stein, is that "it does automatic resource discovery. Napster publishes the route to the user's information. Not just the IP address, which may change, but the port . . . This is very different from conventional Web and FTP servers, in which you have to know the IP address and port numbers in advance."[15] And Stein himself became so enthusiastic about Napster technology that he began exploring "how to use Napster-style automated resource discovery to enable scientists to publish their discoveries" in the Human Genome Project.

Needless to say, the proliferation of Napster users generated an even greater outcry from the record industry regarding an MP3 problem that appeared to be spiraling even more out of control. But since in the original Napster system none of the files actually resided on anyone's server, but only on individual users' hard drives, the traditional pressure tactics employed by the RIAA against server owners and operators did not work. No files were posted on FTP servers or Web sites, and thus, there were no files that could be taken down.

While the Napster litigation led to a wide ranging debate concerning the legal and policy implications of file sharing activities, most commentators predicted that such activities were likely to continue long after the Napster case had concluded. Gnutella and Freenet were the most prominent examples of alternative file sharing options in early 2001, but it was generally expected that further advances would inevitably lead to new and unresolved issues.

As discussed above, the file-sharing technology employed by Gnutella was even more anarchic than Napster because it is so diffuse. While Napster relied on a central server to act as a directory, Gnutella was a serverless system based on a true "distributed" or "peer-to-peer" approach. In its features, Gnutella was also strikingly similar to both the DIRT and BAIT programs used by law enforcement officials to monitor a suspect's hard drive and the TRIN00 and "Tribal Flood Network" (TFN) programs that enabled perpetrators to take over unwitting computers and use them in "distributed DoS attacks." All these programs enable one user to directly access another user's computer, and Gnutella also takes advantage of the distributed nature of the Internet in much the same fashion as TRIN00 and TFN.

Gnutella was originally designed by the programmers who founded Nullsoft, the same company that developed the highly popular Winamp MP3 player. In March 2000, they released a beta version and posted it on the Web as a demo. However, AOL—which had acquired Nullsoft a few months before these events—quickly shut down work on the program, demanded that Nullsoft remove the "unauthorized freelance project" from its site, and essentially washed its hands of the whole matter. It is important to note that AOL at the time was in the process of merging with Time Warner, which owned the giant Warner Music Group.[16]

Even though the program was immediately removed, a good number of online users had already copied the software, and it began appearing on other Web sites as well as in newsgroups and Internet Relay Chats. In addition, other programmers were able to reverse-engineer what they had already seen of Gnutella and come up with their own versions.

Not only did Gnutella enable users to share copies of nearly every kind of digital file—including MP3s, executables, zip files, video files, spreadsheets, word processing programs, and picture files—but there was arguably no company at all behind this serverless software after the series of events that unfolded in the spring of 2000. The program itself was distributed in much the same anarchic manner that had served as the model for the file-sharing software in the first place. And Gnutella thus became even harder to control than Napster. In light of these realities, some experts suggested that there would in fact be almost no way to stop this activity "short of finding and unplugging every single connected machine." Indeed, shutting down a Gnutella-style network appeared at the time to be the equivalent of "trying to stop every phone conversation on the planet."[17]

By mid-2000, programmers continued to develop file sharing software based on the Napster-Gnutella model, and the mutual automated copying of digital files enabled by this software only increased in both amount and scope. File sharing programs released during this era included Wrapster, iMesh, Spinfrenzy, VBGNUtella, and Freenet. The first three were Napster-like programs and services, and VBGNUtella was a version of Gnutella developed by a sixteen-year-old Pennsylvania high school student, who reported to the *San Francisco Chronicle* that he wrote his version in Visual Basic programming language, and that he continued to regularly chat and collaborate online with other Gnutella programmers "to help create better versions."[18]

Freenet was a peer-to-peer alternative to the Web released by several young programmers in early 2000. According to the *Wall Street Journal,* the Freenet System was very similar to Gnutella, and anyone could make their computer a "node" on its network by installing a piece of software. Information posted on Freenet would be automatically replicated and stored on multiple member nodes. If someone wanted to search for something—such as an academic paper or a photograph—the request would move from one computer to the next until it encountered and accessed the desired information. Such an approach would also foil tracking efforts and make it nearly impossible for someone to remove information from the network. British programmer Ian Clarke, who worked on Freenet for a period of eighteen months, envisioned it as a way for political dissidents to publish their views without fear of being found out. "This system is, in a sense, above the law," he says.[19]

Commentators note that the concept of distributed networks exemplified by Napster, Gnutella, and Freenet has a long history, since the Internet itself was constructed as a distributed network. When the user-friendly World Wide Web came along, it created a new layer on top of the Net, centered around the servers that host Web sites. These new programs are therefore viewed by many as a "return to the Net's roots."[20]

And the Napster-Gnutella model may herald the beginnings of even more unique activity. According to Louis, Gnutella could potentially enable persons to massively distribute files across a large network because it facilitates both downloading and streaming. He also suggests that

Gnutella technology could be the backbone of the next generation of search engines. "Not only would it index the pages for the server administrator," he writes, "but it could also report back to a mainstream search engine." With a service such as Gnutella, every Web site could automatically "call back the search-engine directory" to post any changes and updates.[21]

But for those already concerned about the proliferation of free and unfettered digital copying online, these latest developments are something akin to a no-holds-barred nightmare. And even those who favor a less restrictive Internet environment have to concede that recent developments only add to the unique hurdles faced by would-be regulators in this context. Indeed, the MP3 dilemma of 1998 and 1999 pales in comparision with the challenges generated by the emergence of Napster and Gnutella.

Private personal copying in cyberspace on a day-to-day basis has thus generated a range of legal and policy issues that may have their roots in the debates of the recent past but have gone far beyond the xeroxing of documents or the videotaping of television programs. The ability to make perfect digital copies in the privacy of one's own home by taking advantage of the Internet's distributed nature and relying on an unprecedented combination of speed, scale, anonymity, automation, ease of operation, and low cost has taken this controversy far beyond anything that has been seen before. Social norms in cyberspace have played a major role in these recent developments, with Netizens demonstrating a disrespect for the law that has arguably not been seen since the days of prohibition. And the technological changes in this area will only serve to further complicate an already uncharted territory. Indeed, there is a symbiotic and reciprocal relationship between these social norms and this technology. Social norms trigger anarchic technological innovations, which then facilitate new and additional ways of circumventing traditional legal restrictions.

In light of this analysis, an initial assessment of how private personal copying might be approached from a regulatory perspective leads to the determination that the traditional national law model not only has not worked, but may in fact be more appropriately characterized a part of the problem than part of the solution. The international agreement model has its advantages here, but it faces many of the same limitations and engenders much of the same criticism as the national law approach. Code-based regulation is viewed as potentially the most effective model for bringing this activity under some sort of control, but—even apart from any philosophical or sociopolitical concerns—technical protection systems are still viewed as too expensive, too intrusive, or too unwieldy by many stakeholders. In addition, such architectural changes may also be subject to a range of legal challenges under a variety of theories that have already been articulated by Internet law scholars in recent years.

In spite of all these hurdles, there may be things that can be done. While the issues are clearly not easily resolvable under traditional law because of their unique nature, the potential applicability of the national law model must still be considered. This analysis must include a recognition that not only is the current law not working with regard to private personal digital copying, but that efforts to implement more restrictive laws have not succeeded in bringing private personal copying under control. In fact, since the passage of the "No Electronic Theft" Act in 1997 and the Digital Millennium Copyright Act in 1998, lawbreaking in this area has apparently only increased.

At the international level, there are also major concerns. The WTO dispute resolution model, for example, and the accompanying intellectual property rules adopted by its members and codified in TRIPS, may work against any possible reforms by restricting the ability of individual nations to make blanket changes in their own copyright laws. On the other hand, reasonable compromises may be more likely under the WTO model than under any other existing framework. And code-based solutions only multiply by the day, providing support for the arguments of those who insist that architectural changes—with all their flaws—will inevitably need to be part of any reasonable long-term solution to the problem of personal copying in cyberspace.

Traditional Regulation of Private Digital Copying under National Law

There are more U.S. laws governing copying in the online world than most people even realize. The rules are complex, and they interface with each other in a variety of unpredictable ways. Basic copyright doctrine that has been on the books for a very long time may still be applicable, and it has been supplemented by new Congressional legislation for the digital age. The average Netizen does not even know where to begin here. Some creators actually believe that nearly all unauthorized reproductions are copyright infringements, while many online users believe that virtually all private, noncommercial copying of copyrighted works is lawful.

The NRC report discussed above identified a number of "copyright-related myths and urban legends" that have circulated on the Internet in recent years. They include the following misconceptions:

- The absence of any copyright notice on a Web site or an MP3 file indicates that the recordings have no copyright protection and are freely available for copying;
- Downloading a copy of a digital file for evaluation purposes is not an infringement if it is only kept for 24 hours or less;
- Posting sound recordings and other copyrighted material for downloading is legally permissible if the server is located outside the United States;
- If the person uploading digital files is not charging for them or otherwise making a profit, this copying is not an infringement;
- Anything posted on the Web or received via e-mail can be freely copied.

As a general rule, *none* of the above misconceptions are true under current U.S. law.[22] Yet these are among the default rules that are followed by many people who have either chosen to observe prevailing social norms or may simply not understand what the laws really say because the interlocking legal principles may have grown too complicated for anyone who is not an intellectual property law specialist.

And these complexities are only exacerbated by copyright-related warnings that often may extend far beyond what the law really says. Such warnings range from overblown admonitions posted above photocopying machines to frightening declarations at the start of videocassettes and DVDs that may lead some people to expect that the FBI will soon be knocking on their door to punish them for even the smallest potential infraction. A particularly egregious example in this context is the warning that appears on the copyright notice page of many books, stating that "no part" of the book "may be reproduced in any form or by any means . . . without permission."

As a general rule, for the typical book, this admonition is no more valid than any of the misconceptions listed above. The true legal status of private copying is somewhere in between the all-or-nothing extremes that are embraced by too many of the stakeholders in this area.

Basic Principles of U.S. Copyright Law under Federal Legislation

U.S. copyright law grants certain exclusive rights to the creator of an original work that has been "fixed in a tangible medium of expression." Ideas are not protected under this statutory scheme—only the expression of ideas. As a general rule, the protection is automatic, and creators do not typically need to register a copyright or even indicate on the work itself that it has been "copyrighted" as of a particular date. The basic term of copyright protection for works completed on or after January 1, 1978 is "the life of the author plus 70 years."[23]

While a copyright infringer can generally always be sued by the copyright owner in civil proceedings, certain egregious copyright violations are also considered crimes, and defendants in such cases—as discussed in chapter 5—can be arrested and prosecuted as criminal suspects. In addition, persons and entities who are not themselves infringers can also be held responsible for certain copyright violations if they help facilitate the copyright infringement.[24]

The five exclusive rights of the copyright owner include (1) the reproduction right, (2) the modification right, (3) the distribution right, (4) the public performance right, and (5) the public display right. Each of these rights embody complex rules and various exceptions, but the basic principle is that a creator is granted a "monopoly privilege" in his or her work, and that only he or she has the right to reproduce, modify, distribute, publicly perform, or publicly display the protected work. Of course, the copyright owner can sell or give away some or even all of these rights. In day-to-day business affairs, for example, copyright owners often agree in writing to share these rights with others. Such agreements are called "express licenses." In addition, others may be entitled to share these rights through "implied licenses," which emerge as a result of certain conditions that have arisen over time.

Several explicit exceptions to the five exclusive rights have been included in the specific text of the law. One of the most relevant of these exceptions for our purposes is the First Sale Doctrine, which allows a person who has legally obtained a copy to sell or dispose of it without authorization from the copyright holder.[25] Under Section 109 of the U.S. Copyright Act, once a copy of a work is sold, the owner has no further right to control the distribution of *that particular copy*.[26] Thus, for example, an individual, library, or other entity is free to give away, lend, rent, or sell copies of books and many other materials. In contrast, the distribution of "phonorecords" and computer programs are subject to certain detailed restrictions.[27]

Works are not protected under any of these laws if they are in the public domain, however. Some works, such as government documents, are automatically in the public domain. Others move into the public domain when their term of protection has expired. As a general rule, for example, the basic texts of the Bible and Shakespeare are both in the public domain. Works in the public domain may be freely copied and distributed by anyone at any time.

In addition, even if a work is protected under one or more of the five exclusive rights, it may be copied, modified, distributed, performed, or displayed *without permission* if the fair use doctrine applies. Particularly in the age of cyberspace, many believe that the fair use doctrine has become the single most important set of legal principles under U.S. copyright law. Yet it remains one of the most nebulous areas of this law, and court decisions in this area are filled with unusual and arguably inconsistent interpretations of what might actually constitute fair use.

The language of the fair use doctrine can be found in Section 107 of the U.S. Copyright Law, and it is instructive to look at the actual wording. The statute begins with an introduction, which establishes the scope of the doctrine and has set the tone for its application by courts of law. Indeed, many judges have quoted from this introduction when faced with difficult questions of interpretation in this area:

> [T]he fair use of a copyrighted work . . . for purposes such as criticism, comment, news reporting, teaching (including multiple copies for classroom use), scholarship, or research, is not an infringement of copyright.

While the use of copyrighted materials without permission for these specified purposes is not automatically a "fair use," it is clear from numerous subsequent court decisions as well as from the discussions in Congress that copying for purposes of criticism, comment, news reporting, teaching, scholarship, or research has achieved favored status under the law.

In any case, no matter what the use, the four "statutory factors" described in Section 107 must be considered when an alleged copyright infringer raises the fair use defense:

> In determining whether the use made of a work in any particular case is a fair use the factors to be considered shall include—
>
> 1. the purpose and character of the use, including whether such use is of a commercial nature or is for nonprofit educational purposes;
> 2. the nature of the copyrighted work;
> 3. the amount and substantiality of the portion used in relation to the copyrighted work as a whole; and
> 4. the effect of the use upon the potential market for or value of the copyrighted work.

While at one time the courts seemed to believe that the fourth factor was the most important, at this point all four factors have been deemed equally important. In addition, no one formula exists for weighing the four factors. Thus it may be the case that only one of the four factors may be decided in favor of a defendant, but that this one factor—under the circumstances—may be sufficient to decide the case, even if the other three factors tilt the other way.

Finally, it must be noted that a court's analysis is not limited to the four statutory factors, but can also include additional factors relevant to the particular case.[28]

As discussed earlier, the U.S. Congress added new provisions explicitly addressing digital copying to the existing body of copyright law in the late 1990s. These provisions—which included the "No Electronic Theft" Act and the Digital Millennium Copyright Act—arguably upset the balance reflected in original U.S. copyright doctrine by strengthening the ability of copyright owners to pursue legal remedies against alleged infringers while providing few if any concurrent rights for online users. The status of the fair use defense in the aftermath of this legislation became a particularly troubling issue for some commentators, although defenders of the NET Act and the DMCA insisted that fair use had not and would not be compromised.[29]

In any case, the legal tools available to prosecute alleged infringers in a digital environment increased significantly after the two legislative packages were signed into law. Under the NET Act, for example, the justice department could now prosecute Netizens for criminal copyright infringement even if the defendants had no discernible profit motive. And under the DMCA, a variety of stringent rules were enacted that strengthened the hand of copyright owners across the board. These included provisions that actually suggest that "online service providers" may be liable if they knowingly link to infringing material.[30] And it has been noted by commentators that the term "online service provider" as used in the DMCA has been defined "extremely broadly" and appears to include more types of online activities than simply those conducted by the typical ISP.[31] In addition, the DMCA House Judiciary Committee Report explains that the definition of "online service provider" includes "services such as providing Internet access, e-mail, chat room and web page hosting . . . ." Thus, according to an analysis of the act by Washington D.C. Attorney Jonathan Band, even a company that "maintains an Intranet for its employees may be a service provider under the statute." Similarly, a company that "maintains a bulletin board where customers can post comments concerning the company's products may qualify as a service provider" and thus be subject to liability for knowingly linking to infringing material.[32]

The DMCA also contained the much debated anticircumvention and "take-down" provisions. Not only was it now a crime for online users to circumvent copyright protection devices,[33] but online service providers were typically required to take down material from users' Web sites if copyright owners complained that the materials even *appeared* to constitute copyright infringement.[34]

Finally, in addition to these specific statutory provisions and the basic general principles of copyright law, it must be noted that legal principles in other areas of law may also apply to certain copyright-related disputes. These would include well-established rules governing trademarks, patents, and trade secrets as well as the broad and wide-ranging doctrine that has been developed over time to address contract violations and First Amendment questions.

U.S. Laws Addressing Private Copying in a Changing Technological Environment

It is generally believed that copyright law is implicitly designed to adapt to a changing technological environment. The U.S. Supreme Court has, in fact, noted that "[f]rom its beginning, the law of copyright . . . developed in response to significant changes in technology."[35]

Indeed, the Court has cited some very interesting examples in support of this view. It has referenced the fact that "it was the invention of a new form of copying equipment—the printing press—that gave rise to the original need for copyright protection," and has noted that this protection "had its early beginning in the British censorship laws." In addition, the Court has traced the response of the law to the development of player pianos, xeroxing techniques, and the ability to retransmit television programs:

> Thus, for example, the development and marketing of player pianos and perforated rolls of music . . . preceded the enactment of the Copyright Act of 1909; innovations in copying techniques gave rise to the statutory exemption for library copying embodied in Section 108 of the 1976 revision of the copyright law; [and] the development of the technology that made it possible to retransmit television programs by cable or by microwave systems . . . prompted the enactment of . . . [complex new provisions] . . . after years of detailed congressional study.

Two noteworthy examples of recent efforts to adapt U.S. law to personal private copying in a changing technological environment include the 1984 Sony "Betamax" case and the 1992 Audio Home Recording Act (AHRA).

Sony v. Universal Studios and Disney The *Sony* case was a watershed decision in several key ways. Up until this case, for example, it was unclear whether persons in the privacy of their own homes could legally videotape programs off their television for any purpose. Afterward, as a result of a hotly contested 5–4 decision, noncommercial taping of television programs in one's home for purposes of "time shifting" was deemed a fair use.[36] In addition, the Court addressed the question of whether Sony's sale of its mid-1970s model VCR (called the "Betamax") could be restricted under the doctrine of contributory copyright infringement. It concluded that such a restriction was inappropriate because Sony had not violated the principles set forth in this doctrine.[37]

The "Betamax" litigation was initiated by Universal Studios and Disney in 1976. Home videotape recording technology had emerged for the first time in the early 1970s, and expensive new systems that could create home movies as well as record television programs began to appear on the market. By the mid-1970s, great advances in this technology had led to the availability of relatively low-cost VCRs that were being purchased and used by large numbers of Americans. Universal and Disney—dominant entertainment companies that produced and held copyrights on "a substantial number of motion pictures and other audiovisual works"—sued Sony, which manufactured millions of Betamax videotape recorders, under the terms of the U.S. Copyright Act.

The decision of the Court turned to a great extent on the result of several surveys—conducted by plaintiffs *and* defendants in 1978—which focused on the way in which the Betamax machine was used at the time. Although there were some differences in the surveys, both showed that the primary use of the machine for most owners was time-shifting—the practice of recording a program to view it once at a later time and then erase it. Plaintiffs' survey revealed that 75.4 percent of the VCR owners used their machines to record "for time-shifting purposes half or most of the time," and defendants' survey showed that "96% of the Betamax owners had used the machine to record programs they otherwise would have missed."

Both surveys also showed that a substantial number of the viewers had accumulated libraries of tapes, but when plaintiffs asked those polled how many cassettes were in their library, 55.8% said there were ten or fewer. And in defendants' survey, 70.4% of the total programs viewed by interviewees over the previous month "had been viewed only that one time and for 57.9% there were no plans for further viewing." Several viewers indicated that when they had originally purchased their VCRs they had intended not only to time-shift (record, play-back and then erase) but also to build libraries of cassettes. Maintaining a library, however, proved too expensive, and they indicated that they were now erasing some earlier tapes and reusing them.

In addition, Sony's survey indicated that "over 80% of the interviewees watched at least as much regular television as they had before owning a Betamax," and the studios offered "no evidence of decreased television viewing by Betamax owners."

These findings proved central to the Court's analysis. Justice Stevens—writing for the majority—applied the longstanding rule that a defendant can be held liable for contributory infringement if he or she causes or permits another to engage in an infringing act.[38] Stevens determined, after borrowing from some basic principles of patent law, that "the sale of copying equipment, like the sale of other articles of commerce, does not constitute contributory infringement if the product is widely used for legitimate, unobjectionable purposes. Indeed, it need merely be capable of substantial noninfringing uses."[39]

After identifying this rule, the Court set out to decide whether "substantial noninfringing uses" of the Betamax actually existed. It did so by returning to the results of the user survey and examining both the authorized and the unauthorized use of time-shifting by typical owners of the machines. The Court found, first, that some uses were indeed authorized and thus noninfringing—either because programs taped were already in the public domain, or because many content providers (such as producers of news, sports, or educational programs) did not object at all to the taping of their shows for later use. And the Court then found that even unauthorized time-shifting was noninfringing because it constituted fair use under the four-factor analysis.[40]

Major U.S. Supreme Court decisions always generate additional debate, with members of the legal community analyzing their implications and seeking to determine their scope. The Sony case was no exception to this pattern, and the controversy regarding both the meaning and the long-term impact of this decision continues even today.

Most people agree, however, that the *Sony* case is noteworthy because it was the first decision to recognize a limited right of private personal copying in the high-tech era of the late-twentieth century. It also foreshadowed the Rio MP3 player case,[41] and appears to have provided a basic foundation for legal analysis in other controversies that focus on products such as Napster and Gnutella, which may facilitate copyright infringement in certain situations.

On the other hand, it must be noted that *Sony* did not say that all private personal copying in this context was fair use. Indeed, the decision appeared to avoid deciding whether and to what extent other prevalent uses—such as the building of small libraries—might be legal under current copyright law. Thus, much day-to-day activity involving VCRs continues to be unresolved from a legal point of view. And even the limited right to tape for time-shifting purposes rests on a close 5–4 decision that has been questioned by many subsequent court decisions in one form or another.

Yet the *Sony* decision cannot be ignored, and the parallels that can be identified in Justice Stevens's majority opinion between the facts of that case and the realities present in recent digital controversies are striking. For example, the *Sony* Court relied to a great extent on the fact that the studios could ultimately benefit from the very taping activity that they were fighting against. "Here," Stevens wrote, "plaintiffs assume that people will view copies when they would otherwise be watching television or going to the movie theater. There is no factual basis for this assumption. It seems equally likely that Betamax owners will play their tapes when there is nothing on television they wish to see and no movie they want to attend. Defendants' survey does not show any negative effect of Betamax ownership on television viewing or theater attendance."

Based on the practices identified in the surveys, Stevens also declared that "original audiences may increase and, given market practices, *this should aid plaintiffs rather than harm them.*" Finally, Stevens quoted approvingly from the district court decision in favor of Sony:

> Harm from time-shifting is speculative and, at best, minimal. The audience benefits from the time-shifting capability have already been discussed. It is not implausible that benefits could also accrue to plaintiffs, broadcasters, and advertisers, as the Betamax makes it possible for more persons to view their broadcasts. . . . Testimony at trial suggested that the Betamax may require adjustments in marketing strategy, but it did not establish even a likelihood of harm. . . . Television production by plaintiffs today is more profitable than it has ever been, and, in five weeks of trial, there was no concrete evidence to suggest that the Betamax will change the studios' financial picture.

In the end, of course, Stevens's opinion proved to be prophetic. The movie industry—by changing its marketing practices to encourage video (and later DVD) rentals and sales—succeeded in transforming the pattern of home VCR use and is today making more money than ever. Such a pattern, as many have argued, may prove central to a resolution of the recent MP3 file sharing controversy. It may very well be the case that the record industry—even if it continues to lose lawsuits in this area—will ultimately find a way to make substantially more money from this new technology than in the past.

The Audio Home Recording Act of 1992 The AHRA is an addition to the U.S. Copyright Act that was passed by Congress in response to intensive lobbying efforts by the record industry. At issue in the industry's push for additional protection was the imminent introduction of a new recording technology—digital audio technology (DAT)—that would for the first time enable the perfect reproduction of sound recordings.

Despite the fact that the threat of mass piracy allegedly posed by DAT technology never materialized,[42] the recording industry's lobbying efforts did pay off in the passage of the AHRA, which included provisions that mandated the inclusion in DAT machines of "copy-control devices that limit the ability of would-be profiteers to create serial copies of protected works." Under *AHRA §1002(a),* a "digital audio recording device" must conform to a Serial Copy Management System (SCMS) designed to prevent multiple copies being created from a single work.[43]

In addition to this new protection, however, Congress also provided consumers with a new benefit: an explicit recognition that certain types of audio recording in the privacy of one's own home would now be considered legal. *AHRA §1008* provides that consumers who make noncommercial copies of musical recordings utilizing a covered device or medium shall not be liable under a copyright infringement theory. Under this provision, consumers may legally make analog music tapes on audiocassettes for noncommercial purposes from other tapes or CDs. In addition, consumers may make digital music copies for noncommercial purposes, if and only if that copying is done using a "digital audio recording device." It is important to note that a computer hard drive is not—as of 2001—a "digital audio recording device."[44]

The record industry also benefited, however, from the granting of this formal new consumer right. Under an arrangement negotiated during consideration of this new statute, it was agreed that a small tax would be assessed whenever a blank CD or mini-disk was purchased. The tax would eventually be funneled back to music composers through a complex bureaucratic procedure. Only devices that might be used without infringing copyright under the AHRA could be taxed.

The AHRA is noteworthy because it is one of the few examples of a legal system attempting to come to grips with private personal copying during the past thirty years. In the end, both copyright owners and consumers benefited from the act, but commentators generally felt that the music industry came away with more direct and concrete advantages as a result of intensive lobbying and negotiating efforts. In fact, some have also noted that this is yet another example of an unequal playing field where consumers simply do not have the time or the resources to compete with an RIAA that in 2001 included such industry titans as Seagram's Universal Music Group, AOL Time Warner, EMI Group, Sony, and Bertelsmann's BMG Entertainment.

The *Sony* case and the AHRA reflect the tradition of attempting to adapt copyright law to the changing technological environment, yet both efforts soon proved to be incomplete, and the new digital technologies quickly created additional issues that—as we have seen—are far from being resolved. Indeed, it can be argued that copyright law is at a crossroads today because it has failed to adequately adapt to either the new high-tech inventions of the 1970s and 1980s or to the Internet-related developments of the 1990s.

A Call for Realism

In response to the problems reflected in the complex intellectual property law frameworks and the inadequate responses of our legal systems to the dramatic technological changes of the past thirty years, commentators have suggested a range of possible solutions outside traditional national copyright law. Ideas on the table include proposals for stepped-up efforts to standardize copyright rules for global commerce through current and prospective international organizations, increased reliance on code to protect digital works, and the encouragement of additional private rule-making by ISPs and content providers under a contract law theory. But while all these proposals may have their place, no reforms in this area will be complete unless and until the cumbersome and overbearing copyright laws addressing private personal day-to-day activity in cyberspace are adjusted for the new century.

Certainly, there have been some noble efforts to adapt these law to the changing digital environment, but Netizens today face the insurmountable challenge of sorting out an increasingly complex set of rules and exceptions. They are asked to make sense out of malleable doctrines and lengthy new acts that present even veteran attorneys with daunting tasks of statutory interpretation. It is no surprise, then, that day-to-day private copying has only increased in spite of congressional efforts to strengthen the laws. The inability of the average Netizen to understand the complexities of intellectual property law combined with the ease of use and the strong prevailing social norms that support widespread and indiscriminate copying together lead to a situation that is both predictable and understandable. MP3 issues—reflected in the recent debates regarding Napster and Gnutella—are only one component of this much larger picture.

If there once was an implicit social contract in this area, it has arguably broken down on a personal, day-to-day level in much the same way that it did during the prohibition of the 1920s. And enforcement of copyright laws remains nearly impossible under existing Internet architecture for the type of private copying that takes place in cyberspace on a daily basis.

The law has not truly come to grips with private personal copying since the advent of the xerox machine and the widespread availability of high-tech tools that could be used for the unrestricted taping of radio and television programs. Certain adjustments have been made, but most of the personal day-to-day copying that takes place in the privacy of an individual's own home remains subject to the vagaries of conflicting interpretation by members of the legal community.

It is completely unrealistic to expect Netizens to stop what they are doing and reflect on whether and to what extent existing copyright laws apply to the facts of their individual situations. Many have suggested, for example, that much of the day-to-day personal copying that goes on in cyberspace is fair use under well-settled U.S. law. But while an application of the fair use doctrine to a given fact pattern may be a gratifying exercise for students in a law school classroom, it can quickly prove impossible for the average Netizen, who cannot and should not be expected to consult the range of case decisions that have interpreted the various factors in specific instances. And in addition to the case law and the extensive scholarship interpreting it, people must also take into account the complex language in the legislative history regarding the scope of the four-factor test. The House Committee Report, which addressed this topic in the 1970s and was quoted by the U.S. Supreme Court in the *Sony* case, made clear just how intricate and subtle the application of this doctrine was expected to be:

> Although the courts have considered and ruled upon the fair use doctrine over and over again, no real definition of the concept has ever emerged. Indeed, since the doctrine is an equitable rule of reason, no generally applicable definition is possible, and each case raising the question must be decided on its own facts.

The committee went on to address in some detail the general intention behind the 1976 fair use provisions:

> The statement of the fair use doctrine in section 107 offers some guidance to users in determining when the principles of the doctrine apply. However, the endless variety of situations and combinations of circumstances that can rise in particular cases precludes the formulation of exact rules in the statute. The bill endorses the purpose and general scope of the judicial doctrine of fair use, but there is no disposition to freeze the doctrine in the statute, especially during a period of rapid technological change. Beyond a very broad statutory explanation of what fair use is and some of the criteria applicable to it, the courts must be free to adapt the doctrine to particular situations on a case-by-case basis.[45]

Such an analysis, notably, does not even begin to address potentially conflicting laws at the international level.

Commentary addressing the current state of digital copyright law has reflected three basic positions. The first position argues that the laws are not strong enough, and that more stringent provisions must be added to existing statutes. The second position argues that current law is malleable enough to adapt to recent technological changes, and that even if not enforceable for the average user on a day-to-day level, these laws have important symbolic value. The third position argues that current law is unrealistic, outdated, and has been superseded by new social norms. As we have noted, the first position has been discredited because private personal copying has only increased in the aftermath of the stronger laws that were passed in the late 1990s. In addition, the second position is also questionable because current law has not proven easily adaptable to the new digital environment. And relying on traditional legal doctrines such as fair use to take care of most day-to-day problems cannot work as long as individual users are not able to understand and apply the rules themselves. Perhaps such an approach was practical in the days when individuals were not as free and not as empowered to conduct such widespread copying on their own, but this strategy is clearly no longer viable today. The third position—that the law is unrealistic—emerges as the most apt characterization of cyberspace in the early twenty-first century.

It is time to heed this call for realism. A pragmatic approach under traditional national law would begin with clear rules that all Netizens can understand. It would anticipate a multifaceted strategy involving all three models of regulation, and would seek to take certain private personal activity off the table by recognizing its inherent legality.

While U.S. law has not yet explicitly stated that such activity is acceptable, a review of recent statutes and the cases interpreting these statutes provides an emerging pattern. Cases addressing the xeroxing of documents in a course reader context, for example, have ruled against copying services, but the rulings have been based on the fact that these services copied large portions of books without permission for the inclusion in commercial course readers. Much more limited copying of documents by private individuals for noncommercial purposes is distinguishable from these decisions, and commentators have suggested that the subtext of the rulings in both *Kinko's* and *Michigan Document Services* is that such private copying would indeed constitute fair use.[46]

Controversies involving more recent high-tech copying provide further support for such a pattern. The *Sony* case, discussed at length earlier in this chapter, expressly recognized the legality of at least certain types of private videotaping by individuals in their own homes. The AHRA, as we have seen, did the same for the taping of music from the radio and from other cassettes or compact disks by means of specific recording devices. The *Rio* case, *RIAA v. Diamond Multimedia Systems,* held that the manufacture and sale of this portable MP3 player could continue, even though a significant percentage of its buyers were apparently using it to download and play unlicensed copies of digital music files.[47]

Read together, these cases and statutes suggest a pattern that favors the private personal copying of small documents and files for noncommercial purposes. Contrary to the views expressed in certain quarters, simple copying and downloading of small files is not automatically analogous to theft. Much of this limited private activity is already justified under recognized exceptions or under the fair use doctrine. It is important to recall that the first fair use factor focuses on purpose, and whether the copying is done for commercial reasons. The third factor focuses on the amount and substantiality of the portion used in relation to the work as a whole.

De minimis is a legal term that refers to the doctrine of *de minimis non curat lex*. Loosely translated, this doctrine states that the law does not take notice of, or concern itself, with very small or trifling matters. Provision is made under certain criminal statutes for dismissing offenses which are *de minimis*.[48] In copyright law, there are already provisions made for dismissing similarly *de minimis* infractions. Not only is such an approach embodied in the third fair use factor, but even the NET Act, which criminalizes certain types of digital copying, recognizes that a felony cannot be committed in this area unless the total retail value of the works that have been reproduced or distributed is more than $2,500. And Internet content providers are increasingly embracing a similar view. By mid-2000, many Web sites included features that enabled online users to display "printer friendly" versions of files and to e-mail copies of posted documents to "a friend." These features recognize that not only will this activity take place anyway, but that the *de minimis* nature of the activity makes it acceptable under a variety of legal and policy-based theories.

The egregiousness analysis set forth earlier in the chapter provides a good foundational basis for drawing clear lines in this context. Recognizing that the two broad types of behavior at issue here are downloading and uploading, and that the variables identified range from small amounts of noncommercial copying to large amounts of copying and distributing that may also be for commercial purposes, it is possible to identify a basic rule for private personal copying in cyberspace.

Under this rule, *de minimis* private personal downloading and forwarding of protected works in a networked environment without permission for noncommercial purposes shall not constitute copyright infringement. This exception to the five basic rights of the copyright owner should appropriately be codified in the federal U.S. Copyright Act.

Precise definitions would need to be worked out by Congress and included in this new statute. *Downloading* must be clearly defined, and must be distinguished from uploading. Many experts have recognized the importance of such a distinction, and the significant difference in the level of egregiousness.[49]

De minimis downloading could refer to documents of less than ten pages, and to small multimedia files that are themselves portions of larger works. It would not include long articles, major portions of books, or copies of software currently for sale. *De minimis* forwarding might consist of no more than five to ten e-mail attachments to friends. *Private personal* downloading and forwarding would refer to activity taking place on one's own private home computer or laptop for such purposes as personal enrichment or recreation.

In adopting such an exception to traditionally recognized rights, Congress must make it very clear that the formal "legalizing" of certain private personal day-to-day copying in cyberspace does not signal that anything goes. In fact, this rule should appropriately be accompanied by increased law enforcement, international cooperation, and code-based adjustments in online architecture to help ensure that egregious reproduction, uploading, and distribution—which would now be precisely distinguished from legal downloading and forwarding—are clearly viewed as unacceptable activity.

Of course, it is not likely that such an explicit new rule will by itself immediately result in major day-to-day changes. A combination of other strategies and approaches is essential, and careful collaborative planning by stakeholders—including Netizens—that builds on this change in the law will be absolutely necessary. But such a rule promises to be an important beginning, and could go a long way toward restoring the balance that is integral to a fair and reasoned copyright law. It provides the benefit of a clear and precise rule that all online users can understand and embrace, transcending the overblown rhetoric that is currently much too prevalent both online and offline. Greater respect for the law may inevitably follow, accompanied by a gradual change in social norms over time that would benefit both the copyright owners and the public at large.

While the "legalization" of private personal *de minimis* copying will certainly not resolve the MP3 file sharing disputes, it can serve to help simplify the problem. Persons who only download limited numbers of music files that may have already been posted will no longer be lumped together with those who are illegally posting such files. Authorities and policymakers will be able to focus on the appropriate level of egregious conduct. And even those using Napster-like technology can be distinguished in this manner. Since Napster, for example, has provided users with the option of choosing to access other files while not sharing their own, those who choose that option are also only downloading, and their actions—assuming they are not sitting in front of a computer all day every day and downloading hundreds of files—would not be considered copyright infringement under the new statute outlined above.

In any case, whether or not Congress adopts a statute such as the one proposed, it appears likely that in the near future it will be the courts—and not Congress—that have the first crack at resolving the overall Napster-Gnutella dilemma. The *A&M v. Napster* case, for example, focused in great part on the doctrine of contributory copyright infringement and the applicability of the *Sony* decision to these new sets of facts.[50] Courts will be required to sort out a range of legal and policy concerns, but in the end generic file-sharing programs are not likely to be seen as any less legal than the Betamax or the Rio. Particular operations may be questionable, but with additional uses being identified for Napster-Gnutella technology that go far beyond the simple sharing of MP3 files, some form of the technology will inevitably continue. Further adjustments in the law will necessarily follow.

It is important to view the record industry's MP3 position in historical context. From the time that audiotaping technology first developed, industry officials have raised the specter of alleged lost profits and have fought to limit the availability and use of products that would enable persons to record music in the privacy of their own homes. Although the industry has not won every battle, it achieved a major victory under the AHRA, when it essentially succeeded in preventing the widespread introduction of devices that could record perfect copies under digital audio technology. The RIAA position has remained unchanged over time. It continues to challenge new technological developments that empower private users in this area, and it always alleges that it has been negatively impacted financially by these innovations. Yet the record companies continue to make large sums of money, and music industry profitability overall has shown no concrete signs of abating.

Industry spokespersons have insisted all along that the record companies are losing millions of dollars as a result of MP3 file sharing by devoted online music lovers. It remains unclear, however, how the RIAA has calculated these numbers. Even if it is possible to estimate how many MP3 files might be downloaded over time, it is not possible to create valid and reliable data based on such estimates. There are a variety of reasons why an individual person might choose to download an MP3 file, and there is no predictable correlation between such *de minimis* action and loss of money by a record company. Downloading a copy of a song for private noncommercial use that may have been posted illegally does not necessarily *take anything away* from a recording artist or a record company. There is no comparison between such activity and CD piracy, where illicit companies make pirated copies of entire CDs for the purpose of making of profit. Such comparisons are not only disingenuous, but they ignore common patterns of use by MP3 afficionados today. Many users download tracks because they are instantly available, and may not have ever gone out and purchased the entire CD. Netizens, in fact, may already have the song—or a version of the song—on tape, CD, or DVD, but may wish to take advantage of the convenience of MP3 by also having a copy on their hard drives or in their portable MP3 player. And, even more importantly, sampling a copy of the song often motivates a user to go out and get the entire CD or DVD, and can generate a level of interest in the artist or the genre of music that would simply not have been there had it not been for the availability of the MP3 file online. Justice Stevens's prescient predictions in the *Sony* case regarding the potential for additional profitability in the entertainment industry through creative marketing and use of video technology is, of course, equally applicable here.[51]

By 2001, use of MP3 technology had become a mainstream activity, no longer limited to college students or members of virtual MP3 communities. Articles in major newspapers advising readers on features to look for in new computers often referred to MP3 files within the context of recommendations regarding speed and hard drive size. Advertisements for new wireless information appliances boasted of such new features as the ability to play MP3 files. In light of these realities, a reasonable solution to the range of MP3 controversies is not only necessary but inevitable. Legislators, policymakers, and jurists can already benefit from a wide range of impressive commentary on the subject, and some logical combination of recent proposals that maintain the balance between the rights of the creator and the rights of the general public might prove surprisingly effective down the road. One thing is certain, however. The MP3 file format and Napster-Gnutella technology is not about to disappear. It may be supplanted by new portable wireless technology that facilitates copying and file sharing on a level that makes current features seem archaic and anachronistic, but what we are seeing today is only the beginning.

As discussed, these issues are likely to be addressed initially through federal litigation, which may very well take years to resolve. While a reliance on such a common law approach is eminently sensible and cannot easily be dismissed, many commentators continue to question the efficacy of litigation as a vehicle for resolving disputes involving cutting-edge technology. Intellectual property law scholar Douglas Baird raised similar questions in the aftermath of the Sony case back in 1984. In an article entitled "Changing Technology and Unchanging Doctrine," Baird argued that "the failure of the Court to confront existing copyright doctrine and existing technology stems in large measure from the nature of litigation."[52] New court decisions will prove useful, but they must inevitably be followed by relevant statutes and implementing policies that reflect the compromises that will be required down the road.

Addressing Private Digital Copying under the International Agreement Model

Many of the issues under the traditional national law model and much of the analysis above are equally applicable on an international level. Recent controversies such as the MP3 file sharing debate are playing out across the globe, raising additional concerns not only for American companies doing business overseas, but for local record companies in other nations as well. Citizens of every country can benefit from realistic approaches to copyright law reform. Beyond expanding the scope of copyright reform, however, international agreement can play a very important role in addressing the more egregious types of private personal reproduction and distribution.

As we have seen in earlier chapters, the main advantage of an international cooperation model in cyberspace is the potential ability of many nations to work together on three interrelated areas—jurisdiction, inconsistent national laws, and enforcement. For some problem categories, such issues are less relevant, but in the area of copyright, they can be central. Fortunately, many people have worked very hard over the years on both international jurisdiction issues and global intellectual property issues, and Internet stakeholders today can benefit greatly from the foundation that has already been built.

In fact, while jurisdiction issues stemming from inconsistent laws have certainly proven problematic, there are a variety of workable approaches available in this context. On a national level in the United States, as we have seen, the courts are developing and refining a workable system for addressing cyberjurisdiction disputes between states. On an international level, as Jack Goldsmith has pointed out in his seminal law review article *Against Cybernanarchy,* there is an established and workable system for addressing many types of global jurisdiction controversies, particularly in an intellectual property context.

Goldsmith argues that the emerging approach to such "transjurisdictional transactions" offline stems from changes over the past fifty years in transportation, communication, and the scope of corporate activity. These changes, which led to an unprecedented increase in multijurisdictional activity, have, in Goldsmith's view, led the global community toward an approach that maximizes legal options even as it requires acceptance of the fact that more than one law might apply to a given transaction.

Today, as a general rule,

> it seems clear that customary international law, like the United States Constitution, permits a nation to apply its law to extraterritorial behavior with substantial local effects. In addition, both the Constitution and international law permit a nation or state to regulate the extraterritorial conduct of a citizen . . . In short, in modern times a transaction can legitimately be regulated by the jurisdiction where the transaction occurs, the jurisdictions where significant effects of the transaction are felt, and the jurisdictions where the parties burdened by the regulation are from.[53]

Thus, persons and companies caught up in global commercial disputes today can benefit from numerous legal options that trigger specific rules regarding which set of laws might in fact be applicable, depending on the court they choose for their litigation. Those doing business on an international level must be aware that the laws of individual nations could overlap, and that more than one set of laws might ultimately apply to them. In addition, beyond this emerging system of "overlapping jurisdictional authority," many global transactions can include built-in provisions for the arbitration of disputes that might arise.

While no one claims that this system for addressing offline commercial activity is perfect, it has proved to be workable, and could arguably apply to many Internet-related disputes as well. In addition, with regard to the specific area of copyright disputes, the international baseline set forth in the Berne Convention can be of particular help in cyberspace. Nations agreeing to the Berne Convention may still adopt inconsistent laws, but certain basic principles will be the same from country to country.

Many hope that the WTO will provide additional benefits in this area. The goal of the WTO Agreement on Trade-Related Aspects of Intellectual Property Rights, as discussed in chapter 6, is to establish and build upon a baseline of minimum standards for the intellectual property laws of individual nations. In addition to a dispute resolution mechanism with meaningful sanctions for those who fail to abide by such a baseline, many see TRIPS as a vehicle for ultimately harmonizing national intellectual property laws over and above the basic minimum guidelines that it establishes.

While the specific provisions and detailed nuances of the TRIPS agreement are beyond the scope of this book, it is important to note that the national law of WTO member nations in the future *must* be consistent with the basic TRIPS standards of copyright protection. As TRIPS begins to take effect among all member nations over the next few years, a very important and potentially contentious task within the global community will focus on the standard of "intellectual property protection" that will ultimately be required. Some commentators have expressed the fear that "developing nations" will seek to institutionalize a "lowest common denominator" standard of protection, rather than the stricter, more protectionist standard favored by many others. On the other hand, it is very important that no one lose sight of the fact that more rigid copyright laws have failed to stem the growth of private personal copying in recent years. Realistically, the most important role that TRIPS can play with regard to international copyright issues will be to foster increased law enforcement activity for the most flagrant violations.

Those who examine these issues on a global level agree that the most significant threat to the rights of copyright owners on the intellectual property front is not from *de minimis* private, noncommercial copying by Netizens, but from widespread piracy for commercial purposes. Christopher Roberts, former director-general of trade policy for the United Kingdom, reported in mid-2000 that "according to estimates by various industry groups, piracy levels in developing countries routinely exceed 50 percent and frequently rise above 75 percent of the market for IP products (books, music, software, movies, etc.)." Roberts emphasizes that "lawful trade in IP products is still the exception rather than the rule in much of the developing world, and current levels of enforcement are not having a deterrent effect."[54]

Even if reasonable reforms are enacted to address some of the personal private copying issues addressed in this chapter, and even if appropriate global legal standards are put in place to counter the more egregious violations, law enforcement is likely to remain a significant day-to-day challenge in cyberspace. While international agreement has already created a solid foundation that can be built upon to help address jurisdiction problems and inconsistent national laws, the global community is much less farther along in the area of intellectual property law enforcement. But here as well, there is great potential for an additional level of cooperation under the organizational frameworks already in place to address intellectual property issues that arise in global commerce. Individual nations have worked together effectively to address terrorism and other safety-related concerns, and these efforts can serve as models for new initiatives to counter flagrant copyright violations.

Employing Code-Based Regulation to Address Egregious Private Personal Copying

Code-based regulation, as we saw in chapter 7, has the potential to effect an unprecedented level of control in areas such as copyright management. Thus, it is imperative that a comprehensive, long-range plan for addressing private personal copying in cyberspace include a focus on prospective approaches in this area. Combined with copyright law reform for *de minimis* personal copying and an increased level of international cooperation and standardization, reasonable code-based adjustments can play an increasingly important role in bringing a semblance of order to this territory.

It must be emphasized that the appropriate goal for code-based adjustments with regard to private personal copying is to focus on countering egregious violations. Realistic and balanced policies that enable *de minimis* day-to-day activity to continue are essential to maintain the character of today's Internet and to rebuild the implicit social contract in the area of copyright law. In addition, such policies would go a long way toward preventing "code wars," in which disgruntled individual users create software solutions to circumvent technical protection systems, forcing the protection systems industry to then create newer and stronger code, which is then inevitably followed by further efforts to circumvent the new code. Policymakers cannot rely upon the laws prohibiting such circumvention, because these laws have proven no easier to enforce than the copyright statutes that came before them.

An Internet architecture with security measures that focus on limiting only the extensive reproduction and distribution of protected works for commercial purposes while continuing to facilitate *de minimis* day-to-day personal copying not only makes sense in general from a policy perspective, but it would have the best chance of helping to foster a consensus in this area. Such a prudent use of technical protection services can help maintain the balance inherent in the copyright law system established under the U.S. Constitution. In fact, all Internet stakeholders could conceivably benefit from such reasonable controls.[55] Individual Netizens are likely to see this as an eminently sensible approach, and IT industry representatives may ultimately concede that in the end, it is the more egregious violations that worry them the most. Of course, the challenge will be to create technical protection systems that can focus on preventing these violations rather than simply blocking everything.

By 2001, a range of workable technical protection services (TPSs) were available in the copy protection context. They included basic security and integrity features of computer operating systems, various methods of encryption, rights management languages that enable computers to determine whether requested actions fall within a permitted range, and digital watermarking.

Cryptography has served as a central enabling technology for technical protection components. Building on this technology, software engineers have created a range of devices that can be employed for intellectual property management, and new ideas are being explored on a daily basis.[56] The "trusted systems" concept described in chapter 7, for example, could conceivably employ encryption to embed copyright protection mechanisms throughout the computer hardware and software at all levels, right down to the basic input/output operating system (BIOS). While not in widespread use as of 2001, trusted systems, in the view of some software engineers, could lead to security becoming "a major influence on the design of computing and communications infrastructure, leading to the development and widespread adoption of hardware-based, technologically comprehensive, end-to-end systems."

Other TPSs, more limited in both their design and the scope of their protection, were in various stages of development and use as of 2001. They include access control in bounded communities (such as systems in corporations or on college campuses that keep track of member identities, data objects, and the privileges that each user has for each object), enforcement of access and use controls in open communities (such as techniques for posting documents that are easily viewed but not easily captured when using existing browsers), copy detection in open communities (such as digital labeling to facilitate monitoring and deter abuse), and protection mechanisms for niches and special-purpose devices (such as DVDs), which were originally designed to limit reproduction and distribution by individual users).[57]

As discussed in earlier sections of this book, such code-based adjustments can be implemented independently, or can work in conjunction with traditional national law and international cooperation. TPSs can serve as the equivalent of private ordering, or they can constitute features of broader private rule-making processes by content providers and ISPs. Alternatively—or in addition—they can be mandated by federal legislation or international treaty.

The interface between code-based adjustments and traditional national law has been the subject of extensive scholarship in recent years, as commentators examine the legal and policy implications of combinations in this context. Positions have been staked out in support of many possible formulas, including laws mandating architectural changes, laws restricting architectural changes, and creative combinations of default rules and private ordering. Given the range of issues that are likely to emerge as the technology continues to develop and circumstances continue to change, this book endorses the position that a wide array of creative combinations employing features of all three basic regulatory models plus some level of private rule-making together constitute the most promising direction for establishing and maintaining an appropriate degree of control in cyberspace.

Despite a growing variety of options, relatively few technical protection services had been put in place by 2001.[58] Product development was still in its infancy, and issues of cost to content providers and convenience to online users had not yet been adequately addressed. But few prognosticators challenged the conventional wisdom that the inevitability of advances in this area will result in more widespread use of these services over time.

The proper use of code-based regulation to address private personal copying promises to be a central ongoing question in the area of cyberspace law and policy over the next three to five years. The NRC report examined this topic at some length, and came to some important conclusions in this regard.

The report emphasized that a technical protection service cannot protect perfectly. A sufficiently determined adversary can either pick the digital lock or find a way around it. Thus, TPS design almost always involves "a trade-off between capability and cost, including the cost of the effort of the content distributor (who must use and maintain the system) and the effort of users, who typically experience inconvenience in dealing with the system." Yet while this trade-off may result in a content provider choosing a TPS of only moderate strength, such a solution is frequently entirely adequate and appropriate. The report kept coming back to the point that TPS's need not be perfect to be useful:

> Most people are not technically knowledgeable enough to defeat even moderately sophisticated systems and, in any case, are law-abiding citizens rather than determined adversaries. TPS's with what might be called "curb-high deterrence"—systems that can be circumvented by a knowledgeable person—are sufficient in many instances. They can deter the average user from engaging in illegal behavior and may deter [others] by causing them to think carefully about the appropriateness of their copying.[59]

In addition, the NRC report suggested that the quality and cost of a TPS should be tailored to the values of and risks to the resources it helps protect. A new movie release, for example, requires different protection than a professor's class notes. Such a focus will be a central feature of a regulatory system that points toward countering egregious reproduction and distribution for commercial purposes while de-emphasizing efforts to address *de minimis* day-to-day personal copying.

At the broader level of copyright law and policy, the report concluded that while technical protection services may have a place in helping to manage intellectual property, copyright holders "should also bear in mind the potential for diminished public access and the costs involved, some of which are imposed on customers and society."[60]

No one familiar with the complexity of these issues expects a quick and easy resolution to the problem of private personal copying in cyberspace, but a series of steps under each of the basic regulatory models, combined with reasonable and consistent private rule-making efforts at the ISP level, may succeed in reestablishing an implicit social contract for this area. Obtaining such a "buy-in" from the average Netizen will go a long way toward enabling both law enforcement officials and policymakers to focus on the most egregious violations.

Comparing our analysis of private copying issues with the examination of representative problems identified in chapters 9 and 10 yields some interesting additional findings. Regulators seeking to address cyberterrorism, online consumer fraud, and day-to-day personal copying can all begin by referencing a comprehensive list of relevant legal principles under the national law model. However, the statutes and case decisions under the first two categories have proven much more viable from a regulatory perspective than the heavy-handed and often inscrutable laws that govern online copyright today. From an international perspective, the level of cooperation thus far has arguably been most significant in the intellectual property area, although recent global law enforcement efforts in the area of online safety have been among the most successful Internet-related regulatory activities to date. In the area of code-based regulation, architectural changes by either the powers-that-be or individual Netizens may have only a limited impact with regard to online consumer fraud, but could have a major influence on the ability of Internet stakeholders to combat cyberterrorism and egregious private reproduction and distribution of protected works. Indeed, there is a remarkable similarity between recent code-based developments that could serve to protect online sites in general and those technical protection services that can protect copyrighted works. Both have the potential to effect a new and unprecedented level of control in cyberspace, but both could result in irreversible changes in the nature of the online world as we know it. Both can work very well in combination with reasonable and balanced legal principles, but both have their costs in lower levels of convenience and higher levels of capital expenditure. And both may also trigger ongoing code wars unless a viable consensus can be reached between and among all Internet stakeholders, including average Netizens.

Few would argue that code-based adjustments are not becoming a central feature of present and future regulatory efforts, but many issues will have to be sorted out over time. On the legal front, for example, Internet law scholar Jonathan Zittrain has suggested that the courts may wish to consider a new "cyber-abstention" doctrine for certain types of intellectual property cases. Under this doctrine, for every case where plaintiffs are alleging copyright infringement, the court might inquire into whether or not plaintiffs had first employed some form of technical protection system to "lock their digital door." If they had not, Zittrain suggests, then courts could abstain from even hearing the case. As a matter of policy, the courts would be saying that if you do not lock your door or at least make a reasonable effort to lock your door under existing technology, you cannot expect to prevail in certain types of copyright infringement cases.

Yet efforts to adjust Internet architecture in this regard may in and of themselves lead to circumstances that few would ultimately support. Karen Heyman, for example, paints a potentially dystopian scenario that would include new Internet browsers that do not allow users "to cut and paste text or print out articles for free, let alone download music and video." For those who think that this could never happen, Heyman notes the existence of a new product called Clever Content Server that "allows graphic images to be seen only through its own viewer"—a viewer that disallows screen captures and disables the "save as" feature on your browser.[61]

In addition, commentators have addressed the possibility that nonpassive, code-based vigilante measures—analogous to the "counter-terrorist" software described in chapter 9—may be employed by copyright owners, either as preemptive measures or for purposes of retaliation. These measures might include the massive pollution of data pools. Since Napster-like networks tend to keep duplicating the same files, and since users of these networks cannot preview the files, copyright owners might seek to infect the online song libraries with mislabeled files or bad versions of songs. Users who think they are downloading the Clash, for example, might instead get Barry Manilow—or they may get songs filled with noise or skips. Such vigilante action, if implemented on a widespread basis over time, might serve to exasperate users and lead them to stop using the file sharing technology.[62]

An even more nightmarish threat, in the eyes of some, would have copyright owners finding security holes in Napster-Gnutella systems and then taking advantage of the technology to root around individual hard drives, disabling files that in their opinion users were not supposed to have in the first place.[63]

Online copyright issues are remarkably complex on a variety of different levels, and everyone agrees that the story is only beginning. The law has clearly failed to come to terms with private personal copying since the advent of the xerox machine, and that failure has only been compounded by the relentless development of newer and more effective technologies for the reproduction and distribution of perfect digital copies with unprecedented speed and on an unprecedented scale. Disrespect for the law is widespread, and social norms that favor private personal copying in cyberspace for noncommercial purposes only serve to exacerbate the problem.

While none of these problems is resolvable overnight, prudent code-based adjustments combined with a solid international baseline and reasonable reforms that legalize *de minimis* noncommercial private copying can make a tremendous difference over time. Enforcement problems will inevitably remain, but with a new social contract, a viable international consensus, and reasonable architectural adjustments that limit the most egregious copyright violations, we will have moved closer toward restoring a sense of order based upon the proverbial balance inherent in both the U.S. Constitution and the major international treaties.

12

Confronting Inappropriate Conduct in Cyberspace: Online Hate and the Inherent Limits of the Law

You've got to be taught before it's too late, before you are six or seven or eight, to hate all the people your relatives hate, you've got to be carefully taught.

—Rodgers and Hammerstein, *South Pacific,* Circa 1949

While impolite behavior has always been a fact of life, there is mounting evidence that incivility not only is on the rise but has become almost the norm in many parts of the culture. A recent . . . [nationwide] . . . survey . . . found that every single person had experienced some type of rude behavior on the job, including insults, curses, [and] nasty e-mails. . . . Gripes about [restaurant] service have tripled over the past five years. . . . Air travel has practically become a combat zone. . . .

Some see all this as the dark side of the New Economy. . . . High-tech gadgets, such as cellular phones, pagers and Palm Pilots, have . . . fostered antisocial tendencies, enabling people to isolate themselves even in public.

—"A Rude Awakening," The *Wall Street Journal,* May 2000

We fancy ourselves to be dealing with some ultramodern controversy, the product of the clash of interests in an industrial society. The problem is laid bare, and at its core are the ancient mysteries crying out for understanding.

—Benjamin N. Cardozo, *The Paradoxes of Legal Science,* Circa 1920

Online hate can serve as a particularly representative problem under the "inappropriate conduct" category. It includes hostile and inappropriate behavior occurring regularly via e-mail and discussion forums as well as the more "permanent" extremist and hate-related Web sites that have proliferated in recent years. In conceptualizing our four categories of problematic conduct, we characterized *inappropriate conduct* as immoral or offensive acts that are typically neither anarchic nor unlawful. Such conduct is viewed as less egregious than other allegedly problematic activity, but it is still likely to trouble the average person. Other representative examples of inappropriate conduct include certain unacceptable behavior in an online education setting and overly aggressive business practices in an e-commerce environment.

It is important to note at the outset that online hate as defined in part I does not include activity that directly threatens physical safety and is already prohibited under current laws. Words constituting a *true threat,* for example, are appropriately placed under the "dangerous conduct" category, but for those who have been targeted by generic online hate, such activity still poses a real threat of danger at some level down the road.

In general, category 4 conduct such as online hate is seen by most Netizens as less problematic than category 3 conduct such as digital copying. One reason for this perception, perhaps, is that hate-related activity may appear less objectionable to those who have not been victimized.[1] The effects of hateful, overly aggressive, and generally inappropriate behavior are often more subtle, and concrete injuries may be much more difficult to identify. In addition, unlike those victimized by unlawful anarchic conduct—who may typically be in positions of great power and influence and can invoke laws that allegedly exist to protect them—those injured by inappropriate conduct are often individual persons who may not only be relatively disenfranchised but often have little or no recourse under current law. Thus category 3 violations tend to be highly publicized, with those who are ostensibly impacted able to call press conferences, fund lawsuits, or mount extensive lobbying efforts. Category 4 victims, in contrast, are often unable to employ such aggressive strategies on their own behalf. Finally, inappropriate conduct is viewed by many as behavior that people must be prepared to tolerate. After all, the argument goes, persons walking down the street in any public area must expect some level of hateful, overly aggressive, or generally inappropriate behavior. If this is the case in the offline world, why should it be any different in the online world?

Yet there are some surprising similarities between private digital copying and online hate. In both cases, the situation only seems to have worsened since the early and mid-1990s, in spite of aggressive efforts by some Netizens and powers-that-be to tighten regulatory structures. And in both cases, there are key forces and perceptions that operate against any efforts to bring the behavior under control. Not only are there very strong social norms operating in cyberspace that serve to perpetuate these activities, but there are many people who believe that the status quo is about the best we can do here. Finally, there are those who fear that any change in the status quo would lead us down a proverbial slippery slope to a new set of circumstances that fly in the face of commonly accepted notions of copyright and free speech—where people would have too much freedom to copy someone else's intellectual property and not enough freedom to speak their mind.

A range of varied positions and perspectives, reflecting significant differences in core values and divergent views of copyright and free speech law, are at the heart of the consensus problem in these areas. And patterns are not always consistent. While the majority of Internet stakeholders would come down on the side of more restrictive intellectual property laws and less restrictive free speech laws, such positions are not necessarily a given. True cyberspace libertarians will favor less restrictions in both areas, and some regulators will favor more restrictions in both. Then there are those who put great emphasis on the free exchange of information but are particularly concerned about the corrosive impact of certain types of online speech. For this last group, less restrictive copyright laws and tighter free speech laws make the most sense.

Consensus Given these persistent and ongoing differences in perspective, it is clear that achieving consensus in the area of online hate will not be any easier than achieving the consensus necessary to come to grips with private digital copying. In fact, the area of online hate is likely to prove even harder to address in this context because of the overwhelming consensus that has already emerged in the United States regarding the value of strong First Amendment guarantees. And while the U.S. Constitution has been held to provide four speech-related rights—the right to speak, the right not to speak, the right to receive information, and the right not to receive information—most Americans continue to view the right to speak as outweighing all the others across the board.

In addition, many people see the Internet as simply a reflection of the real world, and are not particularly concerned about the growth of online hate because they see it as only one component of a larger reality. Hate, they argue, has been around from time immemorial, and it has spread across large geographical areas in the past even in the absence of high-tech communications media such as the Internet. There are those, in fact, who view the openness of cyberspace as an advantage in this regard. If people tend to be more willing to express hateful thoughts online, the argument goes, we will then be able to learn more about just who is behind much of the extremist thought and how hate-related propaganda is constructed. By gaining a better understanding of all these things, we will then be able to do a better job countering hate in our schools and communities.

Yet while such a view cannot and should not be easily dismissed, it is important to note the corrosive and debilitating effects of ongoing day-to-day activity in this area. The widespread dissemination of hate-related expression in cyberspace is unprecedented in scope, and it may be having a destructive effect on our culture in subtle ways that are still not completely understood. Indeed, commentators have already suggested that the growing lack of civility may be traced at least in part to the impact of "less than civil" online speech on society as a whole.[2]

Just a short time ago, many believed that great progress had been made in the fight against bigotry and hateful activity. Commentators emphasized the fact that society no longer tolerated open expressions of prejudice, and that although this was not the end of the battle, it was an important step in the right direction. Yet we seem to have gone backwards over the past ten years. It is now acceptable in many parts of cyberspace to be openly hateful and to refer to immutable characteristics of individuals in the most derogatory manner possible. Throughout history, such increases in hateful expression have foreshadowed dangerous shifts in the political climate. And while such shifts may not in fact be imminent today, historical patterns cannot be dismissed out of hand.

Cognizant of these patterns, international experts on hate-related issues are making plans for the first United Nations world conference on racism, racial discrimination and xenophobia in 2001. A key objective of this conference is to prepare recommendations on international actions to counter online hate. And European leaders continue to call for "international cooperation to stop the Internet's use as a tool" in this regard. For example, at a January 2000 gathering in Stockholm of seven hundred delegates from forty-six countries, speakers expressed concern about both the rise of neo-Nazi activity in Europe and the growing role of high technology in spreading messages of hate. Ruth Dreifuss, head of Switzerland's Federal Home Affairs Department, declared that "unfortunately the Internet is . . . a cross-border vector for racist theories and the fermentation of hatred and discrimination. Worse still," she added, "the web enables those who support such ideas to network and promote their products, books and so-called 'scientific' and other reports by means of e-commerce, or even to coordinate their subversive activities."

At the same gathering, German Chancellor Gerhard Schroeder called for international efforts to address neo-Nazi use of the Internet. "At a time when neo-Nazi groups are using the modern globe-encompassing means of communication to disseminate their inhumane ideas, we have to improve our international cooperation to fight their propaganda of hatred and their glorification of violence," he told the audience.[3]

Major advocacy groups in the United States also continue to work toward these same goals, monitoring online hate and urging additional efforts on all fronts to counter such negative messages. In addition, the U.S. Department of Housing and Urban Development (HUD) launched a major initiative in the spring of 2000 to investigate hate speech on the Internet.[4] HUD Secretary Andrew Cuomo, accompanied by representatives from advocacy groups and online companies, announced that HUD would provide $200,000 to fund a task force on this matter.[5]

In the United States, however, efforts to address hateful expression continue to be severely restricted by societal norms that tolerate such speech in the interests of maintaining broad First Amendment protections. Judicial decisions in this area have reflected the majoritarian view, although it must be recognized that First Amendment jurisprudence is still flexible enough to be adjusted to changing circumstances. In addition, it must be noted that U.S. free speech law is typically viewed as outside the international mainstream since most major industrial nations today prohibit hateful expression.

One way to begin moving in a more logical direction and bring the U.S. law more in line with the prevailing international view is to focus specifically on the most egregious hate-related activity and examine what it would take to prohibit extremist Web sites. As discussed previously, laws prohibiting true threats already exist, and such laws can be used to address the more extreme day-to-day activity. But under current U.S. law, extremist Web sites cannot be taken down by government officials, and arguably this should change.

Realistically, however, the lack of consensus in the United States and on the Internet today may make any prospective changes highly unlikely under any of the three basic regulatory models we identified in part 2. It may very well prove impossible to buck the prevailing social norms and achieve any level of effective control over inappropriate online hate. Stepped-up efforts in schools and communities to counter hate through traditional grass roots, education-related strategies may be the best that we can do. Still, it is instructive to apply our conceptual framework to this area, and follow the same roadmap we employed in our analysis of cyberterrorism, online fraud, and private personal copying. Circumstances may change, and at some point in the future, a growing percentage of Netizens may come to feel that the current regulatory structure is inadequate and needs to be adjusted.

A change in consensus down the road will only be possible if it reflects a reasonable middle ground with respect for the value of free and open expression combined with genuine concern about the unprecedented level of hate-related communication taking place at any given moment across the globe. Policy initiatives built upon such a balanced view can then lead to reasonable adjustments in the law. There is no reason, for example, why egregious hateful speech cannot be precisely identified and prohibited if other types of speech—such as obscenity—are in fact prohibited. It has become a cliche in many quarters to argue that hateful speech is no less obscene than prurient sexual activity, but this point needs to be made again and again if reasonable adjustments in the law are ultimately going to be made.

As we have seen throughout the book, of course, changes in the law are only one possible step, and do not necessarily have a great deal of impact unless they are combined with other strategies and approaches. But changes in the law are an important beginning, particularly in an area where the law does not provide a great deal of guidance for those who wish to address an increasingly unacceptable status quo.

Uniqueness In addition to the scale of the activity made possible by digital technology, online hate is different from similar offline activity in that it takes advantage of two other unique aspects of cyberspace— unprecedented speed and relative anonymity. Purveyors of hateful messages not only take advantage of the technology to disseminate their thoughts quickly and easily, but they are invariably more willing to be openly hateful in cyberspace. This is also the case with extremist Web sites. People and groups who typically hesitate—for a variety of reasons—to espouse bigoted and racist messages on street corners or in public parks, for example, are generally much more willing to do so online. The fact that a Web site is more permanent and, thus, may allow easy identification of the source does not typically act as a deterrent. The relative anonymity of cyberspace, combined with the general absence of any form of online retribution, can provide just enough of a cover for extremists to feel comfortable expressing their views.

Thus, we witness the continuation of a very interesting paradigm shift in the U.S. regarding First Amendment values and causes. While in the 1960s, for example, the most vocal defenders of free speech were leftist antiwar demonstrators and members of the hippie counterculture, today many vocal defenders of the same principles may be members of the Ku Klux Klan, the White Aryan Resistance, or other right-wing hate groups.

In chapter 3, we noted that not only has discriminatory harassment not abated during the past twenty years, but that Web sites espousing racism, hate, and hate-related violence have increased significantly since the mid-1990s. The Southern Poverty Law Center, for example, has published several valuable reports identifying a range of hateful web activities, from militia sites to general hate sites. SPLC investigative studies have revealed that many of these sites often portray themselves as patriotic, academic, or religious in nature, and that it may be necessary to look below the surface to identify the dangerous and divisive messages. Too often, such messages appeal to impressionable young people and to disenfranchised members of society.

The general hate sites are arguably the most egregious. Representing such groups as the Klan, neo-Nazis, and Racist Skinheads, they range from the more informational in nature to Web pages that actively promote goals which can only be accomplished through racial violence, ethnic cleansing, and "holy wars."

Beyond the challenge of building a consensus in this area, would-be regulators face practical considerations on a day-to-day level. Even if U.S. law can be changed, such changes would take years to implement. And, as we have seen in other contexts, there are so many messages being sent and received at any given moment in cyberspace that it is impossible under the current Internet architecture to implement widespread limitations. But these messages do often lead to the creation of a written record, which can then be used—in particularly egregious cases—as evidence against a person in a court of law. And if U.S. law is adjusted to fit within current international norms, extremist Web sites can be taken down either by Internet Service Providers *or* law enforcement officials. In fact, under a generally accepted view of current law, ISPs are often not limited by the First Amendment and may be able to set forth much more aggressive "acceptable use policies" in this context.

Online hate presents would-be regulators with an unusual combination of factors at play. Its unique aspects suggest the need for nontraditional regulatory approaches. But the conventional features of generic bigotry and racism that have always been with us suggest the need for a more traditional, law-based approach. In the end, there is a clear need for a combination of strategies and approaches that take advantage of all three regulatory models, private rule-making, *and* an increased emphasis on this area in schools and communities.

Traditional U.S. Law and Its Impact on Prospective Regulation of Extremist, Hate-Related Web Sites

Should a consensus emerge at some point in support of reasonable adjustments in laws addressing hate speech, an analysis of possible directions would begin with an examination of constitutional principles, relevant case law, and applicable statutes in this area.

Highlights of U.S. First Amendment Law: Basic Principles and Major Exceptions

Two basic principles of U.S. free speech law as interpreted by the courts under the Constitution are particularly relevant to online hate. The first is that statutes and policies designed by public entities to regulate speech are unconstitutional if vague or overbroad.[6] The second is that speech cannot generally be regulated on the basis of its content, unless the regulation falls within some recognized exception or some other related rule of law.

Under well-settled constitutional law, a statute or policy is unconstitutionally *vague* when "men of common intelligence must necessarily guess at its meaning. . . . [It] must give adequate warning of the conduct which is to be prohibited and must set out explicit standards for those who apply it."[7] A statute or policy regulating speech will be deemed *overbroad* "if it sweeps within its ambit a substantial amount of protected speech along with that which it may legitimately regulate."[8] As we saw in chapter 5, the U.S. Supreme Court in *Reno v. ACLU* addressed arguments set forth by the plaintiffs under these principles, and invalidated disputed portions of the Communications Decency Act because it found them to be overbroad.[9] Justice Stevens determined that by seeking to "deny minors access to potentially harmful speech, the CDA effectively suppresses a large amount of speech that adults have a constitutional right to receive and to address to one another." Such suppression was held by the Court to be "unnecessarily broad."[10]

Any attempt by a governmental entity to restrict speech on the basis of its hateful content would be deemed *content-based regulation,* a type of regulation that is disfavored and presumed unconstitutional under First Amendment law.[11] Yet speech can indeed be regulated on the basis of its content if it is found to be (1) obscene, (2) child pornography, (3) fighting words, (4) incitement to imminent lawless conduct, (5) defamation (libel or slander), (6) an invasion of privacy under tort law, (7) harassment, (8) a true threat, (9) copyright infringement, or (10) another recognized tort or crime.

Each of these legal concepts has been analyzed and debated at great length by commentators, legislators, and jurists, and current definitions reflect the consensus that has emerged over time. It is important to review these definitions in order that we might ascertain exactly how online hate can be addressed by current U.S. law.

Obscenity While Justice Potter Stewart's famous line "I know it when I see it" is still quoted in this context, the U.S. Supreme Court in the 1973 case of *Miller v. California*[12] developed a three-part test for obscenity that is still being used today. A court will inquire whether

(a) "the average person applying contemporary community standards would find that the work, taken as a whole appeals to the prurient interest";

(b) it "depicts or describes, in a patently offensive way, sexual conduct specifically defined by applicable state law"; *and*

(c) "the work, taken as a whole, lacks serious literary, artistic, political, or scientific value."

Child Pornography The definition of child pornography, as set forth by the U.S. Congress, was originally limited to visual depictions of real children. It was expanded in 1996, however, to include both "computer-generated images" and pictures of people who only appear to be under eighteen. Under Title 18 of the U.S. Code, Section 2256, child pornography is defined as:

> any visual depiction, including any photograph, film, video, picture, or computer or computer generated image or picture, whether made or produced by electronic, mechanical, or other means, of sexually explicit conduct, where
>
> (a) the production of such visual depiction involves the use of a minor engaging in sexually explicit conduct;
>
> (b) such visual depiction is, or appears to be, of a minor engaging in sexually explicit conduct;
>
> (c) such visual depiction has been created, adapted, or modified to appear that an identifiable minor is engaging in sexually explicit conduct; or
>
> (d) such visual depiction is advertised, promoted, presented, described, or distributed in such a manner that conveys the impression that the material is or contains a visual depiction of a minor engaging in sexually explicit conduct.

In several recent criminal cases filed under this statute, defendants have argued that the 1996 changes were unconstitutional, and the federal courts of appeal have come down with conflicting rulings. In the 1999 case of *United States v. Hilton,* for example, the First Circuit Court of Appeals held that the statutory changes were consistent with the First Amendment.[13] But in *Free Speech Coalition v. Reno,* a decision handed down in December 1999, the Ninth Circuit Court of Appeals found that the changes violated basic free speech principles.[14] In *Ashcroft v. Free Speech Coalition*, the U.S. Supreme Court is expected to address this volatile question.

Fighting Words The U.S. Supreme Court in the 1942 case of *Chaplinsky v. New Hampshire* set out a two-part definition for fighting words: (a) words which by their very utterance inflict injury and (b) words which by their very utterance tend to incite an immediate breach of the peace.[15]

Since *Chaplinsky,* the Supreme Court has narrowed and clarified the scope of the doctrine in at least three ways. First, the Court has arguably limited the definition so that it now only includes the second half. Second, the Court has stated that in order for words to meet the second half of the definition they must "naturally tend to provoke violent resentment." Finally, the Court has held that fighting words must be "directed at the person of the hearer."[16]

Chaplinsky himself was distributing religious literature on a public sidewalk and was led away by the city marshal because of fear that his acts were causing or would cause a public disturbance. As he was led away, he called the marshal a "G-ddamned racketeer and a damned fascist." His breach of peace conviction was upheld because of the danger that the listener would be incited to violence. The test was whether men of common intelligence would understand the words as likely to cause the average addressee to fight. For speech to be restricted under this doctrine, it had to be "words and expressions which by general consent are fighting words when said without a disarming smile." And the Court referred to words that would produce an "uncontrollable impulse."

It must be noted that since *Chaplinsky* not one conviction under the fighting words exception has been upheld by the U.S. Supreme Court.[17] And after the Court's decision in the 1992 case of *R.A.V. v. City of St. Paul,*[18] many commentators argued that the fighting words doctrine had become a relic of another age. The doctrine, however, has not been explicitly overruled, and it remains on the books as a recognized exception to the rule that speech cannot be regulated on the basis of its content.

Incitement to Imminent Lawless Conduct Under the rule set forth by the U.S. Supreme Court in *Brandenburg v. Ohio,* speech can be restricted on the basis of its content if it is "directed to inciting or producing imminent lawless action and is likely to incite or produce such action."[19] As the Court further explained in a subsequent case, "[W]e have not permitted the government to assume that every expression of a provocative idea will incite a riot, but have instead required careful consideration of the actual circumstances surrounding such expression."[20]

Brandenburg focused on circumstances surrounding a rally and speeches by members of the Ku Klux Klan. During the rally, "re-vengeance'" was threatened, and the defendant—who had organized the event—added that "the n——r should be returned to Africa" and "the Jew returned to Israel." The defendant was convicted under a 1919 Ohio statute that forbids "advocating . . . the duty, necessity, or propriety of crime, sabotage, violence, or unlawful methods of terrorism as a means of accomplishing industrial or political reform." In a relatively short opinion, the Court found in favor of the defendant, holding that the statute was unconstitutional because the First Amendment does not permit a state "to forbid or proscribe advocacy of the use of force or of law violation except where such advocacy is directed to inciting or producing *imminent* lawless action and is likely to incite or produce such action."[21]

Commentators have noted that the distinction drawn between "mere advocacy" and "incitement to imminent lawless action" parallels the reasoning in *Chaplinsky* and indicates that in the U.S. the "public peace" can only be protected against speech that is likely to produce immediate violence.[22]

Defamation In general, defamatory statements—which include libel (the written word) and slander (the spoken word)—are not protected by the First Amendment. Rules of defamation have evolved under the common law and vary from state to state, but typically, to qualify as defamation, a statement must be (a) a defamatory communication about the plaintiff, (b) published to third persons, and (c) false at the time it is made.[23]

A *defamatory communication* has been defined as one that "tends so to harm the reputation of another as to lower him in the estimation of the community or to deter third persons from associating or dealing with him."[24] *Published to third persons* means that the communication (oral or written) must be to someone other than the person allegedly defamed. As for the *falsity* requirement, virtually all states today require that the communication be untrue before a defamation action can proceed.

Over the years, the law of defamation has been bolstered by many special rules. For example, under the First Amendment, if the subject of the communication is a public figure,[25] defendant can be held liable for defamation only if the statement was made with actual malice or reckless disregard for the truth.[26] Even if the subject is a private figure, media defendants focusing on matters of *public concern* must also have acted with actual malice or reckless disregard for the truth to be found liable.[27]

In addition, a statement that is only an opinion—and not fact—cannot be considered defamatory under the First Amendment if it (a) addresses matters of public concern, (b) is expressed in a manner that is not provably false, and (c) cannot be reasonably interpreted as stating actual facts about a person.[28]

Finally, it should be noted that a "republisher" of defamatory statements is also liable under the same basic framework. *Republishers* are "those who participate in distributing a libel," and can include, for example, newspapers that print op-ed pieces or even letters to the editor. As a general rule, if the original author is liable for defamation, republishers can also be found liable for defamation for the same defamation.[29]

Invasion of Privacy Statements that constitute an invasion of privacy under tort law are also not protected by the First Amendment. Four separate torts (or civil wrongs) have actually emerged in this context over the past one hundred years. They include *appropriation* of a person's picture or name, *intrusion* upon a person's private affairs or seclusion, publication of facts placing a person in a *false light,* and public disclosure of *private facts.* Each tort has its own basic requirements.[30]

An *appropriation* is an unauthorized use by the defendant of the plaintiff's picture or name for commercial advantage. The plaintiff can be a celebrity or a private person, but a celebrity typically stands a better chance of winning a large monetary award by suing under the related "right of publicity."[31]

An *intrusion* is an intentional or negligent act of prying or intruding by the defendant into a private area of the plaintiff's life. The intrusion must be something that would be objectionable to a reasonable person. It can be physical (such as entering private property uninvited) or nonphysical (such as repeatedly calling a person late at night). In any case, the plaintiff cannot prevail in such a lawsuit unless it can be shown that a person could reasonably expect that he or she would not be intruded upon in this manner by someone in the defendant's position.

False light invasion of privacy is the publication of facts about the plaintiff placing him or her in a false light in the public eye. As with an intrusion, it must be objectionable to a reasonable person under the circumstances. False light invasion of privacy may include views that a person does not hold, or a description of actions that he or she did not take. It should be noted that such behavior may also constitute defamation if the falsity affects a person's reputation.

Public disclosure of private facts is the disclosure of private information about the plaintiff. Disclosure must be highly offensive, such that a reasonable person of ordinary sensibilities would object to having the information made public. Private facts under this tort must involve aspects of the plaintiff's private life that have not already received publicity and are not open to public observation.[32]

Any statements that fall within the definitions of one or more of these four torts can be restricted by governmental entities without violating the First Amendment.

Harassment Rules prohibiting racial, religious, or sexual harassment evolved in the workplace under Title VII of the U.S. Civil Rights Act of 1964. At this point in time, sexual harassment laws are arguably the most highly developed,[33] and they include prohibitions against both *quid pro quo* harassment and *hostile environment* harassment.[34]

Hostile environment claims were first recognized by the U.S. Supreme Court in 1986,[35] and over the next ten to fifteen years, the rules were fine tuned by subsequent judicial opinions. 1998 proved to be a turning point, with the Court deciding four sexual harassment cases in one year.[36] Commentators have raised questions in recent years regarding the extent to which the First Amendment can or should be employed to limit the scope of harassment law,[37] but as of 2001, as long as certain expression falls within the definitions outlined by the Court, it is not protected speech and can be restricted accordingly.

The basic hostile environment claim under Title VII can only be filed by a person who alleges harassment in the workplace. Sexual harassment is not a crime, but an act or series of acts that can lead to large monetary awards for aggrieved employees who have sued their employers under Title VII. To win such lawsuits, plaintiffs must follow a two-step process.

First, they must establish actionable harassment. Second, they must show that the employer should be held liable for this harassment.[38]

To establish actionable hostile environment harassment, plaintiffs must prove that the activity in question was unwelcome and that it constituted "a sexually objectionable environment" that was (a) objectively offensive and (b) subjectively offensive. An environment is deemed *objectively offensive* if a "reasonable person" would find it hostile or abusive, and it will be found *subjectively offensive* if the victim in fact perceived it to be so.

The objectively offensive inquiry is inevitably the most complex. Courts must look at

> all the circumstances, including the frequency of the discriminatory conduct; its severity; whether it is physically threatening or humiliating, or a mere offensive utterance; and whether it unreasonably interferes with an employee's work performance.[39]

Increasingly, the Court has worked very hard to try to distinguish between simple teasing on the one hand and hostile environment sexual harassment on the other. "A recurring point" in recent court opinions, Justice Souter noted in *Faragher v. Boca Raton,* is that "simple teasing, offhand comments, and isolated incidents (unless extremely serious) will not amount to discriminatory changes in the terms and conditions of employment. These standards for judging hostility," he continued, "are sufficiently demanding to ensure that Title VII does not become a 'general civility code.'"[40]

A version of this framework has recently been applied by the courts in federally funded education programs under Title IX of the Education Amendments of 1972 to the Civil Rights Act of 1964. In *Davis v. Monroe County Board of Education,* the Court held that educational institutions can be held liable for peer-to-peer hostile environment sexual harassment "that is so severe, pervasive, and objectively offensive that it effectively bars the victim's access to an educational opportunity or benefit." But even if plaintiff can meet the requirements of this stringent test for actionable harassment, he or she can only prevail if the education officials in charge acted "with deliberate indifference to known acts of harassment."[41]

True Threats As discussed in earlier chapters, threatening speech can be restricted by governmental entities only if it constitutes a "true threat."

The U.S. courts have disagreed over the years regarding the exact contours of an appropriate test to determine whether words amount to a *true* threat, but there is general agreement in most jurisdictions regarding certain basic principles:

1. The threat must be "against the physical safety or freedom of some individual or class of persons,"[42] *and*
2. The communication would lead a reasonable, objective recipient to believe that the person expressing the threat "was serious about his threat . . . regardless of the subjective intent of the speaker to make an actual threat or whether anyone actually felt frightened, intimidated, or coerced by the threat."[43]

As with many other legal tests, then, the courts here inquire into the state of mind of a hypothetical objective reasonable person. The key question is whether such a hypothetical person would feel threatened, regardless of whether the real-life recipient of the threat actually did. If the communication is objectively threatening, it is deemed to be a true threat.[44]

Copyright Infringement On some level, copyright laws act to restrict freedom of expression on the basis of content, because limitations on expressive activity that infringes one or more of the five exclusive rights of a copyright owner have, of course, been deemed acceptable if they reflect the balance of interests required by the U.S. Constitution.

There has been a significant amount of scholarship over the years addressing the interface between First Amendment law and copyright law. Certain disputes have been characterized as pitting one body of law against the other, and commentators have set out a range of interesting positions in these debates, with some favoring the primacy of the free speech guarantees and others favoring the primacy of intellectual property protection. Although interpretations still vary, most believe that the U.S. Supreme Court decision in *Harper & Row v. Nation Enterprises*[45] ended this debate, or at least significantly limited the impact of any future arguments in favor of loosening copyright restrictions on free speech grounds.

In *Harper,* the defendants, who had reproduced excerpts of President Ford's biography in their magazine prior to the biography's formal publication, invoked First Amendment principles in an effort to excuse their actions.[46] The Court rejected their argument, finding that current copyright law "strikes a definitional balance" in this context "by permitting free communications of facts while still protecting an author's expression."[47]

An early cyberlaw case, *Religious Technology Center v. Netcom,*[48] also addressed the viability of First Amendment arguments by defendants accused of copyright infringement. Netcom, an Internet Service Provider, had been charged by the Church of Scientology with contributory copyright infringement for the posting of protected church documents via its server. Although the case was eventually settled, the federal district court opinion addressing this lawsuit is viewed as a notable contribution to emerging Internet law.

Netcom argued, in part, that if it were found liable for copyright infringement, First Amendment principles would be contravened "as it would chill the use of the Internet because every access provider or user would be subject to liability when a user posts an infringing work to a Usenet newsgroup." The court, however, disagreed, declaring that "while an overbroad injunction might implicate the First Amendment . . . imposing liability for infringement where it is otherwise appropriate does not necessarily raise a First Amendment issue."[49] In addition, since Netcom admitted that "its First Amendment argument is merely a consideration in the fair use argument," the court took this statement as a reason to move away from any further consideration of First Amendment issues and on to a more traditional analysis of fair use under the four-factor test.

Intellectual property law attorney Stephen Fraser, after conducting an extensive analysis of the *Harper* and *Netcom* cases, concluded by arguing in 1998 that the tension between First Amendment law and copyright law should be reexamined. Emphasizing the unique nature of Internet communication, he expressed concern that the aggressive enforcement of copyright laws could chill speech on the Internet. "If Congress insists on asserting control in a centralizing manner that is inconsistent with the structure of the Internet," he wrote, "the First Amendment concerns are subtler because copyright law is a creature suited to a system where works must pass through some editorial intermediary before being disseminated to the public. The Internet allows circumvention of this historical/institutional construct and makes those with access to its networks contributors to a new public forum."[50]

Although Fraser concluded by arguing for an "independent First Amendment privilege outside the copyright fair use doctrine," it is generally believed that such a change is not likely in the near future. Words constituting copyright infringement can still be restricted as they have been in the past despite the imperatives of recent free speech law.

Another Recognized Tort or Crime Other expressive activity can also be regulated on the basis of content if it is a crime or a tort under U.S. law. The crimes and torts we discuss in this section are typically among the most prominent examples, but different circumstances may trigger the application of other legal principles in this area.

Beyond these ten categories, additional restrictions on freedom of expression may be implemented in certain environments, such as on K-12 public school campuses. While the U.S. Supreme Court has recognized that students do not "shed their constitutional rights to freedom of speech or expression at the schoolhouse gate," student speech may be regulated if it materially and substantially interferes with schoolwork, discipline, or the rights of others.[51] In addition, the Court has given school officials substantial leeway to determine "the boundaries of socially appropriate behavior."[52] And school-sponsored expressive activity that might reasonably be perceived to bear the imprimatur of the school—such as school newspapers and dramatic productions—can be restricted by school officials as long as the restrictions are "reasonably related to legitimate pedagogical concerns."[53]

Finally, it must be noted again that all these First Amendment rules and exceptions generally apply only to the public sector. Nonpublic entities such as private universities, corporations, and ISPs are typically not under any obligation to comply with the limits imposed by case law in this context. As a matter of policy, however, most private institutions of higher education and a good number of ISPs do in fact choose to follow these same rules and regulations.

Restricting Extremist, Hate-Related Web Sites under One or More of the Recognized Exceptions

Many members of the U.S. legal community have tried under existing law to limit hate-related speech. However, because there is no content-based exception for hate-related speech per se, it must be shown that the expressive activity in a particular situation falls within one or more of the ten exceptions identified.

Governmental entities face a number of challenges if they wish to take down the typical extremist, hate-related Web site. Such a site generally contains a variety of racial and religious slurs, often accompanied by extensive deprecatory remarks and highly offensive visual imagery regarding the alleged inferiority of certain groups. Many of these sites also contain rhetoric indicating the site owner's belief that "Hitler was right," and often extol the virtues of other extremist and bigoted persons and groups as well. Threatening invective may also be found, ranging from warnings that only certain people should feel free to visit the site to predictions that only through violence and holy war will the "problem" ultimately be resolved. In addition, upcoming organization events may be publicized, and kindred spirits are generally urged to "spread the word."

Going down the list of exceptions to the First Amendment presumption against regulation of speech on the basis of content, it might conceivably be argued that expressive activity on such a Web site constitutes a true threat, incitement to imminent lawless conduct, fighting words, defamation, or harassment. Yet absent additional facts unique to a particular hate-related Web site, each of these arguments is likely to prove fruitless in the end under currently recognized legal doctrine.

True threats, for example, require not only a threat against the physical safety of a particular person or persons, but a communication that would lead a reasonable, objective recipient to believe that the Web site owner was serious about his threat. Unlike the UC Irvine hate speech case described in chapter 3—in which the defendant sent an e-mail message to fifty-nine specific students with Asian last names, explicitly stating that he would personally make it his life's work to "find and kill every one" of them "personally"—the typical extremist, hate-filled Web site contains at most only generalized threats directed toward a broad class of persons. Such threatening language might include warnings of a forthcoming holy war, or admonitions to certain groups to beware because a new Fourth Reich will soon be established. But these expressions do not generally constitute "true" threats under any reasonable definition of the term in U.S. case law.

Incitement to imminent lawless conduct would not typically apply to Web sites, because the rules require that the conduct incited be imminent.

Even the most inflammatory language on such extremist sites does not result in online users dropping everything and immediately going out and disturbing the peace. The incitement exception to the rule that speech cannot be regulated on the basis of content is designed to protect against speech that would immediately result in a disturbance, and it is highly unlikely that hate-related Web sites would be the direct cause of such an event. A causal link may be shown in certain cases between the invective on such Web sites and the subsequent commission of hate crimes by certain individuals, but even this sort of proof would not be sufficient to establish the level of imminence required by First Amendment case law.

Fighting words may appear at first glance to be a more promising category, since so much of what appears on hate-related sites constitutes fighting words to members of targeted groups. Yet the legal definition of fighting words is very technical, and requires that the words be "directed at the person of the hearer." Thus, like incitement to imminent lawless conduct, the focus is on protecting against disturbances of the peace. For expression to constitute fighting words, it must be "in your face." Under current First Amendment doctrine, then, online words of any kind cannot fall within this category.

Defamation triggers a more detailed analysis, since two major cases—both coming out of Illinois—have wrestled directly with hate-related expressive activity in this context. In the 1952 case of *Beauharnais v. Illinois,* the U.S. Supreme Court considered the question of whether defamatory expression directed against an entire group could be restricted by a public entity. The defendant, who was president of the White Circle League, arranged for the distribution in downtown Chicago of highly offensive and inflammatory leaflets that called on the mayor and the city council "to halt the further encroachment, harassment and invasion of white people, their property, neighborhoods and persons, by the Negro." It also called for "one million self respecting white people in Chicago to unite," and added that "if persuasion and the need to prevent the white race from becoming mongrelized by the Negro will not unite us, then the aggressions . . . rapes, robberies, knives, guns and marijuana of the Negro, surely will." Attached to the leaflet was an application for membership in the White Circle League of America.

The defendant was arrested and convicted under an Illinois statute prohibiting the public distribution of material that "exposes the citizens of any race, color, creed or religion to contempt, derision, or obloquy *or* which is productive of breach of the peace or riots." He challenged the conviction as violative of his rights, took the case all the way to the U.S. Supreme Court, and lost by one vote. Writing for a divided court, Justice Frankfurter, repeating the rule from earlier cases that certain "well-defined and narrowly limited classes of speech" such as libel "have never been thought to raise any Constitutional problem," analyzed the question of whether the Constitution allows a state to punish defamatory utterances directed not merely at an individual but "at a defined group." He determined that, given the large number of violent, race-related conflicts that had taken place in Illinois over the previous 150 years, the state was justified "in seeking ways to curb false or malicious defamation of racial and religious groups." Frankfurter concluded that such speech could therefore be outlawed as both fighting words and "group libel."[54]

After *Beauharnais,* however, U.S. First Amendment case law gradually became much more indulgent of free and unfettered expression, moving away from doctrine that at one time served to limit such things as *group defamation.* First, in 1964, the Court determined that defamation would no longer be viewed as completely outside First Amendment limitations, but that it needed to be analyzed under "the principle that debate on public issues should be uninhibited, robust, and wide-open."[55] Then, in 1969, the Court concluded that advocacy of certain offensive, hate-related conduct could be punished only if the speech is likely to produce an *immediate* breach of the peace.[56] Finally, in 1992, the Court decided that a prohibition against hate-related expression could not be justified under the fighting words exception unless the law prohibited *all* fighting words, not just those that a public entity might deem offensive at a particular moment in time.[57] Since the reasoning in the *Beauharnais* opinion was based on a set of rules that were quite different in 1952, First Amendment scholars have generally agreed that even if *Beauharnais* were a correct expression of the law at the time, it cannot be employed to justify restrictions on hate-related speech in the twenty-first century.

Such a change in the law was already apparent in the highly publicized 1978 case of *Collin v. Smith,* which focused on the attempt to prohibit a neo-Nazi group from marching in the village of Skokie, Illinois.[58] In the Skokie case, as it has come to be known, the village attempted to block the march, first by obtaining a preliminary injunction in court and then by enacting several ordinances prohibiting hate-related demonstrations. Among other things, the ordinances specified that a parade or assembly permit could not be granted if the planned activity would "incite violence, hatred, abuse or hostility toward a person or group . . . by reason of reference to religious, racial . . . [or] . . . ethnic affiliation."

An important aspect of the controversy was the fact that Skokie at the time had a large Jewish population, including "as many as several thousand survivors of the Nazi holocaust in Europe before and during World War II." And the National Socialist Party of America (NSPA), which sought to obtain the permit, was described by its leader, Frank Collin, "as a Nazi party." According to the court,

> [A]mong NSPA's more controversial and generally unacceptable beliefs are that black persons are biologically inferior to white persons, and should be expatriated to Africa as soon as possible; that American Jews have "inordinate . . . political and financial power" in the world and are "in the forefront of the international Communist revolution." NSPA members affect a uniform reminiscent of those worn by members of the German Nazi Party during the Third Reich, and display a swastika thereon and on a red, white, and black flag they frequently carry.[59]

It was clear from the record established by the defendant Village that the NSPA's plan to march in Skokie was not a coincidence. According to a highly offensive and inflammatory NSPA leaflet obtained by the defendant, the Nazi group "decided to relocate in areas heavily populated by the real enemy—the Jews."[60]

The Seventh Circuit Court of Appeals first rejected the possibility that the NSPA's planned march might constitute either incitement to imminent lawless conduct or fighting words. Apparently, the Village's brief itself conceded that there was little or no fear of a breach of the peace. The group's parade permit did indicate that thirty to fifty demonstrators would be "wearing uniforms including swastikas and carrying a party banner with a swastika and placards with statements . . . such as 'White Free Speech,' 'Free Speech for the White Man,' and 'Free Speech for White America.'" But the march was to be "silent." No speeches were planned, and no leaflets were to be distributed.

The Village's major argument in favor of its ordinance relied on the *Beauharnais* decision, in which a conviction under an ordinance that also prohibited hate-related expression had been upheld. The federal court of appeals, however, rejected the argument, finding that decisions in First

Amendment cases over a twenty-five-year period "expressed doubt . . . that *Beauharnais* remain[ed] good law at all." And in a very forceful articulation of current free speech law, the court declared:

> Legislating against the content of First Amendment activity . . . launches the government on a slippery and precarious path.
>
> Above all else, the First Amendment means that government has no power to restrict expression because of its message, its ideas, its subject matter, or its content. To permit the continued building of our politics and culture, and to assure self-fulfillment for each individual, our people are guaranteed the right to express any thought, free from government censorship. The essence of this forbidden censorship is content control. Any restriction on expressive activity because of its content would completely undercut the "profound national commitment to the principle that debate on public issues should be uninhibited, robust, and wide-open."[61]

Although the Skokie case was ultimately decided by the federal court of appeals and did not reach the U.S. Supreme Court,[62] it is a decision that has been given great deference over the years.[63] Accordingly, any effort to justify the taking down of an extremist, hate-related Web site by claiming that it constitutes *group defamation* is almost certain to be unsuccessful.

Harassment is the last of the possible justifications that might be employed in defense of restrictions on hate-related Web sites in cyberspace. Assuming that a site does not specifically target individual persons within the definition of the antiharassment provisions of the Communications Decency Act,[64] the only possible theory under this category, however, would be based on the emerging law of hostile environment harassment. It might be argued, then, that extremist, hate-related Web sites create a hostile online environment, and that those in charge could be held liable unless the sites are taken down. Although hostile environment law developed in the workplace and was recently extended only to the education setting, it can be argued that cyberspace is, in fact, a workplace for some and an education setting for others. Thus, the same rules would apply in the online world.[65]

There are several major problems with this line of reasoning, however. First, for many people, it is a stretch to equate cyberspace with a workplace environment or an education setting. Although it is not unusual to use the Internet for work or for education purposes, the workplace or the education setting is arguably not the networked environment itself but the physical reality accompanying the experience. The computer is only one aspect of that reality. Second, even if it is conceded that in some cases, cyberspace does constitute the work environment, who should be held liable if the environment remains hostile? The employer who required the work? The ISP? The government? Third, unlike other hostile environment scenarios, where the victim subjected to unwelcome intimidation or abuse has no control over the circumstances, persons do not have to visit extremist, hate-related Web sites. Knowing that the sites are there would arguably not be sufficient to constitute hostile environment harassment. Fourth, the federal courts have not looked kindly on broad campus speech codes that have sought to ban generic "hate speech," with the judges questioning both the legality and efficacy of extending hostile environment harassment law beyond the scope of its original intent. Finally, along the same lines, recent sexual harassment decisions in this area have continued to emphasize the importance of not expanding hostile environment principles beyond the specific and narrow fact patterns addressed by the law. Justice Souter in *Faragher* and Justice Kennedy in the *Davis* dissent warned against any attempts to interpret hostile environment law as mandating a "general civility code."

Thus, it is clear that under current U.S. First Amendment law—which is based on many court decisions interpreting the parameters of the free speech guarantees—extremist, hate-related Web sites cannot generally be restricted. And if Web sites cannot be restricted, then online hate in general cannot be restricted. The other typical form of online hate—individual communication via e-mail or in chat rooms—is arguably similar in nature to phone conversation. And no one believes it is possible, legally or practically, to restrict what people say to each other over the phone in this regard unless it constitutes harassment on an individual level. Absent additional facts, then, basic online hate in the U.S. is legal and cannot be limited in any way.

Restricting Hate-Related Web Sites on an International Level

On the international level, the picture is very different. Most major countries restrict hate-related speech. Indeed, as mentioned above, the U.S. is significantly outside of the international mainstream in this regard.[66]

In personal discussions with members of the international community, I have been struck by the growing concern about the U.S. position on this issue. At a recent meeting focusing on emerging technology issues with Egyptian Judge Mohamed Ibrahim, who was in the United States as an Eisenhower Fellow, I was told that online hate is one of his country's most pressing Internet-related concerns. While Egypt, like most other nations, expressly prohibits speech targeting ethnic or religious groups in a deprecating manner, the freedom that exists under current U.S. law has led to a troubling increase in such speech . . . directed in cyberspace toward specific Egyptian persons and groups. It is one thing, Judge Ibrahim said, to have laws that only apply in one's own country, but when an individual country's laws impact people from all over the world, the legal terrain must be reconsidered. Judge Ibrahim feels very strongly that international standards must be established here.

As discussed at length in previous chapters, many nations have established such standards in the area of copyright law. Relying on global agreement to develop a consensus and define an international baseline, these standards do not and should not require every country to do exactly the same thing, but they establish minimum requirements for the protection of other nations. If we have been able to formulate standards in the area of intellectual property, perhaps it is possible to do something similar with regard to hate-related online activity.

One possible way to approach the development of such a baseline would be to focus on a specifically identified target such as extremist, hate-related Web sites. Any rules developed to restrict these sites must at the outset be consistent with U.S. First Amendment law, for although international treaties can override inconsistent U.S. statutory law, they cannot override the First Amendment.

Even though the First Amendment, as we have seen, has been interpreted very broadly over the past fifty years to provide wide-ranging free speech rights for all Americans, there are basic First Amendment principles that are compatible with an international agreement to restrict hate-related Web sites should the United States decide at some point to go in that direction. Courts, for example, still uphold the principle that certain utterances "are no essential part of any exposition of ideas, and are of such slight social value as a step to truth that any benefit that may be derived from them is clearly outweighed by the social interest in order and morality. "Justices who have opposed restrictions on hate-related speech in certain settings have nevertheless noted that "a conspiracy . . . which . . . [is] . . . aimed at destroying a race by exposing it to contempt, derision, and obloquy . . . could be made an indictable offense."[67] Enhancing punishments for the commission of crimes that have been deemed hate-related has also been upheld by the U.S. Supreme Court as recently as the 1990s.[68] And the U.S. courts have remained willing to recognize certain exceptions to the rule that speech cannot be regulated on the basis of its content for particular categories of expression that the country has generally viewed as unacceptable.

Such an exception, for example, has been established for obscenity. It was made possible not because of a fear that obscenity might disturb the peace, but rather because the great majority of Americans believe that obscenity in public settings is inappropriate. If public opinion somehow changes in the U.S. and a majority of Americans decide that they can support an international baseline restricting hate-related Web sites, the obscenity exception might serve as a reasonable model. After all, most Americans would certainly agree that—as a starting point—hate-related Web sites are inappropriate.

It is interesting to note that the arguments against restricting obscenity under the law are very similar to those that have been set forth against restricting hate-related speech. They include assertions that it cannot be defined, and that any attempts to define it will be vague and overbroad. But, as we have seen, the courts have indeed come up with a workable definition of obscenity—one that goes far beyond Justice Stewart's "I know it when I see it."

In addition, some of same arguments that are used in favor of restricting obscene speech can be used to justify similar restrictions on extremist, hate-related Web sites. They include assertions that it is immoral, that it could have a bad influence on young people, and that it could negatively impact day-to-day interpersonal relations and activities. And although it is now something of a cliche to say that hate and violence are no less obscene than prurient sexual activity, it can be argued that restrictions on hate-related Web sites that follow the same pattern established by the courts for obscenity can still fit within the generally accepted parameters of First Amendment law. This would be the case whether the current definition of obscenity were expanded or a new exception were carved out for the content-based regulation of certain narrowly defined categories of online hate.

In either case, restrictions on hate-related Web sites must avoid the pitfalls that led courts to rule in favor of the neo-Nazis in the Skokie case and against discriminatory harassment codes in the campus hate-speech cases. The language of a new rule must be drawn so that it carefully restricts only those websites that not only contain racial or religious slurs, extol the virtues of extremist and hateful leaders, and contain extensive deprecatory remarks and highly offensive visual imagery regarding the alleged inferiority of certain groups, but also seek through the existence of the site to publicize and encourage events geared toward action that would resolve the "problem" generated by the mere existence of a particular group that may have immutable characteristics. The type of action encouraged by such sites might include removal, quarantine, or simply elimination of a group through some action like the establishment of a Fourth Reich, ethnic cleansing, or the prosecution of a holy war.

Web sites of this type are distinguishable from the planned Skokie demonstration, in which the National Socialist Party of America, although desiring to march in full Nazi regalia, planned only to conduct a single, silent march. No speeches were to be made, and no leaflets were to be distributed. Such an incident is significantly different from an aggressive ongoing Web presence that contains extensive hate-related propaganda and invective. In addition, the Skokie court noted that it would have been "a very different case" had the NSPA "conspir[ed] to harass or intimidate others and subject them . . . to racial or religious hatred."[69] Arguably, the type of extremist, hate-related Web site described in the previous paragraph is a conspiratorial effort aimed at effecting just the sort of intimidation accompanied by racial or religious hatred that the court indicated it would be willing to prohibit.

New restrictions prohibiting an extremist, hate-related Web presence would also need to be distinguishable from the prototypical campus speech codes of the late 1980s and early 1980s. Codes such as the one at the University of Michigan that prohibited the stigmatizing and victimizing of individuals on the basis of certain immutable characteristics and was accompanied by student conduct guides that identified a wide range of behavior as constituting such stigmatization and victimization were often confusing to students and faculty alike. In fact, it became so difficult to distinguish between types of expressive conduct described in the university's guidelines that attorneys for the university were themselves at a loss to explain them. During the oral argument, the federal district court judge asked the university's counsel how he would distinguish between speech that was merely offensive, which the judge conceded was protected, and speech that "stigmatizes or victimizes" on the basis of an invidious factor. Counsel replied, "very carefully."[70]

By carefully limiting the new international baseline to a single type of activity—the posting and maintaining of a Web presence—and to online speech that, when viewed through a "totality of circumstances" analysis, would constitute a new type of obscenity, nations could avoid the type of pitfalls that were the eventual downfall of campus speech codes at major universities.

The majority of Americans would not support such an international agreement today. Americans and especially U.S. Netizens love their free speech rights, and as much as they would agree that extremist, hate-related Web sites are highly offensive, they are not likely to favor restrictions that might in their view lead to the proverbial slippery slope, where other First Amendment rights would then be in danger of restriction.

The situation might change, however, as globalization and interconnectedness lead toward greater acceptance of basic international standards in controversial areas that affect human interaction online. If such a pattern of consensus emerges, and a new international agreement in this area becomes possible, there are a number of governance and enforcement models that might be implemented. A new or current international organization, for example, might be designated as the governing authority. The WTO model, with its international baselines and its aggressive dispute resolution formula, could be one possible approach. International law enforcement cooperation, such as that currently in place to fight child pornography, would be another. The take-down provisions of the Digital Millennium Copyright Act, which require ISPs to take down sites that "appear to constitute copyright infringement," would be a third approach. And the FTC model, as reflected in the *Pereira* case, in which the offending party was simply ordered off the Internet by the court, would be a fourth. Some combination of all these models might be adopted by the global community, based on a workable consensus that would have to emerge.

The Role of Code-Based Restrictions in This Area

As discussed in earlier chapters, filtering software built into the architecture of cyberspace at various points has been identified as a potential tool in the fight against both obscenity and online hate. Certainly, in light of the analysis above, such software can serve a protective function, but it would at best provide a narrow and short-term remedy for a much larger problem.

Unlike the prospective use of code-based restrictions to counter cyberterrorism or to protect against unauthorized copying and distribution—areas where architectural changes can actually succeed in helping to end the problem—the use of code in an online hate setting does little to address the actual problem of online hate itself. The long-term goal of any restriction on hate-related activity in cyberspace should be a society where such activity is completely unacceptable. As long as it is allowed to flourish openly on the Internet, even behind filters, the message is that it is not completely unacceptable. There will always be some level of hate-related activity on this planet, but every effort must be made to marginalize it. Code-based restrictions of the type currently in use would not truly serve this purpose.

Other Strategies and Approaches to Counter Online Hate

Beyond the three basic regulatory models, there is much that can be done on a community level to counter online hate. Especially if U.S. First Amendment law does not change, and it is not likely to change any time soon, then it is only through individual and group efforts outside the three basic models that any significant progress can take place. Such endeavors can include private rule-making at the ISP level, education at the K-12 and higher education levels, a policy-neutral focus on the inherent value of diversity in all walks of life, and increased efforts to combat hate-related activity through strategies at the family level, in religious institutions, and throughout local communities.

The ability of private ISPs to establish online policies is not generally limited by First Amendment rules that govern public entities. Thus, for example, AOL has been able to establish an uncompromising acceptable use policy that prohibits certain inappropriate subscriber speech.[71] And ISPs that do not currently have such policies may decide at some point to follow suit, at least with regard to prohibiting the posting of extremist, hate-related Web sites. Such actions may not be completely effective, and arguably, there will always be some ISP that chooses to allow the type of online hate that others prohibit, but an aggressive stance by the private sector in this context could go a long way toward changing the dynamic in cyberspace.

Education also has a very important ongoing role to play. It is an undisputed fact that programs implemented by educational institutions with the specific purpose of combating hate can have a significant positive impact on future adult members of our society. Excellent learning activities of this type are available on the Internet at little or no cost to K-12 educators. Such materials can be integrated into English and social studies units from the primary grades through high school.[72]

In addition, a policy-neutral focus on the inherent value of diversity can make a major difference in this area as well. The word *diversity* has come to mean different things to different people, and misunderstandings can arise when its use is linked to a particular political cause.[73] But at the simplest level, the word describes the range of differences in background, perspective, and immutable characteristics that people bring to the table. Valuing these differences, encouraging respect, and facilitating contact between and among people from all walks of life in a policy-neutral fashion may ultimately be the most important things that can be done to counter hate.

The single greatest benefit of policy-neutral diversity is its impact on the debunking of negative stereotypes while promoting a greater understanding of others. The legendary Olympic athlete Jesse Owens, for example, was reportedly fond of saying that if people walk together and talk together, then over a period of time, they eventually come to understand each other. Hate may not completely disappear, but personal day-to-day contact of this type can make a world of difference in the long run.

Finally, these efforts must necessarily be supplemented by strategies to counter hate that can be implemented in individual family units, via religious networks, and through the local community. The Southern Poverty Law Center, for example, has been in the forefront of such efforts for a long time. Through its ongoing commitment to combat extremist and hateful groups such as the Klan and the White Aryan Resistance, the SPLC has gained a tremendous amount of firsthand knowledge regarding both the causes of hate-related activity and what might be done to counter it.[74]

After an increase in hate-related violence over the past five years,[75] the center released a publication entitled "Ten Ways to Counter Hate: A Community Response Guide." This guide, which is also available on the Internet, documents a range of basic steps that can be taken by any person or group interested in countering hate-related violence. Strategies include determining who is behind the activity, providing legal and moral support for those who have been injured, and taking advantage of First Amendment rights to report incidents, sign petitions, attend vigils, lead prayers, buy ads, lobby leaders, build Web sites, and create alternatives to hate.[76]

It has been suggested in this chapter that Americans may wish to consider revisions to their free speech laws that would enable officials to take down extremist, hate-related Web sites. Realistically, such changes are not likely to happen any time soon. The U.S. commitment to free and open dialogue has its roots in the colonial revolutionary activities of the 1700s and has only been reinforced by the unprecedented opportunity for unrestricted expression that is available in cyberspace today. Any suggestion that hate-related activity should be viewed as the equivalent of obscenity and thus restricted in some way may find support in many quarters, but it is likely to be rejected by a clear majority of Americans.

At some point, however, the forces of globalization and the unprecedented level of regular ongoing contact with members of the international community may require a reconsideration of this issue. As discussed, the United States is clearly outside the international mainstream in the area of free speech. It may become increasingly difficult for the U.S. to advocate a baseline of allowable online activity in the areas of cyberterrorism and copyright infringement while rejecting any effort to establish a similar international baseline for hate-related expression. It must also be recognized, however, that the dominant U.S. presence on the Internet may have the opposite effect, forcing other nations to reconsider their own restrictive rules and ultimately resulting in a baseline that ends up *resembling* current U.S. law.

At least in the immediate future, then, our three major regulatory approaches are not likely to prove particularly effective in countering online hate. The national and international law models are severely limited by a lack of consensus, and code-based filtering is at best a band-aid approach that does nothing to directly address the larger problem. But there is more that can be done here outside the three models than in any other representative problem area that we have discussed. Indeed, both the characteristics of the Internet and the behavior enabled by the First Amendment itself can be used to great advantage in combating hate-related activity. Through cyberspace, an unprecedented amount of information is openly available regarding extremist and hateful groups. This information can be used effectively by those willing to take the next step and pursue time-tested, grassroots strategies such as those successfully employed by the Southern Poverty Law Center.

And each individual person can begin doing this today, without waiting for lawsuits to be filed, statutes to be approved, international agreements to be concluded, or new software solutions to be developed.

Conclusion

> In the Psionic Age, people will require very different cities from anything they have today. . . . You will be able to teleport to London for the January sales, to Bangkok to buy your furniture, to Ireland to do your grocery shopping, and to Tierra del Fuego for an unusual low cost holiday. . . .
>
> The entire earth would thus become a single city. . . . Teleportation would encourage a Distanced style of life. You might have your kitchen in France, your bedroom in Sweden, your garden in Italy . . . or any other arrangement you choose. Each person's city would be unique, a conceptual city made up of the bits of the Earth that he wanted to spend time in.
>
> —Robert Sheckley, *Futuropolis,* Circa 1978

> For I dipt into the future, far as human eye could see,
> Saw the Vision of the world, and all the wonder that would be;
> . . . There the common sense of most shall hold a fretful realm in awe,
> And the kindly earth shall slumber, lapt in universal law.
>
> —Alfred Lord Tennyson, "Locksley Hall," Circa 1842

Cyberspace regulation continues to mean different things to different people. For many stakeholders, particularly in the libertarian atmosphere of the online world, the mere mention of the word *regulation* is enough to generate extremely negative reaction. Dystopian predictions of pervasive monitoring and dictatorial control over every aspect of our cyber-lives are inevitably set forth in this context, and government is typically portrayed as the ultimate enemy.

For others, *cyberspace regulation* generates images of a return to a simpler and more circumscribed lifestyle, when human action seemed much more predictable and when people could more easily rely on certain time-tested principles to guide their daily affairs. Those holding such a view do not feel threatened by government action in cyberspace, but rather by lawbreakers and anarchists who might use this new communications medium to further their own nefarious ends. On some level, particularly for certain problem areas, the Internet itself is seen as the enemy here. *Regulation* is viewed as a panacea, and the government is perceived as not doing enough.

Yet these opposing positions are constantly being eroded by emerging events and changing realities. Those who maintain libertarian positions may be confronted by a new problem that leads them to argue for some sort of regulatory solution. And those who have been lobbying for additional, restrictive laws may find themselves in the surprising position of responding to a new issue by arguing that things should simply be left alone. Legislative staff members in Washington, D.C., for example, increasingly joke about how everyone in the IT industry is against regulation until code writers and Netizens combine forces to generate new online activities that may negatively impact established business interests.

And architectural considerations, as we have seen, further complicate this picture. No matter what view of cyberspace one adopts, it must be recognized that on some level this is not a physical reality, but an audio-visual representation created and made possible by software code. Any discussion of regulation issues in this area can therefore lead quickly to central questions regarding appropriate analogies. For example, it has been argued that every communication taking place in a networked environment should be viewed as analogous to a phone conversation, and that both e-mail and the World Wide Web are nothing more than graphic representations of the conversation created through the magic of software code. According to this view, the regulation question is very simple. All the rules we need are those that have already been worked out for telephones.

But this view is typically countered by noting that digital technology has enabled online users to accomplish many things in a networked environment that were simply not possible on a traditional phone, such as taking virtual tours of museums, viewing live scenes from distant locations, and creating digital copies of other people's work. In addition, on some level, an online presence can quickly become very much akin to an offline presence. Establishing an interactive business in cyberspace, for example, is in many ways no different than opening a new commercial enterprise in the building down the street. Which rules should then apply? Those for telemarketing, or those for brick-and-mortar operations? And how should the unique, code-based aspects of online communication be factored in? Should speed, scale, and a greater level of anonymity make any difference in the end? Or can it be expected that at some point new software code will adjust for speed, scale, and anonymity?

In light of these complications and inconsistencies, many people are beginning to gravitate away from all-or-nothing positions regarding regulation. Yet the continued rhetoric accompanying these debates has led to the persistence of certain overarching generalizations regarding the current state of affairs. In the aftermath of the February 2000 denial-of-service attacks against major commercial Web sites, for example, the media was filled with comments purporting to explain the parameters of governmental control. Major newspapers declared that the Internet is neither owned nor regulated by the government. Security experts described the online world as "an open system without set standards of regulation." And President Clinton himself, speaking at a hastily convened "cyber security summit," declared that one of the reasons the Internet "has worked so well is that it has been free of government regulation."

A review of basic definitions, common usage, and recent history quickly demonstrates that none of these statements is true. *Black's Law Dictionary*, for example, defines the term *regulate* in the following manner:

> To fix, establish, or control; to adjust by rule, method, or established mode; to direct by rule or restriction; to subject to governing principles or laws. The power of Congress to *regulate* commerce is the power to enact all appropriate legislation for its protection or advancement; to adopt measures to promote its growth and insure its safety; to foster, protect, control, and restrain. *Regulate* means to govern or direct according to rule or to bring under control of constituted authority, to limit and prohibit, to arrange in proper order, and to control that which already exists. (citations omitted)

WordNet, an online dictionary, defines *regulate* as "to shape or influence; give direction to." And typical synonyms for the term in *Roget's Thesaurus* include *adjust, methodize, systematize, guide, readjust, harmonize, and coordinate.*

As we have seen throughout this book, the U.S. government built the Internet. It did not just let it happen. In addition, it has been involved directly or indirectly in an entire range of *regulatory* activities. Not only have government officials *shaped and influenced* the growth and development of the online world, but a variety of federal agencies have *given direction* to it by *guiding, adjusting, harmonizing,* and *coordinating* its operations. In addition, Congress continues to *enact appropriate legislation for its protection and advancement,* and the White House has *adopted measures to promote its growth* and *insure its safety.* These rules, requirements, and policies continue to impact our day-to-day online experiences in a variety of important ways.

Giving the benefit of the doubt to those who insist that cyberspace is not regulated, it can be argued that they might merely be defining the term narrowly, and could be referring to the regulation of specific stakeholders (such as the IT industry, which remains substantially unregulated), particular types of communication services (such as those monitored by the FCC, which has generally adopted a hands-off approach), or specific problem areas (such as pornography, which the U.S. Congress continues to have difficulty controlling).

But by failing to specify particular entities, services, or problems, these statements only lend credence to the recurring and omnipresent myth that the Internet is not under control and cannot in fact be brought under control. Such expansive and anachronistic generalizations today add little to the inquiry. Many issues clearly remain unresolved, and key problem areas may correctly be viewed as beyond our control at the present time. But cyberspace as a whole remains too large, too complex, and too varied to support grand generalizations of this kind. From the beginning, this book has taken the position that the online world is made up of many different cyber spaces, and that an analysis which might be appropriate in certain instances may turn out to be completely inappropriate for other cyber realities. This point cannot be overemphasized, and must remain a central feature of any Internet-related discussion in this area.

In the end, this book takes the position that regulation is a neutral term, and that in a vacuum it should be viewed as neither a curse nor a panacea. Every situation is different, and a framework for addressing alleged problems in the online world must take all this into account. Such a framework must be built, therefore, on a definition of regulation that is both neutral and broad-based, one which recognizes that the term includes case decisions, legislation, relevant policies, administrative agency activity, international cooperation, architectural changes, private ordering, self-regulation, and any other methods that might be employed to control various portions of cyberspace.

By defining regulation in this broad and objective manner, we can more precisely identify the contours of the debate for individual problem areas. A definition that recognizes that regulation can include everything from action by the powers-that-be to steps that can be taken by individual Netizens is essential here. Cyberspace regulation is not necessarily something that is invariably carried out by *someone else,* but rather a series of steps that anyone can accomplish on an individual basis in particular circumstances. A broad definition recognizes the variety of meanings and the range of manifestations inherent in the term.

Metaphors invoking comparisons with analogous settings can be a useful starting point for any analysis of regulation questions. Thus, in the early chapters, we not only explored the similarities between cyberspace and the quasi-mythical world of the western film, but also emphasized the importance of examining the formulaic events that followed the transformative inventions of other eras. Looking at the classic western, for example, we were able to ascertain patterns in repetitive settings, plot lines, and portrayals of community that provided us with a useful context for our inquiry into which persons and groups might be in charge of the online world. And the scenario that played out in the aftermath of the invention of the harness lent itself to an analysis of whether and to what extent the creation and development of the Internet is in fact a watershed event.

Building on these initial inquiries, we set out to develop a framework that was informed by a growing body of legal and policy research and that could be employed to address Internet-related problems that might arise in our era. By the end of chapter 8, we were able to identify a roadmap for prospective regulation comprised of four interrelated parts: (a) classification of the problem, (b) ability to establish consensus, (c) impact of differences between the online activity and similar offline behavior, and (d) application of regulatory models.

In the final chapters, this framework was then applied to certain representative problem areas: cyberterrorism, online consumer fraud, private personal copying, and extremist, hate-related Web sites. The three major regulatory models at the heart of the roadmap—traditional national law, international agreement, and code-based regulation—played a central role in each case.

In retrospect, the analysis in the final chapters reveals that traditional national law is alive and well in cyberspace, in spite of the inherent limits of our legal system. All four representative problem areas can be addressed in some manner by either applying or changing existing laws. But the pivotal role of consensus in this highly participatory and distributed anarchic environment—bolstered by an unprecedented level of speed, scale, and anonymity—clearly requires adjustments to the traditional formulas. National law will continue to play an important part in this picture, but it will rarely be sufficient. For every problem area discussed in this book, a regulatory approach rooted in national law is only one component of a prospective solution. Given the global nature of the Internet, international agreement and cooperation is often essential. And the centrality of software code in cyberspace requires would-be regulators to address the possibility that an architectural adjustment might prove to be *the* turning point in a particular situation.

Thus we have found that no single regulatory formula is appropriate for the online world.

When addressing cyberterrorism or private personal copying, for example, a creative combination of all three models offers the best possibility for a reasonable regulatory approach. Online consumer fraud, at the present time, is best addressed by a combination of traditional national law and international cooperation. And while efforts to combat hate-related activity can benefit greatly from an international baseline, a more realistic approach at the present time would be to rely on strategies outside the three models, such as education, private rule-making, and grassroots initiatives within local communities.

In addition, we have found that it is important to keep our categories of allegedly problematic conduct in perspective. In chapter 3, we took the first step toward establishing a roadmap by identifying four major problem areas—dangerous conduct, fraudulent conduct, unlawful anarchic conduct, and inappropriate conduct. And throughout the remainder of the book, we suggested that certain patterns might be identified within each of these categories that could provide helpful signposts for would-be regulators. Yet it is clear that these patterns are not applicable across the board.

In the unlawful anarchic category, for example, we were able to pinpoint many useful parallels between personal copying, obscenity, and online defamation. And it is likely that for each of the three cases some creative combination of all three regulatory models might work best. But the nature of these combinations might vary considerably depending on which one of the representative problems is being addressed.

Finally, there is clearly no general rule regarding the inviolability of the status quo. For some cyber spaces, the best approach is to do nothing, and allow things to evolve over time. In other cases, existing regulatory strategies—either by the powers-that-be or private persons and groups—are likely to be sufficient to address the alleged problems. But for certain areas, significant changes in the status quo at the national level, the international level, or the software code level may be the only effective way to bring a particular problem under control.

On one level, this book may be viewed as a recent history of the Internet, documenting key legal and policy developments from 1994 through 2001. On another level, it is a snapshot in time, providing a detailed analysis of cyberspace regulation issues at the beginning of the twenty-first century. Ultimately, however, the book looks toward the future, providing a four-part framework that can be employed to address Internet-related problems that may arise down the road.

Thus, in light of the analysis set forth throughout the book, we conclude by reviewing certain basic principles that can inform any future-oriented approach to cyberspace regulation. Several of these principles have been identified in other works, but it is important to mention them again. Some have been recognized as conventional wisdom, while others may fly in the face of what certain commentators continue to view as conventional wisdom. Still others are derived directly from the inquiry in this book. Taken together, these twenty regulatory principles can serve as important guidelines for the resolution of Internet-related problems in the coming decade.

1. Beware of grand generalizations regarding the current state of cyberspace regulation and the advantages or disadvantages of regulation across the board. Some cyber spaces are, in fact, beyond our control at the present

time, but many others are not. For some situations, regulatory solutions make sense, while other problem areas should simply be left alone.

2. When addressing a particular problem area, consider the entire range of regulatory approaches, including litigation, legislation, policy changes, administrative agency activity, international cooperation, architectural changes, private ordering, and self-regulation. In cyberspace, it is reasonable to assume that a creative combination of approaches will be more effective than any single regulatory strategy.

3. In order to ensure that the Internet retains its ability to serve as a dramatic and unique marketplace of ideas, it is essential that would-be regulators continue to respect the autonomy of individuals and groups in the online world.

4. The status quo, however, should not necessarily be viewed as inviolable. Certain aspects of the online world can and should be changed. And solutions can be crafted for individual cyber spaces that will not impact other cyber spaces. Beware of all-or-nothing arguments that view any change in the law for a particular situation as the first step down a slippery slope. Cutting back the rights of either the powers-that-be or individual Netizens in certain areas does not have to mean that it will be this way across the board.

5. No analysis of prospective regulatory approaches to specific problems is complete without reviewing the academic journal databases to take advantage of the many creative proposals and recommendations in the cyberspace regulation literature of the past six to eight years.

6. Care must be taken to avoid viewing cyberspace regulation issues in a vacuum, and the classification of problematic activity into one of four categories is an important first step in this process. By determining whether certain online behavior constitutes dangerous conduct, fraudulent conduct, unlawful anarchic conduct, or inappropriate conduct, patterns can be identified and helpful signposts can be pinpointed within a larger context. In addition, such an approach recognizes that Internet-related problems can be as varied as the range of issues that must be addressed by legislators and policymakers in the offline world.

7. If we are committed to maintaining the present-day version of the Internet, then consensus among the various stakeholders will be an essential

component of any effective problem-solving approach. Under current conditions, given the highly participatory nature of online activity and the distributed, anarchic design of cyberspace itself, there are a host of ways to get around most restrictions that may be imposed. In addition, new architectural changes can often be countered by other code-based solutions. Thus a proposed regulatory approach may not be possible unless those that have the ability to resist agree to go along with the plan. And the list of such persons and entities would include not just the powers-that-be, but also Internet advocacy groups, virtual communities, and individual Netizens.

8. Any decision regarding how to regulate an online activity must necessarily begin with a determination of just how unique the particular setting and specific behavior might be. Certain conduct may be no different in cyberspace than it is in the offline world, while other conduct may be so dependent on speed, scale, and anonymity that it may require a very new regulatory approach.

9. The inherent limits of our legal system must always be addressed by would-be regulators of the online world. These limits are especially important in cyberspace, and range from the difficulties of establishing a rule of law in complex territory with many variables to the practical limits of any effort to bring everything and everybody under control.

10. In spite of these limitations, however, both the existing rules and any prospective new strategies that might be developed under the traditional national law model should invariably be considered first. Statutes, case decisions, and administrative agency activity have already made a difference in certain key areas. And while no law enforcement operation is ever completely successful, a rule of law that modifies the behavior of most people can indeed constitute a reasonable solution in the end.

11. Particularly from a U.S. perspective, it is important to note the centrality of the federal regulatory approach. State laws may have value in some areas that are typically regulated on that level, but given the ease with which borders can be crossed in cyberspace, a legal structure that can impact a larger geographic entity will often be more effective.

12. Even though the United States has continued to dominate both access to cyberspace and the nature of online content, the Internet must

inevitably be viewed at least on some level as a global communications medium. Given the fact that at any particular moment persons may be connected to the Internet from anywhere in the world and through servers located across the globe, international agreement and cooperation has become an essential component of any regulatory strategy. As the Internet continues to foster globalization and as nations move toward the identification of international baselines for certain key areas of the law, the prospects for international cooperation are surprisingly good here.

13. Code-based change at various levels of the Internet architecture has emerged as potentially the single most powerful regulatory strategy available. Especially when combined with one or more of the other models, software solutions can have a dramatic impact in a setting that is in fact comprised solely of binary code. Yet even as caution must be exercised in this area so that the essential nature of cyberspace does not change, it must be recognized that code-based changes in the online world have often been successfully countered by other code-based changes.

14. Private ordering continues to be set forth as a viable regulatory option by many stakeholders, and its potential effectiveness either by itself or in creative combination with other approaches should not be overlooked. It is in fact useful to identify two types of private ordering. The first—private architectural adjustment through the use of filtering, firewalls, and other security measures—can serve a protective function for individuals and groups against unlawful or inappropriate activity. The second—private rule-making by networks, content providers, and institutions—will typically dictate what others can and cannot do. While the former is appropriately viewed as a subcomponent of the broad architectural change model, the latter can generally be seen as a type of self-regulation.

15. Whatever strategies or combination of strategies that are ultimately adopted, regulators must set forth guidelines that are clear, direct, and understandable. Intellectual property laws, for example, have proven notoriously difficult for the average online user to comprehend, and the new statutory schemes that were added in the late 1990s have served to further complicate this territory. Everyone benefits from rules that are simple and straightforward.

16. In addition, regulatory approaches must be realistic. While this may seem inherently obvious, we have noted, for example, that the law has not

truly come to grips with private personal copying since the advent of the xerox machine and the widespread availability of audiotaping and videotaping technology. Certain adjustments have been made, but most of the personal day-to-day copying that takes place in the privacy of an individual's own home has remained subject to the vagaries of conflicting legal interpretation.

17. As a related corollary, the importance of the implicit social contract in cyberspace must also be taken into account. Clear and realistic rules are an important beginning, but it must also be recognized that, on some level, our legal system is often based upon an implicit social contract. People must want to follow the law, and if they decide they no longer wish to do so, the implicit social contract breaks down. Particularly in certain cyber spaces, where law-breaking is still very easy, steps must be taken to foster a spirit of cooperation between and among all online users.

18. To this end, regulators must recognize and build on existing social norms. While there has been much debate in the legal and policy literature regarding the extent to which Internet norms can be pinpointed, most commentators agree that—at least for specific areas of the law and in particular cyber spaces—identifiable traditions and clear community standards do exist. Examples of generally accepted activity that may have already influenced the development of the law in this regard include linking without permission, a commitment to a libertarian view of free speech rights, an ongoing consensus regarding a perceived right to remain anonymous, and a broad acceptance of file sharing technology to create new digital copies of previously protected works.

19. Ultimately, in the area of cyberspace regulation, there is no magic formula and no quick fix. Particularly for certain intractable problems, solutions simply may not be imminent. In these cases, it is important to identify combinations of approaches that may serve to move things in the right direction. Compromises that may seem unacceptable now could become central features of such new approaches under one or more of the three major regulatory models— traditional national law, international agreement, and code-based change.

20. The Internet today is one of the great achievements of the modern era, and any attempt to adjust its realities for regulatory purposes must proceed slowly and with great caution. Perhaps the most important of all the

inherent limits of our legal system is the rule of unintended consequences. Especially in light of the fact that cyberspace technology will inevitably continue to change, it is essential that we seek to avoid modifications that may have unanticipated effects. While there are no guarantees, since such effects are not always obvious at the time a new strategy is adopted, a regulatory approach that builds upon these twenty principles will begin with a good chance of success.

Given the dramatic innovations we have witnessed over the past ten years, it is particularly difficult to predict how cyberspace might look down the road. Most agree that wireless access will become more prevalent, and that a range of smaller and lighter information appliances will enable people to connect more easily to networked environments. Indeed, if anything is certain, it is the fact that we will continue to become even more interconnected in the future.

Beyond these basic certainties, however, a range of predictions abound. Prognosticators focusing on the technology have set forth dazzling scenarios that expand the limits of human potential. Those who focus on lifestyle envision an Internet that is so much a part of our daily affairs that we no longer think of it as something separate and apart. At that point, many argue, there will be no such thing as cyberspace law because the online world will be virtually indistinguishable from the offline world. There will be no separate Internet specialization in law and public policy, because every member of the legal profession will be an Internet lawyer, and everyone engaged in public policy will be an Internet policymaker.

When and if this level of integration occurs, many of the questions discussed in this book will undoubtedly have been resolved. Yet other Internet-related issues will inevitably emerge even in such a setting, with events seemingly beyond our control and solutions seemingly beyond our reach. But creative strategies informed by the principles identified in these pages can go a long way toward resolving such issues. And the law can continue to be a key feature of such a process, with problem-solving efforts building on the strengths of our legal system even as we recognize its inherent limits.

Notes

Chapter 1

1. See, e.g., Llewellyn Joseph Gibbons, No Regulation, Government Regulation, or Self-Regulation: Social Enforcement or Social Contracting for Governance in Cyberspace, *Cornell Journal of Law and Public Policy* 6 (1997): 475, 490. For a popular timeline of the Internet's development, see Robert Hobbes Zakon, Hobbes' Internet Timeline, v5.3, <http://www.zakon.org/robert/internet/timeline> (visited May 22, 2001).

2. See, generally, Brian Kahin and Charles Nesson, eds., *Borders in Cyberspace: Information Policy and the Global Information Infrastructure* (MIT Press, 1997); Henry H. Perritt, *Law and the Information Superhighway* (Wiley, 1996); and Brian D. Loader, ed., *The Governance of Cyberspace: Politics, Technology and Global Restructuring,* (Routledge, 1997).

Activity that can be characterized as Internet "vigilantism" continues to arise in a variety of contexts. The Mail Abuse Prevention System (MAPS), for example, developed by Paul Vixie to fight unsolicited mass e-mail, has been the subject of much debate in recent years. As described by Internet law scholar David Post, MAPS attacks the problem of spam by coordinating a boycott of Internet service providers (ISPs) by other ISPs. MAPS creates a blacklist—the Realtime Blackhole List (RBL)—of ISPs that are, in its view, fostering the distribution of spam. MAPS then makes the RBL list available to other ISPs on a subscription basis. "The ISPs who subscribe to the RBL can, if they choose, set their mail handlers to delete all e-mail originating from, or going to, an address appearing on the list; the blackholed address, in a sense, disappears from the Internet as far as the subscribing ISP (and its customers) are concerned."

Particularly interesting is MAPS' own definition of *fostering the distribution of spam.* According to Post, it can include "hosting web pages that are listed as destination addresses in bulk e-mails, providing e-mail forwarders or auto-responders that can be used by bulk e-mailers, or allowing mail handling servers to be used by non-subscribers which allows bulk e-mailers to 'launder' e-mail by launching it from a site to which they cannot be traced."

Post notes that although many have criticized the RBL system as unauthorized and unacceptable Net "vigilantism," this activity can just as easily be characterized as positive activism. In addition, "the kind of 'bottom-up,' uncoordinated, decentralized process of which the RBL is a part" strikes Post as "a perfectly reasonable way to make 'network policy' and to 'answer fundamental policy questions about how the Net will work.'" See David G. Post, What Larry Doesn't Get: Code, Law, and Liberty in Cyberspace, *Stanford Law Review* 52(2000): 1439.

3. See Robert Warshow's 1954 essay "The Westerner," in *The Immediate Experience: Movies, Comics, Theatre, and Other Aspects of Popular Culture* 91 (Anchor Books ed., 1962), and, also, William K. Everson, *A Pictorial History of the Western Film* (Citadel Press, 1969); Debra D. Burke, Cybersmut and the First Amendment: A Call for a New Obscenity Standard, *Harvard Journal of Law and Technology* 9 (1996): 87, 92; Xuan-Thao N. Nguyen, The New Wild West: Measuring and Proving Fame and Dilution Under the Federal Trademark Dilution Act, *Albany Law Review* 63 (1999): 201; Michael Meyer and Anne Underwood, Crimes of the 'Net, *Newsweek,* November 14, 1994: 46.

4. See, e.g., Joseph P. Liu, Legitimacy and Authority in Internet Coordination: A Domain Name Case, *Indiana Law Journal* 74 (1999): 587, 599. "The government, through the Department of Defense's Advanced Research Projects Agency ('ARPA') and the NSF," writes Liu, "played a significant role in the initial funding and development of the Internet and plays a continuing role in the funding of various parties."

5. See, e.g., Rivals Cede Throne to AOL, *Washington Post,* April 8, 1999.

6. Kara Swisher and Dean Takahashi, Technology Journal: Gadgets Move In On PC's Turf, *Wall Street Journal,* November 12, 1998.

7. See, e.g., United States v. Microsoft, 84 F. Supp. 2d 9 (D.D.C. 1999) (findings of fact); 87 F. Supp. 2d 30 (D.D.C. 2000) (conclusions of law).

8. See Jonathan Zittrain, The Rise and Fall of Sysopdom, *Harvard Journal of Law and Technology* 10 (1997): 495.

9. Stuart Biegel, Space Stations: Persons and Groups That "Control" the Internet, *UCLA Online Institute for Cyberspace Law and Policy,* November 29, 1996, <http://www.gseis.ucla.edu/iclp/nov96.html> (visited March 1, 2001).

10. Peter Wayner, Net Metaphors Stretch to Fit the Evolution of Data Flow, *New York Times,* May 14, 1998.

11. Steve Bickerstaff, Shackles on the Giant: How the Federal Government Created Microsoft, Personal Computers, and the Internet, *Texas Law Review* 78 (1999): 1, 44. Barbara Esbin, Internet over Cable: Defining the Future in Terms of the Past, 19 n.96 (OPP Working Paper Series, no. 30, Aug. 1998).

12. Denise Caruso, Technology: As Companies That Provide Access to the Internet Consolidate, Users May Run into Roadblocks, *New York Times,* July 6, 1998.

13. See, generally, Esther Dyson, *Release 2.0: A Design for Living in the Digital Age* (Broadway, 1997).

14. David P. Hamilton, Redesigning the Internet: Can It Be Made Less Vulnerable? *Wall Street Journal,* February 11, 2000.

15. A. Michael Froomkin, The Internet as a Source of Regulatory Arbitrage, in Brian Kahin and Charles Nesson, eds., *Borders in Cyberspace* (MIT Press, 1997) at p 129, <www.law.miami.edu/~froomkin/articles/arbitr.htm> (visited May 19, 2000).

16. Hamilton, supra, note 14.

17. Domain names—such as abc.com, pbs.org, or ucla.edu—serve as identifiers for Internet computers, and thus for given entities in the online world. Internet Protocol addresses are numbers (e.g., 98.37.241.30) that serve as routing addresses on the Internet.

18. See, e.g., Neil Weinstock Netanel, Cyberspace Self-Governance: A Skeptical View from Liberal Democratic Theory, *California Law Review* 88 (2000): 395, 484–487. See, generally, Yochai Benkler, Net Regulation: Taking Stock and Looking Forward, *University of Colorado Law Review* 71 (2000): 1203, 1256–1257.

Harvard Law School's Berkman Center for Internet and Society has done a wonderful job of monitoring ICANN-related developments from the start. Berkman Center representatives attend ICANN meetings across the globe, and ICANN decisions are documented in great detail at <http://cyber.law.harvard.edu/projects/governance.html> (visited August 25, 2000).

The evolving role of ICANN is discussed at some length in chapter 6, infra.

19. *Federal Bureau of Investigation National Computer Crime Squad,* <http://www.emergency.com/fbi-nccs.htm> (visited February 2, 2000).

20. National Infrastructure Protection Center, *Message from Michael Vatis, Chief of the National Infrastructure Protection Center,* <http://www.fbi.gov/nipc/welcome.htm> (visited February 2, 2000).

21. Dominic Bencivenga, Internet Cyberforce: SEC and FTC Crack Down on Online Fraud, *New York Law Journal* 220 (1998): 46.

22. John D. McClain, After Net Scam Sweep, U.S. Warns 180 Web site Operators, *Austin American-Statesman,* November 18, 1997.

23. Linus Gregoriadis, Police to Publish Child-Sex Pictures, *The Independent,* November 2, 1998.

24. *Cyberangels Mission Statement,* <http://www.cyberangels.org/about/mission.html> (visited February 2, 2000).

25. Deborah Shapley, Corporate Web Police Hunt Down E-Pirates, *New York Times,* May 19, 1997.

26. John Dodge, Searching for "Net Pirates": Firms Turn to Cyber Dick Tracys to Protect Products, Nab Bad Guys, *The Boston Globe,* April 15, 1998.

27. See Joseph M. Olivenbaum, Rethinking Federal Computer Crime Legislation, *Seton Hall Law Review* 27 (1997): 574, 581; Nicholas W. Allard and David A. Kass, Law and Order in Cyberspace: Washington Report, *Hastings Communications and Entertainment Law Journal* 19 (1997): 563, 569.

28. Jim Kitses, *Horizons West: Anthony Mann, Budd Boetticher, Sam Peckinpah: Studies of Authorship Within the Western* (Thames and Hudson, 1969).

29. See William Golding, *Lord of the Flies* (Perigee, 1954).

30. *Shane,* George Stevens, dir., with Alan Ladd, Jean Arthur, Van Heflin, Brandon de Wilde. Paramount Pictures, 1952.

31. *The Man Who Shot Liberty Valance,* dir. John Ford, with James Stewart, John Wayne, Vera Miles, Lee Marvin. Paramount Pictures, 1962.

32. Id.

33. *Cimarron,* dir. Anthony Mann, with Glenn Ford, Maria Schell. MGM/Universal Studios, 1960.

34. Kitses, supra, note 28.

35. See Reno v. ACLU, 521 U.S. 844 (1997).

36. See, e.g., Lawrence Lessig, The Law of the Horse: What Cyberlaw Might Teach, *Harvard Law Review* 113 (1999): 501.

37. Robert C. Ellickson, *Order Without Law: How Neighbors Settle Disputes* (Harvard University Press, 1991).

38. Robert D. Cooter, Against Legal Centrism, Rev. of *Order Without Law: How Neighbors Settle Disputes,* by Robert C. Ellickson, *California Law Review* 81 (1993): 417.

39. Mark Lemley, The Law and Economics of Internet Norms, *Chicago-Kent Law Review* 73 (1998): 1257, 1270.

40. Online Interview with Mark Lemley, May 23, 2000.

41. Lemley, supra, note 39, at 1271–1272.

42. Amitai Etzioni, E-Communities Build New Ties, but Ties That Bind, *New York Times,* February 10, 2000.

43. Gary Chapman, Efforts Urging Responsibility on Net Call for a Pause to Reflect, Teach, *Los Angeles Times,* February 28, 2000.

44. By late 2000, for example, cultural acceptance of active participation in file sharing activities via Napster, Gnutella, and others may not have amounted to a new Net-wide norm, but the number of persons engaged in such activity was certainly too large to be ignored by the legal community.

Chapter 2

1. 521 U.S. 844 (1997).

2. See Oral Argument of Seth P. Waxman, Esq. On Behalf of the Appellants, *Cyber-Liberties: American Civil Liberties Union,* <http://www.aclu.org/issues/cyber/trial/sctran.html#waxman> (visited May 17, 2000) [hereinafter *Reno v. ACLU Oral Argument*].

3. Stuart Biegel, Reno v. ACLU in the Supreme Court: Justices Hear Oral Argument in Communication Decency Act Case, *UCLA Online Institute for Cyber-*

space Law and Policy, March 27, 1997, <http://www.gseis.ucla.edu/iclp/mar97.html> (visited August 28 2000).

4. See Reno v. ACLU Oral Argument, supra, note 2.

5. See id.

6. See, e.g., PruneYard Shopping Center v. Robins, 447 U.S. 74 (1980).

7. 438 U.S. 726 (1978).

8. Id. at 748.

9. See Reno v. ACLU Oral Argument, supra, note 2.

10. See Biegel, supra, note 3.

11. Lessig, supra, note 36 (chapter 1), at 501, 503; Jerry Kang, Cyber-Race, *Harvard Law Review* 113 (2000): 1130, 1137.

12. Nearly Half of Internet Users Say Internet Becoming a Necessity According to America Online/Roper Starch Cyberstudy, *RoperStarch Worldwide: In the News 1998,* <http://www.roper.com/news/content/news86.htm> (visited August 28, 2000).

13. See Steve Lohr, Information Technology Field Is Rated Largest U.S. Industry, *New York Times,* November 18, 1997.

14. See, e.g., Eleanore C. Sanchez, Don't Discount Online Advertising Just Yet, *BusinessWorld,* March 1, 2001; Ellis Booker, Overseas Expansion Vital to Build U.S. E-Companies, *B to B,* November 20, 2000; Andrea Ahles, Online Trading Communities Spring Up to Meet Growing Demand for Business-to-Business Transactions, Fort Worth Star-Telegram, September 13, 1999. See, generally, Forrester Research <www.forrester.com> (visited March 1, 2001).

In addition to Forrester's intensive monitoring of Internet-related activity, numerous other sources containing Internet-related statistics and projections are available online. See, e.g., the U.S. Department of Commerce's report "Digital Economy 2000," <http://www.esa.doc.gov/de2k.htm> (visited August 27, 2000); The Organization for Economic Cooperation and Development's e-commerce statistics, <http://www.oecd.org/dsti/sti/it/ec/index.htm> (visited August 27, 2000); NUA's Internet surveys, <http://www.nua.ie/surveys/> (visited August 27, 2000). With all of these surveys, questions persist regarding both methodology and validity. In addition, statistical projections cannot account for unexpected events, such as the "e-tailing" shakeout that occurred during the year 2000.

15. The Technological Reshaping of Metropolitan America, *Office of Technology Assessment, Congress of the United States,* September 1995, <http://www.wws.princeton.edu/~ota/ns20/year_f.html> (visited August 28, 2000).

16. See, e.g., *Nolo.Com: Self-Help Law Center,* <http://www.nolo.com/index.html> (visited March 1, 2001).

17. See Stephanie Simon, Internet Changing the Way Some Lawyers Do Business, *Los Angeles Times,* July 8, 1996.

18. See Michael Simonsen, Physicians' Office Market Grows with Changing Health Care Delivery, *The RBI Newsletter,* November 1, 2000. See, generally,

Derek F. Meek, Telemedicine: How an Apple (or Another Computer) May Bring Your Doctor Closer, *Cumberland Law Review* 29 (1998): 173.

19. See James J. O'Donnell, Tools for Teaching: Personal Encounters in Cyberspace, *The Chronicle of Higher Education,* February 13, 1998. See also Michael A. Geist, Where Can You Go Today? The Computerization of Legal Education from Workbooks to the Web, *Harvard Journal of Law and Technology* 11 (Fall 1997): 141.

20. See Jack McGarvey, But Computers Are Clearly the Future, *New York Times,* May 25, 1997.

21. See David Koeppel, Distance Learning; A Sampler of Cyberschools, *New York Times,* April 4, 1999.

22. See Peter Applebome, Distance Learning: Education.com, *New York Times,* April 4, 1999; Katie Hafner, Between Tech Fans and Naysayers, Scholarly Skeptics, *New York Times,* April 1, 1999.

23. See, e.g., Rob Bernstein and David Sheff, How America Uses the Net, *Yahoo Internet Life,* Special Report, September 1999, <http://www.zdnet.com/yil/content/mag/9909/america.html> (visited May 19, 2000); Bilge Ebiri, How the World Uses the Net, *Yahoo Internet Life,* September 1999, <http://www.zdnet.com/yil/content/mag/9909/world.html> (visited May 19, 2000).

24. See, e.g., James Brook and Ian Boal, *Resisting the Virtual Life: The Culture and Politics of Information* (City Lights, 1996); Andrew Leonard, *Bots: The Origin of a New Species* (Penguin, 1997); John Seabrook, *Deeper: My Two-Year Odyssey in Cyberspace* (Simon & Schuster, 1997). See also Jon Katz, How the Net Changed America, *Yahoo Internet Life,* September 1999, <http://www.zdnet.com/yil/content/mag/9909/changed.html> (visited May 19, 2000).

See, generally, Michael L. Dertouzos, *What Will Be: How the New World of Information Will Change Our Lives* (Harper, 1997); Christine L. Borgman, *From Gutenberg to the Global Information Infrastructure: Access to Information in the Networked World* (MIT Press, 2000).

25. See, e.g., Jane Ginsburg, Putting Cars on the 'Information Superhighway': Authors, Exploiters, and Copyright in Cyberspace, *Columbia Law Review* 95 (1995): 1466.

26. See Lawrence Lessig, The Path of Cyberlaw, *Yale Law Journal* 104 (1995): 1743.

27. See M. Ethan Katsh, *Law in a Digital World* (Oxford University Press, 1995); John P. Barlow, *Barlow Home(stead)Page, The Electronic Frontier Foundation,* <http://www.eff.org/~barlow> (visited March 1, 2001).

28. See, e.g., Jack L. Goldsmith, Against Cyberanarchy, *University of Chicago Law Review* 65 (1998): 1199.

29. Eugene Volokh, Technology and the Future of Law, Rev. of *Law in a Digital World,* by Ethan Katsh, *Stanford Law Review* 47 (1995): 1375.

30. See Jane Kaufman Winn, Open Systems, Free Markets, and Regulation of Internet Commerce, *Tulane Law Review* 72 (1998): 1177.

31. Howard Rheingold, *The Virtual Community: Homesteading on the Electronic Frontier* (Addison-Wesley Publishing Co., 1993).

32. Symposium announcement, *Chicago-Kent Law Review,* Symposium on Internet Law and Legal Theory, 73, (4) (1998) (on file with the author).

33. Buford Terrell, post to CyberProf mailing list, December 28, 1998 (on file with the author).

34. I Don't Even Have A Modem, interview with William Gibson, *William Gibson Interview Page #1/4,* <http://www.josefsson.net/gibson/index.html> (visited February 16, 2000).

35. Jerry Kang, Cyber-Race, supra, note 11, at 1131.

36. Lawrence Lessig, Reading the Constitution in Cyberspace, *Emory Law Journal* 45 (1996): 869, 872.

37. Lawrence Lessig, Surveying Law and Borders: The Zones of Cyberspace, *Stanford Law Review* 48 (1996): 1403, 1407.

38. David R. Johnson and David G. Post, Law and Borders: The Rise of Law in Cyberspace, *Stanford Law Review* 48 (1996): 1367.

39. Online interview with David Post (1998).

40. Even the U.S. Government suggested, in the *Reno v. ACLU* oral argument, that the Internet be viewed as akin to a city, with its obscene and pornographic material equivalent to adult bookstores and video stores. Deputy Solicitor General Waxman argued that the dispute regarding the regulation of online "decency" could appropriately be viewed as "a zoning issue," with the case of *Renton v. Playtime Theaters* directly on point. In Renton, theater owners had argued unsuccessfully that their First and Fourteenth Amendment rights had been violated by a zoning regulation that forbade the building of X-rated theaters near residential areas, schools, churches, and parks. The court found that the city was rightly concerned about the "secondary effects" of pornographic theaters and that, in fact, quality of life issues were at stake. By analogy, the quality of life of online users is likewise affected by the presence of obscene and pornographic material.

On the other hand, it must be noted that the government arguably adopted this metaphor to take advantage of the *Renton* "secondary effects" doctrine, not necessarily because it had adopted Post's view of cyberspace.

41. Digital Equipment Corporation v. Alta Vista Technology, Inc., 960 F. Supp. 456 (1997). See also Stuart Biegel, The Ubiquitous PC: Courts and Commentators Alike Recognize That Technology Is Changing Society, *UCLA Online Institute for Cyberspace Law and Policy,* June 26, 1997, <http://www.gseis.ucla.edu/iclp/jun97.html> (visited March 1, 2001).

42. Andrew L. Shapiro, The Disappearance of Cyberspace and the Rise of Code, *Seton Hall Constitutional Law Journal* 8 (1998): 703; See also Andrew L. Shapiro and Richard C. Leone, *The Control Revolution: How the Internet Is Putting Individuals in Charge and Changing the World We Know* (Public Affairs, 1999).

43. See Phillip E. Agre, *Computation and Human Experience* (Cambridge University Press, 1997).

44. Phillip E. Agre, Yesterday's Tomorrow, *Times Literary Supplement,* July 3, 1998.

45. M. Ethan Katsh, Cybertime, Cyberspace, and Cyberlaw, *The Journal of Online Law,* Article 1, Para. 56 (1995) <http://www.law.cornell.edu/jol/katsh.htm> (visited March 1, 2001).

46. Id.

47. Online interview with John Perry Barlow, December 22, 1998. As Barlow described it to me, his first use of the term was very similar to the view expressed by Gibson four years later: "Cyberspace is where you are when you're on the phone." In late 1998, however, he explained that he did not just mean that "Alexander Graham Bell met Mr. Watson there in March of 1876." He also meant "any 'space' in which people can gather their minds without bringing their bodies."

48. Id.

49. See John Perry Barlow, The Economy of Ideas: A Framework for Rethinking Patents and Copyrights in the Digital World, *Wired* 2.03 (1994).

50. John Perry Barlow, A Declaration of the Independence of Cyberspace, *Electronic Frontier Foundation,* <http://www.eff.org/~barlow/Declaration-Final.html> (visited August 28, 2000).

51. Some scholars have even begun to argue that the debate in this context has become anachronistic. See, e.g. Timothy Wu, Application-Centered Internet Analysis, *Virginia Law Review* 85: 1163–1164, 1194–1203 (1999).

52. U.S. v. Thomas, 74 F. 3d. 701 (6th Cir. 1996). For an analysis of the implications of this decision, see, e.g., Eric B. Easton, Closing the Barn Door After the Genie Is Out of the Bag: Recognizing a "Futility Principle" in First Amendment Jurisprudence, *DePaul Law Review* 45: 1 (1995). See, generally, Jonathan Wallace and Mark Mangan, *Sex, Laws and Cyberspace* (Henry Holt, 1996).

53. U.S. v. Thomas, 74 F. 3d. at 706.

54. Other controversies at the time of the decision focused on the fact that the Thomases were convicted of a crime involving "transportation" of computer files even though the actual digital picture files that the defendants created arguably never left their computers in Northern California. BBS members in other locations who made an affirmative choice to do so could then view, print, or download copies to their own personal computers. Still, it can be argued that no transportation actually occurred.

55. Miller v. California, 413 U.S. 15 (1973).

56. See Brock Lunsford, Current Developments in the Law: U.S. v. Thomas, *Boston University Public Interest Law Journal* 6 (1999): 805; Stuart Biegel, *Constitutional Issues in Cyberspace Focus on Community Standards,* UCLA Online Institute for Cyberspace Law and Policy, <http://www.gseis.ucla.edu/iclp/feb96.html> (visited August 27, 2000).

57. See, generally, Wallace and Mangan, supra, note 52.

58. See the English translation of the CompuServe Germany case, *Cyber-Rights and Cyber-Liberties* (United Kingdom), <http://www.cyber-rights.org/isps/somm-dec.htm> (visited August 28, 2000).

59. See Edmund L. Andrews, CompuServe Executive Indicted in Germany on Pornography Charges, *New York Times,* April 17, 1997; Stuart Biegel, Indictment of CompuServe Official in Germany Brings Volatile Issues of CyberJurisdiction into Focus, *UCLA Online Institute for Cyberspace and Policy,* <http://www.gse.ucla.edu/iclp/apr97.html> (visited August 28, 2000).

60. See Roger Boyes, Computer Firm to Fight Bavarian Charges of Internet Pornography, *The Times* (London), April 18, 1997.

61. Relying on a new multimedia law passed shortly after Mr. Somm had been convicted, the court ruled that Mr. Somm could not have done much more than he did and could not be held responsible. Chief Judge Laszlo Ember took note of the fact that Somm had briefly tried to block access to a number of Internet sites, later giving up because the blockade proved unmanageable. Judge Ember then declared that Somm had done all he could. See Edmund L. Andrews, German Court Overturns Pornography Ruling against CompuServe, *New York Times,* November 18, 1999.

Similar issues arose in France in 2000, when *Ligue Internationale Contre le Racisme et l'Antisemitisme* filed suit against Yahoo, claiming that it hosts online auctions of Nazi paraphernalia in violation of French law. LICRA sought a court order requiring Yahoo to make such auctions inaccessible to Internet users in France. See, generally, Jim Hu and Evan Hansen, Yahoo Auction Case May Reveal Borders of Cyberspace, <http://news.cnet.com/news/0-1005-202-2495751.html> (visited August 24, 2000).

62. United States v. Kammersell, 7 F. Supp. 2d 1196 (D. Utah 1998).

63. Ray Rivera, Cyber-Prank Earns Prison Term, *Salt Lake Tribune,* October 16, 1998.

64. Stephen Hunt, 64-Year-Old Statute Spells Big Trouble for High-Tech Prankster, *Salt Lake Tribune,* June 6, 1998. See also Kammersell, 7 F. Supp. 2d 1196 (D. Utah 1998).

The Kammersell decision was affirmed by the U.S. Court of Appeals for the Tenth Circuit. See U.S. v. Kammersell, 196 F.3d 1137 (10th Cir. 1999).

65. AP, Postal Worker Guilty in Threat Via E-mail, *New York Times,* December 13, 1998.

66. Diane Cabell, Post to Cyberprof Mailing List, December 23, 1998 (on file with the author).

67. Steven Millhauser, *Martin Dressler* (New York: Crown, 1996).

68. James Halperin, *The Truth Machine* (Delrey, 1996).

69. Ray Kurzweil, *The Age of Spiritual Machines* (Viking Press, 1999).

Chapter 3

1. Gary Chapman, Net Gain, *The New Republic*, July 31, 1995.

2. Timothy Wu, Application-Centered Internet Analysis, *Virginia Law Review* 85 (1999): 1163.

3. United States v. Machado, No. SACR 96–142–AHS (S.D.Cal. 1998). See also Davan Maharaj, Anti-Asian E-Mail Was Hate Crime, Jury Finds, *Los Angeles Times*, February 11, 1998.

4. David Rosenzweig, Man Charged in Sending Hate E-mail to Latinos Across U.S., *Los Angeles Times*, January 29, 1999.

5. See Planned Parenthood of Columbia/Willamette, Inc. v. American Coalition of Life Activists, 41 F. Supp. 2d 1130 (D. Or 1999) (amended order and permanent injunction).

6. Planned Parenthood of Columbia/Willamette, Inc. v. American Coalition of Life Activists, 244 F.3d 1007 (9th Cir. 2001).

7. See Defending Abortion Rights, *New York Times* (editorial), March 31, 2001; Henry Weinstein, 43 in Congress Ask Court to Revisit Clinic Threat Issue, *Los Angeles Times*, April 13, 2001.

8. See Lisa A. Karczewski, Stalking in Cyberspace: The Expansion of California's Current Anti-Stalking Laws in the Age of the Internet, *McGeorge Law Review* 30 (1999): 517, 527 fn. 48; *1999 Report on Cyberstalking: A New Challenge for Law Enforcement and Industry*, <http://www.usdoj.gov/criminal/cybercrime/cyberstalking.htm> (visited February 28, 2000), which contains a report from the Attorney General to the Vice President; Governor Signs Cyberstalking Legislation, Associated Press, December 28, 1999, a report on the Michigan governor's signing of a new cyberstalking statute.

9. See Greg Miller, Man Pleads Guilty to Using Net to Solicit Rape, *Los Angeles Times*, April 29, 1999.

10. See Marty Rimm, Marketing Pornography on the Information Superhighway: A Survey of 917,410 Images, Descriptions, Short Stories, and Animations Downloaded 8.5 Million Times by Consumers in over 2000 Cities in Forty Countries, Provinces, and Territories, *Georgetown Law Journal* 83 (1995): 1849, 1892. According to Rimm, "Pedo/hebephilic and paraphilic imagery accounts for 2,685,777 downloads, or 48.4%, of all downloads from commercial 'adult' BBS's." See also Carlin Meyer, Reclaiming Sex from the Pornographers: Cybersexual Possibilities, Georgetown Law Journal 83 (1995): 1969.

11. Rahul Sharma, Experts Call for Laws to Curb Internet Child Abuse, Reuters, February 14, 1999.

12. See, generally, 18 U.S.C., secs. 2251–2260, Sexual Exploitation and Other Abuse of Children.

13. See USSG 2G2.4(b)(1). In practice, however, it should be noted that federal prosecutors are highly unlikely to charge possession of child pornography involving seventeen-year-olds.

14. See 18 U.S.C., sec. 2256. See generally infra, chapter 12 of this book.

15. See *Ashcroft v. Free Speech Coalition,* forthcoming (2001–2002), where the U.S. Supreme Court will address the dispute litigated in *Free Speech Coalition v. Reno,* 198 F.3d 1083 (9th Cir. 1999). See also *United States v. Hilton,* 167 F.3d 61 (1st Cir. 1999), *cert. denied,* Hilton v. United States, 120 S.Ct. 115 (1999). The *Free Speech Coalition* case and the *Hilton* case had reached opposite conclusions on the constitutionality of the child pornography statute.

16. See, e.g., Robert Pear, Online Sales Spur Illegal Importing of Medicine to U.S., *New York Times,* January 10, 2000. At the turn of the century, many online prescription drug sales often originated in other countries.

17. Most of the lawsuits currently filed against health care professionals are based on negligence law. Negligence is not typically a crime, but simply a civil wrong (a "tort") that our legal system has recognized. Under negligence law, every person owes every other person a duty to act reasonably. The standard of care for such reasonable action varies depending on the circumstances. And professionals are typically held to a higher standard of care. Thus, the level of care that doctors provide is measured objectively against the level of care that an ordinary reasonable (or "average") doctor would typically provide to a patient. If the doctor's actions fall below this level, and the patient is injured or her condition deteriorates as a result of these actions, then the doctor can be found negligent.

What should the standard of care be for health care professionals in the online world? Should they simply be held to the same standard as any ordinary citizen who posts information online, or should they be held to the higher standard of a doctor interacting with a patient? From a legal perspective, this is a very important question because if they are held to the higher standard, it will often be much easier to find them negligent if injuries occur as a result of their action or inaction.

And even if health care professionals are held to the higher standard of doctors interacting with patients, should this standard of care be the same in the online world as it might be in a clinic or a hospital? Will we expect doctors to be as careful in the virtual world as they are in the real world? Should it depend on the nature of the interaction? Will we expect more from health care professionals who answer our questions and perhaps even view videos of our conditions than from those who simply post standard boilerplate advice in newsletter format online? At what point might online care be seen as equivalent to real-time care? These are the sorts of questions that are currently being debated.

Many additional questions also arise in this context. Does a person who sets up a Web site, for example, have an obligation to check the validity of all factual statements he might post? At what point is it the responsibility of the online user, and not the Web site owner, to ascertain the truth? Should it depend on the nature of the Web site? Should it depend on who the Web site owner is? Will we be expecting more from an apparent expert posting information online than we might from, say, a high school student posting information online? Should there be any difference under the law?

18. See, e.g., Alissa R. Spielberg, Online Without a Net: Physician-Patient Communication by Electronic Mail, *American Journal of Law & Medicine* 25 (1999):

267, 291–292. See generally Glenn Wachter, Interstate Licensure for Telemedicine Practitioners, Telemedicine Information Exchange, March 10, 2000, <http://tie.telemed.org/legal/issues/licensure0300.pdf> (visited February 28, 2001).

19. Interview with Dr. Alan H. Heilpern, President, Los Angeles County Medical Association (LACMA), Spring 1998. See generally Ross D. Silverman, The Changing Face of Law and Medicine in the New Millennium: Regulating Medical Practice in the Cyber Age: Issues and Challenges for State Medical Boards, *American Journal of Law & Medicine* 26 (2000): 255.

20. As quoted by Wade Roush, Hackers: Taking a Byte Out of Computer Crime, *MIT Technology Review,* April 1995, <http://www.techreview.com/articles/apr95/Roush.html> (visited February 28, 2000).

21. Id.

22. See Richard Power, *Current and Future Danger: A CSI Primer on Computer Crime and Information Warfare* 12–13 (2d ed., 1996); Walter A. Effross, High-Tech Heroes, Virtual Villains, and Jacked-In Justice: Visions of Law and Lawyers in Cyberpunk Science Fiction, *Buffalo Law Review* 45 (1997): 931; Catherine Therese Clarke, Innovation and the Information Environment, From Criminet to Cyber-Perp: Toward an Inclusive Approach to Policing the Evolving Criminal Mens Rea on the Internet, *Oregon Law Review* 75 (1996): 191, 221; Michael Lee et al., Electronic Commerce, Hackers, and the Search for Legitimacy: A Regulatory Proposal, *Berkeley Technology Law Journal* 14 (1999): 839, 884–85.

23. See Joel R. Reidenberg and Francoise Gamet-Pol, The Fundamental Role of Privacy and Confidence in the Network, *Wake Forest Law Review* 30 (1995): 105; Joel R. Reidenberg, Rules of the Road for Global Electronic Highways: Merging the Trade and Technical Paradigms, *Harvard Journal of Law and Technology* 6 (1993): 287.

24. See Benjamin J. Fox, *Hackers and the U.S. Secret Service,* <http://www.gseis.ucla.edu/iclp/bfox.html> (visited March 1, 2001).

25. See Hanan Sher, The Weapons of Infowar, *The Jerusalem Report,* June 8, 1998.

26. *Critical Foundations: Protecting America's Infrastructures,* Report of the U.S. President's Commission on Critical Infrastructure, <http://www.info-sec.com/pccip/pccip2/report_index.html> (visited March 9, 2000).

27. Hackers Tell a Senate Committee Internet Has Serious Weaknesses, Associated Press, May 19, 1998.

28. Mark Grossman, Terrorism Stalks Cyberspace, *American Lawyer,* February 12, 1999.

29. Janet Naylor and Jody Upton, Medical Industry Lax on Internet Security, *Detroit News,* February 12, 1999.

30. See Sher, supra, note 25.

31. Amy Harmon, "Hacktivists" of All Persuasions Take Their Struggle to the Web, *New York Times,* October 31, 1998.

32. Some ten days later, however, representatives of the LoU "disavowed any association with people who had called on computer hackers to bring down the data networks of Iraq and China." David Akin, Hackers Call Off Their Cyberwar Against Iraq and China, *The Financial Post,* January 11, 1999.

33. See Marie Woolf, Cabinet Calls in GCHQ to Foil Hackers, *The Independent* (London), February 7, 1999.

34. See Ian Brodie, Clinton Agenda Targets Terrorist Hackers, *The Times* (London), January 20, 1999.

35. See Amy Harmon, supra, note 31.

36. Don Clark, Buying the Goods, *Wall Street Journal,* December 7, 1998.

37. See John F. McGuire, Note, When Speech is Heard Around the World: Internet Content Regulation in the United States and Germany, *NYU Law Review* 74 (1999): 750, 779 n. 160.

38. See U.S. Interagency Working Group on Electronic Commerce, *The Framework for Global Electronic Commerce* <http://www.whitehouse.gov/WH/New/Commerce/read.html> (visited April 6, 2000).

39. This analysis does not address what hackers might be able to do.

40. Jerry Kang, Information Privacy in Cyberspace Transactions, *Stanford Law Review* 50 (1998): 1193.

41. The Junkbusters Web site provides an excellent fundamental overview of cookies and related issues on the World Wide Web. See <http://www.junkbusters.com/ht/en/cookies.html> (visited September 8, 2000).

42. See, e.g., Simson Garfinkel, *Database Nation: The Death of Privacy in the 21st Century* (O'Reilly, 2000); Jeffrey Rosen, *The Unwanted Gaze: The Destruction of Privacy in America* (Random House, 2000). See generally David Brin, *The Transparent Society: Will Technology Force Us to Choose between Privacy and Freedom* (Perseus, 1998).

43. The URL of the EPIC Web site is www.epic.org, whereas Junkbusters may be accessed at www.junkbusters.com.

44. See, e.g., Net Privacy Now! Who's Tracking You? How Do You Stop Them? (*PC World,* cover story, June 2000); Why Privacy Matters (*New York Times Magazine,* cover story, April 30, 2000).

45. Glenn R. Simpson, Clinton Is Unlikely to Back FTC Efforts for New Power to Regulate Web Privacy, *Wall Street Journal,* May 22, 2000.

46. See, e.g., Sporty's Farm, L.L.C. v. Sportsman's Market, 202 F.3d 489 (2d Cir. 2000). See generally Kevin Eng, Note, Breaking Through the Looking Glass: An Analysis of Trademark Rights in Domain Names Across Top Level Domains, Boston University Journal of Science and Technology Law 6 (2000): 7; Jessica

Litman, The DNS Wars: Trademarks and the Internet Domain Name System, *Journal of Small and Emerging Business Law* 4 (2000): 149.

47. See, e.g., Luke A. Walker, ICANN's Uniform Domain Name Dispute Resolution Policy, *Berkeley Technology Law Journal* 15 (2000): 289; David G. Post, Juries and the New Common Law of Cyberspace, *Plugging In,* September 2000, <http://www.temple.edu/lawschool/dpost/Juries.html> (visited September 8, 2000).

48. See, e.g., Raymond T. Nimmer, UCITA: A Commercial Contract Code, *Computer Lawyer* 17 (May 2000); but see Rochelle Cooper Dreyfuss, UCITA in the International Marketplace: Are We About to Export Bad Innovation Policy? *Brooklyn Journal of International Law* 26 (2000): 49. See generally UCITA Online, <http://www.ucitaonline.com/ucita.html> (visited September 8, 2000).

49. See, e.g., Barnaby J. Feder, E-Signing Law Seen as a Boon to E-Business, *New York Times,* July 4, 2000. See generally U.S. Code, Title 15, Sections 7001 et seq.

50. Id.

51. See W. Page Keeton et al., *Prosser and Keeton on the Law of Torts* (5th ed., West Publishing Company, 1984).

52. See Rollin M. Perkins and Ronald N. Boyce, *Criminal Law* (3d ed., Foundation Press, 1982).

53. Scott Glover, Grand Theft Auto Enters the Computer Age, *Los Angeles Times,* October 23, 1998.

54. Benjamin Pimentel, "Cyberspace Bandit" Could Have Stolen $1 Million, Cops Say, *San Francisco Chronicle,* November 9, 1998.

55. See James M. Snyder, Online Auction Fraud: Are the Auction Houses Doing All They Should or Could to Stop Online Fraud? *Federal Communications Law Journal* 52 (2000): 453. See also Lisa Guernsey, A New Caveat for eBay Users: Seller Beware, *New York Times,* August 3, 2000; Sara Nathan, Internet Fraud, *USA Today,* February 24, 1999.

It should also be noted that concerns have been raised regarding the sale of illegal items in this context. See, e.g., Jamie Beckett and Jon Swartz, Clicking For Contraband: The Law Can't Catch Up to the Internet, Where Any Desire Can Be Satisfied for a Price, *San Francisco Chronicle,* March 1, 1999. Indeed, the U.S. Bureau of Alcohol, Tobacco & Firearms (BATF) announced in early 1999 that they were investigating the "alleged sale of contraband" on its Web site. See Online Auction Site Target of Investigation, *Associated Press,* March 2, 1999. See also Monua Jana, Online Auction Users Struggle with Variety of Scams, *San Jose Mercury News,* August 11, 1999; David L. Wilson, Illicit Online Underworld Thrives Below the Surface of the Web, *San Jose Mercury News,* May 23, 1999.

56. Andrew Fraser, Regulators Struggle to Keep Up With Explosion of Online Fraud, *Wall Street Journal,* March 1, 1999.

57. David Barboza, SEC Accuses 44 Stock Promoters of Internet Fraud, *New York Times,* October 29, 1998. In a study released soon after the SEC announcement,

university researchers concluded that concerns about online stock fraud appear to be well founded. "These chat rooms should be a matter of concern. People do seem to be taken in by what they hear," said Robert Forsythe, a senior associate dean of the University of Iowa's business school and co-author of "Cheap Talk: Fraud and Adverse Selection in Financial Markets." See Study Upholds Regulators' Fears About Deceptive Practices Online, *Dow Jones Newswires,* November 18, 1998.

58. Michael Schroeder, Defendant Gets Prison Sentence in Internet Case, *Wall Street Journal,* September 15, 1997.

59. Mark Harrington, On the Web, It's Easy to Deceive Investors, *Newsday,* March 16, 2000. Several high profile Web sites have also been set up to monitor SEC activity in this regard. See, e.g., EnforceNet.Com, which is "devoted to collecting and organizing links . . . related to the rapidly developing relationship between securities regulation and the Internet." <www.enforcenet.com> (visited May 29, 2000).

60. Expert Warns: Criminals Beating Police in Cyberspace, Reuters, March 1, 1999.

61. 18 U.S.C. §2319(c). See also *U.S. Department of Justice Analysis of the NET Act,* <http://www.usdoj.gov/criminal/cybercrime/> (visited March 9, 2000). For a more thorough analysis of the NET Act, see infra, chapter 5.

62. See Pamela Samuelson, The U.S. Digital Agenda at WIPO, *Virginia Journal of International Law* 37 (1997). See also Jessica Litman, Reforming Information Law in Copyright's Image, *Dayton Law Review* 22 (1997): 588.

63. Eric Goldman (aka Schlachter), The Intellectual Property Renaissance in Cyberspace: Why Copyright Law Could Be Unimportant on the Internet, 12 *Berkeley Technology Law Journal* 12 (1997): 15, 36.

64. See Mark A. Lemley, Rights of Attribution and Integrity in Online Communications, Journal of Online Law (1995): Article 2, <http://www.wm.edu/law/publications/jol/lemley.html> (visited May 23, 2001).

65. "As many as 500,000 MP3 files are estimated to be on the Web," wrote Stephanie Schorow in Net Life: If a Computer Lets You Download Music, Does That Make It Stealing?, *Boston Herald,* April 4, 2000. "One report estimated that there are 70,000 new copyright-infringing MP3 music files appearing every month on the Web." Alan Kohler, Record Companies Losing To Net, *Australian Financial Review,* March 28, 2000. For a discussion on whether an implied license applies in these situations, see Bruce A. Lehman, *U.S. Dept. of Commerce, Intellectual Property and the National Information Infrastructure: The Report of the Working Group on Intellectual Property Rights,* 129 n. 424 (1995), where it is suggested that an implied license may arise when a copyrighted work is posted to a newsgroup, but might not extend to activities such as distributing copies of the work to other newsgroups. See also Goldman (aka Schlachter), supra, note 63, 15, 46, where the author discusses the argument that uploading a copyrighted work onto the Internet might grant an implied license to provide hypertext links to the work.

66. See Goldman (aka Schlachter), supra, note 63.

67. See, e.g., Jason Epstein, The Rattle of Pebbles, *New York Review of Books,* April 27, 2000; Eugene Volokh, Cheap Speech and What It Will Do, *Yale Law Journal* 104 (1995): 1805.

68. It should be noted, however, that works already in the public domain have become available in great quantity online, thus removing an additional possible source of income for publishers.

69. Tasini v. New York Times Co., 1999 WL 753966 (2d Cir. 1999).

70. Joseph Gelmis, Industry Watchdog Battles the Pirates, *Newsday,* February 10, 1999.

71. See Karla Haworth, Publishers Press Colleges to Stop Piracy by Students, *Chronicle of Higher Education,* July 11, 1997.

72. See Stuart Biegel, After Image: Regulation Battles Are Just Beginning Following the Decency Act Decision, *UCLA Online Institute for Cyberspace Law and Policy,* July 24, 1997, <http://www.gseis.ucla.edu/iclp/jul97.html> (visited March 1, 2001).

73. Eben Shapiro, PC Matinee: The Race Is On to Make Web a Cyber-Cinema, *Wall Street Journal,* March 2, 1999.

74. See id.

75. See Frank Rich, Naked Capitalists, *New York Times Magazine,* May 20, 2001.

For an overview of legal and policy issues that have been identified in this area, see, e.g., Peter Johnson, Pornography Drives Technology: Why Not to Censor the Internet, *Federal Communications Law Journal* 49 (1996): 217; Lydia W. Lee, Child Pornography Prevention Act of 1996: Confronting the Challenges of Virtual Reality, *Southern California Interdisciplinary Law Journal* 8 (1999): 639. See, generally, Charles Nesson and David Marglin, The Day the Internet Met the First Amendment: Time and the Communications Decency Act, *Harvard Journal of Law and Technology* 10 (1996): 383.

76. Reno v. ACLU, 521 U.S. 844, 854 (1997).

77. See Jaime Wilson-Chiru, U. California-Los Angeles: Web Site Infringes upon UCLA's Trademark, *UCLA Daily Bruin,* February 26, 1999 (also available at 1999 WL 15035325).

78. See, e.g., the Pagejacking-Mousetrapping case, described in detail in chapter 10, infra.

79. See chapter 5 of this book, infra, for a more detailed analysis of *Reno I* and *Reno II.*

80. In a high-profile lawsuit focusing on Internet filtering in public libraries, Judge Leonie Brinkema denied defendant's motion to dismiss and motion for summary judgment, and scheduled a trial on the substantive issues. In late 1997, the Loudoun County Library Board had voted to adopt a "Policy on Internet Sexual Harassment," which required that "[s]ite-blocking software . . . be installed on all [library] computers" so as to: "a. block child pornography and obscene material (hard core pornography)"; and "b. block material deemed harmful to juveniles un-

der applicable Virginia statutes and legal precedents (soft core pornography)." To implement the policy, the Library Board chose "X-Stop," a commercial software product. Plaintiffs challenged this policy under the free speech clause of the First Amendment, alleging that it impermissibly blocked their access to protected speech. In her ruling denying the defendants' motion to dismiss and motion for summary judgment, Judge Brinkema—after analyzing relevant First Amendment cases (and particularly Board of Education v. Pico, 457 U.S. 853)—declared that "the Library Board may not adopt and enforce content-based restrictions on access to protected Internet speech absent a compelling state interest and means narrowly drawn to achieve that end." Mainstream Loudoun v. Board of Trustees of the Loudoun County Library, 2 F. Supp. 2d 783 (E.D. Va. 1998). The same reasoning carried the day in the actual trial later that year. See 24 F. Supp. 2d 552 (E.D. Va. 1998).

81. See Robert Scheer, Internet Sewage King Spews Up a Sordid Clinton Calumny, Aided by the Press Lord's Smut-Meisters, *Los Angeles Times,* January 12, 1999.

82. See, e.g., Jonathan Zittrain, The Rise and Fall of Sysopdom, *Harvard Journal Law and Technology* 10 (1997): 495.

83. Two U.S. district court decisions that came to very different conclusions in cases with very similar fact patterns brought the issue of online defamation to the forefront by the mid-1990s. Both cases focused not on the liability of persons who originally made the libelous statements, but on the liability of commercial online services for defamatory conduct in moderated bulletin board discussions. The disputes were litigated under the legal principle that "one who repeats or otherwise republishes defamatory matter is subject to liability as if he had originally published it" (Restatement [Second] of Torts, sec. 578).

In the first case, *Cubby v. CompuServe* (1991), the commercial online service was absolved of any responsibility for the defamatory comments posted in an online newsletter called "Rumorville." The newsletter, which appeared on CompuServe's Journalism Forum, had been moderated by an independent company under contract with the online service. The court found that posts to the forum were uploaded instantly, and that CompuServe had no more ability to monitor and control the transmission of the defamatory material than a public library, bookstore, or newsstand (776 F. Supp. 135 [S.D.N.Y. 1991]).

Four years later, however, in the case of *Stratton Oakmont v. Prodigy,* the commercial online service was held responsible for defamatory comments posted on its "Money Talk" bulletin board. While it did refer to the *Cubby* case, the court went on to explain that it had ruled differently in this instance because Prodigy—unlike CompuServe—had "held itself out to the public . . . as controlling the content of its . . . bulletin boards, . . . and . . . implemented this control through its automatic screening software . . . and its guidelines. . . ." (1995 N.Y. Misc. Lexis 229, 1995 WL 323710 [N.Y. 1995]). The court held that Prodigy was more like a publisher than a distributor because it "[had] uniquely arrogated to itself the role of determining what is proper for its members to post and read on its bulletin boards."

Many commentators and policymakers, however, found the *Stratton Oakmont* court's distinction to be highly flawed. See, e.g., Eugene Volokh, Freedom of Speech in Cyberspace from the Listener's Perspective: Private Speech Restrictions,

Libel, State Action, Harassment, and Sex, *University of Chicago Legal Forum* (1996): 377 (also available at <http://www.law.ucla.edu/faculty/volokh/listener.htm> [visited March 1, 2001]). And in the Telecommunications Act of 1996 the U.S. Congress included a provision expressly designed to overrule *Stratton Oakmont* and "any other similar decisions which have treated such providers as publishers or speakers of content that is not their own."

For an excellent analysis of the parallels and distinctions in the CompuServe and Prodigy cases generally, see Yochai Benkler, *Rules of the Road for the Information Superhighway: Electronic Communications and the Law,* Section 17.3 (1996).

84. 47 U.S.C., sec. 230(c)(1).

85. 47 U.S.C., sec. 230(e)(3).

The U.S. Circuit Court of Appeals for the Fourth Circuit has since said that this section "creates a federal immunity to any cause of action that would make service providers liable for information originating with a third-party user of the service. Specifically, Section 230 precludes courts from entertaining claims that would place a computer service provider in a publisher's role. Thus, lawsuits seeking to hold a service provider liable for its exercise of a publisher's traditional editorial functions—such as deciding whether to publish, withdraw, postpone or alter content—are barred." Zeran v. America Online, 129 F.3d 327 (4th Cir. 1997).

86. 129 F.3d 327 (4th Cir. 1997).

87. 992 F. Supp. 44 (D.D.C. 1998).

88. Id. The court went on to state that "[i]n some sort of tacit quid pro quo arrangement with the service provider community, Congress has conferred immunity from tort liability as an incentive to Internet service providers to self-police the Internet for obscenity and other offensive material, even where the self-policing is unsuccessful or not even attempted."

89. See, e.g., Doe v. University of Michigan, 721 F. Supp. 852–853, 856 (E.D. Mich. 1989).

90. Under Title 47, Section 223 of the Telecommunications Act—in the portion commonly known as the Communications Decency Act—lawmakers set forth several provisions forbidding online harassment. Section 223(a)(1)(C) prohibits the utilization of a telecommunications device—whether or not conversation or communication ensues and without disclosing one's identity—"with intent to annoy, abuse, threaten, or harass any person . . . who receives the communications." Section 223(a)(1)(E) prohibits persons from "repeatedly initiat[ing] communication with a telecommunications device, during which a conversation or communication ensues, solely to harass any person . . . who receives the communication." And Section 223(a)(2) prohibits anyone from knowingly permitting "any telecommunications facility under his control" to be used for such activity. Criminal penalties for the violation of these federal statutes include fines or imprisonment for up to two years. Although disputed portions of this act were struck down by the U.S. courts, the antiharassment provisions continue in effect.

91. Members were warned that their subscriptions may be terminated if they "transmit any unlawful, harmful, threatening, abusive, harassing, defamatory,

vulgar, obscene, hateful, racially, ethnically, or otherwise objectionable content," and were told that they "may not use the service to harass." See David Cay Johnston, The Fine Print in Cyberspace, *New York Times,* August 11, 1996.

92. See 163 and Counting: Hate Groups find Home on the Net, *Southern Poverty Law Center Intelligence Report,* Winter 1998.

93. U.S. v. Jake Baker, 890 F. Supp. 1375 (E.D. Mich. 1995).

94. Loving v. Boren, 956 F.Supp. 953, 955 (W.D. Okla. 1997).

95. See id.

96. Loving v. Boren, 133 F.3d 771 (10th Cir. 1998).

97. Section 2.1–805 of the 1996 Virginia Act provides that:

Except to the extent required in conjunction with a bona fide, agency-approved research project or other agency-approved undertaking, no agency employee shall utilize agency-owned or agency-leased computer equipment to access, download, print or store any information infrastructure files or services having sexually explicit content. Such agency approvals shall be given in writing by agency heads, and any such approvals shall be [*3] available to the public under the provisions of the Virginia Freedom of Information Act.

Section 2.1–804 defines "sexually explicit" content broadly to include:

(i) any description of or (ii) any picture, photograph, drawing, motion picture film, digital image or similar visual representation depicting sexual bestiality, a lewd exhibition of nudity, as nudity is defined in § 18.2–390, sexual excitement, sexual conduct or sadomasochistic abuse, as also defined in § 18.2–390, coprophilia, urophilia, or fetishism.

98. Urofsky v. Allen, 995 F. Supp. 634 (E.D. Va. 1998).

99. Urofsky v. Gilmore, 216 F.3d 401 (4th Cir. 2000).

100. See Stuart Biegel, Easy Access: Legal Protection for E-Mail Lags Behind the Law Covering Its Nontechnical Counterparts, *Los Angeles Daily Journal,* April 25, 1996.

101. See David Brin, *The Transparent Society: Will Technology Force Us to Choose Between Privacy and Freedom* (Perseus, 1998).

102. John Markoff, Microsoft to Alter Software in Response to Privacy Concerns, *New York Times,* March 7, 1999.

103. John Markoff, When Privacy Is More Perilous Than the Lack of It, *New York Times,* April 4, 1999.

104. See the Boycott Intel site at <www.bigbrotherinside.com> (visited March 28, 1999).

105. See <http://www.junkbusters.com/ht/en/new.html#year> (visited July 2, 2000).

106. John Markoff, A Growing Compatibility Issue in the Digital Age: Computers and Their Users' Privacy, *New York Times,* March 3, 1999.

Chapter 4

1. Charles Dickens, *Bleak House* (1853; rpt. Penguin Classics, 1997), chapter 1, In Chancery. See also chapter 8, Covering a Multitude of Sins, documenting the initial legal theories underlying this Wills and Trusts dispute.

2. Oliver W. Holmes, The Path of the Law, *Harvard Law Review* 10 (1897): 457, 458–64.

3. J. Roland Pennock and John W. Chapman, *The Limits of Law,* (Lieber-Atherton, 1974).

4. David J. Danelski, The Limits of Law, in Pennock and Chapman, supra.

5. Julius Cohen, Perspectives on the Limits of Law, in Pennock and Chapman, supra.

6. Kent Greenwalt, Some Related Limits of Law, in Pennock and Chapman, supra.

7. See Ruth Gavison, Privacy and the Limits of Law, *Yale Law Journal* 89 (1980): 421, 424.

8. See, generally, Hans Zeisel, *The Limits of Law Enforcement,* (University of Chicago Press, 1983).

9. See Davison M. Douglas, The Limits of Law in Accomplishing Racial Change: School Segregation in the Pre-Brown North, *UCLA Law Review* 44 (1997): 677; Sionaidh Douglas-Scott, The Hatefulness of Protected Speech: A Comparison of the American and European Approaches, *William & Mary Bill of Rights Journal* 7 (1999): 305.

10. See John Gillespie, The Role of the Bureaucracy in Managing Urban Land in Vietnam, *Pacific Rim Law and Policy Journal* 5 (1995): 59, 124: "Eliminating discrimination is not as simple as passing legislation. In the debate over the effectiveness of legislation as a tool of social change, the crudely instrumentalist view that legal change translates directly into social change has been discarded." See also L. Lustgarten, Racial Inequality and the Limits of Law, *Modern Law Review* 49 (1986): 68.

11. Roger B. Dworkin, *Limits: The Role of the Law in Bioethical Decision Making* (Indiana University Press, 1996).

12. See id.

13. See Anita M. Allen, Social Contract Theory in American Case Law, *Florida Law Review* 51 (1999): 1.

14. Id. at p. 20. In these cases, the term *social contract* is used to refer to "(a) principles of just and fair government with which rational persons should agree, would agree, or have in fact agreed; (b) the American Revolution and the United States Constitution; (c) a polity's entire body of positive law, including its constitutional law; or (d) specific quotidian bargains, agreements, and commercial contracts struck between, for example, employers and workers."

15. See Monarch Insurance Co. v. District of Columbia, 353 F. Supp. 1249, 1259 (D.D.C. 1973).

16. See *Sandarac Ass'n v. W. R. Frizzell Architects, Inc.*, 609 So. 2d 1349, 1353 n.4 (Fla. 2d DCA 1992).

17. Microsoft Encarta Online, <www.encarta.com> (visited May 30, 1999).

18. See id. "At this point in history, most Protestant nations had come to regard drinking as a social evil. The British government limited the sale of alcoholic drinks to a few early evening hours. In Sweden, where the movement had been strong since the 1830s, the government abolished both the profit motive and the competition from the liquor traffic after 1922 by nationalizing it. In 1919 the Finnish government banned the sale of any drink of more than 2 percent alcohol. Canada outlawed the sale of liquor in all provinces."

19. Id. These events have been documented in one form or another in most comprehensive histories of the United States.

20. See John Kaplan, *Marijuana: The New Prohibition* (World Publishing Company, 1970).

21. See Marijuana: Millions of Turned-On Users, *Life* Magazine, July 7, 1967.

22. See The Marijuana Problem, *Newsweek,* July 24, 1967.

23. These statistics were reported in *Life* Magazine, supra, July 7, 1967.

24. Walt Anderson, The High Cost of Cannabis, *West Magazine,* Los Angeles Times, 1970.

25. These statistics were reported in *Newsweek,* supra, July 24, 1967.

26. Some Say Police Can't Cope with Dope Problem, *Los Angeles Times,* 1968.

27. Marijuana: Is It Time for a Change in Our Laws? *Newsweek,* Sept. 7, 1970.

28. Sam Blum, Marijuana: New Attraction for Middle-Class Adults, *Los Angeles Times,* 1970.

29. See, generally, Kaplan, supra, note 20.

30. AP, Jail Now Less Likely for Marijuana Users, *Los Angeles Times,* June 9, 1971.

31. Adult Drug Use Stable, But More Youths Using Marijuana, Poll Finds, *Education Week,* September 9, 1998.

32. National Center on Addiction and Substance Abuse at Columbia University, Annual Back to School Survey, <http://www.casacolumbia.org/newsletter1457/newsletter_show.htm?doc_id=5788> (visited May 31, 1999).

33. Julie L. Nicklin, Colleges Report Increases in Arrests for Drug and Alcohol Violations, *Chronicle of Higher Education,* May 28, 1999.

34. See Serrano v. Priest, 5 Cal. 3d 584, 594 (1971): "Although equalization aid and supplemental aid temper the disparities which result from the vast variations in real property assessed valuation, wide differentials remain in the revenue available to individual districts and, consequently, in the level of educational expenditures."

35. Jonathan Harr, *A Civil Action* (Random House, 1995), at 369 in Vintage Books Paperback Edition (1996).

36. See id.

37. See Gary Chapman, Net Gain, *The New Republic,* July 31, 1995.

38. Johnson and Post, supra, note 38 (chapter 2), at 1367, 1374: "[Usenet discussion groups] . . . exist, in effect, everywhere, nowhere in particular, and only on the Net." See, generally, Chip Salzenberg, What Is Usenet? <http://www.faqs.org/faqs/usenet/what-is/part1/> (visited March 1, 2001).

See also Paul K. Ohm, On Regulating the Internet: Usenet, A Case Study, *UCLA Law Review* 46 (1999): 1941.

39. Steve Lohr, Privacy on the Internet Poses Legal Puzzle, *New York Times,* April 19, 1999.

40. Anonymity: Should the LCS Anonymous Remailer Be Shut Down? April 1999, <http://www.lcs.mit.edu/anniv/speakers/presentation?id=041399-15> (visited June 4, 1999). Mazieres described at some length the results of an anonymous survey of MIT's anonymous remailer users: "At the most critical end of the spectrum were people who used nym.alias.net because they need protection from oppressive governments. One particularly compelling story came from a person who was a humanitarian aid worker in a country with a fairly oppressive government and that person said that he or she did not feel comfortable communicating back home to friends via e-mail without the availability of a service like this. Another large class of people use the service because they're worried about losing their jobs, potential harassment or just simply being embarrassed for uses such as discussing alcoholism, depression, being a sexual minority. Some people said that they used nym.alias.net to blow the whistle on illegal activities. And a few people said that they found it incredibly useful for fighting harmful cults and helping people escape those cults.

"Another class of people simply wanted protection from mail logs. Right now on most systems if you have an e-mail account, even if no one is sitting there reading your mail, the system is building up a log file of all the mail messages that come and go. And someone can derive from that a list of all the people you've exchanged e-mail with. And people who don't feel comfortable with that use this service to keep the identity of their correspondence secret from the system administrators. And, finally, some people simply use this service for protection from search engines. The fact is right now you could make a statement in a public forum under your real name and 10 years from now people may call up your name on a search engine and be looking at statements you made 10 years ago. Do you still want to be associated with those statements? And, in particular, one person gave a story of a candidate at a job interview whose news posting history came up as a subject for the job interview and that person was obviously very uncomfortable with that.

"Finally, a few people admitted to using the service for admittedly marginal purposes. And probably the most common of these were people who said they used it to discuss marijuana cultivation. There are also a couple of people who said that they used it for software piracy and for virus development."

41. Johnson and Post, supra, note 38 (chapter 2), at 1370.

42. Jack L. Goldsmith, Against Cyberanarchy, *University of Chicago Law Review* 65 (1998): 1199, 1205–1211.

43. Id. at 1233.

44. Id. at 1250.

45. Johnson and Post, supra, note 38 (chapter 2), at 1394–1400.

46. Zippo Manufacturing Co. v. Zippo Dot Com, Inc., 952 F. Supp. 1119 (W.D. Pa. 1997).

47. See, e.g., Cybersell, Inc., an Arizona Corp. v. Cybersell, Inc., a Florida Corp., 130 F.3d 414 (9th Cir. 1997).

48. See Hans Zeisel, *The Limits of Law Enforcement,* supra. See also Richard S. Frase, Defining the Limits of Crime Control and Due Process, California Law Review 73 (1985): 212, 213.

49. Goldsmith, supra, note 42, at 1216–1217. The problem of enforcement is further compounded by the regulation evasion that can occur both in the offline and the online world. See id. at 1221–1222. As described, online users may relocate in geographical space or employ encryption or anonymous remailers to evade the reach of the legal system.

Chapter 5

1. See Justin Brown, Surfing Serbs Fight to Keep Their Access to the Internet's Flow of Information, *The Scotsman,* May 15, 1999; Carlota Gall, Yugoslavs' Web Lifeline Grows More Tenuous, *International Herald-Tribune,* May 17, 1999. See, generally, Jonathan Bing, Pen Is Mightier with the Net, *The Village Voice,* June 8, 1999.

2. Mark Lemley and Lawrence Lessig have both extolled the virtues of common law in a cyberlaw context. See, e.g., Mark Lemley, The Law and Economics of Internet Norms, *Chicago-Kent Law Review* 73 (1998): 1257, 1293–1294: "In 1995, essentially before there were any cases in the field, Lessig extolled the virtues of the slow, adaptive common law development process for the Net. We now have hundreds of reported decisions in various aspects of 'Internet law' ranging from jurisdiction to trademark law to the First Amendment. As I look at these cases, it seems to me that Lessig's intuition was right. Whether or not the common law naturally tends towards efficiency over time, as some have suggested, it's arguably doing a pretty good job of adapting existing law to the new and uncertain circumstances of the Net. Perhaps before we proclaim the law to be a failure, we ought to give it a chance to work. And certainly before we abdicate responsibility for governance to informal social groups or to programmers, we ought to have a much better sense than we do of whether the world that would result is one we would want to live in."

See, generally, Lawrence Lessig, The Path of Cyberlaw, *Yale Law Journal* 104 (1995): 1743, 1745.

A traditional definition of *common law* is found in *Black's Law Dictionary:*

As distinguished from statutory law created by the enactment of legislatures, the common law comprises the body of those principles and rules of action, relating to the government and security of persons and property, which derive their authority solely from usages and customs of immemorial antiquity, or from the judgments and decrees of the courts recognizing, affirming, and enforcing such usages and customs; and, in this sense, particularly the ancient unwritten law of England. In general, it is a body of law that develops and derives through judicial decisions, as distinguished from legislative enactments.

3. It must be noted that even the disputed provisions of Section 223 actually remain "on the books," but that the government has been "enjoined from enforcing, prosecuting, investigating or reviewing any matter premised upon: (a) Sections 223(a)(1)(B) and 223(a)(2) of the Communications Decency Act of 1996, Pub.L. No. 104–104, sec. 502, 110 Stat. 133, 133–36, to the extent such enforcement, prosecution, investigation, or review are based upon allegations other than obscenity or child pornography; and (b) Sections 223(d)(1) and 223(d)(2) of the CDA." See ACLU v. Reno I, 929 F. Supp. 824, 883 (E.D. Pa. 1996).

4. In addition to the provisions of Section 230, which essentially insulate ISPs from civil liability in this context, the CDA created several defenses to liability, including the portions of Section 223 that provide a defense to criminal liability. This defense is intended to protect those who provide access to the Internet and other interactive computer services from liability for obscene material accessed by means of their services. But the defense is generally unavailable to those who also serve as content providers, if the content is itself illegal. See, e.g., Developments in the Law—The Law of Cyberspace II. Communities Virtual and Real: Social and Political Dynamics of Law in Cyberspace, *Harvard Law Review* 112: 1586 (1999). "[S]ection 230 ... [of the CDA] ... granted broad immunity from liability to ISPs that merely carried content generated by others. See also David J. Loundy, Computer Information Systems Law and System Operator Liability, *Seattle U. Law Review* 21: 1075, 1089–90 (1998). "[W]ith this safe-harbor provision, Congress is stating that whatever service providers are, they are not to be treated as republishers of other people's content. In fact, this section would seem to provide immunity even when a system operator sees questionable content on a system and actively decides to leave the content publicly accessible". See generally John F. McGuire, When Speech Is Heard around the World: Internet Content Regulation in the U.S. and Germany, *N.Y.U. Law Review* 74: 750 (1999):

The CDA provided three main defenses for ISP's. ISP's could claim a "good Samaritan" defense if they did not create or assist in the creation of prohibited content, but merely provided "access or connection to or from a facility, system, or network not under that person's control." Id. § 223(e)(1). Further, ISP's could invoke a "good faith" defense if they made "reasonable, effective, and appropriate" efforts using "any method which is feasible under available technology" to prevent minors from accessing prohibited material. Id. § 223(e)(5)(A).... Lastly, ISP's could be insulated from liability if they restricted access of minors by requiring the use of a "verified credit card, debit account, adult access code, or adult personal identification number." 47 U.S.C., sec. 223(e)(5)(B).

5. As discussed in chapter 1, plaintiffs in the initial lawsuit included the Electronic Privacy Information Center, the Electronic Frontier Foundation, Computer Professionals for Social Responsibility, the National Writers Union, and the Planned Parenthood Federation of America.

6. Section 502 of the CDA, for example, provided that whoever "in interstate or foreign communications . . . by means of a telecommunications device knowingly . . . initiates the transmission of, any comment, request, suggestion, proposal, image, or other communication which is obscene or indecent knowing that the recipient of the communication is under 18 years of age regardless of whether the maker of such communication placed the call or initiated the communication . . . shall be fined under title 18, United States Code, or imprisoned not more than two years, or both." 47 U.S.C., sec. 223 (a) (1) (B) (ii).

The act also provided similar criminal penalties for those who in interstate or foreign communications knowingly use an interactive computer service to "send to a specific person or persons under 18 years of age, or . . . display in a manner available to a person under 18 years of age, any comment, request, suggestion, proposal, image, or other communication that, in context, depicts or describes, in terms patently offensive as measured by contemporary community standards, sexual or excretory activities or organs, regardless of whether the user of such service placed the call or initiated the communication; or knowingly . . . [and intentionally] . . . permits any telecommunications facility under such person's control to be used for such activity." 47 U.S.C., sec. 223 (d).

7. Plaintiffs in this second lawsuit included not only such highly respected groups as the ALA, the American Booksellers Association, the American Society of Newspaper Editors, the Association of American Publishers, and the Center for Democracy and Technology, but also such major companies as America Online, Apple Computer, CompuServe, Microsoft Corporation, Netcom, Prodigy, and Wired Ventures, Inc.

8. Plaintiffs continued to focus on 47 U.S.C., sec. 223 (a) (1) (B), (a) (2), and (d).

9. See, generally, Stuart Biegel, Decent Treatment: In Cyberlaw "Trial of the Century," Federal Court Decision Probably Won't Be the Last Word, *UCLA Online Institute for Cyberspace Law and Policy*, May 23, 1996 <http://www.gseis.ucla.edu/iclp/may96.html> (visited September 10, 2000).

10. ACLU v. Reno I, 929 F. Supp. 824 (E.D. Pa. 1996).

11. Under the statute, those accused of violating the law could raise the affirmative defense that they had either (1) taken "good faith, reasonable, effective, and appropriate actions" to restrict access by minors to the prohibited communications, and/or (2) restricted access to covered material by requiring certain designated forms of age proof, such as a verified credit card or an adult identification number or code. See sec. 223(e)(5)(A), sec. 223(e)(5)(B).

Sloviter concluded that these affirmative defenses were not "technologically or economically feasible for most providers," specifically considering and rejecting an argument that providers could avoid liability by "tagging" their material in a manner that would allow potential readers to screen out unwanted transmissions. Id. at 856.

12. See, generally, Judge Dalzell's "Medium-Specific Analysis," 929 F. Supp. at 872 and ff.

13. Id. at 879, 883. See also 929 F. Supp., at 877: "Four related characteristics of Internet communication have a transcendent importance to our shared holding that the CDA is unconstitutional on its face. We explain these characteristics in our findings of fact above, and I only rehearse them briefly here. First, the Internet presents very low barriers to entry. Second, these barriers to entry are identical for both speakers and listeners. Third, as a result of these low barriers, astoundingly diverse content is available on the Internet. Fourth, the Internet provides significant access to all who wish to speak in the medium, and even creates a relative parity among speakers." According to Judge Dalzell, these characteristics and the rest of the District Court's findings "lead to the conclusion that Congress may not regulate indecency on the Internet at all. Ibid. Because appellees do not press this argument before this Court, we do not consider it. Appellees also do not dispute that the Government generally has a compelling interest in protecting minors from 'indecent' and 'patently offensive' speech."

14. Challenges to the Communications Decency Act are eligible for "expedited review." Section 561 of Pub.L. 104–104 provided for the following:

(a) Three-Judge District Court Hearing.—Notwithstanding any other provision of law, any civil action challenging the constitutionality, on its face, of this title or any amendment made by this title [Title V of Pub.L. 104–104, Feb. 8, 1996, 110 Stat. 133, the Communications Decency Act of 1996, for distribution of which, see Short Title note set out under section 609 of this title] or any provision thereof, shall be heard by a district court of 3 judges convened pursuant to the provisions of section 2284 of title 28, United States Code [section 2284 of Title 28, Judiciary and Judicial Procedure].

(b) Appellate Review.—Notwithstanding any other provision of law, an interlocutory or final judgment, decree, or order of the court of 3 judges in an action under subsection (a) holding this title or an amendment made by this title, or any provision thereof, unconstitutional shall be reviewable as a matter of right by direct appeal to the Supreme Court. Any such appeal shall be filed not more than 20 days after entry of such judgment, decree, or order.

15. Transcript of Oral Argument. "In [the Sable Case]," Ennis continued, "this Court, in the telephone context, struck down a law that had precisely that effect. It banned telephone indecent speech. And that had the unlawful effect of banning that speech from adults, as well as from minors. This Court unanimously struck that down."

16. Reno v. ACLU, 521 U.S. 844 (1997). Even Justice O'Connor, who wrote separately—joined by Chief Justice Rehnquist—concurred in the judgment in part but dissented in part. "I write separately," O'Connor said, "to explain why I view the Communications Decency Act of 1996 (CDA) as little more than an attempt by

Congress to create 'adult zones' on the Internet. Our precedent indicates that the creation of such zones can be constitutionally sound. Despite the soundness of its purpose, however, portions of the CDA are unconstitutional because they stray from the blueprint our prior cases have developed for constructing a 'zoning law' that passes constitutional muster."

O'Connor went on to explain that, in her view, "our cases make clear that a 'zoning' law is valid only if adults are still able to obtain the regulated speech." She argued that in cyberspace, in 1997, this was not necessarily possible under the rules set forth in the CDA. However, she indicated that she did not believe this would always be so. And her words may take on greater significance as advances in the technology make it easier to change the architecture of the online world:

> Cyberspace differs from the physical world in another basic way: Cyberspace is malleable. Thus, it is possible to construct barriers in cyberspace and use them to screen for identity, making cyberspace more like the physical world and, consequently, more amenable to zoning laws. This transformation of cyberspace is already underway. (Lessig, supra, at 888–889)
>
> Cyberspace "is moving . . . from a relatively unzoned place to a universe that is extraordinarily well zoned." Internet speakers (users who post material on the Internet) have begun to zone cyberspace itself through the use of "gateway" technology. Such technology requires Internet users to enter information about themselves—perhaps an adult identification number or a credit card number—before they can access certain areas of cyberspace, 929 F. Supp. 824, 845 (ED Pa. 1996), much like a bouncer checks a person's driver's license before admitting him to a nightclub. Internet users who access information have not attempted to zone cyberspace itself, but have tried to limit their own power to access information in cyberspace, much as a parent controls what her children watch on television by installing a lock box. This user-based zoning is accomplished through the use of screening software (such as Cyber Patrol or SurfWatch) or browsers with screening capabilities, both of which search addresses and text for keywords that are associated with "adult" sites and, if the user wishes, blocks access to such sites. Id., at 839–842. The Platform for Internet Content Selection project is designed to facilitate user-based zoning by encouraging Internet speakers to rate the content of their speech using codes recognized by all screening programs. Id., at 838–839.
>
> Despite this progress, the transformation of cyberspace is not complete. Although gateway technology has been available on the World Wide Web for some time now, id., at 845; Shea v. Reno, 930 F. Supp. 916, 933–934 (SDNY 1996), it is not available to all Web speakers, 929 F. Supp. at 845–846, and is just now becoming technologically feasible for chat rooms and USENET newsgroups, Brief for Federal Parties 37–38. Gateway technology is not ubiquitous in cyberspace, and because without it, "there is no means of age verification," cyberspace still remains largely unzoned—and unzoneable. 929 F. Supp. at 846; Shea, supra, at 934. User-based zoning is also in its infancy. For it to be effective, (i) an agreed-upon code (or "tag") would have to exist; (ii) screening software or browsers with screening capabilities would have to be able to recognize the "tag"; and (iii) those programs would have to be widely available—and widely used—by Internet users. At

present, none of these conditions is true. Screening software "is not in wide use today" and "only a handful of browsers have screening capabilities." Shea, supra, at 945–946. There is, moreover, no agreed-upon "tag" for those programs to recognize. 929 F. Supp. at 848; Shea, supra, at 945.

Although the prospects for the eventual zoning of the Internet appear promising, I agree with the Court that we must evaluate the constitutionality of the CDA as it applies to the Internet as it exists today. Ante, at 36. Given the present state of cyberspace, I agree with the Court that the "display" provision cannot pass muster. Until gateway technology is available throughout cyberspace, and it is not in 1997, a speaker cannot be reasonably assured that the speech he displays will reach only adults because it is impossible to confine speech to an "adult zone." 521 U.S. at 886–893.

17. See Sable Communications of Cal., Inc. v. FCC, 492 U.S. 115 (1989).

18. See 47 U.S.C., sec. 223(a)(1)(A)(ii) and 47 U.S.C., sec. 223(a)(2).

19. ApolloMedia Corp. v. Reno, 19 F. Supp. 2d 1081 (N.D. Cal 1998) at n. 5.

20. Id. Judge Illston, dissenting, felt that the same reasoning applied by the U.S. Supreme Court in the Reno case was applicable here, and that the word *indecent* should be severed from the statute.

21. AOL began operating in the early 1990s as a commercial online service, providing its subscribers with a variety of original content, access to a range of AOL chat rooms and discussion forums, and a gateway to the Internet. As the World Wide Web grew in both size and scope, much of this content and many similar interactive forums could also be found outside of AOL, but AOL adjusted its focus and continued to grow, becoming the largest Internet service provider in the world. Yet even as it provided a gateway to the online world, it continued to feature its own content and its own discussion forums.

22. AOL allows its subscribers to choose several different "screen names" to identify themselves in chat rooms and discussion forums. Only AOL knows to whom these screen names belong.

23. Zeran v. AOL, 958 F. Supp. 1124, 1127 (E.D. Va. 1997).

24. It should be noted that by using the screen name "KenZZ03," the perpetrator could also be viewed as impersonating Zeran.

25. The parties disputed the date on which AOL removed this original posting from its bulletin board.

26. In the lawsuit, Zeran sued AOL for negligence, under the theory that distributors of information are liable for the distribution of material that they knew or should have known was of a defamatory character. But the courts characterized the lawsuit as "merely a species or type of liability for publishing defamatory material." See, e.g., 129 F.3d 327, 322 (4th Cir. 1997).

27. Section 230 of the CDA provides, in pertinent part: "No provider or user of an interactive computer service shall be treated as the publisher or speaker of any information provided by another information content provider." 47 U.S.C., sec. 230(c)(1).

28. 129 F.3d at 330.

29. Id. "Another important purpose of § 230," the court wrote, "was to encourage service providers to self-regulate the dissemination of offensive material over their services." Id. at 331.

30. Many commentators added that in their view the drafters of the act did not really understand the Internet.

31. 47 U.S.C., sec. 231.

32. Id. at 231(e)(7).

33. Id. at 231(e)(6).

34. See Ginsberg v. N.Y., 390 U.S. 629 (1968). In Ginsberg, a New York statute with the following language was upheld by the court:

"Harmful to minors" means that quality of any description or representation, in whatever form, of nudity, sexual conduct, sexual excitement, or sadomasochistic abuse, when it:

(i) predominantly appeals to the prurient, shameful or morbid interest of minors, and

(ii) is patently offensive to prevailing standards in the adult community as a whole with respect to what is suitable material for minors, and

(iii) is utterly without redeeming social importance for minors.

The Child Online Protection Act used a hybrid definition, incorporating elements of the U.S. Supreme Court's 1973 test for obscenity—under Miller v. California, 413 U.S. 15—into the structure of the statute upheld in Ginsberg.

35. Internet Censorship Battle Moves to Appeals Court, ACLU Freedom Network, April 2, 1999, <www.aclu.org/features/f101698a.html> (visited September 5, 1999).

36. ACLU v. Reno II, 31 F. Supp. 2d 473, 478–479, 493–495.

37. "There is nothing in the text of COPA," Judge Reed wrote, ". . . that limits its applicability to so-called commercial pornographers only." The court reasoned that because COPA (1) imposed liability on someone whose communication "*includes any material* that is harmful to minors," (2) defined a "communication for commercial purposes" very broadly, and (3) expressly indicated that it is neither necessary "that the person make a profit" from the communication nor that such communications be the person's sole or principal business or source of income," the prohibitions could apply to a very wide range of Web sites that contain only some potentially "harmful to minors" material. Id. at 480.

The court also agreed with the plaintiffs that COPA would probably not meet the First Amendment requirement that such types of regulation must be "narrowly tailored" and must be the "least restrictive means" of achieving an objective.

38. Id. at 496–497.

39. See chapter 2 of this book, supra.

40. ACLU v. Reno, 274 F.3d 162, 174–175 (3d Cir. 2000) (citations omitted). The court went on to explain that "Unlike a 'brick and mortar outlet' with a

specific geographic locale, and unlike the voluntary physical mailing of material from one geographic location to another, as in Miller, the uncontroverted facts indicate that the Web is not geographically constrained. Indeed, and of extreme significance, is the fact, as found by the District Court, that Web publishers are without any means to limit access to their sites based on the geographic location of particular Internet users. As soon as information is published on a Web site, it is accessible to all other Web visitors. Current technology prevents Web publishers from circumventing particular jurisdictions or limiting their site's content from entering any specific geographic community." Id. at 175.

41. See 17 U.S.C., sec. 506(a) (1976).

42. United States v. Cross, 816 F.2d 297 (7th Cir. 1987).

43. Indeed, many commentators have recognized the interrelationship between First Amendment law and copyright law in this context. Restrictions on copying are on some level tantamount to restrictions on speech. See, e.g., Stephen Fraser, The Conflict between the First Amendment and Copyright Law and Its Impact on the Internet, *Cardozo Arts and Entertainment Law Journal* 16 (1998): 1.

44. The No Electronic Theft Act, originally known as *H.R. 2265,* was signed into law by President Clinton on December 16, 1997. See <http://www.gseis.ucla.edu/iclp/hr2265.html> (visited March 9, 2000).

45. 17 U.S.C., sec. 506(a).

46. The act confirms that "willful" infringement must consist of evidence of more than the mere intentional reproduction or distribution of copyrighted works. See 17 U.S.C., sec. 506 (a)(2): "For purposes of this subsection, evidence of reproduction or distribution of a copyrighted work, by itself, shall not be sufficient to establish willful infringement."

47. See 17 U.S.C., secs. 101, 506–507; 18 U.S.C., secs. 2319, 2319A, 2320. See also U.S. Dept. of Justice, *Prosecuting Intellectual Property Crimes,* January 2001 (principal author—David Goldstone), <http://www.cybercrime.gov/ipmanual.htm> (visited May 20, 2001).

Other features of this act include the clarification that reproduction and distribution can be by electronic as well as by tangible means, the extension of the statue of limitations from three to five years, and the enhanced sentencing guidelines that allow courts to consider the quantity of infringing goods and the retail value of the good infringed upon—rather than the often lower value of the infringing good—when sentencing defendants. But the most significant change is the provision that enables the DOJ to prosecute defendants who had no discernible profit motive.

48. 143 Cong. Rec. S12689-01 (daily ed. Nov. 13, 1997) (statement of Sen. Hatch).

49. See also infra, chapter 11 of this book.

50. House Panel Investigates DOJ Failure to Enforce NET Act, *Tech Law Journal,* May 13, 1999, <http://www.techlawjournal.com/intelpro/19990513a.htm> (visited October 3, 1999). DiGregory also indicated that an additional problem was

the failure of the U.S. Sentencing Commission to adopt sentencing guidelines for the NET Act; however, he also testified that this did not bar prosecutions.

51. Ashbel S. Green, Net Piracy Law Gets First Conviction, *The Oregonian,* August 21, 1999.

52. Section 1203 of the Internet Tax Freedom Act described negotiating objectives as follows:

(b) Negotiating Objectives.—The negotiating objectives of the United States shall be—

(1) to assure that electronic commerce is free from—

(A) tariff and nontariff barriers;
(B) burdensome and discriminatory regulation and standards; and
(C) discriminatory taxation; and

(2) to accelerate the growth of electronic commerce by expanding market access opportunities for—

(A) the development of telecommunications infrastructure;
(B) the procurement of telecommunications equipment;
(C) the provision of Internet access and telecommunications services; and
(D) the exchange of goods, services, and digitalized information.

53. See <http://www.whitehouse.gov/WH/New/Commerce/> (visited October 10, 1999).

54. See, e.g., chapter 9 of this book, infra.

55. Persons appointed by Congress pursuant to the ITFA included eight business representatives, eight politicians from state and local governments, and three members of the Clinton Administration. Virginia Governor James Gilmore was designated as chairman of the commission, and other members included Utah Governor Mike Leavitt, Washington Governor Gary Locke and industry representatives such as C. Michael Armstrong, chairman and chief executive of AT&T; Theodore Waitt, chairman and chief executive of Gateway; David Pottruck, president of Charles Schwab; John Sidgmore, Vice Chairman of MCI WorldCom; and Robert Pittman, President of America Online.

Even after the first commission meetings, reports indicated that consensus would prove difficult to establish. Governor Gilmore, for example, a Republican with an aggressive antitax agenda, was apparently not convinced that the Internet should be taxed at all. Business leaders, however, apparently voiced support for taxing Internet commerce as long as a new, simpler, and equitable system could be devised.

See Rajiv Chandrasekaran, Advisory Panel Divided on Issue of Taxing Online Commerce, *Washington Post,* September 16, 1999.

For example, a proposal on the table in the fall of 1999 apparently called for businesses "to collect sales taxes on Internet commerce if state and local governments agree to adopt a single tax rate for each state or commit to new technologies in the form of free, easy-to-use software to enable companies to calculate any tax rate." But there was no guarantee that the commission would be able to reach a consensus on this plan, or indeed on any plan, by the deadline set forth in the act.

According to Governor Gilmore, even if no proposal can be finalized, at least the commission might be able to define both the national and the international issues for Congress. Id.

56. See Rob Wells, Panel to Ask Congress to Extend Internet Tax Ban, *Los Angeles Times,* March 30, 2000; John Schwartz, Web Tax Panel Falls Short of Goal: After 18 Months, Commission Gives Issue Back to Hill, *Washington Post,* March 31, 2000.

57. See id.

58. David Cay Johnston, Governors Criticize Internet Tax Panel, *New York Times,* April 12, 2000.

59. Lizette Alvarez, House Votes to Extend Ban on New Internet Taxes, *New York Times,* May 11, 2000.

60. Jason Anders, Net Capitol: Congress Can't Ignore the Web Any Longer, But Is It Up to the Task? *Wall Street Journal,* July 17, 2000.

61. See, e.g., Lisa I. Fried, Internet Taxation: An Advisory Commission Is Embroiled in a Debate, *N.Y. Law Journal,* September 23, 1999.

62. ALA v. Pataki, 969 F. Supp. 160 (S.D.N.Y. 1997).

63. A ruling overturning a similar Georgia statute was also not appealed on substantive grounds, although attorney fee issues took this case to the appellate court level. See ACLU v. Miller, 977 F. Supp. 1228 (N.D. Ga. 1997); 168 F.3d 423 (11th Cir. 1999).

64. Urofsky v. Gilmore, 216 F.3d 401 (4th Cir. 2000).

65. 4 F. Supp. 2d 1029 (D. New Mexico 1998); Affirmed, 194 F.3d 1149 (10th Cir. 1999).

66. 55 F. Supp. 2d 737 (S.D. Mich. 1999). Affirmed, 238 F.3d 420 (6th Cir. 2000).

67. Id. at 744–745.

Chapter 6

1. A recent example of the hurdles posed by the ratification process is the volatile debate over the U.S. Senate's refusal to ratify the Comprehensive Test Ban Treaty. See, e.g., Brian Whitmore, Russia Soundly Ratifies Nuclear Test Ban Treaty: Putin Seen Taking Upper Hand in Coming Talks with U.S., *Boston Globe,* April 22, 2000. See, generally, Henry A. Kissinger, Arms Control To Suit a New World, *Los Angeles Times,* November 21, 1999.

2. The Four Commentaries of Gaius on the Institutes of the Civil War, 1 The Civil Law 81 (Scott, ed. 1973).

3. See, generally, Joel R. Reidenberg, Lex Informatica: The Formulation of Information Policy Rules Through Technology, *Texas Law Review* 76 (1998): 553: "During the middle ages, itinerant merchants traveling across Europe to trade at fairs, markets, and sea ports needed common ground rules to create trust and confidence for robust international trade. The differences among local, feudal, royal,

and ecclesiastical law provided a significant degree of uncertainty and difficulty for merchants. Custom and practices evolved into a distinct body of law known as the 'Lex Mercatoria,' which was independent of local sovereign rules and assured commercial participants of basic fairness in their relationships."

4. H. Grotius, *De Juri Belli ac Pacis Libri Tres* (Kelsey, trans. 1925).

5. J. Bentham, *An Introduction to the Principles of Morals and Legislation,* 296 (Burns and Hart, ed. 1970).

6. William V. O'Brien, *International Law and the Outbreak of War in the Middle East* (Orbis, 1967) (on file with the author). Professor Ruth Lapidot, former legal adviser to the Israeli Foreign Ministry, noted that warlike declarations by Egypt, the closing of the Strait of Tiran, the mobilization of Egyptian forces, and the evacuation of UNEF were among the threatening actions cited by the Israeli government at the time. Yet Lapidot also noted that "anticipatory self-defense" is a questionable doctrine, and that not all would agree that such actions were legal under international law. Ruth Lapidot, Legal Aspects of the Middle East Conflict and Its Resolution, A Series of Lectures at Hebrew University in Jerusalem, August 1979 (notes on file with the author).

7. See, generally, The Legality of U.S. Participation in the Defense of Vietnam, Memorandum Prepared by the Legal Adviser of the Dept. of State, *U.S. Dept. of State Bulletin* 54 (1966): 474; Kovalev, Sovereignty and International Duties of Socialist Countries, Reprinted from *Pravda, New York Times,* September 27, 1968.

8. Mark W. Janis, *An Introduction to International Law* (Little, Brown & Co., 1993).

9. Id. at 19 (describing the Vienna Convention, art. 9).

10. See, e.g., Curtis A. Bradley, Chevron Deference and Foreign Affairs, *Virginia Law Review* 86 (2000): 649. The U.S. Constitution, Article VI, Clause 2 states: "[A]ll Treaties made, or which shall be made, under the Authority of the United States, shall be the supreme Law of the Land.").

11. E. de Vattel, *The Law of Nations,* xv (1797).

12. See generally Janis, supra, note 8, for an extensive overview of these basic principles.

13. See, e.g., Telford Taylor, *The Anatomy of the Nuremberg Trials: A Personal Memoir* (Alfred A. Knopf, 1992).

14. Montesquieu, *L'esprit des Lois,* Oeuvres Completes 527, 531 (Editions de Seuil, 1964).

15. Aristotle, *Nicomachean Ethics,* 141–142 (book 5, chapter 10) (Ostwald trans., 1962).

16. See, e.g., F. L. Kirgis, *International Organizations in Their Legal Setting* (1977). Examples of areas that are the focus of these organizations today include international peacekeeping, education, promotion of science and cultural activities, health, economic development, monetary affairs, international trade, civil aviation, postal services, telecommunications, meteorology, maritime commerce, protection of intellectual property, and nuclear energy. Id. at xv.

17. See, generally, "A Profile of the EU," <http://www.eurunion.org/legislat/index.htm> (visited December 14, 1999).

18. Janis, supra, note 8, chapter 7.

19. See, generally, "About the United Nations: An Introduction to the Structure and Work of the UN," <http://www.un.org/aboutun/> (visited December 14, 1999).

20. See, e.g., George Smirnoff III, A Critique of the White Paper's Recommendation for Updating the Copyright Act and How the Courts Are Already Filling in its Most Important Shortcoming, On-Line Service Provider Liability, *Cleveland State Law Review* 44 (1996) 197; Pamela Samuleson, The Copyright Grab, *Wired* Magazine, January 1996. But see Gary W. Glisson, A Practitioner's Defense of the White Paper, *Oregon Law Review* 75 (1996): 277.

21. Pamela Samuelson, The U.S. Digital Agenda at WIPO, *Virginia Journal of International Law* 37 (1997): 369, 434–435.

22. Id. at 438.

23. For an overview of the Digital Millennium Copyright Act and links to the entire text, see <http://www.gseis.ucla.edu/iclp/dmca1.htm> (visited September 10, 2000).

24. See WIPO Copyright Treaty, Ratifications and Accessions, <www.wipo.org/eng/main.htm> (visited November 28, 1999).

25. For a detailed discussion of the domain name system, see David J. Loundy's classic overview, A Primer on Trademark Law and Internet Addresses, *John Marshall Journal of Computer and Information Law* 15 (1997): 465, available at <http://www.loundy.com/JMLS-Trademark.html> (visited September 10, 2000). See also infra, chapter 7 of this book.

26. Memorandum of Understanding between the U.S. Dept. of Commerce and ICANN, November 1998, <www.ntia.doc.gov/ntiahome/domainname/icann-memorandum.htm> (visited December 5, 1999).

27. Bylaws for Internet Corporation for Assigned Names and Numbers, amended and restated October 29, 1999, <http://www.icann.org/general/bylaws.htm#II> (visited December 5, 1999).

28. For example, in November 1999, ICANN announced that the Markle Foundation had pledged one million dollars to help recruit an active membership of five thousand Net users who would then vote for nine elected "at-large" representatives on ICANN's permanent governing board. Joe Salkowski, On Net, You Can Make a Difference with ICANN, *Chicago Tribune,* November 15, 1999.

29. See UDRP Resource Page, <http://www.icann.org/udrp/udrp.htm> (visited May 22, 2001).

30. Of the four, the World Intellectual Property Organization ended up hearing most of the cases at that time.

31. Critics noted, for example, that under the UDRP, only trademark holders could bring their case to an arbitration center. See, e.g., Laurie J Flynn, Whose

Name Is It Anyway? Arbitration Panels Favoring Trademark Holders in Disputes over Web Names, *New York Times*, September 4, 2000.

For an excellent overview of recent ICANN-related issues, e.g., the conflicting Congressional Testimony of Michael Roberts and Michael Froomkin before the Senate Commerce, Science & Transportation Committee Communications Subcommittee, February 14, 2001, 2001 WL 2005387 & 2001 WL 2005384. See, generally, Jonathan Weinberg, ICANN and the Problem of Legitimacy, *Duke Law Journal* 50 (2000): 187.

32. See Jonathan Zittrain, ICANN: Between the Public and the Private Comments Before Congress, *Berkeley Technology Law Journal* 14 (1999): 1071.

33. C. Archer, *International Organizations,* 124–126 (2d ed., 1992).

34. H. Grotius, *The Freedom of the Seas,* 7 (Magoffin, trans. 1916).

35. Convention on the Law of the Sea: Overview, <www.un.org/Depts/los/losconv2.htm> (visited November 14, 1999). Highlights of the agreement include the following:

• Coastal states have sovereignty over their territorial sea up to a limit of 12 nautical miles, and foreign vessels are allowed "innocent passage" through those waters.

• Coastal states have sovereign rights in a 200-nautical mile exclusive economic zone (EEZ) with respect to natural resources and certain economic activities, and exercise jurisdiction over marine science research and environmental protection. All other states have freedom of navigation and overflight in the EEZ, as well as freedom to lay submarine cables and pipelines.

• Land-locked and geographically disadvantaged states have the right to participate on an equitable basis in exploitation of an appropriate part of the surplus of the living resources of the EEZ's of coastal States of the same region or sub-region; highly migratory species of fish and marine mammals are accorded special protection.

• Coastal states have sovereign rights over the continental shelf (the national area of the seabed) for exploring and exploiting it; the shelf can extend at least 200 nautical miles from the shore, and more under specified circumstances.

• Coastal states will share with the international community part of the revenue derived from exploiting resources from any part of their shelf beyond 200 miles.

• All states enjoy the traditional freedoms of navigation, overflight, scientific research and fishing on the high seas; they are obliged to adopt, or cooperate with other States in adopting, measures to manage and conserve living resources.

• States bordering on enclosed or semi-enclosed seas are expected to cooperate in managing living resources, environmental and research policies and activities. Land-locked states have the right of access to and from the sea and enjoy freedom of transit through the territory of transit states.

• States are bound to prevent and control marine pollution and are liable for damage caused by violation of their international obligations to combat such pollution;

• Disputes can be submitted to the International Tribunal for the Law of the Sea established under the convention, to the International Court of Justice, or to arbitration. The Tribunal has exclusive jurisdiction over deep seabed mining disputes.

36. See Janis, supra, note 8, at 211.

37. Heeding the Law of the Sea, *Boston Globe* (editorial), September 20, 1999.

38. Treaty on Principles Governing the Activities of States in the Exploration and Use of Outer Space, including the Moon and Other Celestial Bodies, <www.un.or.at/OOSA/treat/ost/ost.html> (visited November 21, 1999).

39. See, e.g., P. C. Jessup and H. J. Taubenfeld, *Controls for Outer Space and the Antarctic Analogy* 201 (1959).

40. This section examines the model where nations may submit voluntarily to some form of judicial deliberation. It should also be noted, however, that another model of international adjudication may exist whereby individual persons are prosecuted by special international tribunals. See, e.g., the UN website description of the International Criminal Tribunal for the Former Yugoslavia, <http://www.un.org/icty/index.html> (visited September 10, 2000). See also the UN website description of the International Criminal Tribunal for Rwanda, <http://www.ictr.org/> (visited September 10, 2000).

41. Michael L. Nash, A Century of Arbitration, *Contemporary Review,* May 1, 1999.

42. See The International Court of Justice: General Information, <http://www.icj-cij.org/icjwww/igeneralinformation/icjgnnot.html> (visited December 15, 1999).

43. See id.

44. Douglass W. Cassel Jr., War and the World Court, *Chicago Daily Law Bulletin,* July 22, 1999.

45. See The International Court of Justice site, supra, note 42.

46. Cassel, supra, note 44.

47. See Janis, supra, note 8, at 275–279, discussing the efforts of UNIDROIT, UNCITRAL, and others.

48. See Introducing the WTO, <http://www.wto.org/wto/inbrief/inbr00.htm> (visited November 25, 1999).

49. See id. at <http://www.wto.org/wto/inbrief/inbr02.htm> (visited November 25, 1999). The top-level decision-making body of the WTO is the Ministerial Conference, which meets at least once every two years. Below this is the General Council (normally ambassadors and heads of delegation in Geneva, but sometimes officials sent from members' capitals), which meets several times a year in the Geneva headquarters. The General Council also meets as the Trade Policy Review Body and the Dispute Settlement Body.

At the next level, the Goods Council, Services Council, and Intellectual Property Council report to the General Council. Numerous specialized committees, working groups, and working parties deal with the individual agreements and other areas such as the environment, development, membership applications, and regional trade agreements. See id.

50. Jonathan Peterson, Bottom Line on WTO Still Shaky for the U.S., *Los Angeles Times,* November 29, 1999.

51. Sara Dillon, Fuji-Kodak, the WTO, and the Death of Domestic Political Constituencies, *Minnesota Journal of Global Trade* 8 (1999): 197.

52. See generally <www.wto.org> (visited September 10, 2000).

53. Pamela Samuelson, Implications of the Agreement on Trade-Related Aspects of Intellectual Property Rights for Cultural Dimensions of National Copyright Laws, *Journal of Cultural Economics* 23 (1999): 95–107.

54. See id. While endorsing the concept of harmonization, Samuelson urges "restraint in pushing for harmonization of national intellectual property laws, especially copyright laws, because national intellectual property policies are often intertwined with cultural values and policies that are deeply connected to national identity."

55. See, generally, Joseph Kahn and David E. Sanger, Impasse on Trade Delivers a Stinging Blow to Clinton, *New York Times,* December 5, 1999.

56. Jonathan Peterson, Activists Bring Turtles' Cause to WTO Fishbowl, *Los Angeles Times,* December 3, 1999.

57. Kevin Phillips, *The Stealth Coup, Los Angeles Times,* November 21, 1999. According to Phillips, many believe that the WTO is about to become an unelected fourth branch of the U.S. government, or that it is a magna carta for U.S. multinational corporations to further decrease their dependence on American employees and loyalties.

"The World Trade Organization, though officially only 4 years old, represents a huge intrusion on U.S. politics and on national, state and local decision-making, largely in the interest of multinational corporations and trade lobbies. Scare talk like this has been exaggerated before. But this is not hyperbole: Legislators in Washington could be on the brink of understanding that they—and the voters—are losing control over the evolution of America's role in the global economy in the 21st century."

58. Martin A. Lee, The Fascist Response to Globalization, *Los Angeles Times,* November 28, 1999. See also Martin A. Lee, *The Beast Reawakens* (Little, Brown & Co., 1997).

59. Alan Murray, The Outlook, *Wall Street Journal,* November 29, 1999.

60. Martin Wolk, WTO Round to Grapple with Vexing E-Commerce Issues, *Reuters,* November 18, 1999.

61. Mary Greczyn and Art Brodsky, WTO Could Renew Consideration of Internet Trade Issues Next Year, *Communications Daily,* December 9, 1999.

62. See, e.g., Jim Landers, Collapse of World Trade Talks Frustrates Delegates, *Dallas Morning News,* December 5, 1999; A Need for Agreements on Tariffs in Cyberspace, *Wyoming Tribune-Eagle,* December 8, 1999.

63. A detailed overview of TRIPS, including its provisions and related matters, is available at <http://www.wto.org/english/tratop_e/trips_e/trips_e.htm> (visited September 10, 2000).

64. On an academic level, major contemporary behavioral theories of international law and international relations include economic liberal institutionalism, structural realism, and soft social construction. See, e.g, Jeffrey L. Dunhoff and Joel P. Trachtman, Economic Analysis of International Law, *Yale Journal of International Law* 24 (1999): 1 (addressing economic liberal institutionalism); Richard H. Steinberg, Trade-Environment Negotiations in the EU, NAFTA, and WTO: Regional Trajectories of Rule Development, *American Journal of International Law* 91 (1997): 231 (addressing structural realism). "Soft" social construction is a label that has been used to describe the area of social norms and the law. See, e.g., Lawrence Lessig, Social Meaning and Social Norms, *University of Pennsylvania Law Review* 144 (1996): 2181; Cass R. Sunstein, Social Norms and Social Roles, *96 Columbia Law Review* 96 (1996): 903.

Economic liberal institutionalism is most useful for justifying the regulation of cyberspace on an international level. *Structural realism* addresses power and interest, and points to the problems that inevitably arise on an international level when some nations have so much greater power and influence than others. *Soft social construction* suggests that international cyberspace regulation will also be dependent on the wishes and—indeed—the activism of Netizens, CyberProfs, and other spokespersons for advocacy groups and electronic communities in this area.

65. It should be noted that not only has it been argued that international cooperation can strengthen the Internet, but also that the Internet can strengthen international cooperation. See, e.g., Henry H. Perritt, Jr., The Internet As a Threat to Sovereignty? Thoughts on the Internet's Role in Strengthening National and Global Governance, *Indiana Journal of Global Legal Studies* 5 (1998): 423.

Chapter 7

1. See, e.g., Internet Regulation through Architectural Modification: The Property Rule Structure of Code Solutions, *Harvard Law Review* 112 (1999): 1634. Also available at <http://www.harvardlawreview.org/issues/112/7_1634.htm> (visited September 10, 2000).

2. In 1998, for example, Cisco announced that it had developed a technology that could enable an ISP to encrypt or decrypt Internet traffic at the router level. See, e.g., Cisco's IPSec White Paper, <http://www.cisco.com/warp/public/cc/techno/protocol/ipsecur/ipsec/tech/ipsec_wp.htm> (visited September 10, 2000).

3. See, e.g., Lawrence Lessig, Intellectual Property and Code, *Saint John's Journal of Legal Commentary* 11 (1996): 635; Lawrence Lessig, The Constitution of Code: Limitations on Choice-Based Critiques of Cyberspace Regulation, 5 *CommLaw Conspectus* (1997). See, generally, Lawrence Lessig, The Law of the Horse: What Cyberlaw Might Teach, supra, note 36 (chapter 1).

4. Lawrence Lessig, *Code and Other Laws of Cyberspace* (Basic Books, 1999).

5. See chapter 1 of this book, supra.

6. See Lessig, chapter 4, at 30 (paperback edition, 2000).

7. See generally chapter 5, 43–60, supra.

8. In an Internet context, the word *proprietary* "[r]efers to collection of data, tools, or applications that are, for all intents and purposes, 'owned.'" See Glossary of Internet Terms, <http://www.abc.gc.ca/abi/8E.HTM#P> (visited September 10, 2000).

For an analysis of the term in context, see, e.g., Dan L. Burk, Proprietary Rights in Hypertext Linkages, *Journal of Information Law and Technology* (1998).

9. See ACLU v. Reno I, 929 F. Supp. 824, 831 (E.D. Pa. 1996).

10. A Brief History of the Internet, by Barry M. Leiner, Vinton G. Cerf, David D. Clark, Robert E. Kahn, Leonard Kleinrock, Daniel C. Lynch, Jon Postel, Larry G. Roberts, and Stephen Wolff, <http://info.isoc.org/internet/history/brief.html> (visited January 3, 2000).

11. ACLU v. Reno I, 929 F. Supp. at 831.

12. See, generally, Barbara Esbin, Internet Over Cable: Defining the Future in Terms of the Past, *CommLaw Conspectus* 7 (1999): 37, 46.

13. See Richard S. Vermut, File Caching on the Internet: Technical Infringement or Safeguard for Efficient Network Operation? *Journal of Intellectual Property Law* 4 (1997): 273, 281–282. According to Vermut, "TCP/IP's acceptance is a result of its development and funding by the United States government and its implementation within UNIX. The Department of Defense needed a network communications standard so all computers connected to the ARPANET could easily communicate with one another. In 1983 the University of California at Berkeley released its version of UNIX known as UNIX 4.2BSD. Embedded within its version of UNIX were the TCP/IP protocols. The use of UNIX as an operating system was widespread, and the availability of the built-in TCP/IP helped achieve its acceptance." Id.

14. The "standard model" for describing layers of a network in this context is the Open Systems Interconnect (OSI) Reference Model. William Hodkowski explains that "this model of network architecture and a suite of protocols (protocol stack) to implement it were developed by the ISO (International Organization for Standardization) in 1978 as a framework for international standards in heterogeneous computer network architecture. The architecture is split between seven layers, from lowest to highest: (1) physical layer, (2) datalink layer, (3) network layer (e.g., IP), (4) transport layer (e.g., TCP), (5) session layer, (6) presentation layer, and (7) application layer. Each layer uses the layer immediately below it and provides a service to the layer above." William A. Hodkowski, Comment: The Future of Internet Security: How New Technologies Will Shape the Internet and Affect the Law, *Computer and High Tech Law Journal* 13 (1997): 217 at n. 277.

Most descriptions of TCP/IP, however, "define three to five functional levels in the protocol architecture," and it is generally viewed as "simplest to describe four." See Lessig, supra, note 4 (chapter 8), at 101.

Timothy Wu describes the layered architecture of TCP/IP as one that can be best understood as a two-layer network. He begins by setting forth the example of a lawyer using the U.S. Postal Service—where one "layer" constitutes the lawyer preparing a legal document but needing to know nothing about how the letter is delivered, and the other "layer" constituting delivery, where the postal workers need to know nothing about how the legal system works. This "network," he writes, is based on an efficient, modular, and flexible architecture:

Notice several things about a network so structured. First, it allows an efficient specialization: That the postal system need not understand law (or the content of any of the messages it carries) dramatically reduces the burden on the post office and allows it to focus on one task: delivering mail. Second, the system is very flexible: The postal system can carry any type of message, and the communication will be successful, provided that the person on the other side understands it. This makes the postal system useful for a wide variety of applications. Finally, the layers are modular: Were the postal system to begin using spaceships to deliver its mail, the lawyers would be unaffected so long as the rules for postage and writing addresses remained the same.

Timothy Wu, Application-Centered Internet Analysis, 85 *Virginia Law Review* 85 (1999): 1163, 1190–91.

The TCP/IP architecture, Wu explains, works in the same way:

The Internet shares this same basic structure. Internet applications—email and so forth—operate separately from and above the set of basic Internet protocols, known as TCP/IP. The Internet's network architecture gives applications their own layer to interpret the data they send to each other without worrying how it got there. And the basic Internet protocols (with some exceptions not important here) are invariable and are used by all applications, much in the way that lawyers, plumbers, and doctors all use the same postal system.

Thus, he concludes, the TCP/IP system can appropriately be characterized as a two-layered architecture, consisting of the "transport" layers and the "interpretation" layers:

So while there are actually four layers in the Internet architecture, for many purposes the most important distinction is between the transport layers, the set of constant Internet protocols that handle the basic data transmissions, and the interpretation layers, the huge variety of possible applications that make use of the data sent around by the transport layers.

Id. at 1191–1192.

15. Vermut, supra, note 13. "Hypertext Transfer Protocol" uses the domain name system to resolve URLs and uses TCP/IP to download HTML documents from servers to client-browsing software.

16. A. Michael Froomkin, The Internet as a Source of Regulatory Arbitrage, in Brian Kahin and Charles Nesson, eds., *Borders in Cyberspace* (MIT Press, 1997), at 129. Also available at <http://www.law.miami.edu/~froomkin/articles/arbitr.htm> (visited May 19, 2000).

Froomkin compares the Internet of the mid-1990s to the mythical Hydra, writing, "Every time one of its heads was cut off it grew two more. To regulators, the Internet may seem like the modern Hydra. Almost every attempt to block access to material on the Internet, indeed anything short of an extraordinarily restrictive access policy, can be circumvented easily." He goes on to argue that three technologies underlie the Internet's resistance to control: "First, the Internet is a *packet switching network,* which makes it difficult for anyone, even a government, to block or monitor information flows originating from large numbers of users. Second, users have access to powerful military-grade cryptography that can, if used properly, make messages unreadable to anyone but the intended recipient. Third, and resulting from the first two, users of the Internet have access to powerful anonymizing tools. Together, these three technologies mean that anonymous communication is within reach of anyone with access to a personal computer and a link to the Internet unless a government practices very strict access control, devotes vast resources to monitoring, or can persuade its population (whether by liability rules or criminal law) to avoid using these tools." Id.

17. Froomkin explains that "it is as if rather than telephoning a friend one were to tape record a message, cut it up into equal pieces, and hand the pieces to people heading in the general direction of the intended recipient. Each time a person carrying tape met anyone going in the right direction, he or she could hand over as many pieces of tape as the recipient could comfortably carry. Eventually the message would get where it needed to go." For additional details regarding the packet-switching functions of TCP/IP, written for those who may have a limited technical background in this area, see, e.g., Michael Specter, Your Mail Has Vanished, *The New Yorker,* December 6, 1999.

18. Vermut, supra, note 13, at 283.

19. Froomkin, supra, note 16.

20. Some have suggested that regulation should indeed take place at the protocol level and/or the lower layers of TCP/IP, but—as Lessig notes—this is not likely at the present time.

21. At the turn of the century, the top-level domain names included ".COM for commercial organizations, .EDU for educational organizations, .GOV for governmental organizations, .MIL for military groups, .NET for major network support centers and Internet service providers, .ORG for other organizations, and .INT for international organizations. Additionally, the top-level domain name can be a two-letter abbreviation for countries, such as .US for United States, .JP for Japan, and .UK for the United Kingdom." Vermut, supra, at n. 60. For a detailed technical description of how the domain name system (DNS) operates within the context of client servers and the World Wide Web, see generally id. at 289–292.

22. See Rajiv Chandrasekaran, Internet Reconfiguration Concerns Federal Officials, *Washington Post,* January 31, 1998. See also Going to the Root, *PC Week,* April 8, 1996, at p. 30: "Called root zone servers, these . . . hosts . . . can access all of the name server hosts that are at the seven top-level domains: .com, .edu, .mil, .gov, .net, .org, and a special one called .arpa . . . The first one, a.root-server.net, is

the primary Internet name server . . . The other name servers are secondaries to the primary, but all of them have copies of the same files so they can serve as alternates or backups for each other . . .

"The root zone files contain all of the host names and IP addresses of the name servers for each subdomain under the top-level domain. For example, in the adobe.com domain, the root zone files for the .com domain contain an entry for the name server for any address that ends with adobe.com."

In other words, each root server knows all the top-level domains, as well as the host name and IP address for at least one name server for each secondary domain in any of the top-level domains. (For the country domains, the database lists the name servers for each country.)

23. Saskia Sassen, The Internet and the Sovereign State: The Role and Impact of Cyberspace on National and Global Governance, *Indiana Journal of Global Legal Studies* 5 (1998): 545. See also Victoria Shannon, Why It's Slow Going on the Net, *Washington Post,* May 24, 1999. For a chart of the thirteen root servers, their locations, and the organizations associated with each one, see Root Nameserver Year 2000 Status, Appendix A, July 15, 1999, <www.icann.org/committees/dns-root/y2k-statement.htm> (visited January 23, 2000). For a geographical diagram of the root server system, see *Internet Domain Name System Root Servers,* <http://www.wia.org/pub/rootserv.html> (visited January 21, 2000).

24. See Policy Needed to Make Web a Power for Life, *China Daily,* September 22, 1999.

25. See Shannon, supra, note 23.

26. See Betsy Hart, Secretive Group Taking Control of Internet's Hub, *Chicago Sun-Times,* June 21, 1999; Ted Bridis, No Major Y2K Effects Expected for Internet, *Chattanooga Times,* August 17, 1999.

27. David G. Post, Governing Cyberspace: Where is James Madison When We Need Him? Webposted on June 6, 1999, <http://www.icannwatch.org/archives/essays/930604982.shtml> (visited January 17, 2000).

28. Sassen, supra, note 23.

29. Post, Governing Cyberspace, supra, note 27. Network Solutions was purchased by Verisign in the year 2000.

30. See, generally, chapter 1 and chapter 6 of this book.

31. See generally supra, chapter 6 of this book, in which the U.S. Department of Commerce's Memorandum of Understanding with ICANN is discussed.

32. See, generally, Marshall Leaffer, Domain Names, Globalization, and Internet Governance, *Indiana Journal of Global Studies* 6 (1998): 139.

33. Joseph I. Liu, Legitimacy and Authority in Internet Coordination: A Domain Name Case Study, *Indiana Law Journal* 74 (1999): 587, 593. "The important point . . . [in this context]," Liu argues, "is that the authority of IANA and NSI over domain name allocation and administration was largely a matter of custom and historical contingency; it was not based on any identifiable legal claim of right." See id.

34. See Approved Agreements among ICANN, the U.S. Department of Commerce, and Network Solutions, Inc., <http://www.icann.org/nsi/nsi-agreements.htm> (visited January 23, 2000). See, generally, Jeri Clausing, Internet Group Approves Domain Name Registration Rules, *New York Times*, November 5, 1999.

35. See Fact Sheet on Tentative Agreements among ICANN, the U.S. Department of Commerce, and Network Solutions, Inc., <http://www.icann.org/nsi/factsheet.htm> (visited January 23, 2000): "Nothing in these agreements affects the current arrangements regarding management of the authoritative root server. NSI will continue to manage the authoritative root server in accordance with the direction of the Department of Commerce. The Department of Commerce expects to receive a technical proposal from ICANN for management of the authoritative root and this management responsibility may be transferred to ICANN at some point in the future. The Department of Commerce has no plans to transfer to any entity its policy authority to direct the authoritative root server."

See, generally, Milton Mueller, ICANN and Internet Governance: Sorting through the Debris of Self-Regulation, *Info*, vol. 1, no. 6, December 1999, <http://www.icannwatch.org/archives/muell.pdf> (visited January 23, 2000).

36. Wu, supra, note 14, at 1193.

37. Timothy Wu takes this analysis even one step further, arguing that legal inquiry with regard to cyberspace should focus on what takes place at the application layer because that is "where the variation that is apparent to the user can actually be found." He even goes so far as to suggest that legal issues in this context are appropriately classified by examining "the universe of existing and possible Internet applications." "Sometimes," he declares, "it makes sense to look at applications individually; other times, applications can be grouped by functional characteristics or by adherence to certain protocols; and in certain cases every application that adheres to the Internet's standards will be affected similarly, making an analysis of the whole Internet reasonable." For Wu, then, all legal questions in cyberspace inevitably begin with a code-based inquiry focusing on the application layer of the Internet architecture. Wu, supra, note 14, at 1164–1166.

38. Passwords, of course, can even be required on an individual user's hard drive, if he or she chooses to protect certain files—or even the entire contents of the computer—from unauthorized use by others.

39. For an overview of digital signature technology, see, e.g., Tara C. Hogan, Now That the Floodgates Have Been Opened, Why Haven't Banks Rushed into the Certification Authority Business? North Carolina Banking Institute 4 (April 2000): 417, 420–427. See, generally, Thomas J. Smedinghoff and Ruth Hill Bro, Moving with Change: Electronic Signature Legislation as a Vehicle for Advancing E-Commerce, *John Marshall Journal of Computer and Information Law* 17 (1999): 723.

40. Leslie Miller, Safe Surfing for Web-Wary Families, *USA Today*, August 18, 1999.

41. See id. See also N2H2 Press Release, November 17, 1999, <http://www.n2h2.com/pressroom/press/pr_020.html> (visited January 27, 2000).

42. See, generally, GetNetWise, a site that lists filtered-access providers of different types and provides an interface that enables online users to sort out various filtering options, <www.getnetwise.org> (visited September 7, 2000).

43. Miller, supra, note 40.

44. For additional details regarding the design and operation of PICS, see Paul Resnick, Filtering Information on the Internet, *Scientific American* 62 (March 1997).

45. See, e.g., Lawrence Lessig, Tyranny in the Infrastructure: The CDA Was Bad, But PICS May Be Worse, *Wired* Magazine, July 1997, <http://www.wired.com/wired/archive/5.07/cyber_rights.html> (visited September 12, 2000). See also *PICS, Censorship, and Intellectual Freedom FAQ,* (Paul Resnick, ed.) (last revised August 4, 1999), <http://www.w3.org/PICS/PICS-FAQ-980126.html> (visited September 12, 2000).

46. For additional exploration of the policy implications of PICS as well as recent developments in that regard, see Lawrence Lessig and Paul Resnick, Zoning Speech on the Internet: A Legal and Technical Model, *Michigan Law Review* 98 (1999): 395.

47. Richard Raysman and Peter Brown, The Disputes Over the Use of Net Filters, *New York Law Journal,* January 12, 1999.

48. See, generally, the National Research Council Report, The Digital Dilemma (2000), regarding the limits of trusted systems, and limitations regarding "technical protection" of copyrighted work in general. The report documents a number of ways that technical protection might work, and references trusted systems in a list that also includes Access Control in Bounded Communities, Enforcement of Access and Use Control in Open Communities, Copy Detection in Open Communities, Protection Technologies for Niches, and Special-Purpose Devices. See <http://books.nap.edu/html/digital_dilemma/> (visited April 2, 2000).

49. See, generally, Mark Stefik, Shifting the Possible: How Trusted Systems and Digital Property Rights Challenge Us to Rethink Digital Publishing, *Berkeley Technology Law Journal* 12 (1997): 137 (a paper based on a keynote address given March 14, 1996 in Washington, D.C. at the meeting of Professional and Scholarly Publishers Group of the American Association of Publishers).

50. Stefik has described several possible ways that encryption might be used in this context, including public key cryptography, "digital envelopes," and combinations of certain hardware and software on a consumer's system. See id.

51. See id.

52. See Julie E. Cohen, A Right to Read Anonymously: A Closer Look at Copyright Management in Cyberspace, *Connecticut Law Review* 28 (1996): 981.

53. See, e.g., Parry Aftab, A Parent's Guide to the Internet, <http://www.cyberangels.org/parentsguide/filtering.html> (visited January 30, 2000). See also Summary of Features of Filtering Software (comparing Net Nanny, CyberPatrol, and CyberSitter), <http://www.cyberangels.org/safetyandprivacy/chart.html> (visited January 30, 2000).

54. Codex also manufactures other software products that provide code-based self-help solutions for security problems. See <www.thecodex.com> (visited January 30, 2000).

55. Tom Spring, Getting DIRT on the Bad Guys, PC World, June 29, 1999, <http://www.pcworld.com/pcwtoday/article/0,1510,11614,00.html> (visited January 30, 2000).

56. For example, in late 2000, the Internet filtering debate continued in the U.S. Congress, as several bills that would require filtering in schools and libraries that benefited from substantial government e-rate discounts were considered. See, e.g., HR 4600, The Children's Internet Protection Act, Introduced in the House, June 8, 2000.

57. Spring, supra, note 55. Also relevant in this context is the uproar that erupted in the summer of 2000 as Netizens learned about the FBI's Carnivore Internet surveillance system. See, e.g., Ted Bridis, FBI Gets Web Guru Cerf's Support for Carnivore, *Wall Street Journal,* September 7, 2000.

58. Dickerson Downing and Kathleen McCarthy, Copyright and the Digital Age, *New York Law Journal,* December 6, 1999.

59. Julie Rosser, Protection of Copyrights in the Age of MP3: How Far Should We Go? December 17, 1999 (research paper on file with the author). See, generally, SDMI Fact Sheet, <www.sdmi.org/public_doc/FinalFactSheet.htm> (visited February 1, 2000).

60. See, e.g., Joel R. Reidenberg, Lex Informatica: The Formulation of Information Policy Rules Through Technology, *Texas Law Review* 76 (1998): 553.

61. See *Code,* chapter 5, at 57 (paperback edition).

62. Wu, supra, note 14, at 1195–1196.

Chapter 8

1. See Mark A. Lemley, The Law and Economics of Internet Norms, *Chicago-Kent Law Review,* 73 (1998): 1257.

2. See Pamela Samuelson, Intellectual Property and the Digital Economy: Why the Anti-Circumvention Regulations Need to be Revised, *Berkeley Technology Law Journal* 14 (1999): 519.

3. See Lawrence Lessig, The Zones of Cyberspace, *Stanford Law Review* 48 (1996): 1403, 1410. "Th[e] next generation of cyberspace," writes Lessig, "will provide individuals with the perfect technology of choice; it will empower individuals to select into the world that they want to see, to select out of the world that they don't."). See also Timothy Wu, Application-Centered Internet Analysis, *Virginia Law Review* 85 (1999): 1163.

4. This legislation, as discussed throughout this book, included both the "No Electronic Theft" Act of 1997 and the Digital Millennium Copyright Act of 1998.

5. The Electronic Privacy Information Center continues to be in the forefront of this battle. See generally <www.epic.org> (visited September 12, 2000). See also Trust and Privacy Online: Why Americans Want to Rewrite the Rules, The Pew Internet and American Life Project, August 20, 2000, <http://www.pewinternet.org/reports/toc.asp?Report=19> (visited September 12, 2000).

6. Neil King Jr. et al., Clinton to Hold Internet Security Summit, *Wall Street Journal,* February 11, 2000.

7. See Lessig, "The Law of the Horse," supra, note 36 (chapter 1), 501, 505–06: "Many believe that cyberspace simply cannot be regulated. Behavior in cyberspace, this meme insists, is beyond government's reach. The anonymity and multi-jurisdictionality of cyberspace makes control by government in cyberspace impossible. The nature of the space makes behavior there unregulable.

"This belief about cyberspace is wrong, but wrong in an interesting way. It assumes either that the nature of cyberspace is fixed—that its architecture, and the control it enables, cannot be changed—or that government cannot take steps to change this architecture. Neither assumption is correct. Cyberspace has no nature; it has no particular architecture that cannot be changed. Its architecture is a function of its design—or, as I will describe it in the section that follows, its code. This code can change, either because it evolves in a different way, or because government or business pushes it to evolve in a particular way. And while particular versions of cyberspace do resist effective regulation, it does not follow that every version of cyberspace does so as well. Or alternatively, there are versions of cyberspace where behavior can be regulated, and the government can take steps to increase this regulability."

8. See Niva Elkin-Koren, Copyrights in Cyberspace—Rights Without Laws?, *Chicago-Kent Law Review* 73 (1998): 1155.

9. See, e.g., David S. Cloud and Neil King Jr., Federal Effort to Protect Web Hampered by a Cultural Chasm, *Wall Street Journal,* February 11, 2000.

10. For an insightful analysis of related issues within this complex territory, see, generally, Post, What Larry Doesn't Get supra, note 2 (chapter 1).

11. Joel R. Reidenberg, Governing Networks and Rule-Making in Cyberspace, *Emory Law Journal* 45 (1996): 911. See also Johnson and Post, supra, note 38 (chapter 2).

12. See, generally, Elkin-Koren, supra, note 8.

13. See Steven G. Gey, Reopening the Public Forum—From Sidewalks to Cyberspace, *Ohio State Law Journal* 51 (1998) 1535, 1620 n. 373; Andrew J. Slitt, Note: The Anonymous Publisher: Defamation on the Internet After Reno v. American Civil Liberties Union and Zeran v. America Online, *Connecticut Law Review* 31 (1998): 389.

14. See, e.g., Stuart Biegel, Hybrid Domain: The First Amendment and the Public-Private Distinction, *UCLA Online Institute for Cyberspace Law and Policy,* September 26, 1996, <http://www.gseis.ucla.edu/iclp/sep96.html> (visited September 11, 2000).

Of course, it is important to note that ISPs may have their own First Amendment rights that prohibit the government from interfering with their ability to restrict speech. See, generally, Eugene Volokh, Freedom of Speech in Cyberspace from the Listener's Perspective: Private Speech Restrictions, Libel, State Action, Harassment, and Sex, *University of Chicago Legal Forum* (1996): 377, 385–401.

15. See chapter 2 of this book, supra, which concludes that the appropriateness of a particular problem-solving approach can be viewed as a function of how unique the setting and the activity are.

16. See Cybersell, Inc., an Arizona corp., v. Cybersell, Inc., a Florida Corp., 130 F.3d 414 (9th Cir. 1997); Zippo Manufacturing Company v. Zippo Dot Com., Inc., 952 F. Supp. 1119 (W.D. Pa. 1997).

17. See Jack L. Goldsmith, Against Cyberanarchy, *University of Chicago Law Review* 65 (1998): 1199.

Chapter 9

1. See, e.g., Declan McCullagh, Was Yahoo Smurfed or Trinooed? *Wired News*, February 8, 2000, <http://www.wired.com/news/business/0,1367,34203,00.html> (visited February 20, 2000):

[Basic smurfing] . . . works this way: A perpetrator sends a stream of 'echo' response-requests and pretends they're coming from the victim's computer. The multiple replies overwhelm the targeted network. They also cause havoc inside the broadcasting (aka smurf amplifying) computers that were used as unwitting reflectors.

Depending on the size of the intermediate network, a clever attacker can easily increase the muscle of his assault. A 768 Kb/s stream of echo packets multiplied by a broadcast network with 100 machines can generate a 76.8 Mb/s flood directed against the target—more than enough to overwhelm any single computer.

The good news is that defenses against this kind of assault are well-known. Computers can be *modified* to ignore echo requests. Cisco and 3Com have both released *instructions* to turn off the broadcasting of them, and the Internet Engineering Task Force *RFC2644* says echo requests 'must' be disabled in routers by default.

2. Computer Incident Advisory Capability—Lawrence Livermore National Laboratory, Distributed System Intruder Tools: Trinoo and Tribe Flood Network, CIAC 00.040, December 21, 1999, <http://ciac.llnl.gov/ciac/papers/Distributed_System_Intruder.html> (visited February 20, 2000).

3. See, generally, Khanh T.L. Tran, Yahoo! Suffers Hacker Attack; Popular Web Site Is Shut Down, *Wall Street Journal*, February 8, 2000.

4. Sites affected by the February 2000 distributed DoS attacks included Yahoo Sites (rated #2 with 42.4 million unique visitors at the time), Microsoft Sites (#3—40.5 million unique visitors), Amazon (#7—16.6 million), About.com Sites (#9—12.6 million), Time Warner Online (#10—12.2 million), Ebay (#14— 10.4 million),

and ZDNet (#16—9.6 million). See Shooting at the Web's Top Guns, *Wall Street Journal,* February 10, 2000.

5. See, generally, Hackers on the Attack Again, Hitting Top Web Sites, *Reuters Online,* February 8, 2000; Lindsey Arent and Declan McCullagh, A Frenzy of Hacker Attacks, *Wired News,* February 9, 2000.

6. Hypertext Webster Gateway, WordNet Definition <http://www.fin.gov.nt.ca/webster.htm> (visited September 15, 2000). See also 18 U.S. Code Section 3077: An "Act of terrorism" means an activity that involves a violent act or an act dangerous to human life that is a violation of the criminal laws of the United States or of any State, or that would be a criminal violation if committed within the jurisdiction of the United States or of any State; and appears to be intended—(i) to intimidate or coerce a civilian population; (ii) to influence the policy of a government by intimidation or coercion, or (iii) to affect the conduct of a government by assassination or kidnapping.

7. See, e.g., M.J. Zuckerman, Targeting Cyberterrorism, *USA Today,* October 20, 1997; Susan Crabtree, Cyberspace: A Terrorist Frontier?, *Washington Times,* August 19, 1996.

8. James Pooley, Litigating Copyright, Trademark and Unfair Competition Cases for the Experienced Practitioner—Update on Trade Secret Law, *Practicing Law Institute,* November-December, 1999.

9. See Greg Miller, Hacker Proud of Program, Denounces Web Attack Use, *Los Angeles Times,* February 12, 2000; Greg Miller, Software Author Offers Insider's View of Attack, *Los Angeles Times,* February 14, 2000.

10. NIPC Information System Alert 00-034: Re-Issue of NIPC Alert 99-029, Originally Issued December 6, 1999, <http://www.fbi.gov/nipc/ddos.htm> (visited February 21, 2000). The NIPC added that it was "concerned that these tools could have been prepared for employment during the Y2K period, and remains concerned this activity could continue targeting other significant commercial, government or national sites." See id.

11. Khanh T. L. Tran and Rhonda L. Rundle, Hackers Attack Major Web Sites, Shutting Amazon, Buy.com, eBay, *Wall Street Journal,* February 9, 2000.

12. UCLA Communications Technology Services-Network Operations Center, Denial of Service Attack on UCLA, January 21, 2000 (on file with the author).

13. UCLA Communications Technology Services-Network Operations Center, Denial of Service Attacks Yesterday, February 9, 2000, <http://www.noc.ucla.edu/operations/messages/msg_2.html> (visited February 21, 2000).

14. Vernon Loeb, Cyberwar's Economic Threat: U.S. Is Vulnerable to Foreign Attacks, Hill Panel Is Told, *Washington Post,* February 24, 2000.

15. 18 U.S. Code Section 1030 (2000).

16. See, e.g., CA Penal Code Section 602—Criminal Trespass.

17. CompuServe, Inc. v. Cyber Promotions, Inc., 962 F. Supp. 1015 (S.D. Ohio 1997).

18. See, e.g., Mark D. Robins, Electronic Trespass: An Old Theory in a New Context, 7 *Computer Lawyer* 7 (July 1998): 1. It should be noted, however, that concerns were raised by numerous scholars regarding an expansive application of the trespass to chattels doctrine in civil litigation focusing on e-commerce. See, e.g., Friend-of-the-Court Brief filed by twenty-eight cyberspace law professors in eBay v. Bidder's Edge, No. C–99–21200 RMW (N.D. Cal. 2000), <http://www.gseis.ucla.edu/iclp/ebay-ml> (visited September 13, 2000). See, generally, Dan L. Burk, The Trouble With Trespass, *Journal of Small and Emerging Business Law* 4 (2000): 27, <http://www.isc.umn.edu/research/papers/trespass-ed2.pdf> (visited September 13, 2000).

19. See Statement of Janet Reno, Attorney General of the U.S., Before the U.S. Senate Committee on Appropriations—Subcommittee on Commerce, Justice, and State, February 16, 2000, 2000 WL 11068228.

20. See Win Schwartau, Striking Back: Corporate Vigilantes Go on the Offensive to Hunt Down Hackers, *Network World,* January 11, 1999. Schwartau notes that, of course, these counteroffensive measures can only succeed if the correct perpetrators have been identified: "No matter what offensive mechanism you choose, the trick is to identify the culprit before returning fire. Should you fail to recognize that the attacker spoofed the identity of another company, you may find yourself attacking J.C. Penney, NBC or General Motors. Innocent companies would not take kindly to that sort of activity—no matter the reason—and ISPs don't appreciate being the vehicle for Internet-based attacks . . . Indeed, one of the big dangers with corporate vigilantism is how easy it is to overreact to an apparent attack."

21. See Id.

22. See "Corporate America's Competitive Edge," a study conducted by Warroom Research, a "competitive intelligence firm" in Annapolis, Maryland, documented in Schwartau, supra.

23. For a discussion of the "ping of death" and related matters, See Eric J. Sinrod and William P. Reilly, Cyber-Crimes: A Practical Approach to the Application of Federal Computer Crime Laws, *Santa Clara Computer and High Technology Law Journal* 16 (2000): 177, 193: "The Ping of Death is a large [Internet Control Message Protocol (ICMP)] packet that is sent to the target server. The target receives the ping in fragments and starts to re-assemble the packets as they arrive. However, the completed size of the packet is larger than the buffer, or than the room the computer has allocated to such packets, and the computer is overwhelmed, often resulting in the server shutting down or freezing up."

24. Schwartau notes that even those with a strong inclination for vigilantism point out that counteroffensive responses are "fraught with danger. Retribution can cause a hair-trigger response that could cause damage to systems in the path from you to the attacker. 'You really have to understand what you're doing,' says Ray Kaplan, a senior information security consultant with Secure Computing. 'Your first response might invite further attack, exactly the opposite of what you intended. You have to consider your firm's public relations posture and how the Internet community as a whole will react to your actions.'" Schwartau, supra, note 20.

25. Traditional common law rules of self-defense, defense of others, defense of habitation, and defense of property are outlined at length in the classic treatises of *Perkins on Criminal Law,* (Foundation Press, 2d ed., 1969), at 993–1030, and *Prosser and Keeton on the Law of Torts,* (West, 5th ed., 1984), at 124–137.

26. See, generally, Stuart P. Green, Castles and Carjackers: Proportionality and the Use of Deadly Force in Defense of Dwellings and Vehicles, *Illinois Law Review* (1999): 1.

27. Founded in 1991, CCIPS worked closely on computer crime cases with Assistant United States Attorneys known as "Computer and Telecommunications Coordinators" (CTCs) in U.S. Attorney's Offices around the country. Each CTC was given special training and equipment, and served as each office's expert in computer crime cases.

28. For example, CCIPS has assisted with wiretaps over computer networks, as well as with "traps and traces that require agents to segregate Internet headers from the content of the packet." CCIPS has also coordinated "an interagency working group consisting of all the federal law enforcement agencies, which developed guidance for law enforcement agents and prosecutors on the many problems of law, jurisdiction, and policy that arise in the online environment."

29. The U.S. Attorney General also lauded the efforts of CCIPS attorneys "to train local, state, and federal agents and prosecutors on the laws governing cybercrime" by giving presentations nationwide, and by chairing the National Cybercrime Training Partnership (NCTP), a "consortium of federal, state, and local entities dedicated to improving the technical competence of law enforcement in the information age." See Reno testimony, supra, note 19.

Reno also explained that "CCIPS works on a number of policy issues raised at the intersection of law and technology." CCIPS attorneys meet regularly with a number of industry groups to discuss issues of common concern, and helped establish the Cybercitizen Partnership in cooperation with high-tech industries to help identify industry expertise which may be needed in a complex investigation, to initiate personnel exchanges and to help safeguard our children. "CCIPS attorneys propose and comment on legislation that affects their high-tech mission."

See, generally, <http://www.cybercrime.gov> (visited March 16, 2000).

30. See, e.g., Richard Ingham, French Leaders Say Internet Self-Regulation Not Enough to Fight Cyber-Crime, Agence France-Presse, May 15, 2000 (describing the May 2000 G8 conference on cybercrime). See, generally, Organised Exploitation of the Information Super-Highway, *Jane's Intelligence Review,* July 1, 2000, available at 2000 WL 11960684.

31. See, generally, chapter 6 of this book, supra.

32. Reno, supra, note 19. In particular, she noted that CCIPS chaired the G-8 Subgroup on High-tech Crime, which has established a "24 hours a day/7 days a week point of contact with 15 countries for mutual assistance in computer crime." She also indicated that CCIPS played "a leadership role in the Council of Europe Experts' Committee on Cybercrime, and in a new cybercrime project at the Organization of American States."

33. There is arguably an inherent contradiction between this statement and the fact that no international representatives were invited to the White House Cyber-Security Summit in February 2000.

34. It should be noted that all WTO disputes have concerned public international law—which is neither civil nor criminal. However, allegations of criminal activity—including routine bribery of customs officials—have found their way into some GATT-related disputes and negotiations, typically within the context of whether a state is complying with its obligations.

35. Taiwan Says Ready If China Launches Internet Attacks, Reuters Online, March 7, 2000.

36. See, e.g., Jacqueline Klossek, The Development of International Police Cooperation Within the EU and Between the EU and Third Party States: A Discussion of the Legal Bases of Such Cooperation and the Problems and Promises Resulting Thereof, *American University International Law Review* 14 (1999): 599, 610–611:

Interpol is the oldest wide-scale mechanism for international police cooperation. Before World War I, international police cooperation was primarily viewed as a means of combating radical and violent political opponents. States were only willing to cooperate on common police and security interests to the extent that their individual sovereignty remained intact. As such, they organized Interpol as a private international association of police chiefs, not as a means of true interstate cooperation.

Since World War II, Interpol has become more of an international public institution, although several of its defining characteristics remain in place. For instance, Interpol's organization is not based upon an international treaty. In addition, Interpol is not embedded in an international political structure such as the United Nations or the Council of Europe. Instead, Interpol is comprised of National Central Bureaux, which are organized around a General Secretariat based in Lyon, France, and provides a far-reaching communications network for the exchange of criminal intelligence and other important information between its members.

There are a number of positive aspects to the internal structure and organization of Interpol. For instance, it has a large membership. Additionally, Interpol includes States from a number of different legal, political, and ideological backgrounds, including those from opposing regimes.

Nonetheless, there are multiple negative aspects of Interpol. First, the organization has a reputation for a relatively low level of security in matters such as terrorism. Second, Interpol can only be effective when the participating States are willing to cooperate and fully engage in the activities of the organization. Some Member States lack a complete commitment to Interpol.

37. See, e.g., Kathleen Murphy et al., Net of the Future, *Internet World,* January 1, 2000.

38. Jim Wolf, Experts Blast Software Makers for Security Lapses, *Reuters,* March 9, 2000.

39. Information about these tools is posted on Cisco's Web site, and configuration guides are also included for those who wish to activate this software. See, generally, <http://www. cisco.com> (visited September 13, 2000).

40. According to Farnsworth,

There are protocols on the Internet that are used primarily for legitimate purposes, but these protocols can be subverted and used to wage the kinds of denial of service attacks we've seen recently. If you send tens of thousands of "ping" packets at a host [computer], you can effectively shut it down. [The "ping" protocol is used to test how long it takes for another computer on the Internet to respond.] Through the use of filtering tools on routers, you could effectively limit the amount and type of these protocols that go through at any one time. It's reasonable to assume that 3% to 4% of traffic might use this protocol, so you can set a limit at 5% [so routers won't pass on "ping" packets once they reach 5% of traffic].

41. Tran and Rundle, supra, note 11.

42. Seamus Phan, How to Forestall Hackers, *Singapore Business Times,* February 21, 2000.

43. See <http://www.nipc.gov> (visited September 13, 2000).

44. Other tools that might help protect individual users were increasingly available for downloading on the Internet. These included both free products and free advice. Zone Labs' ZoneAlarm, for example, was available for no cost and performed essentially the same function as Symantec's Internet Security. See <http://www.zonealarm.com>. And sites providing helpful information and advice in this regard have proliferated in recent years. They include CERT or Computer Emergency Response Team (<http://www.cert.org>), Gibson Research Corp.'s Shields up! (<http://grc.com>), the International Computer Security Association (<http://www.icsa.net>), Microsoft Security Advisor (<http://www.microsoft.com/security>), and ZDNet's Security page (<http://www.zdnet.com/enterprise/security>). Some of these sites provide both information and a variety of special services. The Shields Up Web page, for example, tests an individual machine to see if privacy or data security is at risk. See <http://www.grc.com>. Another Gibson web page describes how Windows users can protect their computers by disabling the Microsoft file and printer sharing from their Internet connection without affecting their ability to access files via a local area network. See <http://grc.com/su-fixit.htm>. Finally, along these same lines, security experts continue to advise individual users to install all the latest software patches and choose "less-than-obvious" passwords.

45. See, e.g., "Slave" Computers Could Be Liable, *Toronto Star,* February 11, 2000; Jim Barlow, Lawsuits Answer to Hack Attacks? *Houston Chronicle,* February 15, 2000. See, generally, Hal R. Varian, Liability for Net Vandalism Should Rest With Those That Can Best Manage the Risk, *New York Times,* June 1, 2000.

46. Nick Wingfield and Scott Thurm, Stalking the Hackers, *Wall Street Journal,* February 10, 2000.

47. William M. Bulkeley, Security Firm Says It Has Web Defense, But It Won't Be Available Right Away, *Wall Street Journal,* February 11, 2000.

48. David P. Hamilton, Redesigning the Internet: Can It Be Made Less Vulnerable? *Wall Street Journal,* February 14, 2000.

49. See Internet Privacy Report Cites Need for Balance, *New York Times,* March 10, 2000: "The ACLU complained that . . . [a new government report on online security and privacy) . . . 'treats the anonymity of Internet users as a *thorny issue,* rather than a constitutional right. An end to Internet anonymity would chill free expression in cyberspace.'"

50. See Hamilton, supra, note 48. It has also been suggested that "short of changing operating systems, software makers and computer companies could simply switch on existing security precautions at the factory . . . If computer systems were set at a more secure level of operation when users buy them, there would be fewer of the loopholes that unwittingly allow hackers to transfer improper traffic or instructions."

51. Jim Wolf, Experts Blast Software Makers for Security Lapses, Reuters, March 9, 2000. In a related matter, many criticized Microsoft for ignoring warnings regarding security flaws in its highly popular Outlook program. See, e.g., Firm Snubs Repeated Virus Infection Warnings: Microsoft Takes Pounding Over Program Flaws, *South China Morning Post,* May 9, 2000.

Chapter 10

1. See, e.g., the FTC's list of "consumer education" topics under the heading "E-Commerce and the Internet," <http://www.ftc.gov/bcp/menu-internet.htm> (visited March 19, 2000).

2. Glenn R. Simpson, FTC Emerges as Chief Enforcer of the Web; Firms Are Worried, *Wall Street Journal,* February 29, 2000.

3. Interview with Paul Luehr, FTC Litigation Attorney, March 16, 2000.

4. See generally chapters 2 and 8 of this book, supra.

5. Such software is typically designed to protect against dangerous conduct, unlawful anarchic conduct, and/or inappropriate conduct, but not typically against fraudulent conduct, which often requires some affirmative activity on the part of the victim.

6. 18 U.S. Code, sec. 1030 (2000).

7. The following is a list of relevant citations for these federal statutes: Fair Packaging and Labeling Act (15 U.S. Code, sec.1451 et seq.), the Consumer Credit Protection Act (15 U.S. Code, sec. 1601 et seq.), the Magnuson Moss Warranty-Federal Trade Commission Improvement Act (15 U.S. Code, sec. 2301 et seq.), the Hobby Protection Act (16 U.S. Code, sec. 2101 et seq.), and the Children's Online Privacy Protection Act, 47 U.S. Code, sec. 231. See, generally, <http://www.ftc.gov/ogc/stat3.htm> (visited March 23, 2000).

8. Under the common law tort of misrepresentation, the victim must also prove that the representation played a substantial part in inducing her to act as she did

(actual reliance), and that the victim was justified in relying on the representation (justifiable reliance). See W. Page Keeton, et al., *Prosser and Keeton on the Law of Torts* (West Publishing Company, 5th ed., 1984).

9. See Rollin M. Perkins and Ronald N. Boyce, *Criminal Law* (3rd ed., Foundation Press, 1982).

10. See the Federal Trade Commission Act, 15 U.S. Code, secs. 41–58.

11. Federal Trade Commission, Vision, Mission and Goals, <http://www.ftc.gov/ftc/mission.htm> (visited March 24, 2000).

12. See, e.g., Simpson, supra, note 2. See also Doug Brown, Bulked-Up FTC: Let's Get Going, *ZDNet Online,* February 18, 2000.

13. See, e.g., *Consumer Protection Policy in the New High-Tech, Global Marketplace,* FTC Staff Report, n. 3 (December 1999).

14. See, e.g., Lawrence Lessig, Online Patents: Leave Them Pending, *Wall Street Journal,* March 24, 2000 (placing the recent controversy over changing rules for patents in cyberspace within the larger framework of government regulation):

In practically every other context of e-commerce regulation, the practice of our government has been not to apply the old rules but to wait and see. Thus Congress supported a moratorium on Internet taxation until we understood what taxing cyberspace would do. The Federal Trade Commission held off regulating online privacy until it saw whether businesses would regulate itself. And the Federal Communications Commission has refused to enforce open-access requirements in broadband cable, in part because we don't yet know how the market will evolve. In each area, the government has hesitated before regulating—at least until officials are satisfied the regulation will do no harm.

15. These organizations include the National Fraud Information Center, a project of the National Consumers League, members of the Better Business Bureau, and Canada's PhoneBusters.

16. A detailed overview of the FTC's accomplishments between 1995 and 2000 can be found in its December 1999 report, *The FTC's First Five Years: Protecting Consumers Online,* <http://www.ftc.gov/os/1999/9912/fiveyearreport.pdf> (visited March 26, 2000).

17. Additional information about these cases can be found in both the December 1999 report, supra, note 13, and in the FTC's digest of recent cases, <http://www.ftc.gov/opa/1999/9912/case-internet.pdf> (visited March 1, 2000). Although, in general, it is traditional law that has been applied, the FTC has noted in its recent documents that

as part of a systematic review of its Rules and Guides to determine whether they are still relevant or should be modified or rescinded, the Commission has analyzed them one-by-one to consider their applicability to online marketing. Where appropriate, the Commission has amended a Rule or Guide to clarify that the scope reaches electronic media, including the Internet. The Commission also has taken steps to ensure compliance with its Rules and Guides so that consumers who shop online are afforded the same protections they enjoy offline.

In addition, however, the agency has noted that "some aspects of the electronic medium—hyperlinking, scrolling, banners, and animation—raise novel questions about the interpretation of common legal terms, such as requirements that disclosures be "clear and conspicuous" and that information be "written," "in writing," or "printed." To seek guidance in this area, the Commission held a Public Workshop on the Interpretation of Rules and Guides for Electronic Media. Representatives of the advertising industry, online businesses, and consumer groups and technology experts discussed the application of particular legal requirements in the online environment in light of technological developments, the way that consumers use the Internet to shop online, and the practical implications of various approaches. December 1999 Report, supra, note 13.

18. See FTC Case Digest, supra, at pages 9–10. See also Interview with Paul Luehr, supra, note 3.

19. Unfortunately, the publicity surrounding the Pereira case has done little to limit mousetrapping practices in and of themselves. In the year 2000, it became a common practice, particularly at pornographic sites. Coding inside the Web page redirects the browser to specific pages against the online user's wishes. It becomes impossible to back out of the page by clicking on the Back arrow, and in some cases users cannot close their browser windows. See, e.g., Tamara E. Holmes, If Your Browser Goes Squirrelly, You've Been Mousetrapped, *USA Today,* April 3, 2000. Users can apparently prevent mousetrapping by disabling Java, Javascript, and ActiveX, but, of course, this process can limit the range of options available to users when visiting other Web pages.

Although the FTC was able to identify regulations that arguably prohibited the pagejacking-mousetrapping activity implicated in the *Pereira* case, basic mousetrapping quickly gets into uncharted legal territory. See, e.g., Richard Guilliatt, Greg Lasrado made his fortune from adult Internet sites, *The Times* (London), September 16, 2000: "[E]ven the FTC admits that mousetrapping itself is not illegal."

20. See, e.g., John Simons, FTC Cracks Down on Three Web Pornographers, *Wall Street Journal,* September 23, 1999.

21. In the Matter of DoubleClick, Before the Federal Trade Commission, February 10, 2000, <http://www.epic.org/privacy/internet/FTC/DCLK_complaint.pdf> (visited September 17, 2000).

22. A major Internet-related privacy dispute beyond the scope of this book focused on the 1998 European Union Privacy Directive and the fact that it provided significantly greater protection for EU consumers than does the U.S. under current national law. After two years of negotiations, an accord was reached in mid-2000 that would "require American companies that gather personal information from Europeans to join so-called 'safe harbor' programs," under which they would agree not to gather or use personal information about European consumers without the consumers' express consent. See, e.g., Jeri Clausing, Europe and U.S. Reach Data Privacy Pact, *New York Times,* March 15, 2000. For a defense of the accord by the former undersecretary of commerce for international trade who negotiated it, see David Aaron, Profiting from Privacy, *Washington Post,* July 31, 2000.

Chapter 11

1. See, e.g., Cyberspace Law Bibliography—Intellectual Property Issues: Copyright Law and the Online World, UCLA Online Institute for Cyberspace Law and Policy, <http://www.gseis.ucla.edu/iclp/bib4.html#Copyright> (visited September 17, 2000).

2. Notable authors of highly influential law review articles in this area include—but are not limited to—Dan Burk, Julie Cohen, Niva Elkin-Koren, Mark Lemley, Jessica Litman, and Pamela Samuelson. See *Cyberspace Law Bibliography,* supra, note 1.

3. See, generally, Dan L. Burk, Virtual Exit in the Global Information Economy, *Chicago-Kent Law Review* 73 (1998): 943.

4. See, e.g., Jane Ginsburg, Putting Cars on the 'Information Superhighway': Authors, Exploiters, and Copyright in Cyberspace, *Columbia Law Review* 95 (1995): 1466. See, generally, Title 17 of the U.S. Code, Section 107 (the "fair use" doctrine).

5. See *The Digital Dilemma: Intellectual Property in the Digital Age,* The Report of the Committee on Intellectual Property Rights and the Emerging Information Infrastructure, National Research Council (2000) [hereinafter the NRC report], <http://books.nap.edu/html/digital_dilemma/index.html> (visited February 27, 2001).

6. See id. See generally supra, chapter 3 of this book.

7. See Sony v. Universal, 464 U.S. 417, 429 (1984), quoting H.R. Rep. No. 2222, 60th Cong., 2d Sess. 7 (1909). See also Justice Hughes' comments on this subject in U.S. v. Paramount, 334 U.S. 131, 158: "The sole interest of the United States and the primary object in conferring the monopoly lie in the general benefit derived by the public from the labors of authors."

8. See, e.g., James Boyle, *Shamans, Software and Spleens: Law and the Construction of the Information Society* (Harvard University Press, 1996).

9. H.R. Rep. No. 2222, 60th Cong., 2d Sess. 7 (1909), quoted in Sony v. Universal, 464 U.S. at 429.

10. In addition to the typical reproduction and distribution of copyrighted materials that occur regularly as a result of affirmative decisions by online users, automatic copies are often created via the caching function of Internet browsers. In addition, some have argued that linking can constitute copyright infringement in certain instances.

11. There have been a range of prospective solutions proposed in this context, however. See, e.g., Paul Veravanich, Rio Grande: The MP3 Showdown at High Noon in Cyberspace, *Fordham Intellectual Property, Media & Entertainment Law Journal* 10 (2000): 433. See generally *Signal or Noise: The Future of Music on the Net,* Berkman Center for Internet & Society Conference materials, May 2000, <http://cyber.law.harvard.edu/events/netmusic.html> (visited September 19, 2000).

12. Indeed, using Napster on a regular basis in early 2001 was as easy as using a basic search engine. Key words identifying the artist and/or the title were entered, and the findings were displayed quickly and efficiently. Clicking on a title generated a process which transferred a copy of the digital file from another user's hard drive to your own. And for online users in 2001 the key to Napster was that it really worked. Unlike many of the MP3 files on lists generated by traditional search engines and located mostly on Web sites and FTP sites, the files on Napster were generally accessible for downloading. In addition, according to a company spokesperson, Napster had taken extreme measures to prevent access to any files on users' computers other than the audio files that users chose to share. Only valid MP3 files were shared. See, generally, Karen Heyman, Pandora's Box, *L.A. Weekly,* March 31, 2000.

13. See id. Heyman explains how the Web has been based on a client-server model: "What makes the World Wide Web work, ditto your office's LAN (local area network), is client-server computing. Your desktop computer (called, in this context, the client) is networked to a larger computer (the server). Generally, in most offices, you'll be able to run your word-processing or spreadsheet programs at your own computer, but you must go on the network in order to print or e-mail. The usual configuration looks like the spokes of a wheel, with the server as the hub, and the PCs at the end of the spokes. Rarely, there is what's called a "peer-to-peer" configuration, where all PCs are linked together, and then hooked up to the server. Keep that term in mind.

"The World Wide Web is a giant client-server system. You at your PC (or Mac, forgive me) log on to the Internet (the network) and, through it, to a favorite site. The site's computer (a server) sends the information you requested back to you. Here's the important part: Even if you e-mail someone, you're still going through a server—there's no direct contact between your computer and someone else's computer. If you want an MP3, you go to a site like MP3.com, request a song, and the site's server sends it to your computer."

14. Tristan Louis, TNL.NET <http://www.tnl.net/newsletter/>.

15. Heyman, supra, note 12. Napster, "when it connects, tells the server what IP address and port number the music can be downloaded from. Both numbers may change from session to session, and the port number may change during a session in order to work around firewall blocks and the like."

16. Several theories circulated regarding AOL's true position in this controversy. Some speculated that AOL had known nothing and was outraged when the software program was released. Others believed that AOL had actually sanctioned the project all along, but decided to pull back after it announced its merger with Time Warner. Cf. Heyman, supra, note 12.

17. See Thomas E. Weber, Maverick Programmers Prepare to Unleash Anarchy on the Web, *Wall Street Journal,* March 27, 2000.

18. See Benny Evangelista, Free For All, *San Francisco Chronicle,* April 3, 2000.

To make matters even worse for the entertainment industry, DivX appeared on the Internet at about the same time as Gnutella. The new program was designed to copy and shrink DVD files down to a size that is easier to transmit and store on a computer hard drive or a writable CD-ROM. It was created by "MaxMorice" and "Gej," who—according to information accompanying the program—"hacked Microsoft MPEG4 video technology and used the MP3 format to reduce a film's audio soundtrack." See id.

At the time, the process of copying an entire movie from a DVD was still complicated and highly technical, and there was no consumer-friendly program like Winamp available for DivX. But Web sites immediately began appearing that included step-by-step instructions along with other news and information. No one expected DivX to have an immediate impact, but commentators noted that playing MP3 files was just as complicated in 1997, until easy-to-use players and copiers started to appear.

19. <http://freenet.sourceforge.net>.

20. Weber, supra, note 17.

21. Louis, supra, note 14.

It should be noted, however, that the serverless file sharing software developed during this era tended to be relatively clumsy and nowhere near as easy to use as Napster. In addition, pointed questions were raised regarding the use and ultimate value of Gnutella that conflicted directly with Louis's optimistic comments. See, e.g., Eytan Adar & Bernardo A. Huberman, Free Riding on Gnutella, Xerox Palo Alto Research Center, October 2000, <www.parc.xerox.com/istl/groups/iea/papers/gnutella/> (visited February 27, 2001).

22. NRC report, supra, chapter 4, <http://books.nap.edu/html/digital_dilemma/ch4.html> (visited February 27, 2001). The Report also points out that "there is also the question of how well informed the public is about intellectual property more generally, including compliance with the private contracts embodied in shrink-wrap licenses, point-and-click licenses, subscriber agreements, and terms-of-service contracts. The intuitive conclusion is that a relatively small portion of the end-user population can be expected to read and fully comprehend all of the restrictions regarding intellectual property protection by which they may be legally bound, and in that sense the public is not well informed about what constitutes legal behavior." Id.

23. With regard to works created for hire and owned by corporations, the protection extends to "the life of the author plus 95 years."

24. Liability for the copyright infringement of others may be found under either a contributory copyright infringement theory or a vicarious liability theory.

25. Other key exceptions include section 108, which addresses reproduction by libraries and archives.

26. Title 17 of the U.S. Code, sec. 109, provides in pertinent part:

(a) Notwithstanding the provisions of sec. *106*(3), the owner of a particular copy or phonorecord lawfully made under this title, or any person authorized by such owner, is entitled, without the authority of the copyright owner, to sell or otherwise dispose of the possession of that copy or phonorecord.

27. See, generally, Title 17, U.S. Code, sec. 109.

28. *Castle Rock Entertainment v. Carroll Publishing Group,* 150 F.3d 132, 146 (2d Cir. 1998); *Byrne v. British Broadcasting Corporation,* 2001 WL 180057, *7 (S.D.N.Y. 2001).

29. See, e.g., David Nimmer, A Riff on Fair Use in the Digital Millennium Copyright Act, *University of Pennsylvania Law Review* 148 (2000): 673.

30. The Digital Millennium Copyright Act (DMCA), Title 17, Section 512 provides in pertinent part:

(d) Information Location Tools.—A service provider shall not be liable for monetary relief, or, except as provided in subsection (j), for injunctive or other equitable relief, for infringement of copyright by reason of the provider referring or linking users to an online location containing infringing material or infringing activity, by using information location tools, including a directory, index, reference, pointer, or hypertext link, if the service provider—

(1) (A) does not have actual knowledge that the material or activity is infringing; (B) in the absence of such actual knowledge, is not aware of facts or circumstances from which infringing activity is apparent; or (C) upon obtaining such knowledge or awareness, acts expeditiously to remove, or disable access to, the material;

(2) does not receive a financial benefit directly attributable to the infringing activity, in a case in which the service provider has the right and ability to control such activity; and

(3) upon notification of claimed infringement as described in subsection (c)(3), responds expeditiously to remove, or disable access to, the material that is claimed to be infringing or to be the subject of infringing activity, except that, for purposes of this paragraph, the information described in subsection (c)(3)(A)(iii) shall be identification of the reference or link, to material or activity claimed to be infringing, that is to be removed or access to which is to be disabled, and information reasonably sufficient to permit the service provider to locate that reference or link.

31. In some portions of the act, for example, the term "online service provider" refers to "providers of online services or network access, or operator[s] of facilities." 17 U.S.Code, sec. 512(k)(1) (1998).

32. Attorney Jonathan Band's excellent overview of the Digital Millennium Copyright Act can be found at <www.dfc.org/issues/wipo/JB-Index/JB-Memo/jb-memo.html> (visited April 23, 2000). Although generic linking from one Web page to another without permission has typically been viewed as legal and has not generally been challenged, issues have been raised in recent years regarding two categories of linking—"deep" linking (where one site links to a Web page other than the home page), and linking to infringing material. Others have raised additional issues regarding links that have been placed in such a manner that they are mischaracterized or misrepresented.

33. The WIPO treaties define copyright management information as "information which identifies the work, the author of the work, the owner of any right in the work, or information about the terms and conditions of use of the work, and any numbers or codes that represent such information, when any of these items of information is attached to a copy of a work or appears in connection with the communication of a work to the public." The anticircumvention provisions of the DMCA are codified at Title 17, U.S. Code, sec. 1201.

34. See Title 17, U.S. Code, sec. 512.

35. See *Sony v. Universal,* 464 U.S. at 430.

36. 464 U.S. 417 (1984).

37. In the early days of VCRs—which were actually called Videotape Recorders (VTRs) by many people at the time—there were two competing products on the market—the VHS recorder and the Betamax recorder. Although both operated in the same manner, the videocassettes differed in size. Sony's model eventually lost out to the larger VHS format.

38. Melville B. Nimmer, 2 Nimmer on Copyright, sec. 12.04 (A). A generally accepted statement of the contributory copyright infringement doctrine as it had evolved over time appeared in Gershwin Publishing Corp. v. Columbia Artists Management, Inc., 443 F.2d 1159 (2d Cir. 1971): "one who, with knowledge of the infringing activity, induces, causes or materially contributes to the infringing conduct of another, may be held liable as a 'contributory' infringer."

39. Sony, 464 U.S. at 442.

40. Id. at 442–456.

41. See RIAA v. Diamond Multimedia Systems, 180 F.3d 1072 (9th Cir. 1999) (the "Rio" Case).

42. See Prof. William Fisher's online MP3 course materials, Harvard Law School, Spring 2000. Fisher reports that, in the eyes of many observers, the record industry's lobbying efforts and the resulting delay was "responsible for the failure of the technology to gain consumer interest. Others blame the lack of consumer enthusiasm on relatively high equipment costs and consumer loyalty to pre-existing audio cassette collections." <http://eon.law.harvard.edu/h2o/property/MP3/main.html> (visited September 19, 2000).

43. A "digital audio recording device" is defined as a device capable of rendering a "digital audio copied recording." The digital audio copied recording must be a digital reproduction of a "digital music recording" and must be produced either directly or from a transmission. See AHRA sec. 1001. Finally, under AHRA sec. 1002(c), it is unlawful to attempt to circumvent the SCMS. See id.

44. See RIAA v. Diamond Multimedia Systems, Inc., 180 F.3d 1072, 1074–1075 (9th Cir. 1999). See generally S. REP. NO. 102-294, at 49 (1992), reprinted at 1992 WL 133198 at 118-19.

45. H. R. Rep. No. 94-1476, at 65–66, quoted in Sony v. Universal, n.31. The court went on to say that "[t]he Senate Committee similarly eschewed a rigid,

bright-line approach to fair use. The Senate Report endorsed the view 'that off-the-air recording for convenience' could be considered 'fair use' under some circumstances, although it then made it clear that it did not intend to suggest that off-the-air recording for convenience should be deemed fair use under any circumstances imaginable." S. Rep. No. 94-473, at 65–66 (1975). The latter qualifying statement is quoted by the dissent, post, at 481, and if read in isolation, would indicate that the Committee intended to condemn all off-the-air recording for convenience. Read in context, however, it is quite clear that that was the farthest thing from the Committee's intention.

46. See, generally, Princeton University Press v. Michigan Document Services, 99 F.3d 1381 (6th Cir. 1996); Basic Books v. Kinko's, 758 F. Supp. 1522 (S.D.N.Y. 1991). Notable examples of legal commentary in this area include Ann Bartow, Educational Fair Use in Copyright: Reclaiming the Right to Photocopy Freely, *University of Pittsburgh Law Review* 60 (1998): 149; Gregory K. Klingsporn, The Conference on Fair Use (CONFU) and the Future of Fair Use Guidelines, *Columbia-VLA Journal of Law and the Arts* 23 (1999): 101; Maureen Ryan, Fair Use and Academic Expression: Rhetoric, Reality and Restriction on Academic Freedom, *Cornell Journal of Law and Public Policy* 8 (1999): 541.

47. See RIAA v. Diamond Multimedia Systems, 180 F.3d 1072 (9th Cir. 1999). The RIAA and the Alliance of Artists & Recording Companies brought the lawsuit against Diamond Multimedia Systems, makers of the Rio, seeking to prevent the sale and distribution of this digital player. The lawsuit was not brought under traditional laws prohibiting copyright infringement, but under the U.S. Audio Home Recording Act of 1992 (AHRA).

48. *Black's Law Dictionary* (West Online Edition).

49. See, generally, William W. Fisher, Property and Contract on the Internet, *Chicago-Kent Law Review* 73 (1998): 1203, 1220, 1225–1226. In this regard, it should be noted that Professor Fisher focuses extensively on suggestions that the legal system might be employed to restrict the ability of private individuals to contract in this area. Although highly relevant, this issue is beyond the scope of this book.

50. See, e.g., A&M Records v. Napster, 2001 WL 115033 (9th Cir. 2001).

51. One commentator, for example, outlined the following prospective scenario in mid-2000:

> At first, the spread of Napster and its clones will stimulate demand for all sorts of "midlist" music that the record industry itself has done a lousy job of promoting, and the music companies will cry over Napster's success all the way to the bank.
>
> Over time . . . a growing number of artists will question their own participation in a system that really doesn't serve the great majority of them. They'll begin to experiment with more direct musician-to-fan schemes—not simply the sell-more-T-shirts approach mocked by artists, but serious new ideas for generating revenue for musicians: ideas like annual fan subscriptions, charges for early access to new music or special deals on collector's items, using online networking to boost attendance at shows and no doubt many others that I can't yet imagine.

The one piece yet to fall into place for . . . [such a] . . . utopian scenario . . . to come true is an easy-to-use micropayments scheme—some nearly universal online system for musicians (and anyone else) to be able to collect very small sums from customers without incurring prohibitive overhead costs. Once such technology becomes available, you can kiss the existing order of the industry goodbye. (Scott Rosenberg, It's Time to Get Rational, and Cool That Napster Rage, *Vancouver Sun,* April 13, 2000.)

52. Douglas Baird, Changing Technology and Unchanging Doctrine, *Supreme Court Review* (1984): 237, 249.

53. Jack L. Goldsmith, Against Cyberanarchy, *University of Chicago Law Review* 65 (1998): 1199, 1207–1208. Goldsmith notes (n. 36) that the Permanent Court of International Justice in the case of the S.S. "Lotus," 1927 P C I J (ser A) No 10 at 1825, "famously established a very weak effects test for extraterritorial jurisdiction and suggested a default rule that favored extraterritorial jurisdiction." He also notes that "Section 403 of the Restatement (Third) of the Foreign Relations Law (ALI 1987) recognized the effects test as a basis for extraterritorial jurisdiction, but added the caveat that a state may not exercise such jurisdiction when it would be 'unreasonable' to do so." But he argues that "[t]his reasonableness requirement has little basis in state practice and does not reflect customary international law." Id. at n.36.

54. Christopher Roberts and Stanford K. McCoy, Trips around the World: Enforcement Goes Global in 2000, *Legal Times,* April 10, 2000.

55. While code-based regulation may be used, for example, to ensure that copyright holders can collect revenue, it can also be used to assist Netizens in verifying the authenticity of information by determining whether it comes from the source claimed and whether it has been altered—either inadvertently or fraudulently. See, e.g., *CIPR Report,* chapter 5, <http://books.nap.edu/html/digital_dilemma/ch5.html> (visited April 28, 2000).

56. See, e.g., Lawrence M. Fisher, Xerox and Microsoft Create Digital Safeguard Company, *New York Times,* April 28, 2000, which describes plans for a new company "to produce and market software that protects copyrighted materials like books, music and video distributed over the Internet."

57. Special purpose devices also include cable-television set-top boxes and portable digital music players. For an extensive overview of technical protection services as of early 2000, see the NRC report, chapter 5, supra, <http://books.nap.edu/html/digital_dilemma/ch5.html/digital_dilemma/ch5.html>, and Appendix E <http://books.nap.edu/html/digital_dilemma/appE.html> (visited April 28, 2000).

58. As of early 2000, technical protection technologies were deployed to varying degrees: "Some, such as encryption and password protection, are widely deployed. Others, such as Web monitoring, watermarking, time stamping, and rights-management languages, are well developed but not yet widely deployed. Copy prevention techniques are deployed to a limited degree. The copy prevention mechanism used in digital video disks provides a notable example of mature development and

consumer market penetration." NRC report, supra, chapter 6, <http://books.nap.edu/html/digital_dilemma/ch6.html> (visited February 27, 2001).

59. Id. The NRC report noted some key points to keep in mind when planning the development and implementation of technical protection systems. First, continuing advances in this area will inevitably be based on cutting edge research in encryption technology. Next, the most effective systems in the near future will continue to be those that combine changes in both hardware and software. Circumvention techniques have proven much easier at the software level, for example, because code-cracking software can easily be distributed online. But circumvention that requires special hardware or hardware-handling expertise is far less easily shared.

In addition, TPS's with hardware components are more effective at making content usable on only one machine, preventing circumvention through redistribution. See id.

60. NRC report, supra, conclusion, <http://books.nap.edu/html/digital_dilemma/ch6.html> (visited February 27, 2001).

61. Heyman, supra, note 12.

62. Rosenberg, supra, note 51.

63. Heyman, supra, note 12.

Chapter 12

1. Of course, such a pattern of perception is consistent with a key rationale for arranging the four categories in their particular order. The list was, in fact, intended to begin with conduct that most would wish to abolish and end with conduct that many would choose not to address at all.

2. See, e.g., James Q. Whitman, Enforcing Civility and Respect: Three Societies, *Yale Law Journal* 109 (2000); 1279.

3. International Action Urged to Drive Racists Offline, Reuters, January 27, 2000 (on file with the author).

4. See Cuomo Announces Task Force to Fight Cyber-Hate and Discrimination, and Investigation of United Klans of America, HUD Press Release No. 00–55, March 16, 2000, <http://www.hud.gov/pressrel/pr00-55.html> (visited May 7, 2000).

5. See HUD Targets Hate Speech on the Internet, *Tech Law Journal,* March 20, 2000 <http://www.techlawjournal.com/censor/20000320.htm> (visited May 7, 2000). According to *Tech Law Journal,* Lee Jones, a spokesperson for HUD, said that they are "not looking for regulation" and that they are "not looking for legislation . . . Jim Dempsey, Senior Legal Counsel at the *Center for Democracy and Technology,* was . . . [also] . . . present at the meeting, and told *Tech Law Journal* that this task force is not a threat to free speech. 'There are sensitive First Amendment free speech issues here, and they recognize that. . . . The message that I took away was a non-regulatory one.'" See id.

6. See, e.g., Doe v. Univ. of Michigan, 721 F. Supp. 852 (E.D. Mich. 1989); UWM Post v. Board of Regents of the University of Wisconsin System, 774 F. Supp. 1163 (E.D. Wis. 1991).

7. See Doe, 721 F. Supp. at 866. The Doe court added: "No one may be required at the peril of life, liberty or property to speculate as to the meaning of penal statutes. All are entitled to be informed as to what the State commands or forbids. These considerations apply with particular force where the challenged statute acts to inhibit freedoms affirmatively protected by the constitution." Id. at 866–867.

8. Id. at 864. See also UWM Post, 774 F. Supp. at 1169:

It is fundamental that statutes regulating First Amendment activities must be narrowly drawn to address only the specific evil at hand. Because First Amendment freedoms need breathing space to survive, government may regulate in the area only with narrow specificity.

In spite of the above, the Supreme Court has held that "the overbreadth doctrine is 'strong medicine'" and that it should be employed "with hesitation, and then only as a last resort." Only a statute that is substantially overbroad may be invalidated on its face. Ferber, at 769. A statute should not be "held invalid on its face merely because it is possible to conceive of a single impermissible application . . ."

9. See Reno v. ACLU, 521 U.S. at 864:

In its appeal, the Government argues that the District Court erred in holding that the CDA violated both the *First Amendment* because it is overbroad and the Fifth Amendment because it is vague. While we discuss the vagueness of the CDA because of its relevance to the *First Amendment* overbreadth inquiry, we conclude that the judgment should be affirmed without reaching the *Fifth Amendment* issue.

10. Id. at 875.

11. Under First Amendment case law, it is often useful to identify two types of speech regulation—content-based regulation and content-neutral regulation. Content-neutral regulation can generally be regulated under reasonable time, place, and manner restrictions. But content-based regulation can only be regulated if the speech falls within one or more recognized exceptions or can be prohibited under other relevant laws. See, e.g., Laurence H. Tribe, American Constitutional Law, chapter 12, *Rights of Communication and Expression* (Foundation Press, 2d. ed. 1988).

12. 413 U.S. 15 (1973).

13. 167 F.3d 61 (1st Cir. 1999).

14. 198 F.3d 1083 (9th Cir. 1999).

15. 315 U.S. 568, 571–572 (1942).

16. See also *UWM Post,* 774 F. Supp. at 1169–1172.

17. An overview of related cases follows.

a. The "hostile audience cases" of the late 1940s and early 1950s cited *Chaplinsky* but appeared to reflect the Court's desire to limit the broad implication of the *Chaplinsky* doctrine:

• *Terminiello v. City of Chicago* focused on a speech denouncing blacks and Jews in Chicago. The statute under which the defendant was convicted was invalidated as vague and overbroad, but strong language in the majority opinion indicated a retreat from *Chaplinsky's* "uncontrollable impulse" test by recognizing that a certain amount of provocative and challenging speech is protected.

• *Feiner v. New York* focused on a speech describing President Truman as a "bum," the mayor of Syracuse as a "champagne sipping bum," and the American Legion as a "Nazi Gestapo." The arrest of the defendant was upheld. The Court said that this was not an effort to regulate content, but an effort to protect the peace.

• *Edwards v. South Carolina* (1963) focused on a civil rights demonstration on the grounds of the state legislature, with demonstrators singing religious and patriotic hymns and speakers urging them to go to segregated lunch counters. The Court refused to label the conduct of the demonstrators "fighting words."

b. *Cohen v. California* (1971) is better known as the "Fuck the Draft" case, and focused on a T-shirt worn by the defendant featuring those words. The decision included Justice Harlan's famous line: "One man's vulgarity is another's lyric." Cohen's victory in this case not only led some to question the precedential value of *Feiner,* but also to question the precedential value of *Chaplinsky* itself.

c. In other cases, decided in the early 1970s, the Court avoided a direct overruling of *Chaplinsky* by employing the vagueness and overbreadth standards to decide in favor of defendants who had originally been convicted for insulting policemen. In *Gooding v. Wilson,* for example, the defendant had said, "[Y]ou son of a bitch . . . I'll choke you to death." In *Lewis v. City of New Orleans,* the defendant had addressed policeman as "you g-damn motherfucking police." Both convictions were overturned, and the local statutes were held to be vague and overbroad.

Even before *R.A.V. v. City of St. Paul* (505 U.S. 377 [1992]), Nadine Strossen stressed that the fighting words doctrine is on very shaky constitutional ground. See 1990 Duke L.J. at 508–514. Charles Lawrence, on the other hand, argues that the police insult cases of the 1970s are distinguishable because in a hate speech context the victim is typically in a subordinated status.

18. 505 U.S. 377 (1992).

19. 395 U.S. 444, 447 (1969).

20. Texas v. Johnson, 491 U.S. 397 (1989).

21. Brandenburg, 395 U.S. at 447. Emphasis added.

22. See, generally, Friedrich Kubler, How Much Freedom for Racist Speech? Transnational Aspects of a Conflict of Human Rights, *Hofstra Law Review* 27 (1998): 335.

23. John Faucher explains that, according to the general rule,

> to prevail in a defamation action, the plaintiff must show that: (1) the defendant published the statement by showing or saying it to a third party, (2) the statement identified the plaintiff, (3) the statement put the plaintiff in a bad light, and (4) it was false at the time that it was made.

Though law schools teach the same defamation law from Hawaii to Maine, state laws vary widely. In particular, state laws vary on standards of fault, distinctions between fact and opinion, application of rules of libel per se and per quod, availability of punitive damages, and statutes of limitations. Any of these laws could affect the outcome of a case. (John D. Faucher, Let the Chips Fall Where They May: Choice of Law in Computer Bulletin Board Defamation Cases, *U.C. Davis Law Review* 26 (1993): 1045, 1052–1054)

24. Restatement 2d Torts, Section 559.

25. Minnesota Attorney Greg Abbott has set forth some additional pertinent information about public figures. According to Abbott,

[A] "public figure" is a person who is publicly prominent, so much so that discussion or commentary about that person amounts to a "public concern." However, such persons are not necessarily public figures for any purpose: status as a public figure may only extend to the particular area in which they are publicly prominent . . .

The U.S. Supreme has established some guidelines on who constitutes a public figure: (1) Involuntary Public Figures: become public figure through no purposeful action of their own, including those who have become especially prominent in the affairs of society; (2) Always Public Figures: those who occupy position of such persuasive power and influence that they are deemed public figures for all purposes; (3) Public Figures on Specific Issues: "those who have thrust themselves to the forefront of particular public controversies in order to influence the resolution of the issues involved." (Gertz v. Robert Welch, Inc., 418 U.S. 323, 345 (1974))

See <http://www.abbottlaw.com/defamation.html> (visited September 20, 2000).

26. New York Times v. Sullivan, 376 U.S. 254 (1964).

27. Gertz v. Robert Welch, 418 U.S. 323 (1974).

28. Milkovich v. Lorain Journal Co., 497 U.S. 1, 17–21 (1990). In determining whether a statement is intended to convey an actual fact about a person, the court looks at (1) whether the language is loose, figurative, or hyperbolic, which would negate the impression that the speaker was seriously maintaining the truth of the underlying facts, (2) whether the general tenor of the article negates the impression that the speaker was seriously maintaining the truth of the underlying fact, and (3) whether the connotation is sufficiently factual to be susceptible of being proved true or false. Id. at 21.

29. See, generally, Eugene Volokh, Freedom of Speech in Cyberspace from the Listener's Perspective: Private Speech Restrictions, Libel, State Action, Harassment, and Sex, *University of Chicago Legal Forum* (1996): 377. Other rules under the law of defamation include certain "privileges" that defendants may invoke against claims of defamation in certain circumstances.

30. In addition, like defamation, certain arguments have been recognized as providing valid defenses to invasion of privacy claims.

31. See, generally, Cristina Fernandez, The Right of Publicity on the Internet, *Marquette Sports Law Journal* 8 (1998): 289.

32. Shibley v. Time, Inc., 321 N.E.2d 791 (Ohio 1974).

33. In Faragher v. Boca Raton, the U.S. Supreme Court noted that hostile environment sexual harassment claims had actually developed from the earlier racial and national origin harassment cases: "In . . . holding that environmental claims are covered by the statute, we drew upon earlier cases recognizing liability for discriminatory harassment based on race and national origin, see, e.g., Rogers v. EEOC, 454 F.2d 234 (CA5 1971); Firefighters Institute for Racial Equality v. St. Louis, 549 F.2d 506 (CA8); Banta v. United States, 434 U.S. 819, 54 L. Ed. 2d 76, 98 S. Ct. 60 (1977), just as we have also followed the lead of such cases in attempting to define the severity of the offensive conditions necessary to constitute actionable sex discrimination under the statute. See, e.g., Rogers, supra, at 238: 'Mere utterance of an ethnic or racial epithet which engenders offensive feelings in an employee' would not sufficiently alter terms and conditions of employment to violate Title VII. See also Daniels v. Essex Group, Inc., 937 F.2d 1264, 1271–1272 (CA7 1991); Davis v. Monsanto Chemical Co., 858 F.2d 345, 349 (CA6 1988); Snell v. Suffolk County, 782 F.2d 1094, 1103 (CA2 1986); 1 B. Lindemann and P. Grossman, Employment Discrimination Law 349, and nn. 36–37 (3d ed., 1996), which cites cases instructing that 'discourtesy or rudeness should not be confused with racial harassment' and that "a lack of racial sensitivity does not, alone, amount to actionable harassment."

In a footnote to this commentary, the Court explained that "Courts of Appeals in sexual harassment cases have properly drawn on standards developed in cases involving racial harassment. See, e.g., Carrero v. New York City Housing Auth., 890 F.2d 569, 577 (CA2 1989), citing Lopez v. S. B. Thomas, Inc., 831 F.2d 1184, 1189 (CA2 1987), a case of racial harassment, for the proposition that incidents of environmental sexual harassment 'must be more than episodic; they must be sufficiently continuous and concerted in order to be deemed pervasive.' Although racial and sexual harassment will often take different forms, and standards may not be entirely interchangeable, we think there is good sense in seeking generally to harmonize the standards of what amounts to actionable harassment."

34. Quid pro quo harassment is the more traditional concept, focusing on such things as the trading of sexual favors for advancement. Hostile environment is a relatively new concept. Although there has been some discussion in the aftermath of recent cases regarding whether the U.S. Supreme Court has moved away from the distinction between quid pro quo and hostile environment harassment, it is important to note that it has not scrapped this distinction. In the 1998 companion cases of *Faragher* and *Ellerth,* the court stated that the distinction is not particularly relevant for the question of when the employer is vicariously liable, but the substantive distinction remains, and is quite important. Unlike hostile environment harassment, quid pro quo harassment does not require an inquiry into hostility, abusiveness, severity, or pervasiveness, either subjective or objective; it merely requires a quid pro quo.

35. See Meritor Savings Bank v. Vinson, 477 U.S. 57 (1986).

36. The four cases were *Oncale v. Sundowner Offshore Services,* 523 U.S. 75 (1998), *Gebser v. Lago Vista Indep. School Dist.,* 524 U.S. 274 (1998), *Faragher v. Boca Raton,* 524 U.S. 775 (1998), and Ellerth v. Burlington Industries, 524 U.S. 951 (1998).

37. See, e.g., Eugene Volokh, Freedom of Speech and Workplace Harassment, *UCLA Law Review* 39 (1992): 1791.

38. Once actionable harassment is shown, the plaintiff still needs to prove that the employer's actions should give rise to liability. Such proof is not necessary if there was a "tangible employment action" as a result of the events in question (such as retaliatory firing after plaintiff complained). However, if no tangible employment action occurs, the employer can prevail if it can be shown that:

a. Employer exercised reasonable care to prevent and correct promptly any sexually harassing behavior, and

b. Plaintiff employee unreasonably failed to take advantage of any preventive or corrective opportunities provided by employer or to avoid harm otherwise. Faragher, 524 U.S. at 807.

39. Id. at 787–788.

40. Id.

41. See Davis v. Monroe County Board of Education, 526 U.S. 629, 633 (1999).

42. U.S. v. Alkhabaz, 104 F.3d 1492, 1506 (6th Cir. 1997) (Krupansky, J., dissenting). This requirement is generally satisfied "irrespective of the identity of the person or group threatened, the originator's motivation for issuing the threat, or the existence or nonexistence of any goal pursued by the threat."

43. Id.

44. See, generally, Anna S. Andrews, When is a Threat "Truly" a Threat Lacking First Amendment Protection? A Proposed True Threats Test to Safeguard Free Speech Rights in the Age of the Internet, *UCLA Online Institute for Cyberspace Law and Policy,* May 1999, <www.gseis.ucla.edu/iclp/aandrews2.htm> (visited May 8, 2000):

Courts over the years have included various elements in their formulations of threats tests. The majority of courts use an "objective" construction. Essentially, an objective test asks whether a reasonable person would construe the defendant's speech or statement as a threat, given the context in which it was made. The point at which courts differ is in deciding who that reasonable person should be. There are three possibilities. The first is to ask whether a reasonable *hearer* of the statement who was not the intended target would interpret the statement as a threat. The second is to ask whether a reasonable *speaker* should have foreseen that his statement would be interpreted as a threat. The third is to ask whether a reasonable *recipient* of the statement would interpret it as a threat. It should be noted that the reasonable hearer and reasonable recipient standards may be confused, as the hearer is often but not necessarily the recipient. Additionally, the reasonable recipient standard is problematic because it invites a jury to consider the unique sensitivities of the particular recipient, whether or not they are supposed to do so; if this happens and the recipient is unusually sensitive, a defendant's speech may be prohibited in that instance, while it would not have been prohibited if it had been directed at a less sensitive recipient.

A few courts have required both an "objective" and a "subjective" element. A subjective element essentially looks at the speaker's intent in making the statement. Some courts ask whether the speaker intended to *threaten,* regardless of intent to carry out the threat. Another approach is to ask whether the speaker intended to *execute* the threat, though this is rarely done as part of the threats test. Confusion over an intent inquiry is amplified by the fact that many statutes include language requiring the speaker to "willfully" or "knowingly" or "intentionally" threaten. This language seems to require specific intent but is ambiguous. The majority of courts do not interpret this as requiring specific intent to actually threaten, but instead view it objectively, asking only whether the speaker voluntarily uttered his speech and whether the speaker knew the meaning of his words.

45. 471 U.S. 539 (1985).

46. See id. at 555–556: "Respondents . . . contend that First Amendment values require a different rule under the circumstances of this case. The thrust of the decision below is that "[the] scope of [fair use] is undoubtedly wider when the information conveyed relates to matters of high public concern."

47. Id. at 556. Justice's Brennan's comments in the *Pentagon Papers* case should also be noted. Addressing the tension between copyright law and First Amendment law in that context, Brennan asserted that "copyright cases have no pertinence here: the Government is not asserting an interest in the particular form of words chosen in the documents, but is seeking to suppress the ideas expressed therein. And the copyright laws, of course, protect only the form of expression and not the ideas expressed." New York Times Co. v. United States, 403 U.S. 713, 726 (1971) (Brennan, J., concurring).

48. 907 F. Supp. 1361 (N.D. Cal. 1995).

49. See id. at 1377. The court added the following: "The copyright concepts of the idea/expression dichotomy and the fair use defense balance the important First Amendment rights with the constitutional authority for 'promoting the progress of science and useful arts,' U.S. CONST. art. I, §8, cl. 8; 1 NIMMER ON COPYRIGHT §1.10[B], at 1–71 to–83. Netcom argues that liability here would force Usenet servers to perform the impossible—screening all the information that comes through their systems. However, the court is not convinced that Usenet servers are directly liable for causing a copy to be made, and absent evidence of knowledge and participation or control and direct profit, they will not be contributorily or vicariously liable. If Usenet servers were responsible for screening all messages coming through their systems, this could have a serious chilling effect on what some say may turn out to be the best public forum for free speech yet devised."

50. Stephen Fraser, The Conflict between the First Amendment and Copyright Law and Its Impact on the Internet, *Cardozo Arts and Entertainment Law Journal* 16 (1998): 1, 50.

51. Tinker v. Des Moines Indep. Community School Dist., 393 U.S. 503 (1969). The students in *Tinker* argued that they had the right to wear black armbands to public high school as a protest against U.S. involvement in the Vietnam War. In the first U.S. Supreme Court case to directly address K-12 student freedom of expression, the justices agreed with the students, declaring that "[i]t can hardly be argued that either students or teachers shed their constitutional rights to freedom of speech or expression at the schoolhouse gate." Under the *Tinker* rule, K-12 students have free speech rights unless their speech materially and substantially interferes with schoolwork, discipline, or the rights of others.

52. Bethel School Dist. No. 403 v. Fraser, 478 U.S. 675 (1986). In the *Bethel District* case, Matthew Fraser was disciplined after giving a lewd and suggestive nominating speech at a public high school assembly. The speech was filled with sexual innuendo and contained numerous double entendres especially popular with junior high school boys. The Court upheld the disciplinary action, indicating that *Tinker* only applied to speech expressing a political viewpoint. It set forth a loose balancing test that apparently gave schools the right to determine "the boundaries of socially appropriate behavior."

53. Hazelwood v. Kuhlmeier, 484 U.S. 260 (1988). In Hazelwood, a public high school principal refused to allow the school newspaper to run articles about teen pregnancy and the effects of divorce on teenagers. The court agreed with the principal, holding that *Tinker* did not apply to school-sponsored expressive activity, and that "[e]ducators do not offend the First Amendment by exercising editorial control over the style and content of student speech in school-sponsored expressive activities, as long as their actions are reasonably related to legitimate pedagogical concerns." School-sponsored expressive activity includes "school-sponsored publications, theatrical productions, and other expressive activities that students, parents, and members of the public might reasonably perceive to bear the imprimatur of the school. These activities may fairly be characterized as part of the school curriculum, whether or not they occur in a traditional classroom setting, so long as they are supervised by faculty members and designed to impart particular knowledge or skills to student participants and audiences."

It should be noted, however, that individual states are able to go beyond this federal "baseline" and grant their students additional free speech rights. California, for example, provides its students with more free speech protection than the *Tinker-Fraser-Hazelwood* line of cases. See, e.g., California Education Code, Section 48907.

54. 343 U.S. 250, 253–266 (1952). Justice Douglas, who dissented, wrote that "Hitler and his Nazis showed how evil a conspiracy could be which was aimed at destroying a race by exposing it to contempt, derision, and obloquy. I would be willing to concede that such conduct directed at a race or group in this country could be made an indictable offense." But he concluded that Beauharnais's speech did not amount to expression "aimed at destroying a race," and, thus, could not and should not be prohibited under U.S. First Amendment law. 343 U.S. at 284–286.

55. See, generally, New York Times v. Sullivan, 376 U.S. 254 (1964).

56. See, generally, Brandenburg v. Ohio, 395 U.S. 444.

57. See, generally, R.A.V. v. City of St. Paul, 505 U.S. 377 (1992).

58. Collin v. Smith, 578 F.2d 1197 (7th Cir. 1978).

59. Id. at 1198–1999.

60. The leaflet continued with the following highly offensive and inflammatory language: "An old maxim goes: 'Where one finds the most Jews, there also shall one find the most Jewhaters.' With this basic truth in mind, we are now planning a number of street demonstrations and even speeches in Evanston, Skokie, Lincolnwood, North Shore, Morton Grove, etc. This leaflet is but the first of a number now being prepared for eventual mass-distribution. A beautiful, full-color poster, 18 inches by 30 inches, with non-removable adhesive on the back, is already in the works. The poster shows three rabbis involved in the ritual murder of an innocent Gentile boy during the hate-fest of Purim." Id. at 1216.

61. Id. Quoting New York Times Co. v. Sullivan, supra, note 55, at 270.

62. Cert. Denied, 439 U.S. 916.

63. In the campus speech code cases of 1989–1994, for example, it was mentioned prominently as supporting evidence in decisions that found those codes unconstitutional.

64. See chapter 5 of this book, supra.

65. See Stuart Biegel, Hostile Connections: Arguably, Workplace Sexual Harassment Principles and Prohibitions Apply Online, *UCLA Online Institute for Cyberspace Law and Policy,* August 22, 1996, <http://www.gseis.ucla.edu/iclp/aug96.html> (visited September 20, 2000).

66. See, generally, Whitman, supra, note 2; Kubler, supra, note 22.

67. See Justice Douglas' comments in his Beauharnais dissert, supra, note 54.

68. See Wisconsin v. Mitchell, 508 U.S. 476 (1993).

69. Collin v. Smith at 1204, n.13.

70. Doe v. University of Michigan, 721 F. Supp. at 867.

71. In mid-2000, America Online expressly prohibited "hate speech," and urged its members to report it using the keyword: "Notify AOL." Its acceptable use policy stated that a subscriber "will be considered in violation of the Terms of Service if he or she or anyone using the account "transmit[s] or facilitate[s] distribution of content that is harmful, abusive, racially or ethnically offensive, vulgar, sexually explicit, or in a reasonable person's view, objectionable. Community standards may vary, but there is no place on the service where hate speech is tolerated." AOL reserved the right "to remove content that does not meet" its "standards." Members were told that they may receive warnings, or . . . "if it's a serious offense" or they've violated the rules before, their account may be terminated. America Online Terms of Service, Visited June 18, 2000.

72. See, e.g., <http://www.teachingtolerance.org> (visited May 14, 2000).

73. See, e.g., Arthur Levine, The Campus Divided, and Divided Again, *New York Times,* June 11, 2000.

74. See <http:www.splcenter.org> (visited March 1, 2001).

75. This increase in hate-related violence included the dragging death of an African American man in Texas, the crucifixion of a gay man in Wyoming, the bombing death of 168 citizens in Oklahoma, and an epidemic of shootings in the U.S. public schools.

76. The entire publication is available online at <http://www.splcenter.org/intelligenceproject/ip-index.html> (visited March 1, 2001).

Subject Index

Index of Cases and Statutes

Cases

Statutes